PRIMARYPLOTS

PRIMARYPLOTS

A Book Talk Guide
for Use with Readers Ages 4–8

By Rebecca L. Thomas

R. R. BOWKER
New York

Published by R. R. Bowker Company
a division of Reed Publishing (USA) Inc.
Copyright © 1989 by Reed Publishing (USA) Inc.
All rights reserved
Printed and bound in the United States of America

Library of Congress Cataloging-in-Publication Data
Thomas, Rebecca L.
    Primaryplots : a book talk guide for use with readers ages 4–8 /
Rebecca L. Thomas.
    p.   cm.
    Includes indexes.
    ISBN 0-8352-2514-3
    1. Children's literature—Stories, plots, etc. 2. Libraries,
Children's—Activity programs. 3. Children—Books and reading.
4. Book talks. I. Title. II. Title: Primaryplots.
Z1037.A1T47 1989   88-34054
011'.62—dc19   CIP

ISBN 0-8352-2514-3

Contents

Preface

Reading aloud and telling stories are the program focus in many public library story hours and school library class visits. Often books are selected that coordinate with a theme or activity, such as a holiday or season. In some cases, one book is read aloud while related titles are presented through brief book talks, thus children are encouraged to select and read them. The brief book talk of a picture book is also a reading guidance activity that many librarians use as a group of children is selecting books. Currently there is a need for materials that can serve as a guide to recent picture books and that will assist teachers and librarians in their program planning.

Primaryplots is designed to meet this need and to expand the range of the reading guidance titles from the R. R. Bowker Company. Since 1967, commencing with *Juniorplots,* and continuing into the late 1980s with *Juniorplots 3* (1987), *Introducing Bookplots 3* (1988), and *Seniorplots* (1989), Bowker has provided librarians and teachers with reference books that promote literature and reading for young people beginning with the middle grades of elementary school and continuing into high school. *Primaryplots* focuses on *recent* picture books that interest children from preschool through age 8. All the featured titles in *Primaryplots* have been selected from books published between 1983 and 1987. In order to focus on high quality materials, the "best books" and "notable" lists from standard reviewing and evaluation sources were consulted, including *School Library Journal*'s "Best Books," the Association of Library Services to Children's "Notable Books," *Booklist*'s "Editor's Choices," and "notable trade books" selected by various science and social studies committees. *Children's Catalog,* 15th edition and supplements (Wilson, 1986–88) were also consulted. The wide range of children's interests was taken into consideration when selecting the featured books. An attempt was made to provide books that could be used at different levels from preschool to the middle grades in elementary school and to correlate the titles with eight themes that serve as chapters. However, the final selection of a title was still in many cases a personal decision.

The citations for all books reflect the information that appears on the title page, thus some books do not list an author (for example, *The Gingerbread Boy*, illustrated by Scott Cook) while other books list the name of an adapter or reteller. Like its companion titles, the purpose of *Primaryplots* is to serve as a guide for book talks, story programs, and reading guidance.

The 150 plots in *Primaryplots* have been organized into eight chapters. They are (1) Enjoying Family and Friends, (2) Developing a Positive Self-Image, (3) Celebrating Everyday Experiences, (4) Finding the Humor in Picture Books, (5) Exploring the Past, (6) Learning about the World Around You, (7) Analyzing Illustrations, and (8) Focusing on Folktales.

Each featured title includes:

1. *Bibliographic Information.* Each main-entry book gives the author(s), title, illustrator(s), publisher, date of publication, paperback information (such as publisher, if different from the hardcover edition, and date of publication), suggested use level, and reading level, if applicable.

The reading level of a picture book is often far beyond the reading ability of the intended audience, thus the Suggested Use Level is included to provide a more specific guide to the children who would be interested in a title. A book such as *The Napping House* by Audrey Wood has a cumulative text in which people and animals pile into the same bed. This makes for long sentences and a high readability (Gr. 8) even though this book is very appropriate for young children. The Suggested Use Level therefore provides librarians and teachers with a more accurate indication of the appropriate audience.

In order to arrive at a readability score, the *School Utilities, Volume 2,* computer program from the Minnesota Educational Computing Consortium was used to calculate a Fry readability level for most of the books. According to the disk directions, three 100 word passages were analyzed for each book (when possible) and an average score was determined for sentence length and syllables, which were then plotted on the Fry graph. The readability score for this program is reported as a single-digit grade level (for example, Gr. 2). A readability level was not calculated for poetry books; alphabet, counting, or other concept books; or for books with incomplete sentence structures. The reading level for these books is listed as "NA" (not available). For example, *Truck Song* by Diane Siebert has a rhyming text that is not punctuated, thus no sentences are available for a readability assessment and the reading level is given as NA.

2. *Plot Summary.* Even though many picture books could be read very quickly, this brief retelling of the plot allows librarians and teachers to make decisions about using a book without having the book at hand.

3. *Thematic Material.* The eight chapter headings represent overall themes for many of the books; however, this section provides more specific information to help librarians and teachers as they select the books.

4. *Book Talk Material and Activities.* Activities have been designed to provide opportunities for children to interact with books in a variety of ways. This section recommends possibilities not only for book talks and discussions, but also for writing, dramatizing, comparing, analyzing, and other extension activities. Some books have been correlated with curriculum areas such as science, social studies, or art. Other books offer opportunities for studying characters, making murals, charting sequential events, or using puppets. Other suggestions include having children use books as models for their own writing and illustrating efforts. Many poems have been highlighted that could be read aloud or rewritten on chart paper (usually 24 inch by 36 inch tagboard). Poetry charts are often illustrated by the children and displayed in libraries and classrooms so the familiar rhymes can be seen. The suggestions for book talks, story programs, and activities are based on personal experience. Ideas are included that could be adapted to the classroom, school, or public library.

5. *Audiovisual Adaptation.* The OCLC (Online Computer Library Center) cataloging database was searched for information about the availability of a title in audiovisual format. Recent catalogs of audiovisual materials were also examined.

6. *Related Titles.* The materials in this section are annotated to describe themes or activities that relate to the featured book. *A to Zoo,* 2nd edition (Bowker, 1986) and *Children's Catalog,* 15th edition and supplements, as well as the "best books" lists were consulted for suggested titles. Many library collections were also consulted. At least five related titles are included for each highlighted book.

7. *About the Author and Illustrator.* Information about the author and illustrator is included, if available. When both an author and illustrator have biographical information, the author's data appears first. Biographical resources that are easily available to school and public libraries were

consulted including *Something about the Author* (Gale, 1971–88), *The Fifth Book of Junior Authors* (Wilson, 1983) and its four companion titles, and *Illustrators of Books for Children, 1967–1976* (Horn Book, 1978).

Young children need many opportunities to interact with books as they learn to read and make decisions about books—such as which type of books they like or dislike. *Primaryplots* is intended to help teachers and librarians provide a variety of books and activities that encourage children to develop a love for books and reading.

Many people have helped with the preparation of this book. Special thanks should be given to Deanna McDaniel and Marvin McDaniel for assisting with the biographical searching. Connie Brown, Kay Dunlap, and Hylah Schwartz read and reacted to many of the chapters. Marilyn Eppich provided technical assistance while Nancy Genger made many corrections to the manuscript. Jeanette Throne evaluated the complete text and made suggestions that reflected her experiences as a kindergarten teacher thus providing additional information on the needs and interests of young children. Professionally, I am indebted to Ellen Stepanian, Director of Library Media for the Shaker Heights City Schools, Ohio, for her ongoing leadership and support. Sheck Cho, Managing Editor at Bowker, has provided invaluable assistance with manuscript preparation. Finally, thanks are due to Marion Sader, Publisher of Professional and Reference Books at Bowker, for encouraging me to become involved with this project.

PRIMARYPLOTS

1

Enjoying Family and Friends

CHILDREN need to develop positive social behavior. Their early experiences are at home with their families. As children become more self-sufficient, they begin to interact with neighbors and friends. Through these experiences, they establish relationships with other people. They learn to be cooperative and caring.

The books in this chapter examine different relationships. There are stories about friends who fight with each other and families that help each other, as well as stories about bedtime, birthdays, holidays, and sharing. Children can compare their experiences with those of the characters in the books.

Bang, Molly. *Ten, Nine, Eight*
Illus. by the author. Greenwillow, 1983; pap., Penguin, 1985
Suggested Use Level: Gr. PreK–1   Reading Level: NA

Plot Summary

As a little girl gets ready for bed, she and her father count backward from 10 and describe some of the things in her room. The rhyming text creates a quiet, restful mood.

Thematic Material

Ten, Nine, Eight could be included in units on counting and on getting ready for bed. It also shows a loving relationship in a black family between a father and daughter.

Book Talk Material and Activities

Every year, teachers in the primary grades and in preschools come to the library to look for simple concept books. *Ten, Nine, Eight* is a good book to highlight. The girl and her father count backward from 10, which provides some variety from the more typical 1 to 10 counting books. The rhyming text captures some of the everyday feelings that the girl shares with her father at bedtime. As the girl prepares for bed, she and her father look around the room and count things. *Goodnight Moon* is another story in which a young character looks around the room and says "good night" to some ordinary objects. Children would enjoy reading and comparing the two books.

Just as the little girl in *Ten, Nine, Eight* looks around her bedroom for things to count, the classroom or library provides another setting for a counting book. Children could count 10 pencils, 9 desks, 8 books, and so on, as they make their own counting books. Other counting books could provide more ideas for children to use in their own books.

Audiovisual Adaptation

Ten, Nine, Eight. Random House Media, cassette/book, 1984; filmstrip/cassette, 1984.

Related Titles

The Balancing Act: A Counting Song illustrated by Merle Peek. Clarion, 1987. The elephants are on the high wire until the tenth elephant comes out and they all fall off. The book ends with a suggestion for a game and the music for a song.

Goodnight Moon by Margaret Wise Brown. Illustrated by Clement Hurd. Harper & Row, 1947. In this classic bedtime book, a little rabbit looks around the room and says "good night" to familiar items.

Roll Over! written and illustrated by Mordicai Gerstein. Crown, 1984. Here is another book that counts back from 10. In this story, a little boy keeps pushing unusual animals from his bed. Children enjoy opening the folded pages to see who falls out.

Roll Over! A Counting Book illustrated by Merle Peek. Clarion, 1981. Different animals are pushed out of bed in this version of the counting rhyme.

Ten Bears in My Bed: A Goodnight Countdown written and illustrated by Stan Mack. Pantheon, 1974. In this version of *Roll Over!* (see above), the 10 animals in the bed are all bears. On the last page, the little boy is trying to fall asleep by counting bears instead of sheep.

Up to Ten and Down Again written and illustrated by Lisa Campbell Ernst. Lothrop, 1986. After all the things at the picnic have been counted, it starts to rain and everyone and everything must leave, except of course the one little duck who is happy to be getting wet in the pond.

About the Author and Illustrator

BANG, MOLLY
Fifth Book of Junior Authors and Illustrators, ed. by Sally Holmes Holtze. Wilson, 1983, pp. 20–21.
Something about the Author, ed. by Anne Commire. Gale, 1981, Vol. 24, pp. 37–39.

Brown, Marc. *Arthur's Baby*
Illus. by the author. Little, Brown, 1987
Suggested Use Level: Gr. K–1   Reading Level: Gr. 2

Plot Summary

The arrival of a new baby is always a source of anticipation and anxiety. For Arthur, the popular hero of the Marc Brown series about Arthur and his family, the news of the coming change in his family brings him unwanted advice from his friends and from D.W., his sister. Arthur's parents try to ease his worries, but he remains ill at ease even after his baby sister, Kate, is born. After Kate is brought home, Arthur's awkwardness continues and he feels even worse because D.W. seems so confident. Arthur's intervention, however, helps stop Kate's crying, and his confidence is restored.

Thematic Material

This story focuses on the natural feelings children have when the family structure changes. Many children experience a new baby in the family, and learning to cope with this change is an important part of growing up. Feeling good about oneself is also a theme in this book.

Book Talk Material and Activities

This book would be useful as part of a discussion on books about siblings. Shel Silverstein's poem "For Sale," in *Where the Sidewalk Ends*, and Mary Ann Hoberman's poem "Brother," in *Yellow Butter, Purple Jelly, Red Jam, Black Bread*, could help set the tone for related booktalking. A natural extension would be to have children talk or write about their feelings about themselves and their siblings. The story could also be retold from the new baby's or D.W.'s point of view.

Marc Brown's illustrations capture Arthur's uncertainty and D.W.'s conceit. They also show Arthur's pride as he helps with Kate and remembers that he has been through this before. The pictures are filled with details of the preparations for the baby and show some of the changes that are taking place. Children could be encouraged to look for details that show the changes going on. They could also draw their own detailed pictures of a special event. Many children will enjoy reading other adventures about Arthur and his family in this series.

Audiovisual Adaptation

Arthur's Baby. Random House Media, cassette/book, 1988; filmstrip/cassette, 1988.

Related Titles

A Baby Sister for Frances by Russell Hoban. Illustrated by Lillian Hoban. Harper & Row, 1964. A classic story of the anxieties that are felt by Frances when a new baby is coming.

The Baby's Catalogue written and illustrated by Janet Ahlberg and Allan Ahlberg. Little, Brown, 1983. The illustrations in this book, which show items associated with a baby, such as diapers and high chairs, would be useful to children as they draw pictures showing details about a new baby.

Nobody Asked Me If I Wanted a Baby Sister written and illustrated by Martha Alexander. Dial, 1971. Similar to *Arthur's Baby* and a good choice for a comparison activity. The companion book, *When the New Baby Comes, I'm Moving Out* (Dial, 1979), shows how Oliver feels before the baby arrives.

Peter's Chair written and illustrated by Ezra Jack Keats. Harper & Row, 1967. Shows how Peter copes with his new baby sister.

Where the Sidewalk Ends written and illustrated by Shel Silverstein. Harper & Row, 1974. A popular collection that includes many poems about everyday worries and concerns.

Yellow Butter, Purple Jelly, Red Jam, Black Bread by Mary Ann Hoberman. Illustrated by Chaya Burstein. Viking, 1981. A collection of poems that captures the playful, imaginative spirit of children.

Other books about Arthur (all published by Little, Brown) are *Arthur Goes to Camp* (1982), *Arthur's April Fool* (1983), *Arthur's Christmas* (1985),

Arthur's Eyes (1979), *Arthur's Halloween* (1982), *Arthur's Nose* (1976), *Arthur's Teacher Trouble* (1986), *Arthur's Thanksgiving* (1983), *Arthur's Tooth* (1985), and *Arthur's Valentine* (1980).

About the Author and Illustrator

BROWN, MARC
Fifth Book of Junior Authors and Illustrators, ed. by Sally Holmes Holtze. Wilson, 1983, pp. 54–55.
Something about the Author, ed. by Anne Commire. Gale, 1976, Vol. 10, pp. 17–18.

Bunting, Eve.   *The Mother's Day Mice*
Illus. by Jan Brett. Clarion, 1986
Suggested Use Level: Gr. K–1   Reading Level: Gr. 3

Plot Summary

Mother's Day is a special day—even for a family of mice. Biggest Mouse, Middle Mouse, and Little Mouse leave their cottage very early to find the perfect surprise gifts for Mother. Biggest Mouse and Middle Mouse already know what they will give; Little Mouse has chosen something very special but unattainable. He would like to give his mother honeysuckle from the cottage porch but he cannot get past the cat. After an adventure outside gathering their gifts, the three mice return home. Little Mouse is empty handed but does have a gift. On his adventure he learned a tune, and he sings a special Mother's Day verse that he has created. This gift is special because it is from Little Mouse's own heart and it helps the mice celebrate their love for each other.

Thematic Material

The Mother's Day Mice shows the strength and love in a family relationship. The young mice want their mother's approval. They want to please her and give her their best even if it means taking risks. Their realization that material gifts are less important and that the best gift is one that comes from within is an important theme for children to hear. There is also the theme of the youngest feeling left out and needing to develop self-confidence.

Book Talk Material and Activities

Mother's Day is the second Sunday in May and it is a time for special story and book talk programs. In *The Mother's Day Mice*, Little Mouse sings his poem to the tune of "Twinkle, Twinkle Little Star." As many children want to make or do something special for their mothers, learning that song—even suggesting their own words to go with it—makes a super gift. The words could also be written on a greeting card.

Jan Brett's illustrations show mice dressed in brightly colored clothes. Their home is filled with intricate details—tiles, cups, seed bins, and carved furniture. The outdoor scenes are from a mouse's perspective and show the dangers of swooping owls and looming foxes and cats. After studying these pictures, children could take a walk outside to look for details in nature. They may enjoy thinking of the world from a mouse's point of view. After they come back from their walk they can draw or write about what they observed.

Related Titles

Ask Mr. Bear written and illustrated by Marjorie Flack. Macmillan, 1932. A little boy wants to find a special gift for his mother and gets some advice from Mr. Bear.

Do Bears Have Mothers, Too? by Aileen Fisher. Illustrated by Eric Carle. Crowell, 1973. Poems about animals and their babies illustrated with large, brightly colored pictures. Some of the animals included are the swan, elephant, kangaroo, penguin, monkey, dolphin, and lion.

Happy Mother's Day by Steven Kroll. Illustrated by Marylin Hafner. Holiday House, 1985. Here's how another family celebrates Mother's Day. Compare the presents that this family gives to the ones given in *The Mother's Day Mice.*

Mr. Rabbit and the Lovely Present by Charlotte Zolotow. Illustrated by Maurice Sendak. Harper & Row, 1962. Mr. Rabbit helps the little girl choose just the right birthday present for her mother.

Mother, Mother, I Want Another by Maria Polushkin. Illustrated by Diane Dawson. Crown, 1978. Another story about a little mouse who loves his mother.

The Runaway Bunny by Margaret Wise Brown. Illustrated by Clement Hurd. Harper & Row, 1942. Little Bunny wants to prove his independence from his mother until she reminds him how much he means to her.

Where Are You Going, Little Mouse? by Robert Kraus. Illustrated by Jose

Aruego and Ariane Dewey. Greenwillow, 1986. After a little mouse runs away, he realizes how much his family means to him.

About the Author and Illustrator

BUNTING, EVE (ANNE EVELYN BUNTING)
Authors of Books for Young People: Supplement to the Second Edition, by Martha E. Ward and Dorothy Marquardt. Scarecrow, 1979, p. 36.
Fifth Book of Junior Authors and Illustrators, ed. by Sally Holmes Holtze. Wilson, 1983, pp. 60–61.
Something about the Author, ed. by Anne Commire. Gale, 1980, Vol. 18, pp. 38–39.
BRETT, JAN
Something about the Author, ed. by Anne Commire. Gale, 1986, Vol. 42, pp. 38–39.

Domanska, Janina. *Busy Monday Morning*
Illus. by the author. Greenwillow, 1985
Suggested Use Level: Gr. PreK–1   Reading Level: Gr. 5

Plot Summary

A boy and his father are busy with their farm chores. Beginning on Monday, they work in the fields each day doing something different. On Sunday, they rest and appreciate what they have accomplished.

Thematic Material

This book presents the concept of the days of the week. The text, which follows a repetitive pattern, is written as verses to a song that is set to music at the back of the book.

Book Talk Material and Activities

The days of the week, months of the year, seasons, and other time concepts are part of many preschool and primary-grade programs. Books with information about time help children become more familiar with the concept. *Busy Monday Morning, No Bath Tonight,* and *Some of the Days of Everett Anderson* all take characters through a week of activities. Children could chart what the characters do on the different days. An example appears in Chart A.

A related activity in a classroom or library program is to make a book showing the group's responsibilities each day. The weekly schedule of

Chart A

Title/Day	Busy Monday Morning	No Bath Tonight	Some of the Days of Everett Anderson
Monday	Father and I mowed hay	Jeremy hurt his foot	Everett is full of joy
Tuesday	Father and I raked hay	Jeremy sat on a pricker bush	Everett won't use his umbrella

library visits, art, music, and physical education classes, and other regular activities could be organized and patterned after *Busy Monday Morning*, with the months of the year treated in a similar manner. Also, just as the boy works with his father, children could talk or write about their activities with different family members.

Related Titles

All Year Long written and illustrated by Nancy Tafuri. Greenwillow, 1983. A look at the days of the week and the months of the year. The illustrations show activities that take place during each season.

Chicken Soup with Rice written and illustrated by Maurice Sendak. Harper & Row, 1962. The months of the year are celebrated in poems. The book is part of the Nutshell Library series, which includes *Pierre* (Harper & Row, 1962); *Alligators All Around* (Harper & Row, 1962); and *One Was Johnny* (Harper & Row, 1962).

No Bath Tonight by Jane Yolen. Illustrated by Nancy Winslow Parker. Crowell, 1978. Something happens to Jeremy each day of the week that keeps him from taking a bath. When it is Sunday and Jeremy still has not had a bath, Grandma comes to visit and has an idea.

One Monday Morning written and illustrated by Uri Shulevitz. Scribner, 1967. On a rainy day, a little boy pretends that the king and his entourage are coming to visit him. Each day of the week adds another person to the group.

Some of the Days of Everett Anderson by Lucille Clifton. Illustrated by Evaline Ness. Holt, Rinehart, 1970. Poems follow Everett Anderson through a very busy week of walking in the rain, visiting the candy shop, talking with his mother, missing his father, and watching the stars.

Through the Year with Harriet written and illustrated by Betsy Maestro and Giulio Maestro. Crown, 1985. Harriet celebrates her birthday in January and then must wait through all the months of the year before her birthday comes again.

The Very Hungry Caterpillar written and illustrated by Eric Carle. Collins-World, 1969. The caterpillar eats something different every day of the week.

About the Author and Illustrator

DOMANSKA, JANINA
Illustrators of Children's Books: 1957–1966, Vol. III, comp. by Lee Kingman, Grace Allen Hogarth, and Harriet Quimby. Horn Book, 1968, pp. 3, 8, 100, 203, 215; *1967–1976, Vol. IV,* 1978, pp. 114, 186.
Something about the Author, ed. by Anne Commire. Gale, 1974, Vol. 6, pp. 65–68.
Third Book of Junior Authors, ed. by Muriel Fuller. Wilson, 1963, pp. 77–78.

Flournoy, Valerie.   *The Patchwork Quilt*
Illus. by Jerry Pinkney. Dial, 1985
Suggested Use Level: Gr. 1–3   Reading Level: Gr. 5

Plot Summary

Tanya is part of a loving family that includes her parents, two brothers, and grandmother. The family history is being remembered by Grandma, who is making a quilt using scraps from the family's favorite old clothes. Grandma sometimes feels that her contributions are not appreciated, and Tanya shows that she cares by offering to help with the quilt. Everyday moments are remembered as Grandma snips patches from faded corduroy pants, and special times are celebrated again with patches from costumes and holiday clothes. When Grandma becomes ill, her quilt is put aside. Tanya realizes the importance of this quilt not just to Grandma but to the entire family. Thus Tanya begins to work on the quilt and is joined by the rest of her family. When Grandma feels stronger, she returns to the quilt, too. The finished quilt is a treasure of memories, and causes the family to share a special moment reflecting on their love for each other.

Thematic Material

The feeling of respect for the elderly is an important theme here. Grandma plays an important role in the family and her contributions are valued. The book presents a positive image of a black family with an emphasis on how much they care for each other.

Book Talk Material and Activities

After hearing this story, children could participate in a family history project. Some could conduct interviews with members of their families and write about what they learned. Children could work together to suggest questions to ask and in pairs or small groups organize the information. Others might decide to illustrate a photo album of family members. Just as the family in *The Patchwork Quilt* works together to finish the quilt, children could work together on their projects to learn about each other and about getting along.

Another activity could focus on special memories. Each child could be given a patch of fabric and asked to imagine the history of that scrap and suggest why it was chosen for a quilt. They could write a story or tell about their fabric.

Audiovisual Adaptation

The Patchwork Quilt. "Reading Rainbow." Great Plains National Instructional Television Library, videorecording, 1985.

Related Titles

Patchwork Tales written and illustrated by Susan L. Roth and Ruth Phang. Atheneum, 1984. Wood block prints represent patches and provide the inspiration for stories about a family.

The Quilt written and illustrated by Ann Jonas. Greenwillow, 1984. Another book where quilt patches bring forth special memories. In this one, a little girl dreams that the patches become places that she visits while she looks for her lost stuffed dog.

The Quilt Story by Tony Johnston. Illustrated by Tomie de Paola. Putnam, 1985. The history of a particular quilt from when it was made during pioneer times until it is found in the attic generations later.

Sam Johnson and the Blue Ribbon Quilt written and illustrated by Lisa Campbell Ernst. Lothrop, 1983. Sam enjoys sewing but finds that others think his behavior is unusual.

A Special Trade by Sally Wittman. Illustrated by Karen Gundersheimer.

Harper & Row, 1978. In *The Patchwork Quilt,* the family helps with the quilt when Grandma is ill. Here, a little girl helps an aging neighbor.

About the Author and Illustrator

PINKNEY, JERRY
Illustrators of Children's Books: 1957–1966, Vol. III, comp. by Lee Kingman, Grace
  Allen Hogarth, and Harriet Quimby. Horn Book, 1968, pp. 158, 235; *Vol. IV,*
  1967–1976, 1978, pp. 151, 205.
Something about the Author, ed. by Anne Commire. Gale, 1983, Vol. 32, p. 145;
  1985, Vol. 41, pp. 164–174.

Griffith, Helen V.   *Grandaddy's Place*
Illus. by James Stevenson. Greenwillow, 1987
Suggested Use Level: Gr. 1–3   Reading Level: Gr. 4

Plot Summary

Janetta and Momma are going to visit Grandaddy. This is the first time that Janetta has met her grandaddy and she is apprehensive about it. She is also worried about staying at his house, which is far out in the country. There are wasps, chickens, a cat, and a mule at his house. Janetta finds that she is afraid of them all, until her grandaddy tells her a story that helps her feel more at home. Janetta and her grandaddy go fishing together and he helps her make friends with the animals. As the story ends, they have developed a special closeness and appreciation for each other.

Thematic Material

Grandaddy understands Janetta's fears and helps her overcome them. Their relationship develops from the love and respect that they feel for each other. This book has a strong positive image of an older adult. It also portrays some of the concerns that come from being in a new situation.

Book Talk Material and Activities

In 1978, the first Sunday after Labor Day was designated National Grandparents' Day. *Grandaddy's Place* should be included in a story or book talk program for this day. Grandparents or senior citizens could be invited to special school or library activities in their honor. They could read favorite stories from when they were children or just tell about what it was like for them to be children. Children need to see the contributions that older people can make, and this would be a special time for sharing.

Grandaddy's Place is a companion book to *Georgia Music*. In *Grandaddy's Place*, Janetta and her grandaddy meet. In *Georgia Music*, her grandaddy's health is failing and he has been brought to live with her in the city. Janetta helps him learn to accept this new situation. In both books there is a strong feeling of caring between Janetta and Grandaddy. Each makes a special effort to help the other. Children need the opportunity to feel useful and to see that they can make a contribution to the world around them. Reading these two books could start a discussion about ways in which children can help others. They might consider a group project, such as making cards or gifts for a nursing home or reading aloud to younger children.

James Stevenson's illustrations are bright and colorful, with a full-page illustration across from each page of text. Children could compare these drawings to those in other books by Stevenson.

Related Titles

Blackberries in the Dark by Mavis Jukes. Illustrated by Thomas B. Allen. Knopf, 1985. This book takes place during the first summer after Austin's grandpa died. Austin's memories of the times he and his grandfather had together show how much he loved his grandfather.

Could Be Worse! written and illustrated by James Stevenson. Greenwillow, 1977. Here is another book about a grandfather that is illustrated by Stevenson. There are several others in this series about Grandpa, Louie, and Mary Ann (see *What's Under My Bed,* Chapter 4). How does this grandfather compare to the one in Griffith's book?

Georgia Music by Helen V. Griffith. Illustrated by James Stevenson. Greenwillow, 1986. Although this book was written before *Grandaddy's Place*, it deals with a later time in the lives of Janetta and Grandaddy.

Grandpa and Bo written and illustrated by Kevin Henkes. Greenwillow, 1986. Bo visits his grandfather in the country. They enjoy walking and talking with each other and, even though it is summer, they celebrate Christmas, because they will not see each other in December.

When Grandpa Came to Stay written and illustrated by Judith Caseley. Greenwillow, 1986. Benny likes spending time with his grandfather and together they remember Grandma.

About the Author and Illustrator

GRIFFITH, HELEN V.

Authors of Books for Young People: Supplement to the Second Edition, by Martha E. Ward and Dorothy Marquardt. Scarecrow, 1979, p. 110.

Fourth Book of Junior Authors and Illustrators, ed. by Doris de Montreville and Elizabeth D. Crawford. Wilson, 1978, pp. 160–161.

Something about the Author, ed. by Anne Commire. Gale, 1985, Vol. 39, pp. 97–98.

STEVENSON, JAMES

Authors of Books for Young People: Supplement to the Second Edition, by Martha E. Ward and Dorothy Marquardt. Scarecrow, 1979, p. 262.

Fifth Book of Junior Authors and Illustrators, ed. by Sally Holmes Holtze. Wilson, 1983, pp. 303–304.

Illustrators of Children's Books: 1967–1976, Vol. IV, comp. by Lee Kingman, Grace Allen Hogarth, and Harriet Quimby. Horn Book, 1978, pp. 161–162, 210.

Something about the Author, ed. by Anne Commire. Gale, 1984, Vol. 34, p. 191; 1986, Vol. 42, pp. 180–184.

Hines, Anna Grossnickle. *Daddy Makes the Best Spaghetti*
Illus. by the author. Clarion, 1986; pap., 1988
Suggested Use Level: Gr. PreK–K   Reading Level: Gr. 1

Plot Summary

A little boy named Corey tells about some of the time he spends with Daddy. They go to the store for groceries and then prepare dinner together. They tease each other and play games. When Mommy comes home, they all eat dinner and then Corey helps Mommy with the dishes. Daddy surprises them when he comes into the kitchen dressed up as "Bathman" and carries Corey off to the tub. Daddy makes bath time fun by splashing with boats and playing monster. When Corey is out of the tub, Daddy surprises him again by pretending to be a dog. Corey gets ready for bed and listens to Mommy read a story before both parents come to kiss him good night.

Thematic Material

There is a feeling of family togetherness in this story. Although the focus is on Daddy, both parents show their love for Corey as they let him be a part of ordinary moments, such as shopping and doing the dishes. This story is also about getting ready for bed.

Book Talk Material and Activities

Including this story in a unit on bedtime would allow children to discuss some of their routines and to relate Corey's experiences to their own. After reading the story to a group of children, ask them to name some of the things that Corey does to get ready for bed. For example, he takes a bath, he puts on his pajamas, and so forth. (It might be helpful to reread all or part of the book.) On a large piece of paper (chart paper), write down the children's suggestions. Leave some space after each item and have each child write his or her name in the column showing if it is part of his or her routine. See Chart B for an example of this activity.

By using simple graphs, children could compare their experiences to Corey's and learn about each other. They could suggest other bedtime routines that are not in the book, such as brushing their teeth, and again chart their participation and find out about each other. As Corey's family shares a story before bed, the children in the group could talk about some of their favorite bedtime stories.

Books that present everyday family experiences allow children to compare their experiences with those of the characters in the books. By allowing children to discuss their feelings and experiences, librarians and teachers can extend the children's understanding of the story and also help them see themselves in relation to their peers.

This book could also be part of a story session for children and their fathers to celebrate Father's Day. *Goodnight Horsey* by Frank Asch is a good companion book, as the father in the book is magically transformed into a horse. Compare the little girl's fantasy vision of her father in *Goodnight Horsey* with the realism in *Daddy Makes the Best Spaghetti*. These

Chart B

GETTING READY FOR BED		
In *Daddy Makes the Best Spaghetti,* Corey	I do this, too.	I don't do this.
1. Takes a bath.		
2. Plays games with Daddy.		

books could be used to help children think about the special times they share with their fathers as they each prepare a Father's Day card.

Related Titles

After Good-Night by Monica Mayper. Illustrated by Peter Sis. Harper & Row, 1987. In her bed, waiting to fall asleep, Nan listens to the sounds in the house.

Bea and Mr. Jones written and illustrated by Amy Schwartz. Bradbury, 1982. Bea and her father decide to trade places for the day. Ask children to think about who they might want to trade places with and what they think might happen.

Bedtime for Frances by Russell Hoban. Illustrated by Garth Williams. Harper & Row, 1960. Frances finds many reasons to keep from going to bed, but her father finally puts an end to her excuses. A favorite for many children.

Goodnight Horsey written and illustrated by Frank Asch. Prentice-Hall, 1981. A patient father answers the bedtime demands of his daughter.

Goodnight Moon by Margaret Wise Brown. Illustrated by Clement Hurd. Harper & Row, 1947. In this classic bedtime story, a little bunny says good night to the room and everything in it.

Jafta's Father by Hugh Lewin. Illustrated by Lisa Kopper. Carolrhoda, 1981. Jafta, who lives in South Africa, thinks of the joy he feels when his father is home and how he misses his father when he is at work.

The Lullaby Songbook edited by Jane Yolen. Illustrated by Charles Mikolaycak. Harcourt, 1986. As part of an evening story session, sing some of the lovely lullabies in this collection.

The Summer Night by Charlotte Zolotow. Illustrated by Ben Shecter. Harper & Row, 1974. A little girl and her father share some special moments together before the little girl goes to sleep. Compare how this little girl gets ready for bed with what Corey does in *Daddy Makes the Best Spaghetti*.

About the Author and Illustrator

HINES, ANNA GROSSNICKLE
Something about the Author, ed. by Anne Commire. Gale, 1986, Vol. 45, p. 111; 1988, Vol. 51, pp. 89–91.

Hopkins, Lee Bennett, ed.   *Best Friends*
Illus. by James Watts. Harper & Row, 1986
Suggested Use Level: Gr. PreK–3   Reading Level: NA

Plot Summary
There are many aspects to being "best friends." The 18 poems in this collection show the moods and moments of friendship. Everyday activities are highlighted. One poem ("The Funny House") is about making a playhouse under a blanket. Two poems ("Slumber Party" and "Song of Triumph") tell about sleeping over. There are poems that show the variety of experiences that friends share: uncontrollable laughter ("Bursting"); talking ("The Telephone Call"); fighting and making up ("Wrestling"); sledding ("Atop"); and even fishing ("Tricia's Fish"). Four poems ("Missing You," "Maurice," "Poem," and "Since Hannah Moved Away") show different interpretations of the feeling that comes from being separated from friends.

Thematic Material
Friendship is the obvious theme here, but Hopkins has selected poems that show the nuances of being friends. Learning to get along with others, accepting changes, and sharing good and bad experiences are all related themes in this collection.

Book Talk Material and Activities
When children hear poetry read aloud, they usually want to join in—to clap to the rhythm or try to say the rhymes. The poems in this collection invite participation. "Noises" by Aileen Fisher has repetition of movements and sounds that will delight children. Reading the four poems about being separated from friends could lead to a discussion of how the poets chose different images to express their feelings. Children could then talk about their feelings about friends. "Changing" by Mary Ann Hoberman encourages children to think about other points of view, and children might enjoy changing roles with one another for a day. An excellent activity is to write many of the poems from this and other poetry books on large chart paper. The poems can be illustrated by children and displayed around the classroom or library. Having poems

displayed encourages beginning readers to focus on the print and try to join in when the poem is read aloud.

Related Titles

Mitchell Is Moving by Marjorie Weinman Sharmat. Illustrated by Jose Aruego and Ariane Dewey. Macmillan, 1978. Mitchell is bored because everything in his life is the same. After he moves, he is lonely but his former neighbor, Margo, has a solution. She moves in next door.

Moving Molly written and illustrated by Shirley Hughes. Prentice-Hall, 1978. A book about moving that would correlate well with the four poems in *Best Friends* regarding being separated from friends.

Rainy Rainy Saturday by Jack Prelutsky. Illustrated by Marylin Hafner. Greenwillow, 1980. A collection of 14 poems about everyday feelings on a rainy day.

Random House Book of Poetry for Children edited by Jack Prelutsky. Illustrated by Arnold Lobel. Random House, 1983. A collection of more than 500 poems that is a great resource for poems to correlate with books or subjects.

Read-Aloud Rhymes for the Very Young edited by Jack Prelutsky. Illustrated by Marc Brown. Knopf, 1986. Some super poems that are just right for young children.

We Are Best Friends written and illustrated by Aliki. Greenwillow, 1982. When Peter moves away, Robert learns how to remain his friend and how to make new friends.

Will I Have a Friend? by Miriam Cohen. Illustrated by Lillian Hoban. Macmillan, 1967. One in a series of books about Jim and his friends. Some of the other titles include *Best Friends* (Macmillan, 1971); *Lost in the Museum* (Greenwillow, 1979); *First Grade Takes a Test* (Greenwillow, 1980); and *Starring First Grade* (Greenwillow, 1985).

About the Author and Illustrator

HOPKINS, LEE BENNETT

Authors of Books for Young People: Supplement to the Second Edition, by Martha E. Ward and Dorothy Marquardt. Scarecrow, 1979, p. 134.

Fifth Book of Junior Authors and Illustrators, ed. by Sally Holmes Holtze. Wilson, 1983, pp. 155–157.

Something about the Author, ed. by Anne Commire. Gale, 1972, Vol. 3, pp. 85–87.

Hutchins, Pat. *The Doorbell Rang*
Illus. by the author. Greenwillow, 1986
Suggested Use Level: Gr. K–1   Reading Level: Gr. 2

Plot Summary

Ma makes a dozen cookies for Sam and Victoria to share, but then the doorbell rings, heralding the arrival of guests. Just as the plate of cookies is divided among the guests, the doorbell rings again and there are more guests. The dilemma of more guests and fewer cookies continues until Grandma arrives, bringing a tray of freshly baked cookies to share with all the children. Everyone agrees that Grandma's cookies are the best, so her arrival is especially satisfying.

Thematic Material

The Doorbell Rang shows children involved with their family and friends with a special focus on the grandmother. The children and Ma show their appreciation for Grandma as they repeat the refrain "No one makes cookies like Grandma." The story also incorporates a simple math concept as the children divide the cookies among the new arrivals; in addition, the importance of sharing and getting along with others is emphasized.

Book Talk Material and Activities

This book could be included in a storytelling or booktalking unit on family relationships with a special emphasis on sharing. Young children would enjoy hearing this story and then talking about special people in their families. Older children might enjoy writing a story about their family, changing the refrain "No one makes cookies like Grandma" to fit their story. For example, "No one reads stories like Mom" or "No one helps me with homework like my brother."

The Doorbell Rang could be correlated with simple math activities; sharing this book might include dividing a plate of cookies among the listeners. Many classroom teachers are trying to incorporate more literature into other curriculum areas, so this math tie-in could be of interest to them.

There is also a story within a story through the illustrations. A bright kitchen/dining area is the setting for the story and Hutchins has included many delightful details, right down to the many footprints the guests leave on Ma's clean floor. Ma's dismayed expression about her floor matches the children's expressions about sharing cookies and provides another point of view.

Related Titles

Frog and Toad Together written and illustrated by Arnold Lobel. Harper & Row, 1971. In the "Cookies" story Frog and Toad can't stop eating cookies. (There are four other stories in this book about these two friends.) Children can compare Frog and Toad's experiences with cookies with those in *The Doorbell Rang*.

I Dance in My Red Pajamas by Edith Thacher Hurd. Illustrated by Emily Arnold McCully. Harper & Row, 1982. A little girl enjoys a visit with her grandparents. This book shows a positive image of the elderly.

If You Give a Mouse a Cookie by Laura Joffe Numeroff. Illustrated by Felicia Bond. Harper & Row, 1985. Sharing a cookie with a mouse leads to many unexpected problems.

Kevin's Grandma by Barbara Williams. Illustrated by Kay Chorao. Dutton, 1975. A boy has a special relationship with a special grandma.

Popcorn written and illustrated by Frank Asch. Parent's Magazine Press, 1979. In *The Doorbell Rang*, there are fewer cookies as more guests arrive. In this book, solving the problem of too much popcorn is fun and filling.

About the Author and Illustrator

HUTCHINS, PAT

Fourth Book of Junior Authors and Illustrators, ed. by Doris de Montreville and Elizabeth D. Crawford. Wilson, 1978, pp. 189–191.

Illustrators of Children's Books: 1967–1976, Vol. IV, comp. by Lee Kingman, Grace Allen Hogarth, and Harriet Quimby. Horn Book, 1978, pp. 20, 129, 193.

Something about the Author, ed. by Anne Commire. Gale, 1979, Vol. 15, pp. 141–143.

Kellogg, Steven. *Best Friends*
Illus. by the author. Dial, 1986
Suggested Use Level: Gr. K–3   Reading Level: Gr. 4

Plot Summary
Kathy and Louise are "best friends." They share everything—their desks at school, chocolate milk, and even a fantasy horse, Golden Silverwind. Louise's aunt and uncle take her on a vacation, and both girls are upset because they will be separated. Left at home, Kathy feels abandoned and she imagines that Louise is lonely, too. A letter from Louise shatters Kathy's visions. Knowing that Louise is having fun makes Kathy decide to have fun, too—just for spite. At first, Kathy is disappointed when her new neighbor is an elderly man. His dog is pregnant and he offers to give her a puppy when his dog gives birth. Kathy is delighted. Now she will have something to show off to Louise. Louise's return home makes Kathy realize that she has been selfish. When each girl asks to have a puppy, but only one puppy is born, Kathy and Louise solve their problem by sharing the puppy. They realize that what is important is that they stay friends.

Thematic Material
As this book shows, there are many aspects of friendship. Close friends usually get along, but at times they disagree. Good friends learn to talk things over, and they remember why they are friends. The theme of learning to get along is evident in the story.

Book Talk Material and Activities
Frequently children want to hear stories about people with lives just like theirs. Reading or hearing about familiar experiences involving friends and family allows children to identify with others and to see similarities and differences. Children also have arguments and misunderstandings with friends. Hearing stories like *Best Friends* helps them see this as a natural part of growing up.

After hearing the story, children could talk or write about their best friends. They might even be willing to describe times when they argued and how they made up. The whole class could write about one imaginary friend, which would provide a fantasy situation for shared feelings.

The postcard that Kathy gets from Louise could be used as a springboard for another writing opportunity. Children could make and write a postcard for a trip (either real or imaginary), for example, a postcard from the moon. This could even tie in with a social studies activity on other countries; students could design postcards for different countries.

Kellogg's illustrations are filled with imaginative details: haunted streets; a clinic with Kathy, Louise, and some surprising animal patients; and pictures of Kathy's fantasies of how she will act toward Louise when she returns home. These illustrations could be compared with those in other Kellogg books to show how he extends the humor of the story through the lively illustrations. The books in the following section, "Related Titles," are useful to compare with *Best Friends*.

Audiovisual Adaptation

Best Friends. "Reading Rainbow." Great Plains National Instructional Television Library, videorecording, 1985.

Related Titles

Frog and Toad Are Friends written and illustrated by Arnold Lobel. Harper & Row, 1970. Five stories about two friends, Frog and Toad.

I'm Not Oscar's Friend Anymore by Marjorie Weinman Sharmat. Illustrated by Tony DeLuna. Dutton, 1975. A boy describes all the reasons why he won't be Oscar's friend, until he realizes that he really does enjoy being with Oscar.

Leo, Zack and Emmie by Amy Ehrlich. Illustrated by Steven Kellogg. Dial, 1981. When Emmie moves into a new neighborhood, it takes some time before the boys, Leo and Zack, will be her friends.

A Letter to Amy written and illustrated by Ezra Jack Keats. Harper & Row, 1968. Peter is having a birthday party and wants to invite someone special.

Rosie and Michael by Judith Viorst. Illustrated by Lorna Tomei. Atheneum, 1974. Rosie and Michael show that sometimes we like people for unusual reasons.

About the Author and Illustrator

KELLOGG, STEVEN
Fourth Book of Junior Authors and Illustrators, ed. by Doris de Montreville and Elizabeth D. Crawford. Wilson, 1978, pp. 208–209.
Illustrators of Children's Books: 1967–1976, Vol. IV, comp. by Lee Kingman, Grace Allen Hogarth, and Harriet Quimby. Horn Book, 1978, pp. 133, 196.
Something about the Author, ed. by Anne Commire. Gale, 1976, Vol. 8, pp. 95–97.

Kellogg, Steven. *Ralph's Secret Weapon*
Illus. by the author. Dial, 1983; pap., 1987
Suggested Use Level: Gr. 1–3   Reading Level: Gr. 6

Plot Summary

Ralph is spending his summer vacation with his flamboyant and eccentric Aunt Georgiana, who has plans for Ralph. He will learn to play the bassoon, enter the snake-charming competition, and save the world from an attacking sea serpent. Ralph goes along with his aunt's plans, although he feels somewhat overwhelmed. Aunt Georgiana is just as involved in projects as Ralph. She makes up her own recipes and creates culinary masterpieces like banana-spinach cream cake, she carves sculptures, and she plays golf. When Ralph and Aunt Georgiana face the sea serpent, Ralph's snake-charming ability is not successful. His "secret weapon," Aunt Georgiana's cake, causes the serpent to hiccup out all the people it has swallowed and to slink away. Ralph, the hero, returns to Aunt Georgiana's house. There, he puts an end to her projects and enjoys the rest of his summer vacation.

Thematic Material

Ralph has a positive relationship with his aunt and he is willing to do things to please her, but he also lets her know when he needs to do things for himself.

Book Talk Material and Activities

Food is a big part of this story, as Ralph saves the world by making the serpent eat the awful banana-spinach cream cake, and food also adds to the fun in many other stories. In *Cloudy with a Chance of Meatballs,* a book that is very popular with children, Grandpa tells a tall tale about a land where the weather is very unusual. Food and beverages fall from the sky instead of rain, sleet, and snow. In *Gregory, the Terrible Eater,* another food story, a goat won't eat nutritious food. Frances the badger takes a lot of food on her picnic in *Best Friends for Frances.* Children could look for other stories where food is important to the narrative. They could keep a list of these books and plan a menu of storybook food. Aunt Georgiana's banana-spinach cream cake would be a great dessert.

Related Titles

Best Friends for Frances by Russell Hoban. Illustrated by Lillian Hoban. Harper & Row, 1969. Frances plans a picnic for her sister, Gloria, and herself, but she hopes to get Albert to come, too. Eggs, tomatoes, carrots, celery, cole slaw, and potato chips are just a few of the foods she puts in her hamper.

Cloudy with a Chance of Meatballs by Judi Barrett. Illustrated by Ron Barrett. Atheneum, 1978. Grandpa tells a story of the faraway town of Chewandswallow, where it rains meatballs, soup, and hamburgers.

Gregory, the Terrible Eater by Mitchell Sharmat. Illustrated by Jose Aruego and Ariane Dewey. Four Winds, 1980. Gregory will only eat from the four food groups, even though his parents want him to eat goat food like newspaper, old clothes, and cardboard.

The Island of the Skog written and illustrated by Steven Kellogg. Dial, 1971. The mice in this story eat a wonderful birthday cake—hot marshmallow cheese cake with raspberry fudge sauce.

Mrs. Pig's Bulk Buy written and illustrated by Mary Rayner. Atheneum, 1981. Mrs. Pig's children put ketchup on everything, but she figures out a way to change their eating habits.

About the Author and Illustrator

KELLOGG, STEVEN

Fourth Book of Junior Authors and Illustrators, ed. by Doris de Montreville and Elizabeth D. Crawford. Wilson, 1978, pp. 208–209.

Illustrators of Children's Books: 1967–1976, Vol. IV, comp. by Lee Kingman, Grace Allen Hogarth, and Harriet Quimby. Horn Book, 1978, pp. 133, 196.

Something about the Author, ed. by Anne Commire. Gale, 1976, Vol. 8, pp. 95–97.

Kent, Jack. *Joey Runs Away*
Illus. by the author. Prentice-Hall, 1985
Suggested Use Level: Gr. 1–3   Reading Level: Gr. 3

Plot Summary

Mother kangaroo wants Joey to clean his room (which is in her pouch), but there is too much mess. Joey runs away instead. When Joey's mother realizes that he is gone, she is distraught. Other animals, however, decide that Joey's empty room might be just right for them. The bear, the elephant, the bull, and the giraffe look at mother's pouch, until she finally tells them the room is not available. Joey is also looking for a place to stay but nothing feels right. He ends up in the mail carrier's sack and is delivered back to his own mother. Joey and his mother realize how much they have missed each other, and Joey agrees to clean his room.

Thematic Material

Children, even kangaroo children, need to get along with their family and friends. In *Joey Runs Away*, Joey finds that leaving home is not the way to solve a problem.

Book Talk Material and Activities

Joey Runs Away is a continuation of the activities of Joey and his mother, who first appeared in *Joey*. Both books show Joey learning to adjust to the needs of others. As part of the socialization process, young children need to develop cooperative attitudes and behavior. *Joey* and *Joey Runs Away* show children how others deal with problems. Other stories about running away could also be presented through brief book talks. Ask children to think about why the character runs away and why he or she decides to return.

Jack Kent's illustrations add to the humor in *Joey Runs Away*, especially when the animals look at the mother kangaroo's pouch, and emphasize how a good picture book uses the text and the illustrations to present a story. Try reading one of the books about Joey without showing the pictures; then read the book and show the pictures. Have children look for humorous details that are presented only in the illustrations. Ask them if their opinion of the book changed when they heard the story and saw the pictures.

Audiovisual Adaptation

Joey Runs Away. Weston Woods, cassette/book, 1986; filmstrip/cassette, 1986.

Related Titles

A Baby Sister for Frances by Russell Hoban. Illustrated by Lillian Hoban. Harper & Row, 1964. Frances decides to run away because her parents pay too much attention to her baby sister, Gloria. Her parents let her know how much they miss her.

Big Sister and Little Sister by Charlotte Zolotow. Illustrated by Martha Alexander. Harper & Row, 1966. Here's a different running away story. The little sister runs away and hides from her big sister, until she realizes that her big sister's bossiness really shows how much she loves her.

Joey written and illustrated by Jack Kent. Prentice-Hall, 1984. Joey's overprotective mother will not let him go out of her pouch. But when all of Joey's friends visit him there, she changes her mind.

Peter's Chair written and illustrated by Ezra Jack Keats. Harper & Row, 1967. Everything that used to belong to Peter is being given to his new baby sister, so Peter decides to run away. When Peter realizes that he has outgrown his baby things, he is ready to come home and be a big brother.

The Runaway Bunny by Margaret Wise Brown. Illustrated by Clement Hurd. Harper & Row, 1942. When this bunny makes plans to run away, his mother tells him how she will follow him.

Runaway Marie Louise by Natalie Savage Carlson. Illustrated by Jose Aruego and Ariane Dewey. Scribner, 1977. Marie Louise is angry at having been punished and decides to run away. She finds that no other mother is as nice as her own.

About the Author and Illustrator

KENT, JACK (JOHN WELLINGTON)
Fifth Book of Junior Authors and Illustrators, ed. by Sally Holmes Holtze. Wilson, 1983, pp. 171–173.
Illustrators of Children's Books: 1967–1976, Vol. IV, comp. by Lee Kingman, Grace Allen Hogarth, and Harriet Quimby. Horn Book, 1978, pp. 134, 196.
Something about the Author, ed. by Anne Commire. Gale, 1981, Vol. 24, pp. 135–137; 1986, Vol. 45, p. 119.

McPhail, David. *Fix-It*

Illus. by the author. Dutton, 1984; pap., 1987
Suggested Use Level: Gr. PreK–1   Reading Level: Gr. 2

Plot Summary

Emma the bear wants to watch television but the set is broken. She wakes up her parents, who cannot seem to fix the set. Emma is distraught. The repairman is called, and he comes to work on the television. Meanwhile, Emma's parents try to entertain her. The repairman cannot fix the television, and he gives up. Emma goes to her room with her doll and her book. When Emma's father finally plugs the set in, Emma is too busy reading to watch television.

Thematic Material

Fix-It is part of a series of books about Emma and her family. Even though the characters are bears, each book focuses on everyday human experiences and shows family relationships.

Book Talk Material and Activities

Emma's warm and loving relationship with her family reflects the emphasis in this book and in *Emma's Pet* and *Emma's Vacation* on family togetherness. A book talk or story program about families provides children with resources on different family situations. The wordless books *Moonlight* and *Sunshine* are especially good to use with a few children at a time. Children could describe what is happening in the pictures and make up their own stories. After sharing their stories with the other children, they should be encouraged to talk about their families.

At the end of *Fix-It*, Emma is too busy reading to watch the television. Of course, the message is that books can be just as involving as television. Ask children to name some of their favorite books and make a chart. In the library use the chart to show children how to look for these "favorite" books on the shelves.

Audiovisual Adaptation

Fix-It. Live Oak Media, cassette/book, 1988; filmstrip/cassette, 1984.

Related Titles

Emma's Pet written and illustrated by David McPhail. Dutton, 1985. When Emma cannot find the pet she wants, she discovers that her father would be the perfect pet.

Emma's Vacation written and illustrated by David McPhail. Dutton, 1987. The bears take a trip and have several adventures, but Emma's favorite time is when she and her parents spend some quiet time together.

Gone Fishing written by Earlene Long. Illustrated by Richard Brown. Houghton Mifflin, 1984. A father and son go fishing and enjoy their time together. Compare this fishing adventure to the one in *Just Like Daddy*.

Just Like Daddy written and illustrated by Frank Asch. Prentice-Hall, 1981. Another story about family togetherness, in which a family goes fishing and Mommy catches the biggest fish.

Moonlight written and illustrated by Jan Ormerod. Lothrop, 1981. In this wordless book, children can follow a little girl on her nighttime routines.

Sunshine written and illustrated by Jan Ormerod. Lothrop, 1982. A companion book to *Moonlight,* which shows the little girl's daytime activities. Children enjoy making up stories to go with the pictures.

About the Author and Illustrator

McPhail, David

Fifth Book of Junior Authors and Illustrators, ed. by Sally Holmes Holtze. Wilson, 1983, pp. 213–214.

Illustrators of Children's Books: 1967–1976, Vol. IV, comp. by Lee Kingman, Grace Allen Hogarth, and Harriet Quimby. Horn Book, 1978, pp. 4, 5, 143, 200.

Something about the Author, ed. by Anne Commire. Gale, 1983, Vol. 32, p. 137; 1987, Vol. 47, pp. 150–165.

Merriam, Eve. *The Birthday Door*
Illus. by Peter J. Thornton. Morrow, 1986
Suggested Use Level: Gr. 1–3   Reading Level: Gr. 4

Plot Summary

Helen awakens from a dream about her birthday only to find that it is Saturday and her birthday has arrived. When a note is slipped under her door, Helen and her cat, Clio, begin to unravel the mystery that will lead to Helen's birthday surprise. Each note is a rhymed couplet that leads Helen and Clio to a door that hides a new message. Finally, they find the clue that takes them to the room with Helen's present—and it is just what she dreamed of!

Thematic Material

The Birthday Door is a story full of imagination and anticipation. It is beautifully illustrated in a manner that reinforces the dreamlike quality of the text. Helen's sense of wonder grows with each new clue, and the author and illustrator include images that display that wonder. There is also a feeling of family in this book, as Helen's parents have planned this special surprise for her.

Book Talk Material and Activities

This book offers many opportunities for involvement. As a discussion book, it allows children to share some of their own feelings about what would be a special gift. The children could talk about their memories of special times and what made them special. They could even do some writing about their feelings or about one special family activity. Children could also try to think of other doors, from among the many different doors around the school and in other locations, that could be used as clues. They could suggest different settings for this story—and how these new settings would influence the feeling of the story. They might even want to try writing some rhymed couplets.

Thornton's beautiful illustrations, in which he used very soft colors to maintain a dreamlike feeling, enhance the mood of anticipation in this story. This is the first picture book that Thornton illustrated. Children could watch for other books illustrated by him—to see if his style changes to fit the mood of other stories—as well as for other books with similar illustrations, noting the kind of mood created through the pictures in each case.

Related Titles

Aunt Nina and Her Nieces and Nephews by Franz Brandenberg. Illustrated by Aliki. Greenwillow, 1983. When visiting Aunt Nina for a birthday party, her nieces and nephews are surprised to celebrate six new birthdays.

Benjamin's 365 Birthdays by Judi Barrett. Illustrated by Ron Barrett.

Atheneum, 1974. Benjamin likes celebrating his birthday so much that he finds a way to celebrate all year.

The Birthday Wish written and illustrated by Chihiro Iwasaki. McGraw-Hill, 1972. A birthday story with beautiful illustrations that was printed in Japan on heavy, grained paper. An excellent companion book to *The Birthday Door*.

Happy Birthday, Sam written and illustrated by Pat Hutchins. Greenwillow, 1978. On his birthday, Sam does not feel older, but a special present from his grandfather shows that he understands what Sam needs.

The Surprise by George Shannon. Illustrated by Jose Aruego and Ariane Dewey. Greenwillow, 1983. Another birthday story about finding a gift, but the mood and tone are very different.

When the Sun Rose written and illustrated by Barbara Helen Berger. Philomel, 1986. The beautiful illustrations in this book glow with a golden light. Berger's use of color could be compared with Thornton's in *The Birthday Door*.

About the Author and Illustrator

MERRIAM, EVE

Authors of Books for Young People: First Supplement, by Martha E. Ward and Dorothy Marquardt. Scarecrow, 1967, p. 204.

Something about the Author, ed. by Anne Commire. Gale, 1972, Vol. 3, pp. 128–129; 1985, Vol. 40, pp. 141–149.

Third Book of Junior Authors, ed. by Doris de Montreville and Donna Hill. Wilson, 1972, pp. 193–194.

Porte, Barbara Ann.   *Harry's Visit*
Illus. by Yossi Abolafia. Greenwillow, 1983
Suggested Use Level: Gr. 1–3   Reading Level: Gr. 3

Plot Summary

Harry's father is taking him to visit the Silversteins, and Harry is dreading it. Harry's father has been friends with the Silversteins for a long time, but Harry barely knows them. He does know, however, that he does not want to spend the day alone with them. As he suspected, everything is very different at the Silversteins. They eat different foods than Harry is used to, their daughter, Judy, likes different games and music, and they don't even eat dessert at lunch. The visit is the disaster that Harry predicted until Jonathan, Judy's brother, takes Harry to play basketball with him. Harry discovers that Mrs. Silverstein's thoughtfulness has made it possible for him to play with the older kids. She has had one hoop lowered so that even younger children like Harry can succeed. In the end, Harry surprises himself by choosing yogurt for a treat instead of his usual ice cream. His visit teaches him about trying new things and meeting new people.

Thematic Material

An important theme here is learning to get along with others. Harry is anxious about the Silversteins because he is in a new situation. As he learns about them, he learns to like them and discovers that he can adapt to their ways.

Book Talk Material and Activities

Many children are concerned about not being liked or about being different. In *Harry's Visit,* Harry shows those same fears and provides a common experience for children to discuss. This is a good book to share at the start of a new situation, for example, at the start of the school year, when everyone is new and worried about getting along. A discussion of similarities and differences could focus on general information about the children in the class or group, such as favorite foods, colors, books, games, and so forth. Seeing the many things they share will help children learn about one another and feel more comfortable together. Children might want to share other situations where they felt "new" and discuss how they learned to get along.

Related Titles

Do You Want to Be My Friend? written and illustrated by Eric Carle. Crowell, 1971. A mouse tentatively asks each animal to be his friend. When he meets another mouse, he finally gets the answer he was hoping for.

The Guest written and illustrated by James Marshall. Houghton Mifflin, 1975. Mona welcomes an uninvited guest into her home and they become close friends.

I Do Not Like It When My Friend Comes to Visit written and illustrated by Ivan Sherman. Harcourt, 1973. A little girl feels inadequate when her friend visits. She finds it difficult to share and to watch her friend be better at activities than she is. This story presents the host's point of view about a visit.

Ira Sleeps Over written and illustrated by Bernard Waber. Houghton Mifflin, 1972. A well-known story of a boy who wonders if his friend will make fun of him for bringing his toy bear along on an overnight visit.

The Popcorn Dragon by Catherine Woolley. Illustrated by Jay Hyde Barnum. Morrow, 1953. Dexter is a dragon who does not know how to make friends. He learns to stop showing off and to share instead.

Visiting Pamela by Norma Klein. Illustrated by Kay Chorao. Dial, 1979. Like Harry in *Harry's Visit,* Carrie worries that her visit with Pamela will be a disaster.

About the Author and Illustrator

PORTE, BARBARA ANN
Something about the Author, ed. by Anne Commire. Gale, 1986, Vol. 45, p. 168.
ABOLAFIA, YOSSI
Something about the Author, ed. by Anne Commire. Gale, 1987, Vol. 46, p. 21.

Rylant, Cynthia. *The Relatives Came*
Illus. by Stephen Gammell. Bradbury, 1985
Suggested Use Level: Gr. 1–3   Reading Level: Gr. 6

Plot Summary

One summer the relatives from Virginia come to visit. Their car is packed for the trip and they enjoy the scenery along the way. When they reach the house there is a joyous celebration of family togetherness— hugging, crying, laughing, talking, and eating. Squeezing together and sharing the space, the relatives stay for a long visit until finally they crowd back into their car and return home.

Thematic Material

The feeling of family togetherness is central here. Written in the form of a reminiscence, the book has a sense of nostalgic yearning for the past. The family members care about each other, and they appreciate their time together. In 1986 Gammell received a Caldecott Honor Medal for his illustrations.

Book Talk Material and Activities

There are several possibilities for discussion. Students could talk or write about trips they have taken, how it feels to stay in someone else's home, or how it feels to have someone stay in your home. Another discussion could focus on times when a family comes together. Children might enjoy sharing information about how many people there are in their family, and a chart could be made with the information they provide, using categories like large families, middle-sized families, and small families.

The Relatives Came could be coordinated with other stories of characters who crowd together, such as *I Go with My Family to Grandma's* and *The Mitten.* Talking about how these characters interact—whether they get along or argue—could get children interested in reading other stories like this one. One project might be a mural depicting the various characters in the different stories.

Gammell's illustrations capture the rollicking fun of this visit. The pictures are crowded with many different characters, and it is a challenge to find the same relatives on different pages.

Audiovisual Adaptation

The Relatives Came. Random House Media, cassette/book, 1986; filmstrip/cassette, 1986; videorecording, 1988.

Related Titles

Brimhall Comes to Stay by Judy Delton. Illustrated by Cyndy Szekeres. Lothrop, 1978. A visit from a relative puts a strain on the relationship between visitor and host.

I Go with My Family to Grandma's by Riki Levinson. Illustrated by Diane Goode. Dutton, 1986. Another family is having a get-together. Each of the five cousins comes by a different mode of transportation from a different part of New York City. As in *The Relatives Came,* this is a crowd of relatives.

It Could Always Be Worse: A Yiddish Folktale retold and illustrated by Margot Zemach. Farrar, Straus, 1976. A peasant is upset by the noise in his crowded house. Compare this crowded family to the ones in *Too Much Noise* and *The Relatives Came.*

Mr. Gumpy's Outing written and illustrated by John Burningham. Holt,

Rinehart, 1970. Mr. Gumpy takes all of his friends for a ride in his car. Another story crowded with characters.

The Mitten: An Old Ukrainian Folktale retold by Alvin Tresselt. Illustrated by Yaroslava. Lothrop, 1964. Animals crowd into a little boy's mitten to try to keep warm.

Picnic written and illustrated by Emily Arnold McCully. Harper & Row, 1984. This wordless story follows a large family of mice on an outing.

Too Much Noise by Ann McGovern. Illustrated by Simms Taback. Houghton Mifflin, 1967. An old man brings farm animals into his noisy house. When he removes these animals, his noisy house seems much less noisy.

About the Author and Illustrator

RYLANT, CYNTHIA
Something about the Author, ed. by Anne Commire. Gale, 1986, Vol. 44, pp. 167–168; 1988, Vol. 50, pp. 182–188.

GAMMELL, STEPHEN
Fifth Book of Junior Authors and Illustrators, ed. by Sally Holmes Holtze. Wilson, 1983, pp. 121–122.

Sharmat, Marjorie Weinman. *Bartholomew the Bossy*
Illus. by Normand Chartier. Macmillan, 1984
Suggested Use Level: Gr. 1–3   Reading Level: Gr. 2

Plot Summary

Bartholomew the skunk has been elected president of the neighborhood club. As president, he tells everyone what they should do and he won't listen to any suggestions. He starts to give everyone orders about how they should act and what they should wear. He even tells his friend the lion how to comb his mane. Pretty soon, no one comes to the club meetings and no one will talk to Bartholomew. Bartholomew goes to Fabian Owl to find out why his friends have deserted him. Fabian gives Bartholomew some strange things to do and when Bartholomew revolts, Fabian tells him that his friends don't like to be told what to do either. Bartholomew goes home and figures out a way to be nice to each of the friends that he has offended, and they all join him back at the clubhouse. When Fabian Owl comes to the meeting and starts to give a boring lecture, Bartholomew is almost bossy again, but he remembers the lesson he has learned and lets Fabian put everyone to sleep.

Thematic Material

Bartholomew does not know how to be in charge of the club. Here, he learns to get along with his friends by accepting them as they are.

Book Talk Material and Activities

Whenever children participate in group activities, they have problems getting along. Learning appropriate behavior is part of the socialization process in schools and libraries, and *Bartholomew the Bossy* could promote a discussion on positive attitudes and behavior. Reading it with some of the related titles in a story program allows children to see how others solve problems with friends. A comparison of *Bartholomew the Bossy, Best Friends for Frances,* and *The Popcorn Dragon* could focus on problem-solving techniques. What do the characters in these books do that causes their problem? What do they do to change the situation? Children could discuss what the characters learn from their experiences, and relate these experiences to their own. From these activities children will develop and express their own opinions about getting along with others.

Related Titles

Addie Meets Max by Joan Robins. Illustrated by Sue Truesdell. Harper & Row, 1985. Addie does not think that Max, her new neighbor, will be her friend. Max's dog barked at Addie, and then Max knocked her off her bike. A discussion could focus on what Addie does to make Max her friend.

Best Friends for Frances by Russell Hoban. Illustrated by Lillian Hoban. Harper & Row, 1969. Like Bartholomew in *Bartholomew the Bossy,* Frances is finding it difficult to be a good friend. She is mean to her sister and then is mad when the boys are mean to her. Discuss with the children what Frances does to make friends.

No Friends written and illustrated by James Stevenson. Greenwillow, 1986. Mary Ann and Louie are worried that they won't make friends in their new neighborhood. Of course, Grandpa has a story to tell about when he and his brother Wainey moved. *What's Under My Bed?* (see Chapter 4) is another adventure with Mary Ann, Louie, and Grandpa.

The Popcorn Dragon by Catherine Woolley. Illustrated by Jay Hyde Barnum. Morrow, 1953. Dexter the dragon is a show-off, and none of the other animals wants to play with him. What does he do to make friends?

Rosie and Michael by Judith Viorst. Illustrated by Lorna Tomei. Atheneum, 1974. Rosie and Michael take turns describing what they like about each other.

About the Author and Illustrator

SHARMAT, MARJORIE WEINMAN

Authors of Books for Young People: Supplement to the Second Edition, by Martha E. Ward and Dorothy Marquardt. Scarecrow, 1979, pp. 247–248.

Fifth Book of Junior Authors and Illustrators, ed. by Sally Holmes Holtze. Wilson, 1983, pp. 282–283.

Something about the Author, ed. by Anne Commire. Gale, 1973, Vol. 4, pp. 187–189; 1983, Vol. 33, pp. 186–194.

Van Leeuwen, Jean.   *Tales of Amanda Pig*
Illus. by Ann Schweninger. Dial, 1983, hb and pap.
Suggested Use Level: Gr. 1–3   Reading Level: Gr. 2

Plot Summary

There are five stories in this book about Amanda Pig and her family. In the first one, Amanda does not want to eat her egg. She waits so long, that the egg is cold. Finally, after Amanda's mother tells her about the fun her father and brother are having outside, Amanda eats her egg and joins them. In the second story, Amanda and her brother, Oliver, are bored, until their mother plays a game with them and their grandmother comes to visit. In the third story, Amanda's father helps Amanda overcome her fear of the dark and of the hall clock that looks like a monster. Amanda and Oliver have a fight in the next story, and the last one shows Amanda getting ready for bed and sharing a quiet moment with her mother.

Thematic Material

These stories show a loving family of pigs that share many quiet moments together. Like ordinary siblings, Amanda and her brother, Oliver, have arguments and their parents get exasperated with them, but there is also much affection in this pig family.

Book Talk Material and Activities

Watching book characters grow and change is always fun. In this series of books about Amanda Pig, Amanda goes from being a baby in a high chair (in *Tales of Oliver Pig*) to a young girl who can help around the house (in *More Tales of Amanda Pig*). Each book about Amanda and her brother has details about their everyday life. Another series in which the character grows up is the one about Peter by Ezra Jack Keats that includes *Peter's Chair* and *Pet Show*. Both series show children how authors develop characters, and may give children ideas for their own writing. Children can also see the way in which characters change in the illustrations and how the illustrator depicts them at different ages.

The chapter format and large, well-spaced print make the books about Amanda accessible to beginning readers. *Oink and Pearl* and *Addie Meets Max* are two other good friendship books in a similar format to include in a book talk program for first- and second-grade classes.

Related Titles

Addie Meets Max by Joan Robins. Illustrated by Sue Truesdell. Harper & Row, 1985. Addie takes a while to feel comfortable with the new boy and his dog who have moved next door. Once they all get to know each other, Addie, Max, and Ginger are glad to be together.

More Tales of Amanda Pig by Jean Van Leeuwen. Illustrated by Ann Schweninger. Dial, 1985. Amanda is older than in *Tales of Amanda Pig*, and she is able to help around the house. She still has time to play "let's pretend" with Oliver and make a mess with bubbles in the bathroom.

Oink and Pearl written and illustrated by Kay Chorao. Harper & Row, 1981. Four stories about Pearl the pig and her little brother, Oink. In one, Oink finds a fishing pole and thinks he would like to go fishing. In another, Pearl and Oink turn a garden party into a mud party. Students can compare the relationship between these pig siblings with Amanda and Oliver's.

Pet Show written and illustrated by Ezra Jack Keats. Viking, 1972. Peter is now much older than he was in *Peter's Chair*. His younger friend, Archie, is the central figure in the story. The children can see how much older Peter's little sister is, too.

Peter's Chair written and illustrated by Ezra Jack Keats. Viking, 1967.

Peter has outgrown his baby chair, but he is not ready to give it to the new baby.

Tales of Oliver Pig by Jean Van Leeuwen. Illustrated by Arnold Lobel. Dial, 1979. Amanda Pig is a baby in this book. She cries, says "gah," and pesters her brother, Oliver.

About the Author and Illustrator

VAN LEEUWEN, JEAN
Fifth Book of Junior Authors and Illustrators, ed. by Sally Holmes Holtze. Wilson, 1983, pp. 317–318.
Something about the Author, ed. by Anne Commire. Gale, 1974, Vol. 6, pp. 212–213.

SCHWENINGER, ANN
Something about the Author, ed. by Anne Commire. Gale, 1982, Vol. 29, pp. 172–173.

Wells, Rosemary. *Max's Christmas*
Illus. by the author. Dial, 1986
Suggested Use Level: Gr. PreK–1   Reading Level: Gr. 2

Plot Summary

It is Christmas Eve and Max the rabbit is waiting for Santa. Even though Max's sister, Ruby, told him not to wait, Max is trying to see Santa. When Santa arrives, he puts Max to sleep on the couch and leaves Max his hat and his blanket. Later, Ruby comes downstairs and is surprised to see Max's new hat, but she is even more surprised when she lifts the blanket that Santa used to cover Max. Under it are all the presents that Santa left them.

Thematic Material

In this Christmas story, Max and Ruby are rabbits that act like humans. Like any older sister, Ruby tries to boss Max around, but he does just as he pleases.

Book Talk Material and Activities

Max the rabbit is a popular character in Rosemary Wells's books. Young children who have seen Max in the cardboard books like *Max's*

Birthday and *Max's First Words* will enjoy this longer story, in which Max celebrates Christmas by waiting for Santa. Christmas is a special time for sharing with family and friends. A program or display could be organized on how other book characters celebrate Christmas, including such books as: *Spot's First Christmas; Georgie's Christmas Carol;* and *Merry Christmas, Amelia Bedelia.* Sharing these books is a good way to encourage children to talk about what they will be doing for the holiday season. Librarians and teachers should be sensitive to the religious and cultural backgrounds of the children and encourage them to share information about other celebrations.

Audiovisual Adaptation

Max's Christmas. Weston Woods, cassette/book, 1987; 16mm film, 1987; filmstrip/cassette, 1987.

Related Titles

The Bear's Christmas written and illustrated by Stan Berenstain and Jan Berenstain. Beginner Books, 1970. Brother Bear gets a sled, skates, and skis for Christmas and, of course, his father takes him out to use them. Each new sport turns into a disastrous experience.

Georgie's Christmas Carol written and illustrated by Robert Bright. Doubleday, 1975. Georgie the ghost and all his friends are excited about Christmas, but his neighbor Mr. Gloams feels like Scrooge. When two children arrive unexpectedly at Mr. Gloams's house, Georgie helps them have a happy Christmas.

Max's Birthday written and illustrated by Rosemary Wells. Dial, 1985. Max copes with a wind-up dinosaur that chases him in this sturdy board book.

Max's First Words written and illustrated by Rosemary Wells. Dial, 1979. In this book with board pages sturdy enough for preschool children, Max's sister, Ruby, tries to teach Max some words.

Merry Christmas, Amelia Bedelia by Peggy Parish. Illustrated by Lynn Sweat. Greenwillow, 1986. Everyone knows how mixed up Amelia Bedelia is. Children can see and discuss how she "stuffs stockings" and "trims the tree."

Merry Christmas, Ernest and Celestine written and illustrated by Gabrielle Vincent. Greenwillow, 1983. Ernest dresses up like Santa Claus to make it a very special Christmas for Celestine.

Merry Christmas, Space Case written and illustrated by James Marshall.

Dial, 1986. Buddy's friend from outer space arrives just in time to rescue Buddy from the bullies who live near Granny's house. A question to ask the children is whether they think they would like being changed into snowmen.

Morris's Disappearing Bag: A Christmas Story written and illustrated by Rosemary Wells. Dial, 1975. Morris the rabbit discovers that he can disappear into a bag. With this special ability, he becomes the envy of his siblings and they let him share their gifts.

Spot's First Christmas written and illustrated by Eric Hill. Putnam, 1983. In this lift-the-flap book, Spot the dog trims the tree, listens to singers, and looks for his presents. Finally he goes to bed. The next morning, he enjoys finding his presents, especially his new collar.

About the Author and Illustrator

WELLS, ROSEMARY
Fourth Book of Junior Authors and Illustrators, ed. by Doris de Montreville and Elizabeth D. Crawford. Wilson, 1978, pp. 343–345.
Illustrators of Children's Books: 1967–1976, Vol. IV, comp. by Lee Kingman, Grace Allen Hogarth, and Harriet Quimby. Horn Book, 1978, pp. 13, 168, 213.
Something about the Author, ed. by Anne Commire. Gale, 1980, Vol. 18, pp. 296–298.

Winthrop, Elizabeth. *Lizzie and Harold*
Illus. by Martha Weston. Lothrop, 1986
Suggested Use Level: Gr. K–1   Reading Level: Gr. 2

Plot Summary

Lizzie cannot wait to have a best friend. She has always wanted one. Her neighbor Harold offers to be her best friend, but Lizzie has other plans. She wants a girl for her best friend and she chooses Christina. Lizzie wears her hair and dresses like Christina, but Christina ignores her. Next, Lizzie decides that she will advertise for a best friend. When Harold answers the advertisement, Lizzie snubs him, but he keeps trying. He even teaches her how to play cat's cradle. Still, Lizzie does not accept him as her best friend. While they are walking to school the next day, Harold tells Lizzie that he has decided to look for a best friend. Lizzie thinks about what Harold means to her and how she has treated him. She is sad when he tells her about his new best friend, until he admits that he likes her more. Lizzie knows that Harold is the best friend she has been looking for.

Thematic Material

Many children wonder who their friends will be and whether anyone will like them. Lizzie learns that friends can't be made to order. She comes to understand the needs of others.

Book Talk Material and Activities

According to *Chase's Annual Events, 1988* (Contemporary, 1987), February is International Friendship Month and June 15 is the annual A Friend in Need Is a Friend Indeed Day. Either time is perfect for sharing this story about two friends. There are many other books that look at the friendship between two characters. Have children suggest "books with two friends" and keep a list of the characters in the library. Some suggestions might be Frog and Toad (*Frog and Toad All Year*), George and Martha (*George and Martha*), and Duck and Bear (*Two Good Friends*). Other categories of friendship books might be "books with three friends" and "books with many friends." During Friendship Month, have children read and report on different friendship books. Ask each child to answer the question "What do friends do?" Encourage the children to use specific details from books they know. Then list the children's answers. The list might look like this:

What Do Friends Do?
Frog brings Toad some ice cream. (*Frog and Toad All Year*)

Harold shows Lizzie how to play cat's cradle. (*Lizzie and Harold*)

George eats Martha's split pea soup even though he hates split pea soup. (*George and Martha*)

When Harold shows Lizzie how to play cat's cradle in *Lizzie and Harold*, a diagram in the book describes the game. *Cat's Cradle, Owl's Eyes: A Book of String Games* gives many more examples of cat's cradle activities. Learning a few simple string games would enhance the telling of this story.

Related Titles

Cat's Cradle, Owl's Eyes: A Book of String Games by Camilla Gryski. Illustrated by Tom Sankey. Morrow, 1983. Clear directions and drawings demonstrate a variety of string games. Have a group of older children learn a few and demonstrate them to younger children.

Ernest and Celestine written and illustrated by Gabrielle Vincent. Greenwillow, 1981. Ernest protects and looks after little Celestine, and when she loses her toy, he finds a way to replace it.

Frog and Toad All Year written and illustrated by Arnold Lobel. Harper & Row, 1976. Follow these two friends through a year of activities. How do they help each other?

George and Martha written and illustrated by James Marshall. Houghton Mifflin, 1972. The first book in the series about two hippo friends.

Goggles written and illustrated by Ezra Jack Keats. Macmillan, 1969. Peter and Archie find some goggles and get chased by some older boys.

Two Good Friends by Judy Delton. Illustrated by Giulio Maestro. Crown, 1974. Sometimes even good friends find it difficult to get along. Bear and Duck find that being helpful is important.

About the Author and Illustrator

WINTHROP, ELIZABETH (MAHONY)
Fifth Book of Junior Authors and Illustrators, ed. by Sally Holmes Holtze. Wilson, 1983, pp. 330–331.
Something about the Author, ed. by Anne Commire. Gale, 1976, Vol. 6, p. 125.

Zolotow, Charlotte. *Some Things Go Together*

Illus. by Karen Gundersheimer. Crowell, 1983; pap., Harper & Row, 1987
Suggested Use Level: Gr. PreK–1   Reading Level: NA

Plot Summary

The rhyming text in this book shows a loving relationship between a mother and a little boy as they share some moments together. The author also lists other things that go together.

Thematic Material

The love that the mother in the story feels for her little boy is very evident, and the rhythmic text creates a gentle mood that celebrates the relationship.

Book Talk Material and Activities

This reassuring story of the love between a mother and a son is especially right for preschool children. The security of the relationship is very satisfying. Children enjoy listening to the pattern of the rhyme and joining in on the closing rhyme. The book should be read several times as part of different story programs. Repeated readings help children become more familiar with books, and through this familiarity, they develop confidence about using books and learning to read. They can join in on refrains, follow patterns, and discuss new words. The children can also see how books are held and how pages are turned. Rereading a book is a satisfying experience, like a visit from a good friend. *Some Things Go Together* deserves to be that friend.

Related Titles

Amifika by Lucille Clifton. Illustrated by Thomas DiGrazia. Dutton, 1977. Amifika's father has been away and now he is coming home. Amifika is not sure if he and his father will "go together."

The Cozy Book by Mary Ann Hoberman. Illustrated by Tony Chen. Viking, 1982. Cozy sounds, smells, clothes, food, and feelings are described in verse.

Pig Pig Rides written and illustrated by David McPhail. Dutton, 1982. Pig Pig fantasizes about having daredevil adventures, but his mother reminds him of the importance of home.

The Runaway Bunny by Margaret Wise Brown. Illustrated by Clement Hurd. Harper & Row, 1942. The bunny tells his mother about his different plans to run away. She tells him how she will always find him. This bunny and his mother "go together."

Say It! by Charlotte Zolotow. Illustrated by James Stevenson. Greenwillow, 1980. As a mother and daughter go for a walk, the mother talks about the beauty of the time they spend together. The little girl wants to hear her mother say "I love you."

About the Author and Illustrator

ZOLOTOW, CHARLOTTE

Authors of Books for Young People, Second Edition, by Martha E. Ward and Dorothy Marquardt. Scarecrow, 1971, p. 575.

More Junior Authors, ed. by Muriel Fuller. Wilson, 1963, p. 235.

Something about the Author, ed. by Anne Commire. Gale, 1971, Vol. 1, p. 233; 1984, Vol. 35, pp. 237–245.

GUNDERSHEIMER, KAREN

Something about the Author, ed. by Anne Commire. Gale, 1986, Vol. 44, p. 86.

2

Developing a Positive
Self-Image

ALTHOUGH many children worry about being accepted in group situations, they are also concerned about developing as individuals. They want to know that others respect their differences and that they have their own identity. They often need to be reassured about changes in their lives, and they want to feel comfortable just being themselves.

The books in this chapter present stories and information about individual needs and interests. Included are nonfiction books about divorce and adoption, as well as fiction books about characters who choose to lead unusual lives and who make independent choices.

Blos, Joan W. *Old Henry*
Illus. by Stephen Gammell. Morrow, 1987
Suggested Use Level: Gr. 1–3   Reading Level: Gr. 3

Plot Summary
Old Henry is an eccentric stranger who moves into a deserted house. At first, the neighbors are pleased to see him because they expect him to repair the dilapidated structure. Their hopeful expectations turn to frustration and disappointment as Henry is content to live in the house as it is. In fact, Henry adds to the clutter with his own belongings. His neighbors are outraged. They entreat him to fix up his house, even threatening him with fines and jail. Henry remains adamant in his opposition until, annoyed by his neighbors' bickering, he packs and leaves. His neighbors are surprised to find that they miss him and they begin to question their own actions. Henry is also having second thoughts. The book ends with Henry writing a letter to the mayor asking if he can come back.

Thematic Material

Old Henry is a man who is "different," yet he is comfortable with himself. He is satisfied with his life and does not feel pressured to conform. Even when his neighbors disapprove, Henry maintains his individuality.

Book Talk Material and Activities

Old Henry is a celebration of one man's independent spirit. Although it is important for children to "fit in," they also like to know that they are special and that their differences will be accepted by those around them. One activity that could correlate with this book is making paper cut-outs. Each child lies down on a large sheet of paper (for example, from a roll of white butcher paper) and other children help trace the child's outline. Children illustrate their outlines to look like themselves, then cut them out and display them. A follow-up activity might have the children suggest positive words or sentences about each other and then write them on the cut-out. The emphasis should be on what the children like about each other. For example, "Evan is . . . caring, helpful, a good friend" or "Tina likes to jump rope and she loves the hula-hoop." This is another way that children can learn about each other.

Older children might want to study Henry's letter and talk or write about a response to it. This could lead to a discussion of values and freedom with questions like "Are the expectations of the group more important then the free choice of an individual?" and "Is conformity a good thing? Why or why not?"

Gammell's illustrations are whimsical, with wild lines around Henry and his house and tightly controlled lines depicting the neighbors. Making children aware of this correlation between text and illustration helps them become more discerning about picture books.

Audiovisual Adaptation

Old Henry. Random House Media, filmstrip/cassette, 1989.

Related Titles

Cornelius written and illustrated by Leo Lionni. Pantheon, 1983. Cornelius feels left out because the other crocodiles don't appreciate his special skills.

Louis the Fish by Arthur Yorinks. Illustrated by Richard Egielski. Farrar, Straus, 1980. Louis is not a happy man. If only he could be a fish, then he would be happy. But such dreams can never come true . . . or can they?

The Man Who Could Call Down Owls by Eve Bunting. Illustrated by Charles Mikolaycak. Macmillan, 1984. The mysterious man who can call down owls is viewed with awe and fear. Like Henry in *Old Henry,* this man is different, but his unusual skills place him in great danger. Older children who see the parallels between the two stories could discuss the danger that an outsider must often face.

Miss Maggie by Cynthia Rylant. Illustrated by Thomas DiGrazia. Dutton, 1983. Like Henry in *Old Henry,* Miss Maggie lives alone in a deteriorating house. Nat is afraid of her until one day, when she needs his help, he discovers that she is lonely and afraid, too.

Miss Rumphius written and illustrated by Barbara Cooney. Viking, 1982. Miss Rumphius lives her life exactly the way she chooses. She shares her happiness by planting lupines and making the world more beautiful.

About the Author and Illustrator

BLOS, JOAN W.
Authors of Books for Young People: Supplement to the Second Edition, by Martha E. Ward and Dorothy Marquardt. Scarecrow, 1979, p. 27.
Fifth Book of Junior Authors and Illustrators, ed. by Sally Holmes Holtze. Wilson, 1983, pp. 35–37.
Something about the Author, ed. by Anne Commire. Gale, 1982, Vol. 27, p. 35; 1983, Vol. 33, pp. 40–42.

GAMMELL, STEPHEN
Fifth Book of Junior Authors and Illustrators, ed. by Sally Holmes Holtze. Wilson, 1983, pp. 121–122.

Brown, Laurene Krasny, and Brown, Marc.   *Dinosaurs Divorce: A Guide for Changing Families*
Illus. by the authors. Little, Brown, 1986
Suggested Use Level: Gr. 3–4   Reading Level: Gr. 5

Plot Summary

Building on their own experiences, Laurene Krasny Brown and Marc Brown have written a book to help children understand the complexities of divorce. The book begins with an explanation of some of the terms that children will need to know, including "divorce," "alimony," "child support," "separation agreement," "stepparents," and "visiting rights." As the authors describe some of the situations that might lead to divorce, they try to reassure young readers that they are not responsible for the problems between their parents. The authors' common sense advice encourages children to talk about their concerns and to ask for help. The cartoon illustrations show dinosaur families learning to cope with the changes that come with a divorce. Some of the chapters in the book discuss "Living with One Parent," "Having Two Homes," "Telling Your Friends," and "Having Stepsisters and Stepbrothers."

Thematic Material

Learning to adapt to change is an important part of growing up. Divorce is a familiar situation for many children, requiring them to cope with their concerns and emotions. This book encourages children to accept the changes while maintaining a positive self-image.

Book Talk Material and Activities

This picture book is good to include in a book talk program of fiction and nonfiction books focusing on children's concerns about growing up, including books that deal with divorce, death, moods and emotions, adoption, and health. Many children in the middle grades (grades 3–4) are interested in reading about how to cope with these problems, and they often find it comforting to read about others who are facing similar situations. Just knowing that they are not alone can be reassuring. *Dinosaurs Divorce* and other related titles also make an excellent book talk program for parents and other adults who work with children.

The cartoon-style illustrations in *Dinosaurs Divorce* are especially interesting. Marc Brown has collaborated with Stephen Krensky on some other self-help books illustrated in the cartoon style, including *Perfect Pigs* and *Dinosaurs Beware!* Children might want to try to imitate the style by illustrating some library or classroom situations in cartoon panels. They could discuss why the Browns chose dinosaurs as the main characters in *Dinosaurs Divorce*.

Audiovisual Adaptation

Dinosaurs Divorce. Random House Media, filmstrip/cassette, 1986.

Marc Brown Video Series, Set III. Random House Media, videorecording, 1986.

Related Titles

Dinosaurs Beware! A Safety Guide written and illustrated by Marc Brown and Stephen Krensky. Little, Brown, 1981. Similar in style to *Dinosaurs Divorce* but with information about safety and how to cope with emergencies.

How It Feels to Be Adopted written and photographed by Jill Krementz. Knopf, 1982. A good book to include in a program about coping with problems. Interviews with 19 children and adolescents provide personal insights into their feelings and concerns about being adopted.

How It Feels When a Parent Dies written and photographed by Jill Krementz. Knopf, 1981. In this photoessay, 18 children tell their personal experiences in coping with the death of a parent.

Perfect Pigs: An Introduction to Manners written and illustrated by Marc Brown and Stephen Krensky. Little, Brown, 1983. Pigs demonstrating proper behavior? Why not? Information about everyday courtesy is presented in an entertaining format.

Slim Goodbody: The Inside Story by John Burstein. Photography by J. Paul Kirouac; illustrated by Craigwood Phillips. McGraw-Hill, 1977. Slim Goodbody is a familiar and popular character who presents information about the human body. Wearing a leotard that illustrates the internal organs, muscles, and bones, Slim discusses good health habits.

About the Author and Illustrator

BROWN, MARC
Fifth Book of Junior Authors and Illustrators, ed. by Sally Holmes Holtze. Wilson, 1983, pp. 54–55.
Something about the Author, ed. by Anne Commire. Gale, 1976, Vol. 10, pp. 17–18.

Carlstrom, Nancy White.   *Jesse Bear, What Will You Wear?*
Illus. by Bruce Degen. Macmillan, 1986
Suggested Use Level: Gr. PreK–K   Reading Level: NA

Plot Summary

In a rhyming text, a young bear celebrates himself and the world around him. After Jesse gets dressed in his shirt and pants, he goes outside and "wears" a flower, the sun, and the sand in his sandbox. Back in the house, he "wears" his chair and his lunch. At bedtime, he "wears" his bath bubbles, his pajamas and blanket, and his dreams.

Thematic Material

This book captures the playful, imaginative spirit that exists between young children and their world. Jesse Bear sees everything in terms of himself. His egocentrism reflects the attitude of most preschool children, who will identify with his nonsense verses and language play.

Book Talk Material and Activities

Jesse Bear, What Will You Wear? could be included in a story session for preschoolers and kindergarteners. Follow it up with *How Do I Put It On? Getting Dressed* and talk about different kinds of clothes. A group project could be to compile a book that lists and illustrates items of clothing. Encourage children to bring in pictures of clothing to use in their illustrations. Another activity could be to suggest categories for clothes and organize the pictures into these categories. A bulletin board or chart could be prepared. Categorizing and manipulating information allows children to use what they already know, while talking about possibilities and working together to make decisions.

Related Titles

Animals Should Definitely Not Wear Clothing by Judi Barrett. Illustrated by Ron Barrett. Atheneum, 1970. How would animals look if they had to wear clothes? Imagine a necktie on a giraffe or a hat on a camel. Here's another book that takes a playful look at clothes.

Better Not Get Wet, Jesse Bear by Nancy White Carlstrom. Illustrated by Bruce Degen. Macmillan, 1988. More rhyming fun with Jesse Bear as he plays with the fish in their tank and the bird in the bird bath, ending up in his own wading pool.

How Do I Put It On? Getting Dressed by Shigeo Watanabe. Illustrated by Yasuo Ohtomo. Philomel, 1979. Like *Jesse Bear, What Will You Wear?*, this book shows a bear getting dressed. What are some of the other similarities and differences between the two bears?

Martin's Hats by Joan W. Blos. Illustrated by Marc Simont. Morrow, 1984. With each new hat, Martin participates in a new activity. Children can think of other hats that correlate with jobs.

Mary Wore Her Red Dress and Henry Wore His Green Sneakers adapted and illustrated by Merle Peek. Clarion, 1985. In this song about clothes, including green shoes, purple pants, and violet ribbons, young children can learn about colors, too. The musical arrangement is included.

Max's New Suit written and illustrated by Rosemary Wells. Dial, 1979. Max the bunny wants to dress himself. The results are not quite right but very funny. Preschoolers will enjoy this series of Very First Books about Max.

Poppy the Panda written and illustrated by Dick Gackenbach. Clarion, 1984. Poppy wants to have clothes like all of Katie's other dolls. Katie's mother comes up with the perfect solution.

Wild, Wild Sunflower Child Anna by Nancy White Carlstrom. Illustrated by Jerry Pinkney. Macmillan, 1987. Like Jesse Bear in *Jesse Bear, What Will You Wear?*, Anna celebrates the world around her. She plays a pretending game as she climbs a hill, then she rolls down to the bottom of the hill.

You'll Soon Grow into Them, Titch written and illustrated by Pat Hutchins. Greenwillow, 1983. Titch gets everyone's hand-me-downs until Dad gets Titch some new clothes of his own. The arrival of a new baby gives Titch the satisfaction of having someone get his clothes.

About the Author and Illustrator

CARLSTROM, NANCY WHITE
Something about the Author, ed. by Anne Commire. Gale, 1987, Vol. 48, pp. 43–44.
DEGEN, BRUCE
Something about the Author, ed. by Anne Commire. Gale, 1987, Vol. 47, p. 73.

Fox, Mem. *Wilfrid Gordon McDonald Partridge*
Illus. by Julie Vivas. Kane/Miller, 1984
Suggested Use Level: Gr. 1–3   Reading Level: Gr. 5

Plot Summary

Wilfrid Gordon McDonald Partridge lives next door to an old people's home. Each resident is slightly eccentric, but Wilfrid enjoys being with them. His favorite is Miss Nancy, whose full name, Miss Nancy Alison Delecourt Cooper, has four names just like Wilfrid's. When Wilfrid hears his parents talking about Miss Nancy's failing memory, he tries to find a way to help her. He asks each of his elderly friends what a memory is, and then he finds an object that captures the essence of their definitions. He gives his collection to Miss Nancy and, as she holds each object, it brings a special memory to her. She and Wilfrid smile and remember together.

Thematic Material

Respect for the elderly is one theme in this book. When Wilfrid helps Miss Nancy remember, he helps her regain her self-respect. The relationship depicted between generations is a very positive one.

Book Talk Material and Activities

Senior citizens play an active role in many communities, often serving as volunteers in schools and libraries. Children need many opportunities to interact with older adults so that they can develop positive attitudes and respect for the elderly. As children discuss this book, they can begin to move beyond their egocentric view of the world and think about other people. Discussion ideas include: "Talk about an older person that you know." "How do you help other people?" and "Have you ever visited a nursing home? What was it like? How did you feel?" A trip could be arranged to a retirement center and children could take cards and gifts that they have made.

Children might also enjoy talking about their own memories. This would be especially appropriate for middle-grade children who are developing a stronger sense of time and place. In a classroom, children could make an end-of-the-year memory book that includes drawings and writings about some of their favorite moments during the year.

Audiovisual Adaptation

Wilfrid Gordon McDonald Partridge. Weston Woods, filmstrip/cassette, 1986.

Related Titles

Happy Birthday, Grampie by Susan Pearson. Illustrated by Ronald Himler. Dial, 1987. Martha and her parents go to visit Grampie at the nursing home, and Martha's special card helps him remember the love they have shared.

I Have Four Names for My Grandfather by Kathryn Lasky. Photographs by Christopher G. Knight. Little, Brown, 1976. In this photoessay, a young boy tells about his grandfather. Compare this portrait of an elderly man with the people in *Wilfrid Gordon McDonald Partridge*. Also, compare it with *My Island Grandma*. How do these grandparents show their love?

I Know a Lady by Charlotte Zolotow. Illustrated by James Stevenson. Greenwillow, 1984. A little girl shares her impressions of her elderly neighbor who lives independently. Contrast this book with Wilfrid's friends in *Wilfrid Gordon McDonald Partridge*.

My Island Grandma by Kathryn Lasky. Illustrated by Emily McCully. Warne, 1978. A little girl shares her feelings of love for her grandmother while she describes the summers they spend together. Ask children to share a special feeling or experience they have had with an older relative.

Now One Foot, Now the Other written and illustrated by Tomie de Paola. Putnam, 1981. After having a stroke, Bobby's grandfather needs his help. As in *A Special Trade*, which is also about special relationships that change, Bobby and his grandfather find that despite many changes their love for each other is still strong.

A Special Trade by Sally Wittman. Illustrated by Karen Gundersheimer. Harper & Row, 1978. A very positive story of the changing relationship between a little girl and her neighbor. Each finds ways to help the other and shows how much they care for the other.

About the Author and Illustrator

Fox, Mem (Merrion Frances Fox)
Something about the Author, ed. by Anne Commire. Gale, 1988, Vol. 51, pp. 65–70.

Geringer, Laura.   *A Three Hat Day*

Illus. by Arnold Lobel. Harper & Row, 1985; pap., 1987
Suggested Use Level: Gr. K–1   Reading Level: Gr. 3

Plot Summary

R. R. Pottle the Third is so fond of hats that he sometimes wears more than one. On sad days, he wears two hats, and on extra sad days, he wears three hats. R. R. Pottle the Third comes from a family of collectors, but now he is all alone and he wishes he could find someone who would appreciate him and his hats. One day, he decides to go shopping.

In the hat store, he cannot resist trying on many different hats until a bad-tempered saleslady makes him stop. A sweet saleslady named Isabel, wearing a very special hat, comes to his defense. R. R. and Isabel are meant for each other. They marry and have a daughter who collects shoes.

Thematic Material

R. R. Pottle the Third is an eccentric character. His search for someone who will accept him is successful. He finds that he does not have to conform to the expectations of others to be appreciated.

Book Talk Material and Activities

Children can select a day as Hat Day and celebrate. They can read stories about hats and vote for their favorites, make pictures of unusual hats, and come to school wearing special hats. Many children study community helpers in social studies, and the hat activities can lead to a discussion of people who help others. Margaret Miller's *Whose Hat?* helps with this discussion.

In *A Three Hat Day,* R. R. Pottle the Third is proud of himself and his hats. Even though others might not understand his fascination with hats, he knows what is right for him. Sharing this book with children lets them see a character who lives an unusual life but is comfortable with himself.

Arnold Lobel's illustrations are delightful. R. R. Pottle the Third's father collected canes and his mother collected umbrellas. The Pottle mansion is depicted with canes and umbrellas incorporated into the architecture. The hat store (shown across from the title page) is shaped like a hat. Children might want to design their own buildings that reflect the interests of different collectors.

Audiovisual Adaptation

A Three Hat Day. Random House Media, cassette/book, 1986; "Reading Rainbow," Great Plains National Instructional Television Library, video-recording, 1987.

Related Titles

Caps for Sale written and illustrated by Esphyr Slobodkina. Young Scott, 1947. What do you do when monkeys steal your hats? The peddler in this story must outsmart the monkeys.

Jennie's Hat written and illustrated by Ezra Jack Keats. Harper & Row,

1966. Jennie is not happy with her plain hat. Her friends, the birds, see this and help make her hat very special. After hearing this story, children like to make their own collage hats.

Martin's Hats by Joan W. Blos. Illustrated by Marc Simont. Morrow, 1984. Whenever Martin changes his hat, he imagines himself in a new adventure, from exploring, to cooking, to working on a farm.

Tan Tan's Hat written and illustrated by Kazuo Imamura. Bradbury, 1978. Tan Tan plays with his hat. He rolls it, throws it, and even catches things with it, including a star.

Whose Hat? written and illustrated by Margaret Miller. Greenwillow, 1988. The text and illustrations in this book follow a pattern, which starts with the question "Whose hat?" and a color photograph of a hat. On the next page are the answer to the question and two color photographs of the hat being worn. This is a good book to use for a discussion of jobs that people do, such as baker, police officer, and construction worker.

About the Author and Illustrator

GERINGER, LAURA
Something about the Author, ed. by Anne Commire. Gale, 1982, Vol. 29, pp. 87–88.

LOBEL, ARNOLD
Authors of Books for Young People: Supplement to the Second Edition, by Martha E. Ward and Dorothy Marquardt. Scarecrow, 1979, p. 321.
Illustrators of Children's Books: 1957–1966, Vol. III, comp. by Lee Kingman, Grace Allen Hogarth, and Harriet Quimby. Horn Book, 1968, pp. xvi, 141, 229; *1967–1976, Vol. IV,* 1978, pp. 17, 18, 140, 173, 199.
Something about the Author, ed. by Anne Commire. Gale, 1974, Vol. 6, pp. 147–148.
Third Book of Junior Authors, ed. by Muriel Fuller. Wilson, 1963, pp. 181–182.

Guthrie, Donna. *The Witch Who Lives Down the Hall*
Illus. by Amy Schwartz. Harcourt, 1985
Suggested Use Level: Gr. 1–3   Reading Level: Gr. 5

Plot Summary

A boy who has moved into a new apartment building speculates about the unusual behavior of his neighbor, Ms. McWee. Is she a witch? She seems to know many things about him, and strange people visit her home. Late at night, sinister noises come from her apartment. The boy's mother has a logical explanation for Ms. McWee's behavior, for example, that the noises in her apartment are from her home computer. The boy is not convinced. To him, the evidence seems overwhelming—Ms. McWee must be a witch. On Halloween night, the boy goes trick-or-treating to the apartments in his building, but most of his neighbors have forgotten that it is Halloween. Ms. McWee hasn't forgotten. Her apartment is decorated with skeletons, bats, and pumpkins. When she asks the boy to do a trick and gives him a treat, the boy is glad to live in a building with the unusual Ms. McWee.

Thematic Material

Learning to accept people who are different is one theme in this Halloween story. A related theme is adjusting to new situations.

Book Talk Material and Activities

Although this story is an obvious choice for sharing at Halloween, it could also lead to a discussion about taking time to really get to know people. Children could see that the boy's expectations are not really correct and talk about how the boy's mother tries to explain Ms. McWee's behavior. *Louanne Pig in Witch Lady* is another similar story where a group of characters decides that an eccentric old lady is a witch. Like the boy in *The Witch Who Lives Down the Hall*, when Louanne gets to know "the witch," all of her unusual behavior is explained. Many scary stories depend on characters being afraid and not investigating the source of their fear. Young children enjoy stories like *The Witch Who Lives Down the Hall* because it is somewhat scary, but the scary parts are explained. The conclusion is satisfying and reassuring.

Related Titles

Humbug Witch written and illustrated by Lorna Balian. Abingdon, 1965. A little girl tries to be a good witch but ends up being a good little girl.

Imogene's Antlers written and illustrated by David Small. Crown, 1985. One morning, Imogene wakes up with antlers on her head. This causes a great commotion in her house. Like Ms. McWee in *The Witch Who Lives Down the Hall*, Imogene likes being different.

Louanne Pig in Witch Lady written and illustrated by Nancy Carlson. Carolrhoda, 1985. Louanne Pig and her friends are afraid of the woman who lives in the spooky house at the top of the hill. When Louanne actually meets the lady, she realizes that she has been wrong.

We Can't Sleep written and illustrated by James Stevenson. Greenwillow, 1982. Louie and Mary Ann can't sleep. Of course, Grandpa remembers a night when he couldn't sleep. Grandpa's experiences make Louie and Mary Ann realize that they are worrying for no reason. *What's Under My Bed?* (see Chapter 4) is another story about these characters.

The Worst Person in the World written and illustrated by James Stevenson. Greenwillow, 1981. The "worst person in the world" meets the "ugliest thing in the world," who helps him learn to be more open and to care about others.

About the Author and Illustrator

SCHWARTZ, AMY
Something about the Author, ed. by Anne Commire. Gale, 1985, Vol. 41, p. 208; 1987, Vol. 47, pp. 190–192.

Haseley, Dennis. *Kite Flier*
Illus. by David Wiesner. Four Winds, 1986
Suggested Use Level: Gr. 1–4   Reading Level: Gr. 5

Plot Summary

The man who makes magnificent kites is admired and respected by the people in the village. When his son is born, his wife dies, and Kite Flier stops making kites, as if all the joy is gone from his world. Slowly, as his son grows, Kite Flier finds happiness again and begins making and flying kites again. Kite Flier expresses his emotions through his kites. When his son decides to leave home, Kite Flier is sad. He makes a huge kite shaped like a bird for them to fly together and set free. Although now far from each other, the father and son set a kite free every year.

Thematic Material

Kite Flier is a man who has chosen an unusual life. He keeps apart from everyone but his son and finds satisfaction and peace through his skill at making kites.

Book Talk Material and Activities

A book talk program for this book could begin with the words: "Many books are written about people who are just like us—people who go to school and play with their friends; people who have arguments and make up. But here are some books about people who are different." *Kite Flier, The Man Who Lived Alone,* and *Miss Rumphius* are three titles that could be presented. Emphasize that being different takes courage and, sometimes, is difficult. As part of a biography study, children in the third and fourth grades could read about some real people who chose to be different, including Martin Luther King, Jr., Elizabeth Blackwell, Sojourner Truth, and Gandhi, and some biographies could be displayed.

Related Titles

The Man Who Lived Alone by Donald Hall. Illustrated by Mary Azarian. Godine, 1984. A man's unhappy childhood leads him to a life of solitude as an adult. He is self-sufficient and satisfied with the life he has chosen.

Miss Rumphius written and illustrated by Barbara Cooney. Viking, 1982. Miss Rumphius is satisfied with her life. She has one important responsibility—to make the world more beautiful.

Nicholas Where Have You Been? written and illustrated by Leo Lionni. Knopf, 1987. Nicholas, a mouse, goes looking for a new berry patch and is befriended by some birds. When he returns home, he helps his friends overcome their prejudices toward birds. The mice and the birds learn to be more tolerant of each other.

Owliver by Robert Kraus. Illustrated by Jose Aruego and Ariane Dewey. Prentice-Hall, 1974. Owliver's parents have plans for him, but Owliver makes his own decision about what is right for him.

Pezzettino written and illustrated by Leo Lionni. Pantheon, 1975. Pezzettino is a little orange square that is searching for where he belongs. None of the mosaic creatures seems to need him, and he realizes that he is just right as he is.

What Are We Going to Do about Andrew? by Marjorie Weinman Sharmat. Illustrated by Ray Cruz. Macmillan, 1980. Andrew can fly and he can turn into a hippopotamus. His parents are proud of his talent but they worry that he is different. When Andrew goes away for a while, his parents realize that being different also means being special.

About the Author and Illustrator

HASELEY, DENNIS
Something about the Author, ed. by Anne Commire. Gale, 1986, Vol. 44, p. 87.

Isadora, Rachel. *Opening Night*
Illus. by the author. Greenwillow, 1984
Suggested Use Level: Gr. 1–3   Reading Level: Gr. 4

Plot Summary

Heather is excited to be going to the ballet. This ballet is special because Heather is in it. She and her friend Libby are thrilled to be backstage because so much is going on. They watch ballerinas doing warm-ups, see characters in costume, and get their own makeup done. As the girls get into their costumes, their excitement builds. Finally, the ballet begins and it is time for Heather and her friends to be on stage. Heather dances her solo and then waits for the ballet to end so that she can return to the stage for the curtain call. Heather and Libby leave the theater satisfied with their "opening night."

Thematic Material

Heather has worked long and hard to be able to perform in the ballet. The story's focus is on Heather's feelings of accomplishment and satisfaction. Heather has earned her applause by practicing. Because of her efforts, she has been able to participate in this important event. The theme of being rewarded for hard work is evident here.

Book Talk Material and Activities

Many children participate in extracurricular activities that let them perform, such as ballet, hockey, and gymnastics. *Opening Night* captures some of the feelings that accompany these experiences: anticipation, excitement, fear, delight, and satisfaction. As children work together in groups, they need to learn about each other. A book like *Opening Night* could promote a discussion about the different talents and experiences of the children in the group. Some children might enjoy performing for the others or for some invited guests.

In a library or classroom, this book could be part of a book talk program on books about the performing arts that includes biographies and other nonfiction books. Children enjoy visiting a theater, even at the local high school. In fact, it is a good opportunity to cooperate with the high school teachers and students. The teachers could talk about the theater program while students discuss the different responsibilities involved in putting on a show. Younger children will be surprised at the variety of activities taking place besides performing. As children visit the theater, they could look for some of the details that are presented in Rachel Isadora's illustrations for *Opening Night*.

Related Titles

The Almost Awful Play by Patricia Reilly Giff. Illustrated by Susanna Natti. Viking, 1984. Ronald Morgan and his classmates put on a play that almost ends in disaster. Ronald's quick thinking helps everything turn out alright.

Oliver Button Is a Sissy written and illustrated by Tomie de Paola. Harcourt, 1979. When Oliver takes dancing classes, his friends make fun of him, until they find out how helpful the classes are.

Perfect Balance: The Story of an Elite Gymnast by Lynn Haney. Photographs by Bruce Curtis. Putnam, 1979. This photoessay focuses on the training and preparation of Leslie Russo, a 15-year-old gymnast.

A Very Young Circus Flyer by Jill Krementz. Photographs by the author. Knopf, 1979. One book in the series about the accomplishments of young people. All the books in the series follow one young person through the rigors of performing.

Wesley Paul, Marathon Runner by Julianna A. Fogel. Photographs by Mary S. Watkins. Lippincott, 1979. A nine-year-old Chinese-American boy prepares to enter the New York City Marathon, providing an interesting perspective on the skills, training, and commitment needed to perform in any athletic competition.

About the Author and Illustrator

ISADORA, RACHEL
Fifth Book of Junior Authors and Illustrators, ed. by Sally Holmes Holtze. Wilson, 1983, pp. 159–160.
Something about the Author, ed. by Anne Commire. Gale, 1983, Vol. 32, p. 100.

Keller, Holly. *Geraldine's Blanket*
Illus. by the author. Greenwillow, 1984
Suggested Use Level: Gr. PreK–K   Reading Level: Gr. 4

Plot Summary

Geraldine the pig loves her blanket. She has carried it with her for years. No matter where she has gone she has taken her blanket. With each year, however, Geraldine's blanket has deteriorated. Geraldine's parents want her to stop carrying her blanket, but Geraldine insists she must have it. Geraldine's parents argue, cajole, and even try to trick her, but it is no use. Finally, Geraldine's blanket is so ragged and small that she knows she must do something. When Geraldine receives a new doll, she trims and sews her blanket into a doll-sized shirt. Happily, Geraldine takes her doll and her blanket and goes out to play.

Thematic Material

Although Geraldine's deteriorating blanket might not seem that important, it is to her. Many children feel that way about their everyday worries. Children will identify with Geraldine's situation and find satisfaction in how she faces and solves her problem.

Book Talk Material and Activities

Did you have a special blanket or toy when you were little? What was it? How did you get it? Where is it now? Using *Geraldine's Blanket* as part of a book talk or story program creates an opportunity for sharing personal experiences, even experiences about one's own childhood. Many children are surprised to hear that the adults they know had experiences similar to theirs. Adults who share personal mementos with children help them develop closer relationships with adults. The bulletin board in a school or public library could be used for a display focusing on staff members as children. Beside photographs of staff members could be a few sentences about "I remember. . . ." This could be a classroom project for children and their parents, grandparents, and other relatives or neighbors—a good project for involving community members in school and library activities.

Related Titles

Alfie Gives a Hand written and illustrated by Shirley Hughes. Lothrop, 1983. Alfie decides to take his blanket to his friend's birthday party. He finds that the blanket gets in the way of his fun and decides that next time he might leave his blanket at home.

The Blanket written and illustrated by John Burningham. Crowell, 1975. A small book that shows the consternation that is felt by a little boy when he loses his blanket. While his father and mother search for it, he finds it and goes to sleep.

The Blanket That Had to Go by Nancy Evans Cooney. Illustrated by Diane Dawson. Putnam, 1981. Susi is worried. What will she do with her blanket when she starts kindergarten? She thinks for a long time and comes up with a perfect solution for her.

Bye-bye, Old Buddy written and illustrated by Deborah Robison. Clarion, 1983. Jenny knows that she must give up her blanket, but she wants to find just the right way to say good-bye.

The Cozy Book by Mary Ann Hoberman. Illustrated by Tony Chen. Viking, 1982. Cozy sounds, smells, clothes, food, and feelings are described in verse. Geraldine needs her blanket to feel cozy. Ask children what makes them feel cozy.

Now We Can Go written and illustrated by Ann Jonas. Greenwillow, 1986. The narrator cannot leave the house without all of his toys. Ask children to talk about their favorite toys or blankets.

Where Can It Be? written and illustrated by Ann Jonas. Greenwillow, 1986. The half-page illustrations are perfect for this story of a little girl's search for something. On the last page, the little girl finds her missing blanket.

About the Author and Illustrator

KELLER, HOLLY
Something about the Author, ed. by Anne Commire. Gale, 1986, Vol. 42, p. 123.

Martin, Bill, Jr., and Archambault, John. *Knots on a Counting Rope*
Illus. by Ted Rand. Henry Holt, 1987
Suggested Use Level: Gr. 3–4   Reading Level: Gr. 3

Plot Summary

A young Native-American boy and his grandfather sit together by a campfire. As the shadows around them deepen, the boy asks to hear a favorite story—the story about himself. The grandfather begins, but the boy interrupts him with details remembered from many tellings. Together, they tell of the birth of a small, frail, blind boy who is welcomed by his family and by the great blue horses. This blind boy, named Boy-Strength-of-Blue-Horses, learns about the world using his other senses. He feels the morning, the sky, and the rainbow. With his horse, he learns the trails. He shows his courage and determination by racing with the other boys on the winding trails. The story ends with the grandfather adding a knot to the counting rope that marks the times this story has been told. The grandfather is preparing the boy to tell his own stories and to celebrate and remember the past.

Thematic Material

Although born blind, Boy-Strength-of-Blue-Horses has developed a sense of self-worth. He has challenged himself to compete with his peers, and his grandfather seems to be preparing him to be a storyteller. The theme of overcoming hardships is evident here. The book also deals with the importance of remembering the past. The relationship between the boy and his grandfather is strong and positive, illustrating the theme of respect for the knowledge and wisdom of the elderly.

Book Talk Material and Activities

Interest in techniques for storytelling is great, and many children enjoy learning and telling favorite stories. This story shows the importance of the oral tradition particularly to Native Americans. It would be a wonderful book to talk about as part of a storytelling activity. Children in a classroom or at a public library program will be interested in its dramatic style. The boy and his grandfather tell the story through a dialogue, and two children may want to try to tell or read the story by taking the two parts.

The storytelling tradition is evident in many folktales, such as *A Story, A Story*. In this African tale, Ananse is the storyteller who describes how he earned the Sky God's stories. Another African tale, *Who's in Rabbit's House*, is presented as a play with members of the tribe wearing masks and acting out the story before an audience. Children may want to look for other examples of storytelling in the books that they read (for example, in *Grandfather Tales* or Uncle Remus in *The Tales of Uncle Remus* and *Jump!*).

As a culminating activity to a program, having the children try telling a story about themselves gives them a chance to get to know each other better. This activity might work better with the children sharing in small groups of three or four, as some might be too intimidated to talk before a larger group. The children could go home and ask their family about a favorite family story, then share it the next time they get together.

Through the book's illustrations, the setting becomes an important part of this book. Ted Rand has captured the purples, blues, and blacks of the night. The bright contrast of the firelight is reflected on the faces of the boy and his grandfather, showing highlights and shadows. By studying different styles, children can become more aware of the ways in which an illustrator can interpret the story. *Knots on a Counting Rope* can be contrasted with *Where the Buffaloes Begin*.

Audiovisual Adaptation

Knots on a Counting Rope. "Reading Rainbow." Great Plains National Instructional Television Library, videorecording, 1987.

Related Titles

Grandfather Tales collected and retold by Richard Chase. Illustrated by Berkeley Williams, Jr. Houghton Mifflin, 1948. Twenty-five tales from North Carolina and Virginia are recounted here as if at a family gathering.

Jump! The Adventures of Brer Rabbit by Joel Chandler Harris. Adapted by Van Dyke Parks and Malcolm Jones. Illustrated by Barry Moser. Harcourt, 1986. A new collection of some of the more well known Brer Rabbit stories.

A Story, A Story retold and illustrated by Gail E. Haley. Atheneum,

1970. Ananse, a storyteller, tells a story about how he won his stories from the Sky God.

The Tales of Uncle Remus as told by Julius Lester. Illustrated by Jerry Pinkney. Dial, 1987. These brief tales are perfect to learn for story-telling.

Where the Buffaloes Begin by Olaf Baker. Illustrated by Stephen Gammell. Warne, 1981. Black-and-white pencil sketches provide a contrast to the bright colors in *Knots on a Counting Rope*. Show both books to children to increase their awareness of how artists interpret different stories.

Who's in Rabbit's House? A Masai Tale retold by Verna Aardema. Illustrated by Leo Dillon and Diane Dillon. Dial, 1977. A folktale told in the form of a play.

About the Author and Illustrator

MARTIN, BILL, JR. (WILLIAM IVAN MARTIN)
Something about the Author, ed. by Anne Commire. Gale, 1985, Vol. 40, p. 128.

Rosenberg, Maxine B. *Being Adopted*
Photographs by George Ancona. Lothrop, 1984
Suggested Use Level: Gr. 3–4   Reading Level: Gr. 7

Plot Summary

This photoessay presents three children who have been adopted. Rebecca, a black child, has been adopted into a multiracial family. Andrei, from India, and Karin, from Korea, are each adopted by white parents. Rosenberg focuses on the kinds of questions that many adopted children ask, such as "Who are my parents?" and "Why didn't they want me?" Because these children and their parents are from different cultures, Rosenberg presents some of the special issues that develop. Appended to the text is a section entitled "About Adoption Today" that gives more details on transracial and transcultural adoptions. George Ancona's photographs capture the diversity of these families with images of many moods and situations.

Thematic Material

This book celebrates the diversity of families. It presents a picture of different people learning to get along. The adopted children share their feelings of insecurity, but they emphasize their desire to get along in their new homes. The book also shows that information can be presented in a variety of formats, in this case, a photoessay.

Book Talk Material and Activities

The photoessay is a type of informational book that should be introduced to children. It presents information in an attractive format and often serves as a springboard for additional reading on a topic. George Ancona has taken photographs for many books. Having children look at other books with his photographs is a valuable activity for them. Some areas to consider are: Does he change his style when working with different authors or different topics? Do the photographs and text match? Is there information in the photographs that is not given in the text? Other photoessays could be compared with Ancona's, for example, Seymour Simon's books about space (see *Saturn* in Chapter 6), and the concept books by Tana Hoban (see *Shapes, Shapes, Shapes* and *26 Letters and 99 Cents* both in Chapter 3).

Related Titles

The First Thanksgiving Feast by Joan Anderson. Photographs by George Ancona. Clarion, 1984. Photographs taken at Plimoth Plantation depict Pilgrims and Native Americans preparing for the first Thanksgiving.

Growing Older written and photographed by George Ancona. Dutton, 1978. Brief excerpts from the reminiscences of older people whom Ancona interviewed about their lives.

Handtalk: An ABC of Finger Spelling and Sign Language by Remy Charlip, Mary Beth, and George Ancona. Photographs. Four Winds, 1974. Bright, colorful photographs clearly depict the finger spelling for each letter of the alphabet.

Handtalk Birthday: A Number and Story Book in Sign Language by Remy Charlip, Mary Beth, and George Ancona. Photographs. Four Winds, 1987. It is Mary Beth's birthday and her friends are giving her a party. Color photographs show words being signed.

I Feel: A Picture Book of Emotions written and photographed by George Ancona. Dutton, 1977. Black-and-white photographs capture moments of joy, fear, pride, and sorrow in this simple concept book, which could be compared to some of the books by Tana Hoban (see *Shapes, Shapes, Shapes* and *26 Letters and 99 Cents*, both in Chapter 3).

Joshua's Westward Journal by Joan Anderson. Photographs by George Ancona. Morrow, 1987. Photographs re-create the experiences of a family traveling to Illinois during the westward expansion of the 1800s. The text is written in the form of a boy's journal.

Monsters on Wheels written and photographed by George Ancona. Dutton, 1974. Describes the operation of a variety of heavy machinery, including the bulldozer, fork truck, tractor, back hoe, lunar rover, and other giant machines.

About the Author and Illustrator

ROSENBERG, MAXINE B.
Something about the Author, ed. by Anne Commire. Gale, 1987, Vol. 47, p. 189.
ANCONA, GEORGE
Authors of Books for Young People: Supplement to the Second Edition, by Martha E. Ward and Dorothy Marquardt. Scarecrow, 1979, p. 5.
Something about the Author, ed. by Anne Commire. Gale, 1977, Vol. 12, pp. 10–12.

Steig, William. *Brave Irene*
Illus. by the author. Farrar, Straus, 1986
Suggested Use Level: Gr. 1–3   Reading Level: Gr. 2

Plot Summary

Irene's mother, Mrs. Bobbin, is a seamstress who has finished sewing a beautiful gown. It is to be delivered to the duchess for a dance that evening, but Mrs. Bobbin feels too ill to make the trip. Irene helps her mother to bed and carefully packs the dress in a box. She puts on her warmest clothes and takes the dress out into the winter storm. With the wind blowing around her, she bravely begins her long walk. The trip becomes a battle between Irene's will and the strength of the wind. When the dress is blown away, it seems as if the wind has won. Irene continues her trip, determined to explain the situation to the duchess. Her perils continue, but she struggles on. As she nears the palace, the impossible occurs. Irene finds the gown. Everyone is delighted with her and they commend her for being so brave. Irene attends the ball and is driven home in grand style. Her mother has been worried and is relieved to see her. Mrs. Bobbin is proud of Irene's accomplishment.

Thematic Material

As the title indicates, this is a story of bravery. Irene's intrepid spirit allows her to persevere even though she is faced with great adversity. The story has elements of melodrama—the long-suffering seamstress, the fierce storm, Irene's determination, and her triumphant return home. Success through hard work is also a theme.

Book Talk Material and Activities

In this story, Irene overcomes insurmountable odds in order to fulfill an obligation. She is brave and heroic. Many other stories could be compared and contrasted with it—traditional stories of heroism, like *Saint George and the Dragon* and *The Loathsome Dragon,* and stories of everyday courage, like *Henry the Explorer.* These stories could be included in book talk or story programs on bravery. Children could talk about situations when they have felt brave. A book like *Eugene the Brave* might promote the discussion.

In *Brave Irene,* Irene is heroic, and it might be interesting to look at heroes in today's world. After reading several books, a group of children could work on a list that describes "What makes this character heroic?" One sample group of students said Irene was heroic because she fought against the wind, she continued her trip to the duchess without the dress, she never quit, and she was proud of her mother's work. In *The Loathsome Dragon,* children felt that Childe Wynd was heroic because he confronted the dragon in the harbor and because he chose to kiss the dragon instead of killing it. In both cases, children felt that being a hero meant standing up to something or someone stronger than you.

Steig's use of language is detailed and descriptive. His illustrations, especially Irene's posture and expressions, help create the changing moods of the story—the warmth of Irene's home, the bleakness of the winter storm, and the opulence of the duchess's ball. Comparing *Brave Irene* with other books by William Steig could encourage children to become more knowledgeable about the author/illustrator. His illustrations have received the Caldecott Medal (1970, *Sylvester and the Magic Pebble*), and his writing has been awarded the Newbery Honor Medal (1977, *Abel's Island* and 1983, *Doctor DeSoto*).

Audiovisual Adaptation

Brave Irene. Weston Woods, cassette/book, 1988; filmstrip/cassette, 1988.

Related Titles

Abel's Island written and illustrated by William Steig. Farrar, Straus, 1976. Abel, a refined mouse, becomes stranded on an island and must learn to survive without the comforts that he has always known.

Doctor DeSoto written and illustrated by William Steig. Farrar, Straus, 1982. Doctor DeSoto, a dentist who is a mouse, will not treat dangerous animals. One day, a fox needs his help and Doctor DeSoto must decide what to do.

Eugene the Brave by Ellen Conford. Illustrated by John M. Larrecq. Little, Brown, 1978. Eugene the possum learns to overcome his fear of the dark.

Henry the Explorer by Mark Taylor. Illustrated by Graham Booth. Atheneum, 1966. Henry and his dog go off on an adventure that is full of surprises. There are several other books in this series.

The Loathsome Dragon retold by David Wiesner and Kim Kahng. Illustrated by David Wiesner. Putnam, 1987. A traditional story of bravery, in which Childe Wynd must rescue his sister from the spell of the evil enchantress.

Ruby the Red Knight written and illustrated by Amy Aitken. Bradbury, 1983. After visiting the museum, Ruby imagines that she is a knight who breaks the enchantment of the wizard.

Saint George and the Dragon retold by Margaret Hodges. Illustrated by Trina Schart Hyman. Little, Brown, 1984. A traditional story of heroism told with dramatic language and 1985 Caldecott-Award-winning illustrations.

Sylvester and the Magic Pebble written and illustrated by William Steig. Simon & Schuster, 1969. Sylvester accidentally wishes to be a rock. How will he become himself again?

About the Author and Illustrator

STEIG, WILLIAM

Illustrators of Children's Books: 1967–1976, Vol. IV, comp. by Lee Kingman, Grace Allen Hogarth, and Harriet Quimby. Horn Book, 1978, pp. 18, 19, 161, 210.

Something about the Author, ed. by Anne Commire. Gale, 1980, Vol. 18, pp. 175–177.

Third Book of Junior Authors, ed. by Doris de Montreville and Donna Hill. Wilson, 1972, pp. 276–277.

Titherington, Jeanne.   *A Place for Ben*
Illus. by the author. Greenwillow, 1987
Suggested Use Level: Gr. PreK–K   Reading Level: Gr. 4

Plot Summary

Ben feels that he needs a place that belongs to him. His baby brother, Ezra, seems to be everywhere, even in Ben's own room. After looking around, Ben finds a good place in the garage and settles down there. Yet, even with his favorite toys to play with, Ben realizes that he is lonely in his own place. He tries to get his cat, his dog, and his parents to join him, but they won't. Ben sits and waits for someone to come to be with him. At last, someone does—Ezra.

Thematic Material

Anyone with younger brothers or sisters can identify with Ben's feelings of being crowded out by Ezra. Ben realizes, though, that being alone can be lonely, and he is very happy to have Ezra join him in his place. Ben finds his own place but also finds the satisfaction that comes with sharing. The themes include needing time alone and getting along with others.

Book Talk Material and Activities

Where do you go when you want to be alone? What makes that place special? These questions could introduce a brief book talk about this book. If the story were read aloud at a story program, the subsequent discussion could focus on specific details. For example, Ben takes several items that he feels are important to his special place. What would you take along with you?

Many children feel frustrated with pestering siblings and ignored by busy adults. This book provides a chance for children to express some of their feelings. For a writing activity, fold a piece of paper in half. On one side write "I like it when" and on the other side write "I don't like it when." This could provide a framework for shared feelings either individually or in small groups.

The pastel illustrations in the book have very few background details. As a result, the focus is clearly on Ben and his immediate concerns. Yet, the illustrations have information that is not in the text. For example, Ezra's appearance in Ben's place is not described in the text. Only through the illustrations does the reader discover that Ezra joins Ben. The illustrations also show Ben's pleased reaction. Once children develop an awareness of the relationship between the text and the illustrations, they may be more discerning about the books they read. They may also enjoy looking for other stories where the illustrations tell important parts of the story.

Related Titles

Amanda Pig and Her Big Brother Oliver by Jean Van Leeuwen. Illustrated by Ann Schweninger. Dial, 1982. Five stories tell some of the everyday activities of two pigs. The other books in this series should be read, too.

Handmade Secret Hiding Places written and illustrated by Nonny Hogrogian. Overlook Press, 1975. Ten different hideouts are described, including "The Cardboard Box House," the "Behind the Stairs Hideout," and "The Four Poster Arabian Tent."

If It Weren't for You by Charlotte Zolotow. Illustrated by Ben Shecter. Harper & Row, 1966. A boy thinks about what he could do if he didn't have a little brother, only to realize how lonely he would be.

I'll Fix Anthony by Judith Viorst. Illustrated by Arnold Lobel. Harper & Row, 1969. Here's a story of how a little brother feels about his big brother. Compare the tone and point of view with *A Place for Ben*.

Rachel and Obadiah written and illustrated by Brinton Turkle. Dutton, 1978. Rachel is Obadiah's little sister. She feels left out, not just because she is smaller, but also because she is a girl. Even in colonial America, however, a girl can carry an important message.

Your Own Best Secret Place by Byrd Baylor. Illustrated by Peter Parnall. Scribner, 1979. A girl remembers the secret places that she and her friends have claimed.

Williams, Vera B.   *Something Special for Me*
Illus. by the author. Greenwillow, 1983
Suggested Use Level: Gr. 1–3   Reading Level: Gr. 6

Plot Summary

Rosa's birthday is coming and Mama and Grandma have agreed that she should use the money in the savings jar to buy something special. Rosa knows that she wants skates, but after she tries them on she decides that they are not special enough. Neither are the polka dot dress and the blue shoes nor the red tent and the blue sleeping bag. Rosa wonders if she will ever find something special for her gift. Her mother reassures her and, while they enjoy a moment together, Rosa finds her present— an accordion. Rosa knows that this is the special present that she has wanted. Rosa's whole family helps her buy it and together they celebrate Rosa's choice. Rosa and her family first appeared in *A Chair for My Mother,* and their story continues in *Music, Music for Everyone.*

Thematic Material

Rosa needs to find the present that is just right for her. At first, she thinks that she will get something that all her friends have, but she decides to demonstrate her independence. Many children are faced with decisions that encourage individualism. Rosa's spirit and emotions provide a model for this experience.

Book Talk Material and Activities

Like Rosa, many children have moments when they want to be different from their friends. They want to feel special. Hearing a book talk on *Something Special for Me* could encourage children to discuss times when they felt special and to share some of their favorite memories. They could write a story about a treasured item. Sharing personal reflections helps children learn about each other. They begin to see and feel a sense of community with their peers.

Music is an important part of this story and of the sequel, *Music, Music for Everyone.* Some children may not be familiar with what an accordion is and, perhaps, a trip to a music store could be arranged or a guest speaker could demonstrate different instruments. Children might even want to share some of their own musical experiences. Several Leo Lionni books celebrate finding what is right for you. Children could compare *Something Special for Me* with Lionni's *Cornelius; Frederick;* or *Geraldine, the Music Mouse.* Like Rosa, these characters learn the importance of their individuality.

One very special feature of *Something Special for Me* is the illustrations. Williams has used bright colors, patterned borders, and personal details to show Rosa's world. The borders help capture the feelings of the story—reminiscences, anticipation, indecision, and excitement. Studying the borders and the details gives additional information about Rosa and her family. Children could try using a border on a picture about their family. They could also look at other illustrations with borders, such as in books illustrated by Jan Brett (for example, *Annie and the Wild Animals*) or Trina Schart Hyman (for example, *Little Red Riding Hood*).

Audiovisual Adaptation

Something Special for Me. Random House Media, cassette/book, 1983.

Related Titles

Annie and the Wild Animals written and illustrated by Jan Brett. Houghton Mifflin, 1985. Annie cannot find her cat, Taffy. The food that Annie leaves out for Taffy attracts many woodland animals instead. The borders that surround the illustrations depict the activities of the animals, including bears searching for food and wolves howling in the woods.

A Chair for My Mother written and illustrated by Vera B. Williams. Greenwillow, 1982. Rosa and her mother use the money in their savings jar to buy a chair. Vera B. Williams received a Caldecott Honor Medal in 1983 for her illustrations.

Cornelius written and illustrated by Leo Lionni. Pantheon, 1983. Cornelius is a crocodile who has seen the world and learned new things. When he returns to his friends, he must learn that he can be proud of himself and what he knows.

Frederick written and illustrated by Leo Lionni. Pantheon, 1967. While the other mice prepare for winter, Frederick does not seem to be helping. Yet when the cold, dreary winter days arrive, Frederick shares his colors, feelings, and words.

Geraldine, the Music Mouse written and illustrated by Leo Lionni. Pantheon, 1979. Like Rosa in *Something Special for Me*, Geraldine is enchanted with music. When Geraldine discovers that she can create her own music it is a special moment.

Little Red Riding Hood by the Brothers Grimm. Retold and illustrated by Trina Schart Hyman. Holiday House, 1983. The illustrations of this classic story have beautiful borders that frame the text. The designs in the borders extend the details of the main illustration.

Music, Music for Everyone written and illustrated by Vera B. Williams. Greenwillow, 1984. Now that Rosa has her accordion she has a delightful time making music.

The Old Banjo by Dennis Haseley. Illustrated by Stephen Gammell. Macmillan, 1983. In this musical fantasy, the long-forgotten instruments play a concert and fill the farm air with their special sounds.

A Piano for Julie written and illustrated by Eleanor Schick. Greenwillow, 1984. Julie loves the piano at her grandmother's house and she longs for one of her own. Like Rosa in *Something Special for Me,* Julie's wish comes true.

About the Author and Illustrator

WILLIAMS, VERA B.
Fifth Book of Junior Authors and Illustrators, ed. by Sally Holmes Holtze. Wilson, 1983, pp. 327–328.
Something about the Author, ed. by Anne Commire. Gale, 1983, Vol. 33, p. 230.

Yorinks, Arthur.   *It Happened in Pinsk*
Illus. by Richard Egielski. Farrar, Straus, 1983, hb and pap.
Suggested Use Level: Gr. 1–4   Reading Level: Gr. 2

Plot Summary

Irv Irving lives in the lovely city of Pinsk. Even though he has a nice home, caring wife, and successful job, Irv is not satisfied. Irv is consumed by envy as he longs for more. Irv's life is transformed when he wakes up and has, literally, lost his head. After his wife makes him a new one, Irv frantically begins to search for his own head. Irv does not feel or look like himself and on the streets of Pinsk, he has some upsetting experiences of mistaken identity. With difficulty, Irv finally finds his head and returns home feeling somewhat better about his own life.

Thematic Material

This book is not just about the importance of being yourself; it is about being happy with yourself. Irv does not realize how good his life is until it is changed. The book also demonstrates the interrelationship between text and illustrations.

Book Talk Material and Activities

Egielski's illustrations contribute details to the story that are not in the text. Yorinks describes Pinsk as a lovely city but does not specify the time period or location. Egielski shows smokestacks and church spires, including the onion dome of an Eastern Orthodox church. He depicts clothing, hairstyles, vehicles, furnishings, and a telephone of the early twentieth century. Try reading the story to a group of children without showing the illustrations. Where do they think the story is set? How would they describe Irv's home? Many children will relate the story to the present and will be surprised by Egielski's illustrations.

The interplay between the matter-of-fact tone of the text and the depiction of these unusual events in the illustrations is wonderful. When Irv loses his head, his wife is not surprised, nor are any of the people that he meets. Much of the humor in this story comes from the way Yorinks and Egielski present Irv's very strange situation as something that could actually happen. Children in grade 3 and up could discuss what makes a book humorous. Each child could find one book that he or she thinks is funny and talk about why, for example, it has zany characters. Different categories of humor could be determined as children begin to refine their critical thinking skills.

Related Titles

How Droofus the Dragon Lost His Head written and illustrated by Bill Peet. Houghton Mifflin, 1971. Like Irv in *It Happened in Pinsk*, Droofus is not satisfied with his life. When he finds a way to be useful, he begins to feel better about himself.

"I Left My Head" by Lilian Moore in *Something New Begins: New and Selected Poems*. Illustrated by Mary Jane Dunton. Atheneum, 1982. A poem that also talks about losing your head.

"The Loser" by Shel Silverstein in *Where the Sidewalk Ends*. Illustrated by the author. Harper & Row, 1974. Compare this poem with "I Left My Head" by Lilian Moore. Put both on poetry charts to read along with *It Happened in Pinsk*. Have children discuss how the different authors and illustrators use the idea of losing your head. Are they just being funny or is a lesson being taught?

Molly's Moe written and illustrated by Kay Chorao. Clarion, 1976. Molly is always losing something. On a shopping trip with her mother, Molly is especially careful and does not lose anything, but when she gets home she cannot find her favorite toy.

The Mystery of the Missing Red Mitten written and illustrated by Steven Kellogg. Dial, 1974. Characters in many stories lose things besides their heads. Here Annie has lost her mitten and imagines where it might be. She is surprised at where it really is. Steven Kellogg has several other mysteries in this series.

Where's Waldo written and illustrated by Martin Handford. Little, Brown, 1987. Waldo is not lost; he is somewhere on every page. But so are hundreds of other characters. Children must look carefully to find Waldo.

About the Author and Illustrator

YORINKS, ARTHUR
Something about the Author, ed. by Anne Commire. Gale, 1983, Vol. 33, pp. 236–237; 1987, Vol. 49, pp. 211–217.

EGIELSKI, RICHARD
Illustrators of Children's Books: 1967–1976, Vol. IV, comp. by Lee Kingman, Grace Allen Hogarth, and Harriet Quimby. Horn Book, 1978, pp. 116, 187.
Something about the Author, ed. by Anne Commire. Gale, 1977, Vol. 11, pp. 89–90; 1987, Vol. 49, pp. 90–96.

Ziefert, Harriet.   *A New Coat for Anna*
Illus. by Anita Lobel. Knopf, 1986; pap., 1987
Suggested Use Level: Gr. 1–3   Reading Level: Gr. 4

Plot Summary

Anna needs a new coat. Now that the war is over, it should be easier to visit the shops and find clothes, but the shops are still empty. Anna and her mother have very little money, so Anna's mother decides to use some of their treasures to have a new coat made. Grandfather's gold watch is traded for the wool, a lamp is traded for spinning the wool, the weaver takes a garnet necklace, and the tailor takes a teapot. During the year that passes while Anna's coat is being made, Anna comes to know each new helper (including the sheep). The book ends with a celebration for the new coat and the new friends.

Thematic Material

Being resourceful is one theme in this book. Anna's mother finds a way to use what they have to get Anna a coat. She also shows her adventurous spirit as she and Anna face the deprivations of war. Anna and her mother have a respectful, loving relationship. The book also presents some information about the process of making a coat.

Book Talk Material and Activities

For many children, buying a coat involves a quick trip to the department store, where there are racks of coats in many colors and styles. *A New Coat for Anna* presents a different time and a different way of life. Life in the 1940s during and after the war was filled with hardships. Although the book does not deal with the war experience, it does show how Anna and her mother must make sacrifices to get Anna's new coat. It also shows how much time and effort goes into making the coat.

Several other books that show the process behind making something could be included in a program on everyday items and how they are made. *"Charlie Needs a Cloak"* and *The Goat in the Rug* are two similar and especially good companion books to discuss. Like *A New Coat for Anna*, they focus on making cloth. Children could make a chart that demonstrates how each book describes the steps in the process. Then they could examine the information, noting what is included and what is left out, and decide which description seems the most helpful.

Many communities have lists of speakers who will visit schools and libraries. Children would enjoy a weaving demonstration followed by some simple projects. They could even try describing the weaving process for themselves by looking at the steps and the sequence. A book talk program about other books that look at the process of making something would be a good follow-up activity.

Audiovisual Adaptation

A New Coat for Anna. Random House Media, cassette/book, 1988; filmstrip/cassette, 1988.

Related Titles

"Charlie Needs a Cloak" written and illustrated by Tomie de Paola. Prentice-Hall, 1973. Charlie looks at his old tattered cloak and decides to make a new one.

The Goat in the Rug by Charles L. Blood. Illustrated by Nancy Winslow Parker. Parent's Magazine Press, 1976. A goat named Geraldine describes the process of weaving a Navajo rug.

How a Book Is Made written and illustrated by Aliki. Crowell, 1986. A clear and well-illustrated description of the process of publishing a book. Specific careers are highlighted.

Louisville Slugger: The Making of a Baseball Bat written and photographed by Jan Arnow. Pantheon, 1984. Did you know that baseball players can have their bats made to order? This book discusses the production of Louisville Slugger baseball bats. It includes details about some famous players as well as information about the factory and bat-making process.

Pelle's New Suit written and illustrated by Elsa Beskow. Harper & Row, 1929. Pelle needs a new suit. Each person he asks for help gives him something to do, but eventually Pelle's suit is finished.

The Purple Coat by Amy Hest. Illustrated by Amy Schwartz. Four Winds, 1986. Gabrielle wants her new coat to be different. She knows she will feel special in a purple coat. Mama has to be reminded of her own childhood before she will agree with Gabrielle.

About the Author and Illustrator

LOBEL, ANITA

Illustrators of Children's Books, 1957–1966, Vol. III, comp. by Lee Kingman, Grace Allen Hogarth, and Harriet Quimby. Horn Book, 1968, pp. 3, 140, 229; *1967–1976, Vol. IV,* 1978, pp. 140, 198–199.

Something about the Author, ed. by Anne Commire. Gale, 1974, Vol. 6, p. 146.

Third Book of Junior Authors, ed. by Muriel Fuller. Wilson, 1963, pp. 180–181.

3

Celebrating Everyday
Experiences

RIDING a bus, being afraid of the dark, having a pet, and learning about
letters, numbers, money, and shapes are some of the everyday experiences of children. They are also some of the experiences presented in
the books in this chapter. As children read about familiar activities, they
see how their lives are similar to those of other children. They see that
books can be about such ordinary things as cars, trucks, and animals.
Sharing these books with children shows them the range of topics and
formats used by authors and illustrators when describing everyday
events.

Asch, Frank. *Goodbye House*
  Illus. by the author. Prentice-Hall, 1986
  Suggested Use Level: Gr. PreK–K   Reading Level: Gr. 3

Plot Summary
  It is moving day for Baby Bear and his family. The van is nearly full
when Baby Bear runs back into the house to find something. All of the
rooms are empty and he feels very sad. His parents join him in the house
and help him think about some of the times they have shared there. Baby
Bear and his father move from room to room remembering and saying
good-bye. As they drive away, Baby Bear is satisfied. He has had the
opportunity to express his regret and to prepare for the changes that are
coming.

Thematic Material

Baby Bear is facing a new experience. He feels sad to be leaving his home and he is apprehensive about his new situation. Many children will identify with these feelings as they watch Baby Bear try to cope with the changes that come from moving to a new house.

Book Talk Material and Activities

In any group of children, some will probably have had an experience with moving. Perhaps neighbors, parents, friends, or relatives have moved away. Taking time to talk about personal experiences helps children get to know one another and feel more comfortable together. In a school or public library, *Goodbye House* could be featured at a story program for preschoolers or kindergarteners. After hearing the story, children could talk about where they live now and what they like about their home. If a map of the city or town is available, the general area of each child's home could be marked on the map. Older children might enjoy hearing this story and then finding out about some of the moves their family has made. Where did their parents grow up? Their grandparents?

Children could discuss what other changes they have experienced. Some possibilities are the start of a new school year or the birth of a new brother or sister. Giving children a chance to talk about their feelings helps them learn to express themselves. They hear how others react to situations and they can build relationships by sharing what they have done. Book discussions can encourage children to think about and react to situations.

Frank Asch has written and illustrated several other bear books, including *Sand Cake* and *Just Like Daddy*.

Related Titles

Just Like Daddy written and illustrated by Frank Asch. Parent's Magazine Press, 1981. Baby Bear likes to do things "just like Daddy." He wakes up, gets dressed, gives mother a flower, and goes fishing. But when he catches a fish, he is "just like Mommy."

I'm Moving by Martha Whitmore Hickman. Illustrated by Leigh Grant. Abingdon, 1974. William describes his family's preparations for moving. He talks about what they take and what they leave behind. This is a companion book to *My Friend William Moved Away*.

Moving Day by Tobi Tobias. Illustrated by William Pene du Bois.

Knopf, 1976. A little girl reassures her stuffed bear (and herself) about their move to a new house.

Moving Molly written and illustrated by Shirley Hughes. Prentice-Hall, 1978. After her family moves, Molly must adjust to her new situation. Everyone is so busy that Molly feels left out, until she discovers a special place to play.

My Friend William Moved Away by Martha Whitmore Hickman. Illustrated by Bill Myers. Abingdon, 1979. When William leaves and Jimmy is left behind, Jimmy misses all the fun he had with William, but he discovers that there are still other friends for him to play with.

Sand Cake written and illustrated by Frank Asch. Parent's Magazine Press, 1978. Baby Bear and his family enjoy a day at the beach. Baby Bear makes a cake out of sand and playfully suggests a way to "eat" the cake.

Teddy Bears' Moving Day written and illustrated by Susanna Gretz. Four Winds, 1981. During the Teddy Bears' move, Robert is more trouble than help. When he gets lost, the other bears find that they really do miss him.

About the Author and Illustrator

ASCH, FRANK

Authors of Books for Young People: Supplement to the Second Edition, by Martha E. Ward and Dorothy Marquardt. Scarecrow, 1979, p. 9.

Fourth Book of Junior Authors and Illustrators, ed. by Doris de Montreville and Elizabeth D. Crawford. Wilson, 1978, pp. 17–18.

Illustrators of Children's Books: 1967–1976, Vol. IV, comp. by Lee Kingman, Grace Allen Hogarth, and Harriet Quimby. Horn Book, 1978, pp. 97, 179.

Something about the Author, ed. by Anne Commire. Gale, 1973, Vol. 5, p. 9.

Bunting, Eve.   *Ghost's Hour, Spook's Hour*
Illus. by Donald Carrick. Clarion, 1987
Suggested Use Level: Gr. PreK–K   Reading Level: Gr. 1

Plot Summary

On the night of the big storm there is a power failure. Jake awakens and is apprehensive about the dark. He hears some sinister noises and wonders what is wrong with the lights. One noise turns out to be his dog,

Biff; together they investigate the dark house. Creaking doors, empty rooms, cracking branches, and ticking clocks seem threatening. When Jake can't find his parents, his concern grows. Walking through the noises and shadows, Jake and Biff come to the dining room where they encounter a blob of whiteness that yells at them. The blob turns out to be Jake and Biff reflected in the mirror, and the yell was Jake's own voice. His yell brings his parents from the living room. They talk about the storm, the noises, and the dark. Jake sleeps with his parents on the fold-out couch feeling safe and reassured.

Thematic Material

Being afraid of the dark with its noises and shadows is a familiar feeling for most children. So is the feeling of reassurance and security that children feel with their parents. Many children will relate to Jake's situation and feel satisfied when he overcomes his fears.

Book Talk Material and Activities

This is a good story to share with younger children at a spooky story time. Young children often enjoy feeling a little frightened, but they do want to know that they are safe. Although there are some scary moments in this book, the overall tone is reassuring. This story is told in the first person, which could encourage children to share some of their own experiences about being afraid.

The book's illustrations add to the suspense of the story. When Jake is hearing noises, the illustrations are colored with dark black, blue, and gray. In some, Jake's face is partially hidden by shadows. When Jake finds his parents, the illustration has a bright glow of yellow and orange. The story actually begins on a wordless page after the title page showing some electrical workers pointing to the darkened house. Before reading the book, show this picture and ask the children to predict what will happen. After reading the book, go back to this picture and see what the children think. This activity will help children learn to examine illustrations carefully for information about the story.

Related Titles

Bumps in the Night by Harry Allard. Illustrated by James Marshall. Doubleday, 1979. Some zany animal characters hold a seance and meet a lonely ghost who becomes their friend.

In a Dark, Dark Room and Other Scary Stories retold by Alvin Schwartz.

Illustrated by Dirk Zimmer. Harper & Row, 1984. Seven scary stories in an easy-to-read format.

Scary, Scary Halloween by Eve Bunting. Illustrated by Jan Brett. Clarion, 1986. The not-too-scary images of Halloween—glowing eyes, skeleton costumes, and ghosts—make this another good book to share with younger children.

See My Lovely Poison Ivy and Other Verses about Witches, Ghosts and Things by Lilian Moore. Illustrated by Diane Dawson. Atheneum, 1975. Read the poem "Something Is There" and have children join in on the poem "Whooo?" for an enjoyably shivery experience.

Spooky Riddles written and illustrated by Marc Brown. Random House, 1983. A collection of riddles about skeletons, ghosts, witches, and other scary creatures that will add to the fun of a spooky activity.

About the Author and Illustrator

BUNTING, EVE (ANNE EVELYN BUNTING)
Authors of Books for Young People: Supplement to the Second Edition, by Martha E. Ward and Dorothy Marquardt. Scarecrow, 1979, p. 36.
Fifth Book of Junior Authors and Illustrators, ed. by Sally Holmes Holtze. Wilson, 1983, pp. 60–61.
Something about the Author, ed. by Anne Commire. Gale, 1980, Vol. 18, pp. 38–39.

CARRICK, DONALD
Fourth Book of Junior Authors and Illustrators, ed. by Doris de Montreville and Elizabeth D. Crawford. Wilson, 1978, pp. 71–72.
Illustrators of Children's Books: 1967–1976, Vol. IV, comp. by Lee Kingman, Grace Allen Hogarth, and Harriet Quimby. Horn Book, 1978, pp. xiii, 106, 183.
Something about the Author, ed. by Anne Commire. Gale, 1975, Vol. 7, p. 40.

Cole, Joanna.   *Cars and How They Go*
Illus. by Gail Gibbons. Crowell, 1983; pap., Harper & Row, 1986
Suggested Use Level: Gr. 1–3   Reading Level: Gr. 4

Plot Summary

Clear illustrations and a well-written text describe how a car works. The internal combustion engine is explained as Cole describes how air and fuel are mixed, how the spark plugs are fired, and how the movement of the pistons turns the crankshaft. Information about the exhaust system, gears, starter, radiator, steering, brakes, headlights, and instrumentation panel is also included. Cole explains some of the differences between cars, for example, front wheel drive and rear wheel drive. She briefly discusses different types of engines and looks at some possibilities for the future. The illustrations correlate with the text and make clear use of labels and arrows to highlight what is being discussed.

Thematic Material

Children are naturally curious about the world around them, and many are fascinated by cars and trucks. This book provides some basic information about cars and could serve as an introduction to nonfiction books.

Book Talk Material and Activities

Cars and How They Go is a nonfiction book in a picture-book format. It demonstrates how a book can be used for information. As children become more experienced with books and reading, they need to know about different kinds of books. Through book talk and story programs, children could learn about picture books, beginning readers, other fiction books, biographies, reference books, and other nonfiction books. If these programs take place in the library, they could also learn about the location of these materials and begin to develop strategies for how to find them.

One way to show the difference between fiction and nonfiction is to share an example of each. Compare *Cars and How They Go* with *Mr. Gumpy's Motor Car.* How is the car presented in each book? What does each book tell you about cars? Suggest some reasons why one might choose each book. A group of children might want to prepare a display of car books for the classroom or library.

Another book that could be included in a comparison activity is *The Wheels on the Bus,* a popular song in picture-book format. Children can list some of the parts of a car and compare them with the parts of a bus that are in the song. They can then rewrite the song for a car and add some verses that show what has been learned about a car. Have the children illustrate the verses that they have written.

Related Titles

Cars written and illustrated by Anne Rockwell. Dutton, 1984. A very simple book about the way people use cars. Rockwell has also written other books about motor vehicles: *Big Wheels* (Dutton, 1986); *Trucks* (Dutton, 1984); and *Things That Go* (Dutton, 1986).

Mr. Gumpy's Motor Car written and illustrated by John Burningham. Macmillan, 1973. Mr. Gumpy takes his friends for a drive. When it begins to rain, his car gets stuck in the mud and everyone must get out and push.

New Road! written and illustrated by Gail Gibbons. Crowell, 1983. An interesting book to compare with *Cars and How They Go,* this book could be part of a social studies unit on transportation.

Tin Lizzie written and illustrated by Peter Spier. Doubleday, 1975. Detailed illustrations help tell the story of a Model T Ford through many years of ownership.

The Wheels on the Bus written and illustrated by Maryann Kovalski. Joy Street Books, 1987. A popular song available in picture-book format.

About the Author and Illustrator

COLE, JOANNA
Fifth Book of Junior Authors and Illustrators, ed. by Sally Holmes Holtze. Wilson, 1983, pp. 77–78.
Something about the Author, ed. by Anne Commire. Gale, 1985, Vol. 37, p. 50; 1987, Vol. 49, pp. 68–74.

GIBBONS, GAIL
Something about the Author, ed. by Anne Commire. Gale, 1981, Vol. 23, pp. 77–78.

Crews, Donald.   *School Bus*

Illus. by the author. Greenwillow, 1984; pap., Penguin, 1985
Suggested Use Level: Gr. PreK–1   Reading Level: NA

Plot Summary

This book describes a typical day for some school buses. It starts with the empty fleet parked in the bus lot. The different buses in various sizes and shapes then move across town through city traffic and residential neighborhoods, adding more school-age passengers to their seats with each stop. After dropping everyone off at school, the empty buses wait again for school to be over. At the end of the day, the buses take everyone home, and then go home themselves.

Thematic Material

School buses are a familiar sight to most children. They are a method of transportation that many children have experienced, sometimes on a daily basis but often on school-sponsored trips. School bus safety is an important part of the curriculum in most elementary schools.

Book Talk Material and Activities

Children like to share information about their everyday experiences. They enjoy finding out about each other. Sharing *School Bus* in a story session could start a discussion about transportation. Some of the questions that could be considered are: How do you travel to school? How long does it take you to get to school? and What are some of the rules to follow when riding a bus? Making a chart on "How We Get to School" would encourage children to use counting and numbers to answer a question, as they begin to see relationships like big and little or more and fewer. For example, on a chart where the answers are "Riding in a Car," "Riding on a School Bus," or "Walking," children could write their names under the appropriate response. Then they could count the responses and talk about which form of transportation is most often used. Charting allows children to see information about themselves and their classmates.

Reading *School Bus* could also lead to a story program about what happens at school. Many school stories are appropriate for sharing with different age groups of children. Some possibilities are the Miss Nelson books (see Harry Allard and James Marshall, *Miss Nelson Has a Field Day*, Chapter 4); *The Day Jimmy's Boa Ate the Wash;* and *The Day the Teacher Went Bananas. The Wheels on the Bus*, adapted from the popular song, is a fun story to read about riding a city bus, and children could join in singing the song and making up new verses about their own experiences.

Related Titles

The Day Jimmy's Boa Ate the Wash by Trinka Hakes Noble. Illustrated by Steven Kellogg. Dial, 1980. A little girl's class rides a bus on a field trip to the farm. At the farm, her friend Jimmy's boa constrictor causes all kinds of problems. What other places have children visited by school bus?

The Day the Teacher Went Bananas by James Howe. Illustrated by Lillian Hoban. Dutton, 1984. A school story where a gorilla comes to teach the class and the teacher is sent to the zoo. The mix-up makes for a very unusual school day.

Louis James Hates School written and illustrated by Bill Morrison.

Houghton Mifflin, 1978. Louis James does not go to school. When he tries to find a job, he realizes how much he needs to know, and he hurries back to school.

Teach Us, Amelia Bedelia by Peggy Parish. Illustrated by Lynn Sweat. Greenwillow, 1977. What would it be like to have Amelia Bedelia for a teacher? It certainly would be different. Imagine her "calling the roll" and "planting a bulb."

Timothy Goes to School written and illustrated by Rosemary Wells. Dial, 1981. Timothy is excited about going to school, but he finds that school is not much fun with Claude around. The children can look at Timothy's expressions as he walks back and forth to school. How do they think he feels?

The Wheels on the Bus written and illustrated by Maryann Kovalski. Joy Street Books, 1987. The popular song is adapted within the framework of a story about a grandmother and her grandchildren on a shopping trip.

Will I Have a Friend? written by Miriam Cohen. Illustrated by Lillian Hoban. Macmillan, 1967. Jim worries about finding a friend at nursery school. Other stories written by Cohen and illustrated by Hoban continue the adventures of Jim and his friends.

About the Author and Illustrator

CREWS, DONALD
Fifth Book of Junior Authors and Illustrators, ed. by Sally Holmes Holtze. Wilson, 1983, pp. 88–90.
Illustrators of Children's Books: 1967–1976, Vol. IV, comp. by Lee Kingman, Grace Allen Hogarth, and Harriet Quimby. Horn Book, 1978, pp. 110, 185.
Something about the Author, ed. by Anne Commire. Gale, 1983, Vol. 30, p. 88; 1983, Vol. 32, pp. 58–60.

Degen, Bruce. *Jamberry*
Illus. by the author. Harper & Row, 1983; pap., 1985
Suggested Use Level: Gr. PreK–K   Reading Level: NA

Plot Summary
A lilting rhyme takes a bear and a boy on a search for berries. Word play and imaginative humor add to the fun, as the bear and the boy find blueberries, strawberries, blackberries, and raspberries.

Thematic Material

In *Jamberry,* the playful attitude of the bear and the boy captures the spirit of young children with its feeling of simple enjoyment.

Book Talk Material and Activities

Many children make up their own nonsense rhymes. *Jamberry* is like some of those playful rhymes. There are made-up words and a lilting rhythm. The rhymes here are fun to say and, after repeated readings, children will be able to join in and say the rhymes, too.

After reading *Jamberry,* share some berries or berry jam and crackers and read another berry book, for example, *Blueberries for Sal.* Children enjoy tasting different berries and voting for their favorite. Other nonsense rhyme books, such as *Jiggle Wiggle Prance* and *Moses Supposes His Toeses Are Roses,* could be booktalked. Children might then borrow similar books.

Audiovisual Adaptation

Jamberry. Live Oak Media, cassette/book, 1986.

Related Titles

Bears in Pairs by Niki Yektai. Illustrated by Diane deGroat. Bradbury, 1987. Rhyming words describe bears of all shapes and sizes. On the last page, the reader sees that all the bears are toy bears belonging to a little girl who is having a tea party.

Blueberries for Sal written and illustrated by Robert McCloskey. Viking, 1948. Little Sal and her mother go blueberry picking. So do Little Bear and his mother. A problem occurs when the little ones end up with the wrong mother.

Jiggle Wiggle Prance written and illustrated by Sally Noll. Greenwillow, 1987. Children might enjoy jiggling, wiggling, and prancing along with the rhyming words in this book, which are all movements.

The Moon Came Too by Nancy White Carlstrom. Illustrated by Stella Ormai. Macmillan, 1987. A little girl is going to visit her grandmother. As she prepares for the trip, she makes up some simple rhymes about what she will take with her.

Moses Supposes His Toeses Are Roses: And Seven Other Silly Old Rhymes retold and illustrated by Nancy Patz. Harcourt, 1983. These nonsense rhymes and tongue twisters appeal to the silly side of children.

Pop Corn and Ma Goodness by Edna Mitchell Preston. Illustrated by

Robert Andrew Parker. Viking, 1969. The title characters meet, fall in love, and get married in this rollicking verse. Children might like to join in and say this singsong rhyme.

Who, Said Sue, Said Whoo? written and illustrated by Ellen Raskin. Atheneum, 1973. Sue is surrounded by different animal noises. She finds out who is making each noise, for example, the owl says "whoo."

About the Author and Illustrator

DEGEN, BRUCE
Something about the Author, ed. by Anne Commire. Gale, 1987, Vol. 47, p. 73.

Gardner, Beau.   *Have You Ever Seen . . .? An ABC Book*
Illus. by the author. Dodd, 1986
Suggested Use Level: Gr. 1–4   Reading Level: NA

Plot Summary

This alphabet book is an opportunity to play with language. For each letter of the alphabet (both capital and lowercase letters are shown), an unusual alliterative item is described and depicted, continuing the title question. For example, "G" is "a Ghost with Glasses." Colorful graphics illustrate each odd combination.

Thematic Material

Gardner's presentation of the letters of the alphabet is inventive.

Book Talk Material and Activities

Alphabet books are written for different age groups. Some are designed to introduce the letters, like Dick Bruna's *B Is for Bear,* in which the illustrations each show just one lowercase letter and one item that illustrates it. The clarity and simplicity of the book are on target for young children. Such other books as *Have You Ever Seen . . .?* are more complex, showing how to play with language. Children who feel comfortable with their knowledge of the alphabet can use *Have You Ever Seen . . .?* to spark their imaginations and expand their vocabularies by trying to create their own combinations. This alphabet book should be booktalked with older children, even those in fourth grade, who have the language fluency to appreciate Gardner's creations and to experiment on their own. *Aster Aardvark's Alphabet Adventures* is another alliterative alphabet presentation as is *Alligator Arrived with Apples. Albert B. Cub and Zebra* is a wordless book, but the illustrations are filled with so many items for each letter that older children often compete to identify the most. Playing with words and language helps children develop confidence in their verbal and written skills. When they see language as something that they control, they feel more comfortable using it.

Related Titles

Albert B. Cub and Zebra: An Alphabet Storybook written and illustrated by Anne Rockwell. Crowell, 1977. On the first page of this wordless book, zebra is abducted. Albert B. Cub searches from A to Z to find him.

Alligator Arrived with Apples: A Potluck Alphabet Feast written by Crescent Dragonwagon. Illustrated by Jose Aruego and Ariane Dewey. Macmillan, 1987. In alphabetical order, animals bring appropriate items to a banquet, so there are animals and food from A to Z. Along with alligator's apples, there are mouse's mousse and zebra's zucchini.

Aster Aardvark's Alphabet Adventures written and illustrated by Steven Kellogg. Morrow, 1987. Kellogg tells a story about Aster Aardvark, Bertha Bear, Cyril Capon, and other alliterative animals. Children will enjoy the antics of "Hermione, a hefty hyperactive hippo" and "Kenilworth, the kind kangaroo."

B Is for Bear: An ABC written and illustrated by Dick Bruna. Methuen, 1967. Each lowercase letter is illustrated with one item. An apple for "a," a lion for "l," and a pig for "p" are some of the combinations.

What's Inside? The Alphabet Book written and illustrated by Satoshi Kitamura. Farrar, Straus, 1985. Clues in the illustrations encourage children to guess what items will depict the letters of the alphabet. For example, the tail of a kite and the bottom of a ladder are depicted on the "K" and "L" page. When the page is turned, there is the kite, and a ladder is being used to get it out of the tree.

About the Author and Illustrator

GARDNER, BEAU
Something about the Author, ed. by Anne Commire. Gale, 1988, Vol. 50, pp. 83–84.

Gibbons, Gail. *The Milk Makers*
Illus. by the author. Macmillan, 1985; pap., 1987
Suggested Use Level: Gr. K–1   Reading Level: Gr. 4

Plot Summary

The Milk Makers follows the production of milk from the cow to the store. Gibbons discusses the different animals that produce milk. She explains that cows are most often used for milk production, and she tells how cows are able to make milk. What cows eat, how their four stomachs digest the food, and how cows are milked are presented through clear text and illustrations. The processing of milk for home use, including how it is pasturized and homogenized, is also described. The last page in the book uses illustrations and captions to show milk and other dairy products.

Thematic Material

Milk is used every day in nearly every home. In describing how milk is produced, Gibbons emphasizes the production process. Her book gives children some background information about something familiar.

Book Talk Material and Activities

In *The Milk Makers,* children see how much effort and attention is given to producing milk. Studying the process behind the preparation of familiar items helps children develop an understanding of the many people who contribute to their lives. Many schools and libraries organize trips to local businesses. *The Milk Makers* and other similar books are good to read and discuss before a trip to any production facility. A chart could be made highlighting the settings and characters that are part of the milk production process. (Chart C shows the setting and characters in *The Milk Makers* and in Donald Carrick's book, *Milk.*) Such a chart could serve as a model for studies of other people and processes, for example, a visit to a bakery or department store. It could also be correlated with the study of farm animals prior to a trip to a farm.

Gail Gibbons has written many similar books that focus on community services, including *Department Store* and *Fire! Fire!* An in-depth study of her books would not only help children learn about their community but would also introduce them to the author/illustrator. Gibbons's books

Chart C

THE MILK MAKERS		MILK	
Setting	Characters	Setting	Characters
Field	Cows	Pasture	Cows
Barn	Farmer and cows	Barn	Farmer and cows
Tank truck	Driver	Tank truck	Farmer and driver
Dairy	Workers (including lab technicians and machine operators)	Dairy	Workers (including technicians and packers)
Delivery truck	Driver and loaders	Delivery truck	Driver
Store	Checkers and stockers	Store	Stockers
Home	Family		

could be compared with the books about communities by Anne Rockwell and Harlow Rockwell, such as *My Barber,* and Anne Rockwell's *Our Garage Sale.*

Audiovisual Adaptation

The Milk Makers. "Reading Rainbow." Great Plains National Instructional Television Library, videorecording, 1986.

Related Titles

Department Store written and illustrated by Gail Gibbons. Crowell, 1984. The text and illustrations feature different people and activities in a department store. Customers, salespeople, stockroom workers, and display artists are some of the people who are included.

Fill It Up! All about Service Stations written and illustrated by Gail Gibbons. Crowell, 1985. Details about what goes on at a service station are presented. Clear, well-labeled illustrations highlight facts like how a hydraulic lift works and where gasoline is stored.

Fire! Fire! written and illustrated by Gail Gibbons. Crowell, 1984.

Firefighting equipment is described as are the different responsibilities of firefighters, including searching for people in a burning building and operating an aerial ladder.

Milk written and illustrated by Donald Carrick. Greenwillow, 1985. Like *The Milk Makers,* this book also describes the process of milk production. Children can compare the two books.

My Barber written and illustrated by Anne Rockwell and Harlow Rockwell. Macmillan, 1981. On a visit to the barbershop, a boy and his father observe what the barber does and the tools being used.

Our Garage Sale written by Anne Rockwell. Illustrated by Harlow Rockwell. Greenwillow, 1984. A boy and his family clean their attic and have a garage sale.

The Post Office Book written and illustrated by Gail Gibbons. Crowell, 1982. Some of the activities of postal employees, including sorting the mail, loading it onto trucks and planes, and delivering it are described.

About the Author and Illustrator

GIBBONS, GAIL
Something about the Author, ed. by Anne Commire. Gale, 1981, Vol. 23, pp. 77–78.

Goffstein, M. B.   *Our Snowman*
Illus. by the author. Harper & Row, 1986
Suggested Use Level: Gr. PreK–1   Reading Level: Gr. 4

Plot Summary

After a blizzard, a girl and her younger brother go outside and build a snowman. The girl instructs her brother on how to roll the big snowballs so that the snow stays clean. They put the snowballs together, make a face, and then go into the house. Once inside, the girl becomes upset when she looks outside and sees the lonely snowman. She mopes around the house. Finally, her mother turns on the porch light so her father can take her outside and make a wife for the snowman.

Thematic Material

The girl and her brother enjoy being outside together. This book could be used to discuss the seasons, focusing on the snowy weather of winter.

Book Talk Material and Activities

Books about winter can be featured at a story program in public or school libraries. By hearing these stories, children find out about how characters enjoy the seasons. *Our Snowman* is both a winter story and a warm family story. The whole family ends up caring about the snowman and making sure that he is happy. A related outdoor activity is making characters out of snow. It is not only fun but also encourages cooperation and allows children to share responsibilities.

A comparison could be made between Mira Lobe's *The Snowman Who Went for a Walk* and *Our Snowman*. The realism of *Our Snowman* contrasts with the fantasy in *The Snowman Who Went for a Walk* (in which a snowman leaves the yard where he was made and finds his way to the cold land in the North where he will never melt). Have children suggest imaginative adventures for the snow couple in *Our Snowman*. Ask them to name some places where these snow people could go. Possible answers are an ice arena or a football game in Green Bay, Wisconsin. In this activity, children could also learn about places where the weather stays cold.

Related Titles

The Biggest Snowstorm Ever written and illustrated by Diane Paterson. Dial, 1974. The Bunche family is excited by the snowstorm and they all go outside to play. As the snow continues, however, their house is covered and they must tunnel into it.

First Snow written and illustrated by Emily Arnold McCully. Harper & Row, 1985. In this wordless book, a family of mice enjoys a day in the snow.

It's Snowing! It's Snowing! by Jack Prelutsky. Illustrated by Jeanne Titherington. Greenwillow, 1984. The 17 poems in this collection present many different images of snow. The poem "My Snowman Has a Noble Head" would go well with *Our Snowman*.

Midnight Snowman by Caroline Feller Bauer. Illustrated by Catherine Stock. Atheneum, 1987. The children in this story live in a climate where it hardly ever snows. One surprising night it snows and everyone in town comes out to make a snowman.

Snow written and illustrated by Kathleen Todd. Addison-Wesley, 1982. A very young child enjoys a walk in the snow. This book could be compared with *The Snowy Day*.

The Snowman written and illustrated by Raymond Briggs. Random

House, 1978. In this wordless book, a snowman comes to life and escorts a little boy on a magical adventure.

The Snowman Who Went for a Walk by Mira Lobe. Illustrated by Winfried Opgenoorth. Morrow, 1984. A snowman realizes that he will soon melt, so he looks for a place that is cold year round.

The Snowy Day written and illustrated by Ezra Jack Keats. Viking, 1962. A little boy named Peter enjoys his day in the snow, making a snowman and snow angels.

Snowy Day: Stories and Poems edited by Caroline Feller Bauer. Illustrated by Margot Tomes. Lippincott, 1986. A collection of stories and poems describes different feelings and activities associated with snow.

About the Author and Illustrator

GOFFSTEIN, M. B. (MARILYN BROOKE)

Authors of Books for Young People: Supplement to the Second Edition, by Martha E. Ward and Dorothy Marquardt. Scarecrow, 1979, p. 101.

Fourth Book of Junior Authors and Illustrators, ed. by Doris de Montreville and Elizabeth D. Crawford. Wilson, 1978, pp. 151–152.

Illustrators of Children's Books: 1967–1976, Vol. IV, comp. by Lee Kingman, Grace Allen Hogarth, and Harriet Quimby. Horn Book, 1978, pp. 122, 123, 190.

Something about the Author, ed. by Anne Commire. Gale, 1976, Vol. 8, pp. 70–71.

Hale, Sarah Josepha. *Mary Had a Little Lamb*
Illus. by Tomie de Paola. Holiday House, 1984, hb and pap.
Suggested Use Level: Gr. PreK–K   Reading Level: NA

Plot Summary

This picture-book version of "Mary Had a Little Lamb" pairs the verses of the familiar rhyme with Tomie de Paola's colorful illustrations. Besides the well-known opening verse, there are additional verses about how the teacher sends the lamb away, how and why the lamb is devoted to Mary, and how all children should be kind to animals. A musical score is included.

Thematic Material

Children learn many simple songs and rhymes in their homes, nursery schools, and preschools.

Book Talk Material and Activities

Tomie de Paola's illustrations use an old-fashioned setting to interpret this familiar nursery rhyme from the nineteenth century, which is part of the early experiences of many children. A related activity would be to organize a display of other picture-book versions of simple rhymes, such as "Little Bo Peep." When children visit the library from preschools or when the librarian visits nursery schools, these books can be shared. Some can be read to the children and others highlighted through brief book talks. Day-care workers, nursery school teachers, and parents would appreciate a list of the titles of available picture-book versions of simple rhymes, so that they can borrow them for their programs. Simple nursery rhymes that have been typed onto paper can be copied and distributed for children to illustrate. Several teachers in the primary grades do this with their classes and then compile a monthly book of poems for each child to take home. The illustrated rhymes are featured around the classroom on enlarged charts and also are part of shared reading activities. Some children even memorize the simple rhymes. For many children, this is an early experience with print and reading. At home, children can share their books with family members and "read" the rhymes that they have memorized.

Audiovisual Adaptation

Mary Had a Little Lamb. Weston Woods, cassette/book, 1985; filmstrip/cassette, 1985.

Related Titles

Cat Goes Fiddle-i-Fee adapted and illustrated by Paul Galdone. Clarion, 1985. The rhyme is also a song, in which animals appear in sequence and make noises. Some are familiar, such as the dog's "bow-wow"; others, such as the goose's "swishy, swashy," are not so familiar. Many children like to follow the pattern of the rhyme.

The Comic Adventures of Old Mother Hubbard and Her Dog illustrated by Arnold Lobel. Bradbury, 1968. Lobel's illustrations and the small size of the book make this version of the familiar rhyme about Old Mother Hubbard a good one to share with small groups.

Little Bo Peep illustrated by Paul Galdone. Clarion, 1986. Many children are delighted to find that there is more to this rhyme than just the familiar verse. The book includes other verses as well.

Old Mother Hubbard and Her Dog illustrated by Evaline Ness. Holt,

Rinehart, 1972. Another familiar rhyme in picture-book format. Compare it with *The Comic Adventures of Old Mother Hubbard and Her Dog*, illustrated by Arnold Lobel.

Sing a Song of Sixpence illustrated by Tracey Campbell Pearson. Dial, 1985. The illustrations of this rhyme are very humorous, as the blackbirds fly out of the pie and wreak havoc on the court of the king and queen.

Three Little Kittens illustrated by Paul Galdone. Clarion, 1986. Children who hear this rhyme may enjoy joining in on the repeated meows and purrs.

About the Author and Illustrator

DE PAOLA, TOMIE (THOMAS ANTHONY)
Fifth Book of Junior Authors and Illustrators, ed. by Sally Holmes Holtze. Wilson, 1983, pp. 98–100.
Illustrators of Children's Books: 1957–1966, Vol. III, comp. by Lee Kingman, Grace Allen Hogarth, and Harriet Quimby. Horn Book, 1968, pp. 99, 215; *1967–1976, Vol. IV*, 1978, pp. 16, 112, 186.
Something about the Author, ed. by Anne Commire. Gale, 1977, Vol. 11, pp. 68–71.

Hayes, Sarah. *This Is the Bear*
Illus. by Helen Craig. Lippincott, 1986; pap., Harper & Row, 1986
Suggested Use Level: Gr. PreK–K   Reading Level: Gr. 3

Plot Summary

In this rhyming story, a stuffed bear named Fred is involved in a series of mishaps. He falls in the trash and is taken away to the dump. His owner searches for him, finds him, and takes him home, where Fred keeps his adventure a secret from the other toys.

Thematic Material

Stories about toys and their adventures are very common in picture books for children, and many involve stuffed bears. Toys that seem to talk, at least to their owners and to other toys, are also a familiar part of many stories.

Chart D

Title	Bear's Name	Bear Talks to	Problem Is	Problem Solved When
Corduroy	Corduroy	Himself	No one will buy Corduroy	Lisa takes him home
This Is the Bear	Fred	The dog, the boy, and the other toys	He is dumped in the trash	The boy and the dog find him

Book Talk Material and Activities

This Is the Bear is very similar to several other stuffed bear stories and would be a fine book to share as part of a stuffed bear parade or party. A look at how other authors and illustrators portray stuffed bears would be interesting. Perhaps a chart of some of the similarities and differences could be made. Some questions to consider are: Does the bear talk? To whom? What problems does the bear face and how are they solved? Chart D provides a sample of this activity using *This Is the Bear* and a related title, *Corduroy*.

Related Titles

Brunus and the New Bear written and illustrated by Ellen Stoll Walsh. Doubleday, 1979. When Benjamin gets a new stuffed bear, Brunus, his old toy, is jealous. Brunus learns that the more love is shared, the more it grows.

Corduroy written and illustrated by Don Freeman. Viking, 1968. Corduroy waits in the department store for someone to buy him. After an adventure in the furniture section, Corduroy is returned to the toy department and Lisa buys him and takes him home. Corduroy's adventures continue in *A Pocket for Corduroy* (Viking, 1978).

Ira Sleeps Over written and illustrated by Bernard Waber. Houghton Mifflin, 1972. Ira has a problem. He is going to sleep over at Reggie's house but doesn't know if he should bring his stuffed bear.

Old Bear written and illustrated by Jane Hissey. Philomel, 1986. A group of toys works together to rescue a stuffed bear who has been stored in the attic and forgotten.

Peabody written and illustrated by Rosemary Wells. Dial, 1983. Annie gets a new doll and she ignores her stuffed bear, Peabody. When the doll breaks, she remembers her old friend and goes to him for comfort.

Teddy Bears Go Shopping written and illustrated by Susanna Gretz. Four Winds, 1982. This is part of a series of books about the antics of a group of teddy bears. Read about *Teddy Bears' Moving Day* (Four Winds, 1981) and *Teddy Bears Cure a Cold* (Four Winds, 1985).

About the Author and Illustrator
CRAIG, HELEN
Something about the Author, ed. by Anne Commire. Gale, 1987, Vol. 46, p. 56; 1987, Vol. 49, pp. 75–77.

Hoban, Tana.   *Shapes, Shapes, Shapes*
Photographs by the author. Greenwillow, 1986
Suggested Use Level: Gr. PreK–1   Reading Level: NA

Plot Summary
   This book begins with a list of 11 shapes and a picture of each shape. Color photographs of 29 everyday scenes and items follow—houses, streets, chairs, construction sites, and even a lunch box. In each photograph, children are encouraged to look for many different shapes and to develop their observation skills.

Thematic Material
   The concept of shapes is paired with the development of observation skills. Another theme is learning about familiar items.

Book Talk Material and Activities
   Tana Hoban has created many concept books, including *Dots, Spots, Speckles, and Stripes; Is It Larger? Is It Smaller?;* and *Round and Round and Round.* Her clear photographs highlight many ordinary objects and encourage close observation. *Shapes, Shapes, Shapes* and other books by Hoban could provide a language experience for preschool and kindergarten children. Present the photographs in *Shapes, Shapes, Shapes* to a group of children and encourage them to talk about the shapes they see.

Then, have them look at other Hoban books in pairs and talk about what they see. This provides each child with the opportunity to develop verbal skills while cooperating with a classmate. By talking to each other, young children improve their social skills. They also learn to use books for information and, with Hoban's books, they learn that books can convey information even when there are no words. Children might enjoy making a collage of shapes using construction paper or pictures from magazines, perhaps cooperatively.

In addition to Tana Hoban's concept books, three books by Marcia Brown could be used to promote sensory perception skills. *Listen to a Shape, Touch Will Tell,* and *Walk with Your Eyes* combine free verse and photographs to encourage observation of the natural world.

Related Titles

Dots, Spots, Speckles, and Stripes written and photographed by Tana Hoban. Greenwillow, 1987. In this wordless book, color photographs of a peacock, a child with freckles, a zebra, confetti, and other familiar objects illustrate the concepts in the title.

Is It Larger? Is It Smaller? written and photographed by Tana Hoban. Greenwillow, 1985. Items in color photographs illustrate the concepts of large and small in this wordless book. For example, one picture shows a sow and some piglets; another a toy car and a real car.

Is It Rough? Is It Smooth? Is It Shiny? written and illustrated by Tana Hoban. Greenwillow, 1984. This wordless book has color photographs of items with different textures, such as cotton candy, a turtle, and bubbles.

Listen to a Shape written and photographed by Marcia Brown. Watts, 1979. Poetic verses and color photographs encourage children to look for shapes in the natural world.

Push, Pull, Empty, Full: A Book of Opposites written and photographed by Tana Hoban. Macmillan, 1972. Black-and-white photographs illustrate 15 pairs of opposites, for example, elephants are shown for the word "thick," and flamingos are depicted for "thin." The illustrated word is printed on the photograph.

Round and Round and Round written and illustrated by Tana Hoban. Greenwillow, 1983. The color photographs in this wordless book show many familiar round things, including the holes in Swiss cheese and a scoop of ice cream.

Touch Will Tell written and photographed by Marcia Brown. Watts,

1979. Photographs of the natural world focus on the feel and texture of items, for example, the rough bark of a tree.

Walk with Your Eyes written and photographed by Marcia Brown. Watts, 1979. Both text and photographs encourage children to be close observers of nature.

About the Author and Illustrator

HOBAN, TANA

Authors of Books for Young People: Supplement to the Second Edition, by Martha E. Ward and Dorothy Marquardt. Scarecrow, 1979, p. 129.

Fourth Book of Junior Authors and Illustrators, ed. by Doris de Montreville and Elizabeth D. Crawford. Wilson, 1978, pp. 178–179.

Illustrators of Children's Books: 1967–1976, Vol. IV, comp. by Lee Kingman, Grace Allen Hogarth, and Harriet Quimby. Horn Book, 1978, p. 176.

Something about the Author, ed. by Anne Commire. Gale, 1981, Vol. 22, pp. 158–159.

Hoban, Tana.   *26 Letters and 99 Cents*
Photographs by the author. Greenwillow, 1987
Suggested Use Level: Gr. PreK–2   Reading Level: NA

Plot Summary

This is actually two books in one. The first seven pages have photographs of the letters of the alphabet (upper- and lowercase) and an item that depicts each letter—an airplane for Aa, a bicycle for Bb, and so on. At the end of the alphabet, the reader is instructed to turn the book upside down and begin again. This part of the book shows the numbers 1 to 30 and then 35, 40, 45, 50, 60, 70, 80, 90, and 99. Next to the numbers are photographs of pennies, nickles, dimes, and quarters in combinations that add up to the number being presented. For example, there is one penny for 1, one penny and one dime for 11, and so on.

Thematic Material

26 Letters and 99 Cents introduces children to the alphabet, numbers, and money.

Book Talk Material and Activities

The brightly colored letters and numbers used in the photographs are very clear and give a feeling of depth. A note from the author describes them as "Soft Touch" letters and numbers, which can be purchased in toy stores. Children could make their own three-dimensional letters out of clay or cookie dough. Tactile experiences with letters and numbers help children become more familiar with their shapes. Children could also fingerpaint letters and numbers in their pictures. *Crictor,* the story of a clever snake that can form letters and numbers with his body, is a good book to share.

The clear photographs of pennies, nickles, dimes, and quarters allow children to see the relationship between the coins and their value. Booktalking stories about money, such as *Arthur's Funny Money* and *Willis,* could extend the discussion of how money is used.

Related Titles

Alexander, Who Used to Be Rich Last Sunday by Judith Viorst. Illustrated by Ray Cruz. Atheneum, 1978. Alexander is irked because his brothers have more money than he does. But Alexander spent his money on unusual things, like renting a snake for an hour.

Arthur's Funny Money written and illustrated by Lillian Hoban. Harper & Row, 1981. Arthur the chimp needs to earn money for a team uniform. When he and his sister go into the bike-washing business, they find out how much it costs to try to earn money.

Bravo, Ernest and Celestine! written and illustrated by Gabrielle Vincent. Greenwillow, 1981. Ernest and Celestine earn money to fix their leaking roof. However, they end up spending it on special gifts for each other.

Crictor written and illustrated by Tomi Ungerer. Harper & Row, 1958. Crictor, the boa constrictor, is an intelligent pet. He bends his body to form letters and numbers, and he catches a robber and holds him until the police arrive.

Dollars and Cents for Harriet written and illustrated by Betsy Maestro and Giulio Maestro. Crown, 1988. Harriet needs $5 to buy something at the toy store. She already has 100 pennies and she is able to earn 20 nickles, 10 dimes, 4 quarters, and 2 half-dollars. The money that she earns is clearly drawn in the book. Children can count the coins along with Harriet.

Rachel and Obadiah written and illustrated by Brinton Turkle. Dutton, 1978. Even in colonial times children tried to earn money. Obadiah

Starbuck does not think his sister, Rachel, can earn the silver coin. He soon discovers that he is wrong.

Willis written and illustrated by James Marshall. Houghton Mifflin, 1974. Willis wants some sunglasses, and his friends want to help him. Their efforts to earn enough money are hilarious and eventually successful.

About the Author and Illustrator

HOBAN, TANA

Authors of Books for Young People: Supplement to the Second Edition, by Martha E. Ward and Dorothy Marquardt. Scarecrow, 1979, p. 129.

Fourth Book of Junior Authors and Illustrators, ed. by Doris de Montreville and Elizabeth D. Crawford. Wilson, 1978, pp. 178–179.

Illustrators of Children's Books: 1967–1976, Vol. IV, comp. by Lee Kingman, Grace Allen Hogarth, and Harriet Quimby. Horn Book, 1978, p. 176.

Something about the Author, ed. by Anne Commire. Gale, 1981, Vol. 22, pp. 158–159.

Hoguet, Susan Ramsey. *I Unpacked My Grandmother's Trunk: A Picture Book Game*

Illus. by the author. Dutton, 1983

Suggested Use Level: Gr. PreK–1   Reading Level: NA

Plot Summary

This book is an illustrated version of the popular alphabet game. As the trunk is unpacked, each new item that is shown begins with the next letter of the alphabet, until the pages are filled, from acrobat to zebra. Some of the pages are only three-quarter size. The end of the page lines up with the lid of the trunk. When the page is lifted, another item appears to have come out of the trunk, giving the illusion of the trunk being unpacked.

Thematic Material

Children love to play games, and this book encourages the use of the alphabet in their activities. It also shows how an unusual page format can add to the impact of the ideas being presented.

Book Talk Material and Activities

Alphabet games are very popular and provide opportunities for children to experiment with language. A familiar game in book format encourages children to participate in the book sharing experience, because they know what is expected. They are able to suggest possibilities for the next item and talk about other times when they played the game. Several children could work on their own version of this book, or a bulletin board display of "Grandmother's Trunk" could be prepared using the children's artwork.

Hoguet's illustrations are especially effective because they make use of an unusual format. The three-quarter-size page on alternate pages turns to reveal the new item that is being unpacked, giving the illusion that the items are coming out of the trunk. Children need to develop their abilities to examine and evaluate books critically. Looking at this and other books with unusual formats could lead to a discussion of how the presentation of ideas enhances their impact.

Related Titles

A My Name Is Alice by Jane Bayer. Illustrated by Steven Kellogg. Dial, 1984. Another alphabet game in picture-book format that could be compared with Hoguet's book.

Bear Hunt by Margaret Siewert and Kathleen Savage. Illustrated by Leonard Shortall. Prentice-Hall, 1976. A popular game that children will enjoy seeing in a book.

Do Your Ears Hang Low? Fifty More Musical Fingerplays by Tom Glazer. Illustrated by Mila Lazarevich. Doubleday, 1980. Fifty finger plays and rhymes set to music. A companion to *Eye Winker, Tom Tinker, Chin Chopper.*

Each Peach Pear Plum written and illustrated by Janet Ahlberg and Allan Ahlberg. Viking, 1978. Like *I Unpacked My Grandmother's Trunk,* this book is based on a game and has an unusual format.

Eye Winker, Tom Tinker, Chin Chopper: Fifty Musical Fingerplays by Tom Glazer. Illustrated by Ronald Himler. Doubleday, 1973. Clear illustrations and musical arrangements for finger plays, action poems, and songs.

Finger Rhymes collected and illustrated by Marc Brown. Dutton, 1980. A clearly presented collection of fun and familiar finger plays.

The Very Hungry Caterpillar written and illustrated by Eric Carle.

Collins-World, 1969. The unusual format really does add to the telling of this story of the caterpillar and what he eats.

We Hide, You Seek written and illustrated by Jose Aruego and Ariane Dewey. Greenwillow, 1979. The jungle animals enjoy a good game of hide-and-seek. The illustrations have to be scrutinized in order to see the animals in their hiding places.

Hopkins, Lee Bennett, ed. *Surprises*
Illus. by Megan Lloyd. Harper & Row, 1984; pap., 1986
Suggested Use Level: Gr. PreK–3   Reading Level: NA

Plot Summary
Lee Bennett Hopkins selected 38 poems on topics of everyday interest to children. The poems are grouped into six sections: "Who to Pet"; "Creep, Crawl, Fly"; "At the Top of My Voice"; "Boats, Trains, and Planes"; "Rain, Sun, and Snow"; and "Good Night." Many familiar poets are represented, including Aileen Fisher, Gwendolyn Brooks, Langston Hughes, Eve Merriam, Karla Kuskin, Myra Cohn Livingston, and Carl Sandburg.

Thematic Material
Surprises really fits the chapter theme "Celebrating Everyday Experiences." The poems that Hopkins has included describe people, places, animals, seasons, and feelings that children will recognize from their own lives.

Book Talk Material and Activities
As part of the I Can Read series (Harper & Row), this book is very accessible to beginning readers because of the enlarged print and wide spacing between lines. The poems that have been selected are very suitable in topic and length to be rewritten onto chart paper and displayed in a library or classroom. Poetry charts make it easier for a group of children to follow along and join in when saying the poem. Even young children benefit from shared reading experiences using enlarged text.

They begin to focus on the print and isolate specific words and phrases. Poetry charts also give children the opportunity to illustrate the poems and to see their work displayed and used.

The poems in *Surprises* contain many features that attract children to poetry. They have rhyme and repetition and are about familiar experiences. "My Dog" by Myra Cohn Livingston is about the independent spirit of a pet. "Freckles" by Aileen Fisher expresses a child's sincere admiration for a friend's features. "Everybody Says" by Dorothy Aldis captures the feeling of needing to be yourself. Correlating poems with programs or saying them aloud just for fun will help children develop an appreciation for the poet's creative use of language.

Related Titles

Bronzeville Boys and Girls by Gwendolyn Brooks. Illustrated by Ronni Solbert. Harper & Row, 1956. Brooks's poems deal with the individual experiences of children. Try comparing "Robert, Who Is a Stranger to Himself" with Dorothy Aldis's "Everybody Says" in *Surprises*.

Feathered Ones and Furry by Aileen Fisher. Illustrated by Eric Carle. Crowell, 1971. These poems are about animals including the pelican, squirrel, robin, duck, and raccoon.

A House Is a House for Me by Mary Ann Hoberman. Illustrated by Betty Fraser. Viking, 1978. The pattern for this poem is easy for children to learn. Many children will join in on the refrain.

Jump All the Morning: A Child's Day in Verse edited and illustrated by P. K. Roche. Viking, 1984. Two young bunnies spend a happy day together. The poems reflect some of their activities.

More Surprises edited by Lee Bennett Hopkins. Illustrated by Megan Lloyd. Harper & Row, 1987. More simple poems from the I Can Read series.

A Song I Sang to You by Myra Cohn Livingston. Illustrated by Margot Tomes. Harcourt, 1984. Running, playing, thinking, worrying, and wondering are some of the experiences reflected in this collection.

Yellow Butter, Purple Jelly, Red Jam, Black Bread by Mary Ann Hoberman. Illustrated by Chaya Burstein. Viking, 1981. Did you ever have a tea party using acorns and leaves? Did you ever wish your little brother would go away? Did you ever play dress up? Hoberman has written poems about these childhood experiences that are sure to strike a familiar chord.

About the Author and Illustrator

HOPKINS, LEE BENNETT

Authors of Books for Young People: Supplement to the Second Edition, by Martha E. Ward and Dorothy Marquardt. Scarecrow, 1979, p. 134.

Fifth Book of Junior Authors and Illustrators, ed. Sally Holmes Holtze. Wilson, 1983, pp. 155–157.

Something about the Author, ed. by Anne Commire. Gale, 1972, Vol. 3, pp. 85–87.

Kitchen, Bert. *Animal Alphabet*

Illus. by the author. Dial, 1984; pap., 1988

Suggested Use Level: Gr. K–4   Reading Level: NA

Plot Summary

In this alphabet book, the capital letters are illustrated by animals. Some are familiar, such as the lion and the zebra, but many, such as the armadillo, the jerboa, and the umbrella bird, are not as well known. The oversized book allows for the letters to be extra large, and the animals interact with the letters. For example, the rhinoceros's horn is piercing the "R," and the bats are hanging in the "B." A list of all the animals is provided at the end of the book.

Thematic Material

Animal Alphabet presents the capital letters of the alphabet as well as large pictures of 26 animals.

Book Talk Material and Activities

In *Animal Numbers,* a companion book to this title, salamanders, squirrels, Irish setters, and the sea horse are some of the animals that illustrate numbers. Following the same idea, children could use animals to illustrate other concepts, such as seasons, opposites, and colors. For example, in an animal colors book, the raven could illustrate black, the flamingo could be used for pink, and so on. Children would need to do research to find unusual animals for the concepts. This is a good cooperative project between older and younger children. For example, fourth graders could help first graders find information about animals. Nonfiction books about animals, such as *Large as Life* and *A Child's Book of Birds,* could be booktalked to the children first.

Other alphabet books, such as *Alphabatics* and *Action Alphabet,* could provide ideas for further alphabet activities. Presenting several different alphabet books allows children to choose their own project.

Related Titles

Action Alphabet written and illustrated by Marty Neumeier and Byron Glaser. Greenwillow, 1984. Letters of the alphabet act out the words that illustrate them, including a "D" that is a "Drip" and an "O" that is in "Orbit."

Alphabatics written and illustrated by Suse MacDonald. Bradbury, 1986. Letters of the alphabet make acrobatic movements to transform themselves into the items that illustrate them. For example, "S" stretches into a "Swan," and "C" curves into the smile of a "Clown." This book received the Caldecott Honor Medal in 1987.

Animal Numbers written and illustrated by Bert Kitchen. Dial, 1987. The numbers from 1 to 10 and then 15, 25, 50, 75, and 100 are illustrated with large, colorful pictures of animals.

A Child's Book of Birds by Kathleen N. Daly. Illustrated by Fred Brenner. Doubleday, 1977. A brief description and an illustration (many in color) of some familiar birds, including the cardinal and the quail.

Giraffe by Caroline Arnold. Photographs by Richard Hewett. Morrow, 1987. The text describes the giraffe's habits, focusing on a group of giraffes in an animal park in New Jersey, of which there are many color photographs. The author and photographer also collaborated on *Koala* (Morrow, 1987) and *Kangaroo* (Morrow, 1987).

Large as Life: Daytime Animals by Joanna Cole. Illustrated by Kenneth Lilly. Knopf, 1985. The illustrations in this oversized book are life-size depictions of several animals, including the ermine, the common tree frog, and the eastern chipmunk. A brief text describes each animal.

Martin, Bill, Jr., and Archambault, John.   *The Ghost-Eye Tree*
Illus. by Ted Rand. Holt, Rinehart, 1985; pap., Henry Holt, 1988
Suggested Use Level: Gr. K–2   Reading Level: Gr. 2

Plot Summary

A mother asks her son and daughter to go to Mr. Cowlander's barn to get some fresh milk. It is very dark and the wind is blowing. The barn is across town, down a deserted country road, along which there is a large oak tree known as the ghost-eye tree. The boy wears his hat and acts tough, and he and his sister arrive at the barn without incident. On the way back, however, when they come to the tree, they seem to have an encounter with the spirit of the tree, and the boy loses his hat. But the boy's sister goes back to get it for him, and they arrive home safely. After that, the boy avoids any trips down the long, dark road.

Thematic Material

The boy and his sister are afraid of the dark, the wind, and the big oak tree. Being afraid and overcoming fears are themes in this story.

Book Talk Material and Activities

Many children are afraid of the dark—of the noises that they hear and the shadows that they see. In *The Ghost-Eye Tree*, the boy and his sister almost let their fears overpower them. The sister goes back to get the boy's hat on the dark, spooky road, facing her fears. The boy, however, hides when his mother calls him to go down the road at night. He is still afraid. Children could share some of their fears and talk about how they deal with them.

The illustrations in the book are full of dark blues and blacks. What light there is casts long shadows. The branches of the tree seem to reach across the page forming grasping claws. Ask children to describe how these pictures complement the story. Look at the illustrations in other scary stories and see what colors and images are used.

Related Titles

A Dark, Dark Tale written and illustrated by Ruth Brown. Dial, 1981. Children can discuss the spooky images in the dark, sinister pictures and the text of this familiar story.

Do Not Open written and illustrated by Brinton Turkle. Dutton, 1981. When Miss Moody opens the bottle (even though it is marked "Do Not Open") a monster appears. Children can examine the transformation that the monster goes through and answer the question, What makes this monster seem scary?

The Gobble-uns'll Git You Ef You Don't Watch Out! by James Whitcomb Riley. Illustrated by Joel Schick. Lippincott, 1975. Have the children look at the various creatures depicted in this picture-book version of the "Little Orphan Annie" rhyme.

Hubnuckles by Emily Herman. Illustrated by Deborah Kogan Ray.

Crown, 1985. Hubnuckles is a ghostly figure that appears on Halloween. The black-and-white sketches in this book have an eerie quality that is very different from the darkly colored illustrations in *The Ghost-Eye Tree*.

Spooky and the Ghost Cat by Natalie Savage Carlson. Illustrated by Andrew Glass. Lothrop, 1985. Spooky meets a strange white cat that is under the spell of a witch. How will Spooky rescue her?

About the Author and Illustrator

MARTIN, BILL, JR. (WILLIAM IVAN MARTIN)
Something about the Author, ed. by Anne Commire. Gale, 1985, Vol. 40, p. 128.

Merriam, Eve. *Blackberry Ink*
Illus. by Hans Wilhelm. Morrow, 1985
Suggested Use Level: Gr. PreK–1   Reading Level: NA

Plot Summary

The 24 poems in this collection cover many subjects, including cats, snow, monsters, the wind, and washing clothes. There are nonsense verses and sing-song chants as well as poems of imagination, word play, and humor.

Thematic Material

Eve Merriam has created poems about the many moods of young children. Images of playful disobedience and youthful egocentrism will bring nods of recognition from young listeners.

Book Talk Material and Activities

The effervescent spirit of the poems in this book could extend the experience of many other books. For example, "Five Little Monsters" could be read in a story program about monsters that includes books like Pat Hutchins's *The Very Worst Monster* (see Chapter 4). "Swish, Swash" could be read with stories about clothes, like *Mary Wore Her Red Dress and Henry Wore His Green Sneakers* and *Mariana May and Nursey*. In "Bella Had a New Umbrella," Bella won't use her umbrella, just like Everett Anderson in *Some of the Days of Everett Anderson*. "Crick! Crack!," a poem about the wind that ends with a mitten being lost, could lead into the book *The Mitten*. And "Bertie, Bertie" is about a character who will not take a bath, just like Jeremy in *No Bath Tonight*. Poetry should be included regularly in story and book talk programs.

Related Titles

Mariana May and Nursey written and illustrated by Tomie de Paola. Holiday House, 1983. Mariana May gets dirty when she plays, until her friends come up with a plan.

Mary Wore Her Red Dress and Henry Wore His Green Sneakers adapted and illustrated by Merle Peek. Clarion, 1985. A song about clothes, including green shoes, purple pants, and violet ribbons.

The Mitten: An Old Ukrainian Folktale retold by Alvin Tresselt. Illustrated by Yaroslava. Lothrop, 1964. A lost mitten becomes the home for many small animals.

No Bath Tonight by Jane Yolen. Illustrated by Nancy Winslow Parker. Crowell, 1978. Every night of the week Jeremy finds a reason for not taking a bath. Soon he'll be as dirty as the character in Eve Merriam's "Bertie" in *Blackberry Ink*.

Some of the Days of Everett Anderson by Lucille Clifton. Illustrated by Evaline Ness. Holt, Rinehart, 1970. On Tuesday, Everett Anderson gets wet because he does not use his umbrella, just like the character in Eve Merriam's "Bella" in *Blackberry Ink*.

About the Author and Illustrator

MERRIAM, EVE

Authors of Books for Young People: First Supplement, by Martha E. Ward and Dorothy Marquardt. Scarecrow, 1967, p. 204.

Something about the Author, ed. by Anne Commire. Gale, 1972, Vol. 3, pp. 128–129; 1985, Vol. 40, pp. 141–149.

Third Book of Junior Authors, ed. by Doris de Montreville and Donna Hill. Wilson, 1972, pp. 193–194.

Merriam, Eve.   *Halloween ABC*
Illus. by Lane Smith. Macmillan, 1987
Suggested Use Level: Gr. K–4   Reading Level: NA

Plot Summary

There are 26 poems in this book—one for each letter of the alphabet. Each poem highlights some aspect of Halloween. From a poison "apple" to a mysterious "key" to an ominously empty "zero," these are poems of fear, suspense, and even some humor.

Thematic Material

These poems correlate with Halloween activities and the alphabet. They could also stimulate language play and creative writing activities.

Book Talk Material and Activities

Poetry can be incorporated into book talk or story programs in many ways. Poems can be read aloud to set the mood or to provide a transition from one book to another. They can be written on charts illustrated by the children and then displayed around the room. Many children find the language and rhythm of poetry so memorable that they join in on repeated readings and naturally read/memorize the poems.

The poems in *Halloween ABC* show some of the scary and fun feelings of this holiday. Some poems could be used with different age levels. "Jack-o'-lantern" would be great to share during a pumpkin-carving activity. The "gooey" sounding words would appeal to younger children as they reach inside their own pumpkins, and children could suggest other slimy words to describe this experience. Older children would appreciate the word play in "Witchery." Read some of these poems at a Halloween program along with some scary stories like *Do Not Open* and *The Tailypo*.

Another related activity would be to make an alphabet book to correlate with another holiday.

Related Titles

Do Not Open written and illustrated by Brinton Turkle. Dutton, 1981. Miss Moody opens the bottle marked "Do Not Open" and a very frightening monster appears. But the conclusion is safe and satisfying.

Hey-How for Halloween! edited by Lee Bennett Hopkins. Illustrated by Janet McCaffrey. Harcourt, 1974. More than 20 poems about witches, goblins, ghosts, and other favorite Halloween creatures.

It's Halloween by Jack Prelutsky. Illustrated by Marylin Hafner. Greenwillow, 1977. The format of the 13 poems in this collection is just right for beginning readers. The large print and wide spacing between the lines make it easier for children to focus on the text. These Halloween poems set just the right spooky mood.

Scary, Scary Halloween by Eve Bunting. Illustrated by Jan Brett. Clarion, 1986. The rhythmic poetic text follows different trick-or-treaters, as a family of cats watches the parade of strange creatures.

The Tailypo: A Ghost Story by Joanna Galdone. Illustrated by Paul Galdone. Clarion, 1977. An old man chops off the tail of an unusual creature, then eats the tail. Later that night, the man is awakened by the creature searching for the tail, and it does get its tail back.

Thump, Thump, Thump written and illustrated by Anne Rockwell. Dutton, 1981. The Thing has lost his hairy toe and the old woman has found it. Now the Thing is looking for his toe.

About the Author and Illustrator

MERRIAM, EVE

Authors of Books for Young People: First Supplement, by Martha E. Ward and Dorothy Marquardt. Scarecrow, 1967, p. 204.

Something about the Author, ed. by Anne Commire. Gale, 1972, Vol. 3, pp. 128–129; 1985, Vol. 40, pp. 141–149.

Third Book of Junior Authors, ed. by Doris de Montreville and Donna Hill. Wilson, 1972, pp. 193–194.

Schwartz, Amy. *Oma and Bobo*
Illus. by the author. Bradbury, 1987
Suggested Use Level: Gr. 1–3   Reading Level: Gr. 4

Plot Summary

On her birthday, Alice is delighted to find that she will be allowed to have a dog. Alice's grandmother, Oma, is not pleased. Alice picks out her dog at the animal shelter and she names him Bobo. Oma expresses her continuing disapproval by muttering in German and locking herself in her room. As Oma predicted, Bobo causes a problem, and he and Alice are sent to obedience school. The lessons don't seem to help Bobo, and Alice fears that they will not win a blue ribbon at the dog show. Oma sees Alice's disappointment and decides to help train Bobo. Alice is amazed, but she wisely allows Oma to become involved. At the dog show, Bobo does very well, but he will not "fetch." From the audience, Oma's command of "Achtung, Bobo! Fetch! Herbringen!" gets Bobo's attention and he wins a blue ribbon.

Thematic Material

Themes of wanting a pet and of family togetherness are evident here. Alice's life is filled with ordinary details—going to school, playing with Bobo, and watching Oma cook breakfast. Alice and her grandmother have a strong relationship.

Book Talk Material and Activities

Caring for a pet is part of the everyday life of many children. Book talk or story programs about adjusting to new pets can introduce children to fiction and nonfiction books about this topic. Judith Viorst's poem "Mother Doesn't Want a Dog" (in the book *If I Were in Charge of the World, and Other Worries*) is a great poem to write and illustrate on a poetry chart for sharing with *Oma and Bobo*. Lee Bennett Hopkins's poetry collection *Surprises* (see this chapter) also has a section of poems about pets. Many activities can be correlated with a program on pets, including a pet show (with real or stuffed animal pets), making a photo album of children and their pets, and a visit from a pet shop owner or a veterinarian.

After hearing a story about a pet dog, children may want more information about pets. The books in the Junior Petkeepers Library series, like *Dogs* by Fiona Henrie, present easy-to-read facts about caring for pets. Sharing this book at a story program provides an opportunity to discuss the kind of information found in nonfiction books and how these books are different from stories. It also demonstrates the variety of materials that are available in a library.

Amy Schwartz's illustrations in *Oma and Bobo* show many details from Alice's everyday life. Children could look for these details and then discuss how they compare with their own lives. How would they describe an ordinary day? Who do they see? Where do they go? Arnold Lobel's story of "A List" in *Frog and Toad Together* also describes some routine activities.

Related Titles

Can I Keep Him? written and illustrated by Steven Kellogg. Dial, 1971. A boy wants a pet but nothing seems quite right until a new boy moves into the neighborhood.

Dogs by Fiona Henrie. Photographs by Marc Henrie. Watts, 1980. Part of the Junior Petkeepers Library series, this book contains information about choosing and caring for a dog. Some of the other books in the series look at cats, gerbils, fish, and rabbits.

Frog and Toad Together written and illustrated by Arnold Lobel. Harper & Row, 1971. Five stories about the everyday activities of two good friends.

Harry's Dog by Barbara Ann Porte. Illustrated by Yossi Abolafia. Greenwillow, 1984. Like Alice in *Oma and Bobo,* Harry wants a dog. His father's allergies make it difficult for Harry and his dog, but his Aunt Rose helps solve the problem.

Hi, Cat! written and illustrated by Ezra Jack Keats. Macmillan, 1970. Does Archie pick his own pet or does the pet pick Archie? In this story, a cat follows Archie and Peter around their neighborhood.

If I Were in Charge of the World, and Other Worries: Poems for Children and Their Parents by Judith Viorst. Illustrated by Lynn Cherry. Atheneum, 1981. Viorst's collection of poems focuses on the everyday concerns, hopes, and emotions of families.

Mine Will, Said John by Helen V. Griffith. Illustrated by Muriel Batherman. Greenwillow, 1980. John has some definite ideas about the pet he wants, but it takes him a while to convince his parents.

Okay, Good Dog written and illustrated by Ursula Landshoff. Harper & Row, 1978. Part of the I Can Read series, this book provides simple instructions for training a dog.

Pinkerton, Behave! written and illustrated by Steven Kellogg. Dial, 1979. Children can compare Pinkerton's behavior at obedience school with Bobo's in *Oma and Bobo.*

About the Author and Illustrator

SCHWARTZ, AMY
Something about the Author, ed. by Anne Commire. Gale, 1985, Vol. 41, p. 208; 1987, Vol. 47, pp. 190–192.

Schwartz, David M.   *How Much Is a Million?*
Illus. by Steven Kellogg. Lothrop, 1985; pap., Scholastic, 1986
Suggested Use Level: Gr. 1–4   Reading Level: Gr. 5

Plot Summary
Using familiar items, David M. Schwartz makes very large numbers understandable to children. In one of the comparisons, readers are asked to imagine children standing on each others' shoulders, and then how high 1 million children would reach. In another comparison using a goldfish bowl, children are asked to imagine how large the goldfish bowl would have to be to hold 1 million goldfish. The same comparisons are proposed for 1 billion and 1 trillion. Kellogg has drawn 100,000 stars on 7 pages, and according to Schwartz it would take 70 pages to show 1 million. Schwartz's note at the end of the book describes the mathematical computations behind the size relationships.

Thematic Material
This book describes millions, billions, and trillions, emphasizing size relationships that children can relate to.

Book Talk Material and Activities
Many children have difficulty understanding very large numbers. *How Much Is a Million?* uses comparisons that children will understand. Teachers and librarians can extend this understanding by providing other opportunities for making comparisons. The concept of "big, bigger, biggest" could be presented with children looking for three similar items to illustrate the concept. Librarians might show three books including an atlas. Children might find three leaves, three balls, or three pencils. Stories about large numbers, like *Millions of Cats,* would be fun to read and discuss, and other math concept stories, such as *Bunches and Bunches of Bunnies,* could be booktalked.

Related Titles
Bunches and Bunches of Bunnies by Louise Mathews. Illustrated by Jeni Bassett. Scholastic, 1978. The rhyming text illustrates some simple multiplication facts, with the final picture showing 144 (12 × 12) bunnies crowded into a house for a reunion. Older children might be able to do

some mathematical computations like those in *How Much Is a Million?* For example, if there are 144 bunnies on two pages, how many pages would it take to show 100,000 bunnies?

Jillions of Gerbils written and illustrated by Arnold Dobrin. Lothrop, 1973. When David grows up, he wants to have "jillions of gerbils." When he loses his 2 gerbils, and then finds them in the basement with 10 baby gerbils, he is well on his way. Librarians and teachers should indicate to the children that "jillion" is not a real number. Children can use *How Much Is a Million?* to look at the real words for numbers.

The King's Flower written and illustrated by Mitsumasa Anno. Collins, 1976. Anno pokes fun at a king who wants everything he owns to be the biggest by humorously depicting his huge bed and kitchen utensils. The book shows that the biggest is not always best.

Millions of Cats written and illustrated by Wanda Gag. Coward, McCann, 1928. A classic picture book tells about a man who finds "millions of cats" and brings them home as pets.

One Zillion Valentines written and illustrated by Frank Modell. Greenwillow, 1981. Two boys, Marvin and Milton, do not actually make a "zillion" valentines, but they do make one for everyone in their neighborhood. Emphasize that "zillion" is not a real number.

One, Two, Three and Many: A First Look at Numbers by Solveig Paulson Russell. Illustrated by Margot Tomes. Walck, 1970. Children may ask about "jillions" (*Jillions of Gerbils*) and "zillions" (*One Zillion Valentines*), but they will be surprised to find out that a "googol" is the number that has a one with 100 zeros after it. Other numbers are described, too.

About the Author and Illustrator

KELLOGG, STEVEN
Fourth Book of Junior Authors and Illustrators, ed. by Doris de Montreville and Elizabeth D. Crawford. Wilson, 1978, pp. 208–209.
Illustrators of Children's Books: 1967–1976, Vol. IV, comp. by Lee Kingman, Grace Allen Hogarth, and Harriet Quimby. Horn Book, 1978, pp. 133, 196.
Something about the Author, ed. by Anne Commire. Gale, 1976, Vol. 8, pp. 95–97.

Siebert, Diane. *Truck Song*
Illus. by Byron Barton. Crowell, 1984; pap., Harper & Row, 1987
Suggested Use Level: Gr. PreK–1   Reading Level: NA

Plot Summary
The rhyming text of this story describes some of the experiences of drivers of big trucks. Talking on their CB radios, planning to meet at rest stops, and listening to music helps the drivers pass the hours behind the wheel. Details are included about checking the load, driving on long stretches of highway, and traveling through rain, up mountains, and in cities. Several different kinds of trucks are mentioned, making the point that many people and vehicles provide services to families and communities. The story ends as the driver delivers his load and plans for his next assignment.

Thematic Material
This book follows a truck and its driver on their delivery route and could be included in programs about workers and their jobs. Although the focus of the story is on trucks and transportation, some attention is given to the driver's feeling of satisfaction with his job.

Book Talk Material and Activities
Many schools include communities and services as part of their social studies curriculum, and *Truck Song* could be correlated with that study. By knowing the school curriculum, school and public librarians can order materials and plan programs that help build a partnership between the classroom and the library. Book talks, story programs, class visits, displays, and bibliographies can be organized to support classroom activities. As part of a library visit, children could work on a collage of trucks using pictures they have brought from home or those found in magazines from the library (of course, using only those that have been canceled). This might even be a good way to talk about how to take care of library materials.

Several other picture books about trucks could be used to examine how other authors and illustrators present the same subject. The text and illustrations in *Trucks* by Anne Rockwell, *Truck* by Donald Crews, *Trucks* by Gail Gibbons, and *Dig Drill Dump Fill* by Tana Hoban could be analyzed, with discussion focusing on what kinds of trucks are presented, how the book is illustrated, what age group might enjoy the book, and whether the children learned anything new about trucks. One way to organize this discussion is to have a small group of children look at one book and then report to the large group. Children could then ask questions and make their own decisions about which books best fit their needs.

Audiovisual Adaptation

Truck Song. Live Oak Media, cassette/book, 1988; AIMS Media, 16mm film, 1987.

Related Titles

Dig Drill Dump Fill written and illustrated by Tana Hoban. Greenwillow, 1975. This is basically a wordless book of photographs about the operation of heavy equipment. Two pages at the end of the book show all the vehicles and describe "What They Are and What They Do."

Truck written and illustrated by Donald Crews. Greenwillow, 1980. Another virtually wordless book, except for signs and the writing on the trucks, this book gives children the opportunity to make their own story.

Trucks written and illustrated by Gail Gibbons. Crowell, 1981. A very simple text and well-labeled illustrations show a variety of trucks and what they do.

Trucks written and illustrated by Anne Rockwell. Dutton, 1984. Colorful illustrations show cats using dump trucks, ice cream trucks, garbage trucks, and more.

Trucks and Supertrucks by Norman Richards and Pat Richards. Doubleday, 1980. Large black-and-white photographs and a brief text present information about different kinds of trucks and how they are used.

About the Author and Illustrator

BARTON, BYRON

Authors of Books for Young People: Supplement to the Second Edition, by Martha E. Ward and Dorothy Marquardt. Scarecrow, 1979, pp. 16–17.

Fifth Book of Junior Authors and Illustrators, ed. by Sally Holmes Holtze. Wilson, 1983, pp. 21–23.

Something about the Author, ed. by Anne Commire. Gale, 1976, Vol. 9, p. 17.

4

Finding the Humor
in Picture Books

WHAT MAKES children laugh? Silly things like pigs that play hide-and-seek. Surprising things like children who shrink. Sometimes, scary things like monsters and their families. Children find humor in illustrations, especially when unexpected events are depicted. They enjoy stories where ordinary characters are in extraordinary circumstances. They laugh at the antics of animals facing human predicaments.

The books in this chapter present a variety of humorous situations. Familiar characters appear, for example, Miss Nelson, Pinkerton, George and Martha, and Pig Pig. In other books, mice, pigs, foxes, wolves, and even a camel are involved in unusual activities. Children will enjoy the many ways that authors and illustrators incorporate humor into their books.

Allard, Harry, and Marshall, James.   *Miss Nelson Has a Field Day*
   Illus. by the authors. Houghton Mifflin, 1985; pap., 1988
   Suggested Use Level: Gr. K–3   Reading Level: Gr. 3

Plot Summary
Things are not right at the Horace B. Smedley School. Everyone is depressed and embarrassed by the awful performance of the football team. The coach is having problems and he must leave school for a long mental rest. The school must find a replacement for him before the big game. But who? Miss Nelson gets an idea after she overhears some kids discussing the tough substitute they once had whose name was Miss Viola Swamp. She hurries home and finds a black sweat suit, but meanwhile a

new Miss Viola Swamp appears. Of course, no one is fooled by the principal, Mr. Blandsworth, in his costume. The team's laughter is interrupted by the appearance of the real Miss Swamp and things begin to change. The team starts to shape up. They exercise, run, and practice plays like never before. Puzzled by Miss Swamp's identity, Mr. Blandsworth wants to check with Miss Nelson but decides not to bother her. When the coach returns from his mental rest, Miss Nelson and Miss Swamp are shown looking out separate windows. Of course, the team wins, but what about the appearance of Miss Nelson and Miss Swamp in the same picture? On the final page, Miss Nelson thanks her look-alike sister for all her assistance.

Thematic Material

The text and illustrations are filled with slapstick humor and zany characters. Some details in the illustrations will also surprise those who are familiar with the two previous books in the series (*Miss Nelson Is Missing* and *Miss Nelson Is Back*).

Book Talk Material and Activities

Miss Nelson Has a Field Day is the third book in the series about the antics at the Horace B. Smedley School. The familiar characters, setting, and style will attract many children to it. Teachers and librarians could use the book to discuss the concept of a series. Most children will be familiar with television series where the same characters and setting appear each week but the plot changes. Many will also be familiar with books that are part of a series. Curious George, Georgie the ghost, Spot, Corduroy, Clifford, Frog and Toad, Little Bear, and Pinkerton are some characters that children might know from series books. Discussing books from different series helps familiarize children with the concepts of setting, character, and plot. Children can also learn how to find some of these books, which contributes to their development as independent library users.

Allard and Marshall include some surprises in their illustrations. Readers of the first two books will feel certain that Miss Viola Swamp is really Miss Nelson in disguise. If that is true, however, how can Miss Nelson and Miss Swamp be together in the same picture? Children will have fun making predictions about this page before finding out about Miss Nelson's sister. Another detail in the illustrations (on page 10) is a poster on the wall commemorating February 19 as National Be Kind to Teachers

Day. This would be a great time for a school or public library program inviting teachers to stop in and learn more about the services available in the library.

Related Titles

Clifford the Small Red Puppy written and illustrated by Norman Bridwell. Scholastic, 1972. Emily Elizabeth tells how she came to own Clifford and how he became the beloved big red dog.

Corduroy written and illustrated by Don Freeman. Viking, 1968. Lisa sees Corduroy in the department store and wants him for her own. *A Pocket for Corduroy* (Viking, 1978) continues their adventures.

Curious George written and illustrated by H. A. Rey. Houghton Mifflin, 1941. In this first book in the popular series about the little monkey and the man in the yellow hat, the man finds George in Africa and brings him to America where his curiosity results in several problems.

Days with Frog and Toad written and illustrated by Arnold Lobel. Harper & Row, 1979. The fourth book in the series about these two good friends. Children can read about how they fly a kite, get the shivers, and show consideration for each other.

Georgie written and illustrated by Robert Bright. Doubleday, 1944. Meet Georgie, the Whittakers, Miss Oliver, and Herman in this first adventure about the little ghost.

Little Bear by Else Holmelund Minarick. Illustrated by Maurice Sendak. Harper & Row, 1957. Little Bear celebrates his birthday and has other adventures in this collection of stories.

Miss Nelson Is Missing written and illustrated by Harry Allard and James Marshall. Houghton Mifflin, 1977. The first book about Miss Nelson and the first appearance of Miss Viola Swamp. Both return in *Miss Nelson Is Back* (Houghton Mifflin, 1982).

A Rose for Pinkerton written and illustrated by Steven Kellogg. Dial, 1981. In this second story about Pinkerton, he meets a kitten named Rose and together they disrupt the International Pet Show.

Spot Goes to the Farm written and illustrated by Eric Hill. Putnam, 1987. Spot and his father look for baby animals at the farm. In this manipulative book, children enjoy guessing what they will find under the flaps.

About the Author and Illustrator

ALLARD, HARRY
Authors of Books for Young People: Supplement to the Second Edition, by Martha E. Ward and Dorothy Marquardt. Scarecrow, 1979, p. 4.

Fifth Book of Junior Authors and Illustrators, ed. by Sally Holmes Holtze. Wilson, 1983, pp. 5–6.
Something about the Author, ed. by Anne Commire. Gale, 1986, Vol. 42, pp. 23–28.
MARSHALL, JAMES
Authors of Books for Young People: Supplement to the Second Edition, by Martha E. Ward and Dorothy Marquardt. Scarecrow, 1979, p. 187.
Fourth Book of Junior Authors and Illustrators, ed. by Doris de Montreville and Elizabeth D. Crawford. Wilson, 1978, pp. 253–254.
Illustrators of Children's Books: 1967–1976, Vol. IV, comp. by Lee Kingman, Grace Allen Hogarth, and Harriet Quimby. Horn Book, 1978, pp. 5, 144, 201.
Something about the Author, ed. by Anne Commire. Gale, 1974, Vol. 6, pp. 160–161; 1988, Vol. 51, pp. 109–121.

Brown, Marc, and Brown, Laurene Krasny. *The Bionic Bunny Show*

Illus. by the authors. Little, Brown, 1984; pap., 1985
Suggested Use Level: Gr. 1–4   Reading Level: Gr. 5

Plot Summary

Wilbur Rabbit is the star of "The Bionic Bunny Show." At the television studio, he goes to the makeup room and the wardrobe department to be transformed into a television superhero. On the set of the show, Wilbur listens to the director, and filming begins on the week's script. In this episode, the Bionic Bunny chases and captures some bank-robbing rats. The filming is interrupted several times as Wilbur needs help with his lines and technicians set up new shots. When the filming is completed, Wilbur takes off his costume, leaves the studio, and goes home, where he is a mild-mannered, somewhat inept father. A chart entitled "Television Words and What They Mean" is on the last page of the book.

Thematic Material

This humorously presented behind-the-scenes look at a television show is a story within a story. Readers see Wilbur's real life as well as an episode of "The Bionic Bunny Show."

Book Talk Material and Activities

The illustrations help make this book humorous. In real life, Wilbur is an ordinary rabbit who wears glasses. As the Bionic Bunny, he is supposed to have superpowers, but Wilbur is actually quite clumsy. He cannot read the teleprompter and, while chasing the rats, he falls out of a boat and must be rescued because he cannot swim. Children often believe that television characters are real; *The Bionic Bunny Show* gives them a look at some of the work that goes into making a television show. One activity that would extend children's understanding of how a television program is made is a videotaping project. The project could be a simple one, such as letting the children say their names and something about themselves and then playing it back for them, or it could be more complex, such as having the children act out a favorite story. Afterward, the children could discuss how they prepared for their appearance, what they would change about the tape, and how they have changed since the tape was made, referring to the glossary at the end of *The Bionic Bunny Show,* to learn some television terminology.

The Browns used two different formats for the illustrations. Throughout the book they used cartoon characters, but scenes from "The Bionic Bunny Show" are in a comic strip with characters' dialogue in cartoon balloons. Children would enjoy seeing other books with comic-strip style illustrations, like *Flicks* and *The Knight and the Dragon,* and they could even try making their own. Librarians and teachers could booktalk some art books that discuss this style of illustration, like *The Art of the Comic Strip* and *Cartooning for Kids.*

Audiovisual Adaptation

The Bionic Bunny Show. "Reading Rainbow." Great Plains National Instructional Television Library, videorecording, 1987.

Related Titles

The Art of the Comic Strip by Shirley Glubok. Illustrated with reproductions of comic strips. Macmillan, 1979. A brief history of the comic strip in American newspapers includes early versions of comics like "Blondie" and "Peanuts."

Cartooning for Kids written and illustrated by Carol Lea Benjamin. Crowell, 1982. Some of the chapters describe "Body Basics," "What's So Funny?," and even "Professional Secrets You Can Use." The book includes easy-to-follow directions for drawing animals and people and for adding details to convey feelings.

Draw 50 Famous Cartoons written and illustrated by Lee J. Ames. Doubleday, 1979. Step-by-step examples demonstrate how to draw characters like Popeye and Dagwood. Ames has created other similar books like *Draw 50 Cats* (Doubleday, 1986) and *Draw 50 Dogs* (Doubleday, 1981).

Flicks written and illustrated by Tomie de Paola. Harcourt, 1979. In this wordless book, five short stories are presented as if they were silent movies. Children can make up their own dialogue to accompany the illustrations.

The Knight and the Dragon written and illustrated by Tomie de Paola. Putnam, 1980. De Paola uses different sizes and layouts of illustrations to tell the story of how a dragon and a knight decide to cooperate.

About the Author and Illustrator

Brown, Marc

Fifth Book of Junior Authors and Illustrators, ed. by Sally Holmes Holtze. Wilson, 1983, pp. 54–55.

Something about the Author, ed. by Anne Commire. Gale, 1976, Vol. 10, pp. 17–18.

Dubanevich, Arlene.   *Pigs in Hiding*
Illus. by the author. Four Winds, 1983
Suggested Use Level: Gr. PreK–1   Reading Level: NA

Plot Summary

A group of pigs is playing a game of hide-and-seek. The pig who is "it" begins to count while the other pigs find places to hide. When he reaches 100, he begins to look for the other pigs, but he cannot find them. He looks in different rooms inside the house and he looks outside without success, yet the other pigs are clearly visible in the illustrations. Finally, the pig seems to give up. He tricks the other pigs into coming from their hiding places. The game is over and the pigs have a party.

Thematic Material

This is a humorous fantasy in which much of the humor is in the illustrations. In fact, the story does not have a narrative text but is presented through the pigs' conversation balloons/captions.

Book Talk Material and Activities

The illustrations in this book show pigs playing hide-and-seek—behaving like humans and enjoying a human game. The pigs live in a house, speak English, ride scooters, and wear bow ties. At their party, they have doughnuts, sandwiches, popcorn, strawberries, peanuts, and punch. Stories that use animals in the illustrations often have a more universal appeal. They also provide librarians and teachers with an opportunity to discuss fantasy and realistic fiction. Comparing them to real pigs helps children begin to make the distinction between fiction and nonfiction and between reality and fantasy. Using a nonfiction or reference book about pigs, answer some questions about how they live, for example: What do they eat? What noises do they make? Where do they live? Then use these same questions to look at some stories about pigs. Children's responses could be charted and referred to when other stories are discussed (see Chart E for an example). Comparing stories and looking for similarities and differences makes children look more closely at their books. Instead of just listening to a story, children read the book again and again to look for more details that will help them make decisions about the characters, setting, plot, and other features. In story programs, teachers and librarians can help children learn to examine books by providing them with opportunities to compare and contrast stories. Through book discussions and charts, teachers and librarians can demonstrate ways to analyze books.

The illustrations in *Pigs in Hiding* have many humorous details. The pigs move and act like humans. Their house has many pig mementos—pictures, bookends, a statue. Also, the reader can see the hiding pigs but the seeking pig cannot, and there is no good reason why not. Children often enjoy feeling superior to the characters that they see, and they will like being able to find the "pigs in hiding."

Related Titles

The Book of Pigericks: Pig Limericks written and illustrated by Arnold Lobel. Harper & Row, 1983. Children like limericks. Lobel's fancy pigs and inventive humor are delightful.

Oink and Pearl written and illustrated by Kay Chorao. Harper & Row, 1981. Here are four stories about Pearl and her little brother. Their adventures continue in *Ups and Downs with Oink and Pearl* (Harper & Row, 1986).

Chart E

WHAT WE KNOW ABOUT PIGS			
	Pigs in *World Book*	*Pigs in Hiding*	*Piggins*
What do pigs eat?	They eat corn and other grains, pasture crops, and garbage	They eat popcorn, doughnuts, sandwiches, strawberries, and peanuts, and drink punch	They eat elegant foods like shrimp soup and drink tea
What noises do pigs make?	They grunt and squeal	They speak English	They speak very proper English
Where do pigs live?	They live on farms	They live in houses	They live in very fancy houses
What do pigs do?	They eat a lot and wallow in mud	They play games and have parties	They work as butlers and solve mysteries

Pig Pig Grows Up written and illustrated by David McPhail. Dutton, 1984. Although Pig Pig is growing out of all his baby things, he refuses to give them up.

Piggins written by Jane Yolen. Illustrated by Jane Dyer. Harcourt, 1987. Piggins is the butler for Mr. and Mrs. Reynard. When Mrs. Reynard's diamonds are stolen, Piggins comes to the rescue.

Pigs from A to Z written and illustrated by Arthur Geisert. Houghton Mifflin, 1986. Seven pigs are hidden on each page of this alphabet book. They do a better job of hiding than the *Pigs in Hiding!*

Poinsettia and Her Family written and illustrated by Felicia Bond. Crowell, 1981. With her large family and small house, Poinsettia cannot find anywhere to call her own. *Poinsettia and the Firefighters* (Crowell, 1984) follows the story of Poinsettia and her family in their new home.

Roger Takes Charge written and illustrated by Susanna Gretz. Dial, 1987. When Roger is in charge of his little brother, his neighbor Flo wants to take over. Flo ends up covered with garbage, but Roger and his brother stay clean.

Fox, Mem. *Hattie and the Fox*
  Illus. by Patricia Mullins. Bradbury, 1987
  Suggested Use Level: Gr. PreK–1   Reading Level: Gr. 1

Plot Summary

Hattie the hen sees something suspicious in the bushes. It is a long, pointed nose. When Hattie tells her barnyard friends—the goose, the pig, the sheep, the horse, and the cow—their replies are polite, but they are not really interested. Hattie continues to watch the creature in the bushes and sees a nose and two eyes. Again, her friends are unconcerned. Hattie becomes more agitated as she sees more of the creature sneaking out of the bushes, and her friends continue to ignore her warnings. When the fox emerges from the bushes, Hattie flies into a tree and her friends panic. The cow's loud "moo" scares the fox away and the barnyard is peaceful again.

Thematic Material

The humor in this story comes from the animals' unconventional and unconcerned responses to Hattie's warnings. There are also anticipation and suspense as the fox slowly emerges from the bushes. The conclusion is safe and satisfying.

Book Talk Material and Activities

The animals in the story do not listen to Hattie's warnings. Children will be able to see the danger along with Hattie, as they anticipate the confrontation with the fox. They will laugh at the animals' lack of concern and their unusual replies. For example, the pig does not say "oink"; he says "well, well!" The sheep says "who cares?" This is an opportunity to talk about the sounds animals are expected to make, and how their unexpected remarks are funny.

Another confrontation between a fox and a hen occurs in *Rosie's Walk*. A comparison with *Hattie and the Fox* could focus on the illustrations and how they add to the humor of the story. In *Hattie and the Fox*, the barnyard animals are shown calmly ignoring Hattie's warnings while she becomes more agitated. In *Rosie's Walk*, only the illustrations show what happens to the fox, as he is hit by a rake, falls into the pond, and experiences other disasters while following Rosie. Comparing similar stories encourages children to look more closely at books. They also begin to notice how authors and illustrators each make a contribution to the story.

Related Titles

Cat Goes Fiddle-i-Fee adapted and illustrated by Paul Galdone. Clarion, 1985. The animals in this book make some unusual sounds, like the hen that goes "chimmy-chuck" and the pig that goes "griffy, gruffy."

One Fine Day written and illustrated by Nonny Hogrogian. Macmillan, 1971. While an old lady is gathering wood, a fox drinks all of her milk. She is so angry that she cuts off his tail. The fox must find a way to get his tail back.

"Quack!" Said the Billy Goat by Charles Causley. Illustrated by Barbara Firth. Lippincott, 1986. Like the animals in *Hattie and the Fox*, these barnyard animals say some unusual things.

Rosie's Walk written and illustrated by Pat Hutchins. Macmillan, 1968. As Rosie the hen goes for a walk, a fox follows her. The illustrations show all the disasters that befall the fox, while Rosie calmly continues her walk.

Silly Goose written and illustrated by Jack Kent. Prentice-Hall, 1983. In this silly story, a goose comes to the aid of a smart fox. The fox shows off his knowledge, but the goose uses common sense.

About the Author and Illustrator

Fox, Mem (Merrion Frances Fox)
Something about the Author, ed. by Anne Commire. Gale, 1988, Vol. 51, pp. 65–70.

Hurd, Thacher.   *The Pea Patch Jig*
Illus. by the author. Crown, 1986
Suggested Use Level: Gr. K–3   Reading Level: Gr. 4

Plot Summary

Farmer Clem spends his day working in his garden. He does not know that a family of mice has a house at the edge of his garden. One day, as Baby Mouse's parents prepare for a party, she wanders away from her home and falls asleep in a head of lettuce. Of course, that is the lettuce that Farmer Clem picks for his salad. Father and Mother Mouse hurry to rescue their baby. At home after this adventure, the party preparations continue and Baby Mouse wanders off again. This time, she decides to play ball with some tomatoes and accidentally hits Grandfather Mouse with one. At last, it is time for the party. The guests arrive and everyone enjoys the evening together. Baby Mouse goes to bed, but she cannot sleep. From her window, she shoots peas at the guests. But then she shoots peas at an uninvited guest. The fox runs away and the party continues. Everyone dresses up as vegetables, with Baby Mouse as a pea, and they dance to the music of Grandfather's fiddle.

Thematic Material

Some of the characters in this family story are mice. Using animals to portray human experiences provides children with the opportunity to relate to the story without feeling it is too personal. The slapstick humor in this one is captured in the illustrations. A musical arrangement is included.

Book Talk Material and Activities

Several aspects of this story make it humorous and these can be discussed with children. There is the relationship between Farmer Clem and the Mouse family. Also, do mice really live in little houses, dress in clothes, and have parties? Baby Mouse's antics are amusing, especially when she hits Grandfather with a tomato and shoots peas at the guests. The author's use of expressive language also adds to the story's appeal. Farmer Clem is hit with a zucchini ("THWACK"), he shouts with surprise ("JAKERS CRAKERS"), Baby Mouse kicks a tomato off a plant ("SPLAT"), and one lands on Grandfather's head ("MMMMMPPPPHHHHH"). After reading the story, go back and look for some of the creative expressions. Reread the story and have the children join in on the sounds and exclamations.

At the end of the book, Hurd includes some music for and a reference to "The Pea Patch Jig" by Dan Emmett, arranged by John Hartford. In a school, the music teacher might be willing to play the song for the children and look at other kinds of country music. Another possibility is to correlate the book with learning country dances in physical education.

Audiovisual Adaptation

The Pea Patch Jig. Random House Media, cassette/book, 1988.

Related Titles

Barn Dance! by Bill Martin, Jr., and John Archambault. Illustrated by Ted Rand. Henry Holt, 1986. On this farm, the scarecrow waits until it is dark and then calls all the animals together. In the barn, they have a rollicking dance until the sun begins to rise.

Do Your Ears Hang Low? Fifty More Musical Fingerplays by Tom Glazer. Illustrated by Mila Lazarevich. Doubleday, 1980. And *Eye Winker, Tom Tinker, Chin Chopper: Fifty Musical Fingerplays* by Tom Glazer. Illustrated by Ronald Himler. Doubleday, 1974. These two books include familiar songs that encourage participation. After reading *The Pea Patch Jig* and singing the song, try singing and doing the movements for "The Barnyard Song" in *Eye Winker, Tom Tinker, Chin Chopper*.

Go Tell Aunt Rhody illustrated by Aliki. Macmillan, 1974. And *Go Tell Aunt Rhody* illustrated by Robert M. Quackenbush. Lippincott, 1973. Two versions of the same song illustrated by different artists. How do they compare?

Hush Little Baby: A Folk Lullaby illustrated by Aliki. Prentice-Hall, 1968. And *Hush Little Baby* illustrated by Margot Zemach. Dutton, 1976. Another opportunity to look at different interpretations of the same song.

Oh, a-Hunting We Will Go by John Langstaff. Illustrated by Nancy Winslow Parker. Atheneum, 1974. Familiar animals are being sought for some amusing purposes. Langstaff has other picture books of songs, including the 1956 Caldecott-Award-winning *Frog Went a-Courting* (Harcourt, 1955).

About the Author and Illustrator

HURD, THACHER
Something about the Author, ed. by Anne Commire. Gale, 1986, Vol. 45, pp. 115–
116; 1987, Vol. 46, pp. 87–90.

Hutchins, Pat.   *The Very Worst Monster*
Illus. by the author. Greenwillow, 1985
Suggested Use Level: Gr. PreK–1   Reading Level: Gr. 3

Plot Summary

When a baby boy monster is born to the Monster family, nearly everyone expects him to grow up to be the Worst Monster in the World. Pa,

Grandpa, and Grandma all dote on Billy and admire his antics. Hazel, Billy's older sister, tries to capture their attention by outperforming Billy, but everyone ignores her. When Billy wins The Worst Baby Monster in the World contest, Hazel is determined to show her ability to be a good monster. She tries to lose Billy and finally she gives him away. Her parents are dismayed by her monstrous behavior but, when Billy is returned to them, they realize that Hazel is "The Very Worst Monster." The adventures of this family continue in *Where's the Baby?*

Thematic Material

Even though the characters are monsters, this is a family story. When new babies arrive, there is often some resentment from the other siblings. Many children will sympathize with Hazel's efforts to get attention. Children will also enjoy the humorous look at the everyday lives of monsters.

Book Talk Material and Activities

How do monsters live? What is a monster home like? Do monsters have toys, clothes, furniture, or other familiar items? What do monsters look like? Pat Hutchins's illustrations answer some of these questions and children will enjoy examining them for details. The humor in this story is enhanced by seeing the monsters living in such human conditions (although their homes do seem a bit cavelike). Their flowered curtains, patterned rugs, and coordinated clothes seem incongruous with their ugly faces and funny feet. One extension activity for *The Very Worst Monster* is to have children design some additional monster paraphernalia or describe some other aspects of monster life, for example, what they eat or where they go on vacation. They could draw or mold a statue commemorating a famous monster for a Monster Hall of Fame. Their pictures and models could be displayed with brief captions describing each monster's accomplishments.

Audiovisual Adaptation

The Very Worst Monster. Weston Woods, cassette, 1986; filmstrip/cassette, 1985.

Related Titles

The Baby Uggs Are Hatching by Jack Prelutsky. Illustrated by James Stevenson. Greenwillow, 1982. Fantastic imaginary creatures are described through Prelutsky's lively poems and Stevenson's humorous illustrations.

Clyde Monster by Robert L. Crowe. Illustrated by Kay Chorao. Dutton, 1976. What are monsters afraid of? People, of course. Compare this with *Four Scary Stories*.

Four Scary Stories by Tony Johnston. Illustrated by Tomie de Paola. Putnam, 1978. A goblin, an imp, and a scalawag tell scary stories about that scariest of creatures—a boy. Another opportunity to talk about point of view as readers see the monsters' side of the story.

How Beastly! A Menagerie of Nonsense Poems by Jane Yolen. Illustrated by James Marshall. Collins, 1980. Jane Yolen has invented some fantastic creatures, and James Marshall's illustrations capture the details of her descriptions.

I'm Coming to Get You written and illustrated by Tony Ross. Dial, 1984. Just when you think that Tommy will be destroyed by the monster, the pictures show a surprise ending.

Monster Poems edited by Daisy Wallace. Illustrated by Kay Chorao. Holiday House, 1976. Another collection of poems about monsters. Read "The Monster Birthday Party" by Lilian Moore and talk about what a monster would want for a gift.

Where's the Baby? written and illustrated by Pat Hutchins. Greenwillow, 1988. Baby Monster creates a huge mess wherever he goes.

About the Author and Illustrator

HUTCHINS, PAT
Fourth Book of Junior Authors and Illustrators, ed. by Doris de Montreville and Elizabeth D. Crawford. Wilson, 1978, pp. 189–191.
Illustrators of Children's Books: 1967–1976, Vol. IV, comp. by Lee Kingman, Grace Allen Hogarth, and Harriet Quimby. Horn Book, 1978, pp. 20, 129, 193.
Something about the Author, ed. by Anne Commire. Gale, 1979, Vol. 15, pp. 141–143.

Johnston, Tony. *The Witch's Hat*
Illus. by Margot Tomes. Putnam, 1984
Suggested Use Level: Gr. K–1   Reading Level: Gr. 1

Plot Summary

While a witch is preparing a brew, her hat falls into her magic pot. She fishes the hat out of the pot but finds that it is now magical. The hat transforms itself into a bat and flies to the bat-filled attic. When the witch finally discovers which bat is her hat, the hat becomes a rat and runs into the rat-filled wall. Again, the witch finds her hat only to have it become a cat. Searching her cat-filled house, the witch finds which cat is her hat and puts it on her head, only to have her hat turn into a frog.

Thematic Material

Even though *The Witch's Hat* is not actually set during Halloween, it has many elements that are associated with the holiday and would be a fun story to share then.

Book Talk Material and Activities

The witch's hat is transformed into some funny, rhyming items that try to run away from the witch. Compare it with the runaway hat in *Who Took the Farmer's Hat?* The wind blows the farmer's hat past a squirrel, a mouse, and other familiar animals. Each animal sees the hat but thinks it is something else. For example, the bird uses it as a nest. Comparing these similar stories encourages children to devise categories for analyzing books. Both *The Witch's Hat* and *Who Took the Farmer's Hat?* have sequential events, and examining the sequence could be one category. Another category could be "What happens to the hat at the end of the story?" Children need many opportunities to discuss books and to think about the ways in which stories are similar or different.

The Witch's Hat uses the rhyming words "hat," "bat," "rat," and "cat." Some teachers may want to share other stories that incorporate rhyming words, such as *Three by the Sea*, which pokes fun at books that sacrifice the sense of a story in order to teach phonics. *The Witch's Hat* succeeds in being entertaining while using many words that are familiar to beginning readers.

Audiovisual Adaptation

The Witch's Hat. Spoken Arts, filmstrip/cassette, 1987.

Related Titles

The Little Witch and the Riddle written and illustrated by Bruce Degen. Harper & Row, 1980. Lily the witch must find the answer to a riddle before she can unlock the book of magic spells. Her friend Otto Ogre helps her solve the riddle.

Pat the Cat written and illustrated by Colin Hawkins and Jacqui Hawkins. Putnam, 1983. The story about Pat is told using the words "cat," "fat," "mat," "hat," "bat," and "rat."

The Teeny, Tiny Witches by Jan Wahl. Illustrated by Margot Tomes. Putnam, 1979. A tiny family of witches must find a home where other creatures will not bother them. The easy-reading format (large type and wide spaces between lines) makes the book accessible to beginning readers.

Three by the Sea by Edward Marshall. Illustrated by James Marshall. Dial, 1981. Lolly, Spider, and Sam tell stories that use the simplified vocabulary from their reading book, but are much more interesting than those in their reader.

Who Took the Farmer's Hat? by Joan L. Nödset. Illustrated by Fritz Siebel. Harper & Row, 1963. As the wind blows the farmer's hat past different animals, each animal thinks of another use for it.

About the Author and Illustrator

JOHNSTON, TONY

Authors of Books for Young People: Supplement to the Second Edition, by Martha E. Ward and Dorothy Marquardt. Scarecrow, 1979, pp. 143–144.

Something about the Author, ed. by Anne Commire. Gale, 1976, Vol. 8, p. 94.

TOMES, MARGOT

Fifth Book of Junior Authors and Illustrators, ed. by Sally Holmes Holtze. Wilson, 1983. pp. 313–314.

Illustrators of Children's Books: 1957–1966, Vol. III, comp. by Lee Kingman, Grace Allen Hogarth, and Harriet Quimby. Horn Book, 1968, pp. 182, 243; *1967–1976, Vol. IV,* 1978, pp. 164, 211.

Something about the Author, ed. by Anne Commire. Gale, 1982, Vol. 27, p. 223.

Joyce, William. *George Shrinks*
Illus. by the author. Harper & Row, 1985; pap., 1987
Suggested Use Level: Gr. K–3   Reading Level: Gr. 2

Plot Summary

After dreaming that he has shrunk, George wakes up to find that his dream has come true. It is difficult for the diminutive George to follow the directions that his parents have left him. It takes all his ingenuity to perform his daily tasks, and the family cat is now an added danger. Mouse-sized George plays with his brother and has an adventure in a toy plane. Suddenly, the cat attacks. Just when George's situation seems hopeless, his parents return home and awaken him from what has been a bad dream.

Thematic Material

Much of the humor comes from the matter-of-fact way Joyce presents George's situation. George just accepts his new size and goes about his daily routine as if nothing is wrong. The illustrations also add details that help make the book funny.

Book Talk Material and Activities

How would you feel if you were suddenly small? What would change about your life? Is there anything good about being small? What problems would you have? These are some questions that children could think about after hearing *George Shrinks*. A teacher can have each child in the class make a small person out of tagboard. The children can name their person, make clothes, and carry him or her around the school. They can also tell and write stories about their person. Class discussions might focus on how it feels to take responsibility for someone else and on learning to see things from the point of view of someone smaller. *George Shrinks* could also be compared with other dream stories, such as *Dreams*, *Ben's Dream*, and *The Quilt*.

The illustrations in *George Shrinks* add to the humor. The text quotes the letter from George's parents, and the illustrations show how George, who has shrunk, follows their instructions. For example, the letter says, "Eat a good breakfast," but George is pictured drinking soda while resting next to a layer cake. His feet are propped up on a cherry. When he and his brother are taking out the garbage, George is riding on his brother's back. His brother is wearing an elephant's nose, and George is dressed like a rajah. Throughout the book, a cat, who is depicted but never discussed, is illustrated providing a threat to George. Helping children learn to see the relationship between text and illustrations allows them to improve their observational skills.

Related Titles

Ben's Dream written and illustrated by Chris Van Allsburg. Houghton Mifflin, 1982. While studying for his social studies test, Ben falls asleep and dreams that he is visiting all of the places he has been studying about. The shifts in perspective provide a challenge to children as they try to identify where Ben is.

Bobo's Dream written and illustrated by Martha Alexander. Dial, 1970. In this wordless story, a dachshund dreams of rescuing his young owner from a gang of older boys.

Dreams written and illustrated by Ezra Jack Keats. Macmillan, 1974. Everyone is asleep and dreaming but Roberto. When his paper mouse falls out of his window, the eerie shadows that are cast save his friend Archie's cat from a threatening dog.

I'm Coming to Get You written and illustrated by Tony Ross. Dial, 1984. The end is a surprise, as the giant monster is really no bigger than a mouse. Children can discuss how the illustrations make the viewer think the monster is big.

Lemon Moon written and illustrated by Kay Chorao. Holiday House, 1983. A little boy tells his grandmother that the animals on his quilt come to life at night. Compare this book with *The Quilt* by Ann Jonas.

Once a Mouse: A Fable Cut in Wood retold and illustrated by Marcia Brown. Scribner, 1961. A hermit transforms a mouse into progressively larger animals until the mouse, overcome with his own pride, thinks about destroying the hermit. The mouse is returned to his original shape, and the hermit ponders the meaning of this fable about size.

The Quilt written and illustrated by Ann Jonas. Greenwillow, 1984. As the little girl sleeps, she dreams that the patches on her quilt are places that she can visit. She imagines that she is looking for her missing stuffed dog, only to wake up and find the dog on the floor.

About the Author and Illustrator

JOYCE, WILLIAM
Something about the Author, ed. by Anne Commire. Gale, 1987, Vol. 46, p. 122.

Kasza, Keiko.   *The Wolf's Chicken Stew*
Illus. by the author. Putnam, 1987
Suggested Use Level: Gr. K–2   Reading Level: Gr. 3

Plot Summary

A wolf, who loves to eat, is planning to make chicken stew. He sees a chicken that is just right for his recipe, but then he decides to fatten her up a bit. First, he makes a batch of pancakes and leaves them on the porch of her house. Next, he leaves her a plate of doughnuts. Finally, he makes her a huge cake. Convinced that she must be fat enough for his stew, he hurries to her house. When she opens the door, the wolf is greeted by 100 chicks who call him "Uncle Wolf" and thank him for all the wonderful treats. The wolf gives up his plan for chicken stew, goes home, and bakes cookies for the chicks.

Thematic Material

In this humorous story, a wolf changes his mind about eating a chicken. The unexpected ending adds to the humor.

Book Talk Material and Activities

In many stories, characters are stereotyped to behave in a certain way. For example, foxes are sly, wolves are violent, beautiful characters are sweet-tempered, and ugly characters are mean. In *The Wolf's Chicken Stew*, a wolf behaves in an unexpected way. He befriends a family of chickens instead of eating them. A discussion of the story could encourage children to see that once the wolf actually knows the chickens, he treats them differently. *Sleeping Ugly* is another book that challenges children to reconsider stereotypes. Other books with wolves as characters could be booktalked to encourage children to see how different authors and illustrators present this animal.

Related Titles

It's So Nice to Have a Wolf Around the House by Harry Allard. Illustrated by James Marshall. Doubleday, 1977. Cuthbert Devine is a wolf who is also a bank robber. He pretends to be a dog and becomes the pet of an elderly man, but eventually his deception is discovered. Ask children how the wolf is portrayed in this story.

Jim and the Beanstalk written and illustrated by Raymond Briggs. Coward, McCann, 1970. Jim climbs up a beanstalk and meets a giant who needs his help. This humorous original story is a takeoff on the familiar folktale about Jack, like Gail E. Haley's *Jack and the Bean Tree* (see Chapter 8).

Sleeping Ugly by Jane Yolen. Illustrated by Diane Stanley. Coward, McCann, 1981. In most traditional stories, beautiful characters are good, and ugly characters are bad. In this one, the beautiful Princess Miserella is a brat and Plain Jane is sweet-tempered. The story pokes fun at stereotypes.

Stone Soup written and illustrated by Tony Ross. Dial, 1987. In Tony Ross's altered version of a familiar folktale, a wolf plans to eat a hen. The hen outwits the wolf by making stone soup, and the wolf ends up too full to eat the hen. *Stone Soup: An Old Tale,* retold and illustrated by Marcia Brown (Scribner, 1957), is a traditional version of the story.

The Three Pigs written and illustrated by Tony Ross. Pantheon, 1983. Three pigs move from an apartment building in the city to three houses in the country. Only the third pig is able to outwit the wolf. *The Three Little Pigs,* retold and illustrated by Paul Galdone (Clarion, 1970), is a traditional version of the story.

Walter the Wolf by Marjorie Weinman Sharmat. Illustrated by Kelly Oechsli. Holiday House, 1975. Walter loves to play the violin and never bites anyone. A fox convinces him to give up the violin and go into the biting business. Walter must decide if biting is really for him. Children can be asked to compare Walter with the wolf in *The Wolf's Chicken Stew.*

Kellogg, Steven. *Prehistoric Pinkerton*
Illus. by the author. Dial, 1987
Suggested Use Level: Gr. 1–3   Reading Level: Gr. 5

Plot Summary

The little girl who owns Pinkerton is studying dinosaurs in school. While she shows Pinkerton her dinosaur book and costume, he chews on pencils, a broom, and her bedpost. The family decides that Pinkerton is teething, and they buy him some rawhide bones, but not before he chews down a tree and the legs of the piano. Finally, just to get Pinkerton out of the house, the little girl dresses him in her stegosaurus costume and takes him to the museum. Of course, Pinkerton starts to chew on a dinosaur bone and the dinosaur display is demolished. No one can be angry with Pinkerton for long and, as his puppy teeth fall out and his teething is done, the children happily crowd around Pinkerton.

Thematic Material

Prehistoric Pinkerton, a humorous story where the humor comes from the problems of owning a very large dog, is part of a series of books about Pinkerton. This story also provides an opportunity to discuss dinosaurs and museums.

Book Talk Material and Activities

What makes a story funny? Some of the humor here comes from the exaggerated problems caused by a very big dog. When a group of children heard this story, they said "It was funny when Pinkerton wrecked the dinosaur. You knew it was going to happen." "I liked it when he ate the piano and the teacher fainted." "Everyone wore funny costumes." After looking more closely at the book, some children commented about all the extra words in the pictures, for example, the labels on the box of bones and the sound of Pinkerton's licking. These extra details provide more humorous moments.

Several follow-up activities are suggested. Children could read other books about Pinkerton to find out more about him. For example, does Pinkerton always create a problem? Reading several books in a series gives children an opportunity to see the same character in different adventures and to find out details about the character's personality. Children also could read other books by Kellogg to study his art and humor and see the other characters he has created. How do they compare to Pinkerton? They could tell their own Pinkerton stories by sending Pinkerton to other places where he would cause some problems—suggestions include the grocery store, an amusement park, and school—or they could tell about the biggest problem that they ever had with their pet. In all of these activities, children should be encouraged to look for or use exaggeration. They could talk about other books that are funny because the characters are exaggerated, including Steven Kellogg's versions of *Paul Bunyan* and *Pecos Bill.*

As previously mentioned, Steven Kellogg has included many words in the illustrations. The little girl and her family use books to learn about their dog, to read for fun, to find a telephone number, and for music for the piano. At the museum, there are signs for the displays, and many of the children have signs to accompany their costumes. Studying these pictures could lead to a discussion of environmental print, and children could collect examples of words they see around them.

Children often take field trips to museums, and this humorous look at Pinkerton's experiences would be fun to share with them before a trip. Other, more serious, museum books could be discussed as well, including *My Visit to the Dinosaurs* and *Visiting the Art Museum*.

Related Books

My Visit to the Dinosaurs (revised edition) written and illustrated by Aliki. Harper & Row, 1985. A much more traditional trip to the natural history museum than Pinkerton's. Some background information is included about archaeology and paleontology as well as facts about several dinosaurs.

Paul Bunyan retold and illustrated by Steven Kellogg. Morrow, 1984. A lively and imaginative retelling of the tall tale. Look at the details in Kellogg's illustrations. How do they add to the humor of the story?

Pecos Bill retold and illustrated by Steven Kellogg. Morrow, 1986. Another fun version of a tall tale. Look closely at the people and animals in the illustrations. Do they look similar to any other Kellogg characters?

Pinkerton, Behave! written and illustrated by Steven Kellogg. Dial, 1979. The first book about Pinkerton. After disrupting everything at home, Pinkerton is enrolled in obedience school and, of course, he causes problems there, too. When a burglar comes to the house, the family is lucky to have Pinkerton.

A Rose for Pinkerton written and illustrated by Steven Kellogg. Dial, 1981. The "Rose" that Pinkerton gets is a kitten. Imagine this oversized dog and little kitten at the pet show.

Tallyho, Pinkerton! written and illustrated by Steven Kellogg. Dial, 1982. Rose and Pinkerton go with their little girl on a nature walk and disrupt a fox hunt, saving the fox. Instead, the hunters corner a skunk!

Visiting the Art Museum written and illustrated by Laurene Krasny Brown and Marc Brown. Dutton, 1986. A family's visit to the museum is told through conversation balloons. The pictures and objects that they see are described more completely in the "More about the Art" section at the end of the book.

About the Author and Illustrator

KELLOGG, STEVEN
Fourth Book of Junior Authors and Illustrators, ed. by Doris de Montreville and Elizabeth D. Crawford. Wilson, 1978, pp. 208–209.
Illustrators of Children's Books: 1967–1976, Vol. IV, comp. by Lee Kingman, Grace Allen Hogarth, and Harriet Quimby. Horn Book, 1978, pp. 133, 196.
Something about the Author, ed. by Anne Commire. Gale, 1976, Vol. 8, pp. 95–97.

McKissack, Patricia. *Flossie and the Fox*
Illus. by Rachel Isadora. Dial, 1986
Suggested Use Level: Gr. 1–3   Reading Level: Gr. 2

Plot Summary

Flossie's grandmother has sent her to deliver a basket of eggs to Miz Viola. Before Flossie leaves, Big Mama warns her to beware of a fox that has been causing trouble. Flossie decides to walk through the woods because it is shorter and cooler. Of course, she meets the fox and, just like Big Mama had warned, the fox is "one sly critter." The fox introduces himself but Flossie acts as if she does not believe he really is a fox. She makes the fox prove himself, first by comparing him to a rabbit, then to a rat, then to a cat, then to a squirrel, and finally to a dog. All the while, Flossie continues on her way to Miz Viola's. When she admits that she is convinced of the fox's identity, Flossie and the fox are at the end of the woods and Mr. McCutchin's hound dogs are there to chase the fox away. Flossie knows that she has outwitted the fox and she continues her journey.

Thematic Material

Flossie and the Fox has ties to storytelling and the oral tradition. In the Author's Note, Patricia McKissack explains how her grandfather would tell her this story when she was a little girl. The language of the story reflects the rural dialect of her grandfather, and the illustrations depict the life of a black family in the South. The illustrations also capture Flossie's spirit and show the fox's sly personality.

Book Talk Material and Activities

This is a good story to share as part of a program on American folk-tales. *Flossie and the Fox* can be coordinated with such other books of folklore and the black experience as *Wiley and the Hairy Man* and *The People Could Fly*. Other genres to discuss include tall tales about characters like Pecos Bill, Paul Bunyan, and John Henry; Native American legends like *Arrow to the Sun* and *Whale in the Sky;* and such American folk songs as *The Erie Canal* and *She'll Be Comin' Round the Mountain*. Look at how these stories and songs reflect the American experience by celebrating the pioneering spirit and heritage of its many peoples.

The dialect of *Flossie and the Fox* makes it a great choice for reading aloud or memorizing for a story program. To capture the cadence and pattern of the language so that the reading or retelling is smooth and expressive takes some practice.

Rachel Isadora's illustrations help delineate the personalities of Flossie and the fox. Before reading this book, show a picture of the two characters—such as the fox sitting on the stump, or the final picture of Flossie—and ask children to suggest how they think each character will act in the story. Write their predictions on a chalkboard or paper and discuss them after the story. Rachel Isadora has used many styles to illustrate picture books. Showing the black-and-white illustrations in *Ben's Trumpet* and the colorful impressions in *Opening Night* (see Rachel Isadora, Chapter 2) allows children to see the variety.

Audiovisual Adaptation

Flossie and the Fox. Weston Woods, cassette/book, 1988; filmstrip/cassette, 1988.

Related Titles

Arrow to the Sun: A Pueblo Indian Tale adapted and illustrated by Gerald McDermott. Viking, 1974. Bright, colorful pictures capture the joy of the boy's discovery of his father.

Ben's Trumpet written and illustrated by Rachel Isadora. Greenwillow, 1979. A musician remembers his own childhood dream as he helps Ben achieve his dream. The black-and-white illustrations are jagged and angular. They extend the jazz theme of the text.

The Erie Canal written and illustrated by Peter Spier. Doubleday, 1970. Spier's illustrations for this popular song are filled with details that capture the action on the canal. A musical arrangement is included for joining in and singing the song.

The People Could Fly: American Black Folktales retold by Virginia Hamilton. Illustrated by Leo Dillon and Diane Dillon. Knopf, 1985. A collection of folktales that includes another version of *Wiley and the Hairy Man,* which could be compared with the version by Molly Bang.

She'll Be Comin' Round the Mountain retold and illustrated by Robert Quackenbush. Lippincott, 1973. A popular folk song in a picture-book format. How does this reflect on life in the Old West?

Whale in the Sky written and illustrated by Anne Siberell. Dutton, 1982. A legend from the Native Americans of the Northwest in which a story is told and then represented in the carving of a totem pole.

Wiley and the Hairy Man adapted from an American folktale and illustrated by Molly Bang. Macmillan, 1976. Just as Flossie must outwit the fox in *Flossie and the Fox,* Wiley and his mother must outwit the Hairy Man. This story has the feel of life in the Deep South.

About the Author and Illustrator

McKISSACK, PATRICIA
Something about the Author, ed. by Anne Commire. Gale, 1988, Vol. 51, p. 122.

ISADORA, RACHEL
Fifth Book of Junior Authors and Illustrators, ed. by Sally Holmes Holtze. Wilson, 1983, pp. 159–160.
Something about the Author, ed. by Anne Commire. Gale, 1983, Vol. 32, p. 100.

McPhail, David.   *Pig Pig and the Magic Photo Album*
Illus. by the author. Dutton, 1986
Suggested Use Level: Gr. PreK–1   Reading Level: Gr. 3

Plot Summary

While Pig Pig is waiting to have his picture taken, he glances through an album of photographs. As he smiles and says "cheese," he suddenly finds himself inside the photograph of a church with a steeple. He is hanging on the steeple. Just as he is about to fall, he enters another picture, then another, and another. Each new photograph puts him into danger. In the last picture, just when it looks as if he will be eaten by some vicious dogs, he is able to enter a picture of his own living room, where his mother tells him to get ready for his photograph. Pig Pig sits quietly for his picture and refuses to touch the photo album again.

Thematic Material

This humorous story has elements of fantasy and magic. Pig Pig's adventure is exciting, and the illustrations of a pig in these unusual circumstances add to the humor.

Book Talk Material and Activities

For National Library Week in April, have an election of the children's favorite book characters. Each class can nominate one character and then the whole school can vote. In one such election, Pig Pig was nominated by one first-grade class. Although he did not win, his nomination demonstrates that children who have heard the Pig Pig books really enjoy them.

In *Pig Pig Grows Up*, one of the other three books about Pig Pig, he stops acting like a baby and learns to care about the needs of others. The illustrations of a big, fat pig riding in a baby stroller and stuffed into a crib appeal to young children's sense of humor. The book could be used to introduce the concept of a series in which a character appears in different books doing different things. The books about Pig Pig could also be part of a story program on how characters grow and change. Jean Van Leeuwen's *Tales of Amanda Pig* (see Chapter 1) also shows a pig character who grows up. Other popular pigs in the series are Louanne Pig and Poinsettia.

Related Titles

Louanne Pig in Making the Team written and illustrated by Nancy Carlson. Carolrhoda, 1985. Louanne Pig is planning to try out for the cheerleading team, and her friend Archie the cat wants to play football. They realize that Louanne plays football better than she cheers, and Archie leads cheers better than he plays football.

Pig Pig Goes to Camp written and illustrated by David McPhail. Dutton, 1983. During his first trip to summer camp, Pig Pig learns to do many new things, like cooking on a campfire and giving first aid. He also learns to make friends with frogs. When he brings his new friends home with him, his mother is delighted.

Pig Pig Grows Up written and illustrated by David McPhail. Dutton, 1980. In this first book about Pig Pig, he has outgrown his crib, baby clothes, high chair, and stroller, but he insists on being "the baby." It takes a real baby to make Pig Pig act his age.

Pig Pig Rides written and illustrated by David McPhail. Dutton, 1982. Pig Pig fantasizes about being in an auto race, riding a motorcycle, and even going on a rocket to outer space. His mother reminds him of the importance of home.

Poinsettia and Her Family written and illustrated by Felicia Bond. Crowell, 1981. Poinsettia the pig thinks that her house is too crowded. When her parents and the rest of the family look for a larger house, Poinsettia enjoys her time alone, but then she starts to think about how empty the house feels and realizes that she loves and misses her family.

About the Author and Illustrator

McPHAIL, DAVID
Fifth Book of Junior Authors and Illustrators, ed. by Sally Holmes Holtze. Wilson, 1983, pp. 213–214.
Illustrators of Children's Books: 1967–1976, Vol. IV, comp. by Lee Kingman, Grace Allen Hogarth, and Harriet Quimby. Horn Book, 1978, pp. 4, 5, 143, 200.
Something about the Author, ed. by Anne Commire. Gale, 1983, Vol. 32, p. 137; 1987, Vol. 47, pp. 150–165.

Marshall, James.   *George and Martha Back in Town*
Illus. by the author. Houghton Mifflin, 1984
Suggested Use Level: Gr. K–2   Reading Level: Gr. 2

Plot Summary

There are five stories in this book from the popular series about two hippo friends, George and Martha. In the first story, George has left a package on his kitchen table with a note that reads "Do Not Open." But Martha cannot resist the temptation and ends up chasing jumping beans. In the next story, George plans to dive off the high diving board. After climbing up the ladder, he finds he cannot do it. Martha comes up with a way for him to get down. In the third story, Martha teaches George a lesson about playing practical jokes, and in the fourth one, George teaches Martha a lesson about following rules. In the final story, George is trying to read a book, but Martha keeps pestering him. Just as George is about to lecture her, he remembers what a good friend she has always been.

Thematic Material

These are humorous and sensitive stories about friendship.

Book Talk Material and Activities

The books about George and Martha provide many stories that could be used for puppet activities. *Glove, Mitten, and Sock Puppets* gives some simple directions for making puppets, one of which, the "Sock Someone," could be adapted to look like George or Martha. Mittens or socks could be used for puppet activities. As all George and Martha books have five stories, children can choose their puppet activities from many different possibilities.

The George and Martha books are also fun for creative dramatics. Older children often enjoy acting out the stories for younger children. One group of fourth graders made a videotape of some George and Martha stories that they showed to a kindergarten class. It demonstrated to the younger children that older children also enjoy books that they know and the older children had an opportunity to use the video equipment and organize a production. After the fourth graders had read all the George and Martha books, they selected the stories that they wanted to use. Then they gathered props and rehearsed. Watching the finished tape together was a positive experience for both the kindergarteners and the fourth graders.

Related Titles

Glove, Mitten, and Sock Puppets written and illustrated by Frieda Gates. Walker, 1978. Gates provides clear directions for making some simple puppets, including a "Glove Monster," a "Sock Someone," a "Silly Animal," and a "Knee Sock Snake."

The following books are all about George and Martha. They were all written and illustrated by James Marshall and published by Houghton Mifflin.

George and Martha (1972). One story tells how George got his gold tooth. Children might want to make two George puppets—one with two white teeth for the first four stories in this book, and one with one white tooth and one gold tooth for the final story.

George and Martha Encore (1973). These five stories include the one where Martha gets sunburned—an opportunity to make another puppet.

George and Martha One Fine Day (1978). Martha and George enjoy a visit to "The Amusement Park," a story with a surprise ending that children will find fun to act out.

George and Martha Rise and Shine (1976). In one story, George turns as white as a sheet after seeing a scary movie. In another, Martha teaches George a lesson about telling fibs. Both stories could be dramatized by the children using very few props.

George and Martha Round and Round (1988). In a story where George gives Martha a birthday present that she does not really like, Martha must decide what to do without hurting his feelings.

George and Martha Tons of Fun (1980). In one story, Martha turns yellow from smoking a cigar. In another, she gives George a photograph of herself. Both stories have a lesson about caring for others.

About the Author and Illustrator

MARSHALL, JAMES

Authors of Books for Young People: Supplement to the Second Edition, by Martha E. Ward and Dorothy Marquardt. Scarecrow, 1979, p. 187.

Fourth Book of Junior Authors and Illustrators, ed. by Doris de Montreville and Elizabeth D. Crawford. Wilson, 1978, pp. 253–254.

Illustrators of Children's Books: 1967–1976, Vol. IV, comp. by Lee Kingman, Grace Allen Hogarth, and Harriet Quimby. Horn Book, 1978, pp. 5, 144, 201.

Something about the Author, ed. by Anne Commire. Gale, 1974, Vol. 6, pp. 160–161; 1988, Vol. 51, pp. 109–121.

Peet, Bill. *Pamela Camel*
Illus. by the author. Houghton Mifflin, 1984; pap., 1986
Suggested Use Level: Gr. 1–3   Reading Level: Gr. 7

Plot Summary

Pamela Camel works for the circus. Because Pamela is clumsy, she is not in a circus act. She is part of the menagerie of wild animals that people stare at and poke. Pamela is not happy with this life and one day she runs away from the circus. Walking through the countryside, Pamela comes to some railroad tracks, which she discovers are broken. She wonders what she should do. When she hears a train coming, she risks her life by standing on the tracks and forcing the engineer to stop the train.

Her courageous act is widely celebrated and the circus owners take her back and make her the star of the circus.

Thematic Material

Pamela bravely risks her life to save others. The circus setting makes this a fun story.

Book Talk Material and Activities

Bill Peet has written and illustrated more than 25 books for children. Youngsters who study them can learn about the characters, settings, and themes that he uses. *Pamela Camel* introduces children to the circus setting that is also seen in *Ella*. Peet's other books show a variety of settings—the sea (in *Kermit the Hermit*), the farm (in *The Whingdingdilly*), the train yard (in *The Caboose Who Got Loose*), and the castle (in *How Droofus the Dragon Lost His Head*). Many of his characters are outsiders who would like to be accepted for themselves. A theme in many of his books is being satisfied with oneself.

Children might enjoy making a mural of "Bill Peet's Worlds." After reading many of Peet's books and identifying different settings, the children can then meet in small groups to work on different sections of the mural, rereading the books to find more details to include and trying to imitate Peet's colorful cartoon style. The finished mural can be used as a backdrop for a display of Peet's books.

Related Titles

The Caboose Who Got Loose written and illustrated by Bill Peet. Houghton Mifflin, 1971. The rhyming text tells about Katy Caboose, who does not like being the last car in the train and who wishes for a better life. An unusual circumstance makes her wish come true.

Ella written and illustrated by Bill Peet. Houghton Mifflin, 1964. Ella the elephant is the star of the circus. When something at the circus annoys Ella, she hides and is left behind when the circus leaves town. Ella finds that her new life is not what she expected.

How Droofus the Dragon Lost His Head written and illustrated by Bill Peet. Houghton Mifflin, 1971. Droofus the dragon is accidentally separated from his family. Although he is lonely, he learns to survive. Unfortunately, one day the king sees him and wants to have Droofus's head on his castle wall. Droofus must use his head, or lose it.

Kermit the Hermit written and illustrated by Bill Peet. Houghton Mifflin, 1965. Kermit is a greedy, mean-spirited crab who learns a lesson about needing help and then helping others.

The Whingdingdilly written and illustrated by Bill Peet. Houghton Mifflin, 1970. Scamp is not happy being a dog. When a witch changes him into a "whingdingdilly," he is even more unhappy. Scamp learns that he should have been satisfied being himself.

About the Author and Illustrator

PEET, BILL
Authors of Books for Young People, second edition, by Martha E. Ward and Dorothy Marquardt. Scarecrow, 1971, p. 405.
Illustrators of Children's Books: 1957–1966, Vol. III, comp. by Lee Kingman, Grace Allen Hogarth, and Harriet Quimby. Horn Book, 1968, pp. 157, 235; *1967–1976, Vol. IV*, 1978, pp. 150, 204.
Something about the Author, ed. by Anne Commire. Gale, 1969, Vol. 2, pp. 201–203; 1985, Vol. 31, pp. 158–164.
Third Book of Junior Authors, ed. by Muriel Fuller. Wilson, 1963, pp. 222–223.

Purdy, Carol.   *Iva Dunnit and the Big Wind*
Illus. by Steven Kellogg. Dial, 1985
Suggested Use Level: Gr. 1–3   Reading Level: Gr. 5

Plot Summary

During pioneer times, Iva Dunnit and her six children were homesteading on the American prairie. Life was difficult for women and children, but Iva and her children were able to survive through hard work and togetherness. Once, they saved their house from a fire. Another time, they outwitted a thief. However, nothing prepared them for coping with the "Big Wind" that started in August. First, it blew away some of the family's best hens. Then while Iva was trying to retrieve them, the wind blew away her petticoats. Also Iva discovered that the roof was starting to blow away, so, carrying the hens, she climbed a ladder to fix the roof. The wind blew down the ladder, and Iva was left hanging from the roof. Although Iva yelled, the children could not hear her over the noise of the wind. Finally, the children became curious about her whereabouts. They rescued Iva from the roof and, as the wind died down, they watched the town doctor coming down the road to visit them wearing Iva's petticoats.

Thematic Material

Iva and her children are high-spirited and resourceful. Their adventures with the wind are humorously presented in both text and illustrations.

Book Talk Material and Activities

Librarians and teachers might want to set aside some windy stories for windy days. *Iva Dunnit and the Big Wind* is a good one to share. Children will enjoy the humorous details in the text and illustrations. The author used descriptive language like "I feel plumb cozy" and "Boy, howdy" to add a rural flavor to the text, and librarians and teachers may want to affect a drawl when reading the story. Iva Dunnit's name is a humorous play on the words "I have done it," which captures her intrepid spirit. Giving all six children names starting with "I" (Ida, Ivan, Ima, Issac, Ira, and Iris) is also humorous and unique. Other books about the wind, such as *The Wind Blew* and *Jack and the Whoopee Wind,* could be booktalked in order for children to borrow them from the library. Poems about the wind, like "Days That the Wind Takes Over" by Karla Kuskin (in *Dogs and Dragons, Trees and Dreams*) and James Reeves's "The Wind" (in *The Random House Book of Poetry for Children*), which present different images of the wind, would also enhance the program.

Related Titles

Dogs and Dragons, Trees and Dreams: A Collection of Poems written and illustrated by Karla Kuskin. Harper & Row, 1980. Many of Kuskin's best-known poems are in this collection, including "Hughbert and the Glue." Some poems, such as "Spring," could be coordinated with the seasons.

Gilberto and the Wind written and illustrated by Marie Hall Ets. Viking, 1963. A little boy describes all the ways that he interacts with the wind, including watching the laundry flap on the line and trying to fly a kite.

Jack and the Whoopee Wind by Mary Calhoun. Illustrated by Dick Gackenbach. Morrow, 1987. Another story about a big wind out on the prairie, in which Jack, a farmer, must find a way to keep the wind from blowing away all of his belongings, including his dog, Mose.

The Random House Book of Poetry for Children edited by Jack Prelutsky.

Illustrated by Arnold Lobel. Random House, 1983. The subject index lists 11 pages with poems about the wind.

The Wind Blew written and illustrated by Pat Hutchins. Macmillan, 1974. In this rhyming story, the wind blows something away from each person and then stops blowing, leaving the people to sort out their belongings.

About the Author and Illustrator

KELLOGG, STEVEN
Fourth Book of Junior Authors and Illustrators, ed. by Doris de Montreville and Elizabeth D. Crawford. Wilson, 1978, pp. 208–209.
Illustrators of Children's Books: 1967–1976, Vol. IV, comp. by Lee Kingman, Grace Allen Hogarth, and Harriet Quimby. Horn Book, 1978, pp. 133, 196.
Something about the Author, ed. by Anne Commire. Gale, 1976, Vol. 8, pp. 95–97.

Rayner, Mary.   *Mrs. Pig Gets Cross*
   Illus. by the author. Dutton, 1986
   Suggested Use Level: Gr. 1–3   Reading Level: Gr. 4

Plot Summary

There are seven stories about the Pig family in this book. In the first one, Mrs. Pig is tired of cleaning up after her 10 piglets. Instead, she lounges on the couch all afternoon. When Mr. Pig arrives home from work, he is annoyed by the mess. Both he and Mrs. Pig go to bed angry, forgetting to lock the door. A fox comes into the house and tries to rob them, but trips over the many toys and leaves with a bag full of blocks. The second story is about one of the piglets, William, and the tricks he plays on his siblings. When one of William's brothers needs help, though, William is there. In the next story, all the piglets climb into bed with their parents, who finally leave their bed and sleep in the piglets' bunk beds. "The Potato Patch" is a story about gardening. Father Pig plants potatoes while Alun and William plant acorns, a felt-tip pen, a squash, and some bananas. In the fifth story, Benjamin Pig, one of the youngest in the family, is in a bad mood. His sister, Sarah, helps him become more cooperative. The next story tells of a contest between the girl and the boy pigs. At the conclusion of the contest, the Pig family is happy to realize that everything is even. In the final story, Mr. and Mrs. Pig have a party, and a wolf in disguise is an uninvited guest. The piglets discover the deception and expose the treachery.

Thematic Material

In each of the seven stories, the Pig family demonstrates the fun they have being together. The humor of the stories is evident in the behavior of the piglets, who combine human and pig characteristics.

Book Talk Material and Activities

The stories in this book continue the series of books about the Pig family that includes *Mr. and Mrs. Pig's Evening Out, Garth Pig and the Ice Cream Lady,* and *Mrs. Pig's Bulk Buy.* The pigs in these stories sometimes act like humans, but they also exhibit characteristics of pigs— squealing, grunting, and overeating. Children enjoy the pig details. Have them look at other books about pigs to see how they are portrayed. In James Marshall's books about Emily Pig (*Yummers!* and *Yummers, Too!*), Emily has some very piglike characteristics. Jane Yolen's *Piggins* is a highly different pig character. Seeing how different authors and illustrators present the same animal in stories can give children ideas for their own writing.

Related Titles

Garth Pig and the Ice Cream Lady written and illustrated by Mary Rayner. Atheneum, 1977. Garth is chosen to buy a treat for his siblings. The sign on the "Volfswagon" reads "Lupino's Icecreams," but Garth is abducted by the wolf who owns the van and must be rescued by the other piglets.

Mr. and Mrs. Pig's Evening Out written and illustrated by Mary Rayner. Atheneum, 1976. While their parents are out, the piglets are supervised by a suspicious-looking babysitter. Mrs. Wolf has cooked up a plan for the piglets.

Mrs. Pig's Bulk Buy written and illustrated by Mary Rayner. Atheneum, 1981. Mrs. Pig has a plan to change the ketchup-eating habits of her piglets. She feeds them only ketchup.

Picnic with Piggins by Jane Yolen. Illustrated by Jane Dyer. Harcourt, 1988. Who abducted Rexy Reynard? Piggins, the butler for Mr. and Mrs. Reynard, must solve this mystery.

Piggins by Jane Yolen. Illustrated by Jane Dyer. Harcourt, 1987. Piggins is the butler for Mr. and Mrs. Reynard. When Mrs. Reynard's diamonds are stolen, Piggins comes to the rescue.

Yummers! written and illustrated by James Marshall. Houghton Mifflin, 1973. Emily Pig is trying to lose weight, so she goes for a walk. On her walk, she finds many things to eat.

Yummers, Too! written and illustrated by James Marshall. Houghton Mifflin, 1986. Emily Pig eats three popsicles but does not have the money to pay for them. She tries earning money, but ends up eating the merchandise she is supposed to sell.

About the Author and Illustrator

RAYNER, MARY

Fifth Book of Junior Authors and Illustrators, ed. by Sally Holmes Holtze. Wilson, 1983, pp. 254–255.

Illustrators of Children's Books: 1967–1976, Vol. IV, comp. by Lee Kingman, Grace Allen Hogarth, and Harriet Quimby. Horn Book, 1978, pp. 36, 152–153, 206.

Something about the Author, ed. by Anne Commire. Gale, 1981, Vol. 22, p. 207.

Stevenson, James. *What's Under My Bed?*
Illus. by the author. Greenwillow, 1983; pap., Penguin, 1984
Suggested Use Level: Gr. K–1   Reading Level: Gr. 2

Plot Summary

After hearing a scary story from Grandpa, Mary Ann and Louie go to bed and begin to wonder about the shadows and noises. A sinister shadow approaches and frightens them, but it is only the dog. Their apprehension is not relieved and they run downstairs to be with Grandpa. Grandpa tells them of a similar experience from when he was growing up. Louie and Mary Ann are able to find reasonable explanations for each scary moment that Grandpa describes, until Grandpa tells them about the witches, dragons, and other creatures that chased him—right into the arms of his own grandparents. Grandpa tells how his grandparents gave him some ice cream, so Louie, Mary Ann, and Grandpa decide to share some ice cream, too.

Thematic Material

Stevenson pokes fun at some of the ordinary fears of childhood. In the illustrations he shows something scary and then depicts it as something ordinary. There is humor in this juxtaposition. There is also humor in the surprise appearance of monsters, creepers, and other creatures.

Book Talk Material and Activities

Stevenson has shown a variety of creatures in this story, and he has used strange creatures in many of the other books that he has written and/or illustrated. The series of books about Grandpa often include moments when Grandpa talks about some monster or beast. Stevenson's illustrations in *The Baby Uggs Are Hatching* by Jack Prelutsky also show his ability to depict unusual animals. Children would enjoy getting to know some of these creatures and deciding which ones are the scariest. Is it "The Quossible" or "The Dreary Dreeze" in *The Baby Uggs Are Hatching,* or the monster in *That Terrible Halloween Night?* What features make the monsters seem scary, or funny, or gross? Byron Barton illustrated Jack Prelutsky's creatures in *The Snopp on the Sidewalk and Other Poems.* Compare Barton's interpretation with Stevenson's.

Children can learn about books in a series by studying the many other books about Grandpa, Louie, and Mary Ann. They can see how Grandpa always tells about his own childhood, and how he has a mustache even when he is shown as a little boy. Children should notice the use of cartoon frames and handwritten remarks. Does every Grandpa book have creatures in it? Have children read them and report back.

Audiovisual Adaptation

What's Under My Bed. Weston Woods, cassette/book, 1984; filmstrip/cassette, 1984.

Related Titles

The Baby Uggs Are Hatching by Jack Prelutsky. Illustrated by James Stevenson. Greenwillow, 1982. How would you draw a "Quossible" or a "Smasheroo?" Read some of these aloud and have children draw their own pictures. Then, take a look at Stevenson's interpretation.

The Snopp on the Sidewalk and Other Poems by Jack Prelutsky. Illustrated by Byron Barton. Greenwillow, 1977. Wild creatures include "The Grobbles" and "The Wozzit." Compare them with those drawn by Stevenson.

Other books about Grandpa, Louie, and Mary Ann (all published by Greenwillow) are: *Could Be Worse!* (1977); *Grandpa's Great City Tour* (1983); *The Great Big Especially Beautiful Easter Egg* (1983); *No Friends*

(1986); *That Dreadful Day* (1985); *That Terrible Halloween Night* (1980); *There's Nothing to Do!* (1986); *We Can't Sleep* (1982); *Will You Please Feed Our Cat?* (1987); and *Worse Than Willy!* (1984).

About the Author and Illustrator

STEVENSON, JAMES
Authors of Books for Young People: Supplement to the Second Edition, by Martha E. Ward and Dorothy Marquardt. Scarecrow, 1979, p. 262.
Fifth Book of Junior Authors and Illustrators, ed. by Sally Holmes Holtze. Wilson, 1983, pp. 303–304.
Illustrators of Children's Books: 1967–1976, Vol. IV, comp. by Lee Kingman, Grace Allen Hogarth, and Harriet Quimby. Horn Book, 1978, pp. 161–162, 210.
Something about the Author, ed. by Anne Commire. Gale, 1984, Vol. 34, p. 191; 1986, Vol. 42, pp. 180–184.

Wood, Audrey. *The Napping House*
Illus. by Don Wood. Harcourt, 1984
Suggested Use Level: Gr. PreK–1   Reading Level: Gr. 8

Plot Summary

In this sequential story, everyone is sleeping. Granny is in her bed, and the other characters join her there. First the child, followed by the dog, the cat, the mouse, and, finally, the flea. When the flea bites the mouse, a series of events results that causes everyone to wake up.

Thematic Material

The events in this story take place in a sequence, as each character joins Granny on the bed. The illustrations use light and color to follow the adventures through the night and into the morning. The surprised expression on the characters' faces as they wake up adds to the humor.

Book Talk Material and Activities

Reading this book in a story program could introduce children to the concepts of sequence and pattern. The events follow a circular pattern. The characters join Granny on the bed one by one, and then, when the flea bites the mouse, they leave the bed in reverse order. Other stories also use this pattern, for example, *One Fine Day*. Learning about the patterns in stories helps familiarize children with literary devices. They become more comfortable with literature as they are able to make predictions about what will happen and then have those predictions confirmed. Sequential stories are fun to put down on a chart and illustrate; children can work independently on individual segments and then add them to the group chart.

In his illustrations, Don Wood uses changes in light, perspective, position, and expression to capture the humorous events. Look at the rug on the floor of the room. As the perspective of the room shifts, more of the rug is visible, as is more of the inside of the pitcher. Look closely at the characters as each changes position throughout the night. Look out the window. The rain is pelting the window, and the background is dark blue. As morning approaches, the rain begins to stop and light begins to fill the room. Children are able to make these observations. They need encouragement to read and reread books and to study the illustrations. They should be guided in group story reading sessions so that they can apply their knowledge to their independent reading. Uri Shulevitz's *Dawn* shows night becoming morning while Barbara Berger's *Grandfather Twilight* shows day becoming night. Both would be good to share with *The Napping House*.

Audiovisual Adaptation

The Napping House. Weston Woods, cassette, 1985; filmstrip/cassette, 1985; 16mm film, 1985; videorecording, 1985.

The Napping House and Other Stories. Caedmon, cassette, 1987.

Related Titles

Dawn written and illustrated by Uri Shulevitz. Farrar, Straus, 1974. A boy and his grandfather spend the night outside, waking just before dawn and watching the sun rise. The illustrations begin as a small blue and black oval and grow in size and color to fill the pages with bright green, blue, and yellow.

Good-Night, Owl! written and illustrated by Pat Hutchins. Macmillan, 1972. Like the characters in *The Napping House*, Owl is trying to sleep, but other characters disturb his rest.

Grandfather Twilight written and illustrated by Barbara Berger. Philomel, 1984. A man carries a special pearl to the sea. As he walks, he leaves the soft light of twilight behind him.

One Fine Day retold and illustrated by Nonny Hogrogian. Macmillan,

1971. After drinking the old woman's milk, the fox loses his tail. He must find a way to repay the old woman. He asks the grass for help, but the grass wants water. He asks the water for help, but the water wants a jug. Everything he asks for help wants something in return. Just as in *The Napping House,* characters appear in sequence and then the sequence is reversed.

Roll Over! written and illustrated by Mordicai Gerstein. Crown, 1984. A little fellow cannot sleep until he gets everyone else out of his bed. Another book where characters crowd together.

Ten Sleepy Sheep written and illustrated by Holly Keller. Greenwillow, 1983. Lewis is having trouble falling asleep until he begins counting sheep. Unfortunately, these sheep just add to Lewis's sleeplessness.

About the Author and Illustrator

WOOD, AUDREY
Something about the Author, ed. by Anne Commire. Gale, 1986, Vol. 44, p. 214; 1988, Vol. 50, pp. 218–224.

WOOD, DON
Something about the Author, ed. by Anne Commire. Gale, 1986, Vol. 44, p. 214; 1988, Vol. 50, pp. 224–231.

5

Exploring the Past

For many children, the past is yesterday or, perhaps, last week. Through text and illustrations, books can help children learn about important events in history that occurred hundreds, even thousands of years ago. The books in this chapter about people and places from the past include personal memoirs of growing up and information books about celebrations and accomplishments. By reading about past experiences of others, children can make connections between life long ago and their own lives.

Aliki. *A Medieval Feast*
    Illus. by the author. Crowell, 1983; pap., Harper & Row, 1986
    Suggested Use Level: Gr. 3–4   Reading Level: Gr. 4

Plot Summary

Camdenton Manor is preparing for a visit from the king, which includes his queen and all the members of his court. Some serfs clean the manor house while others get ready for the feast. They hunt, trap, fish, and gather food from the garden, then they prepare the food in the great kitchen. When the king arrives, everything is ready. The guests assemble in the great hall in the morning and begin to eat. Throughout the day they eat, talk, and are entertained. When it is dark, they go to bed.

Thematic Material

This nonfiction book uses text and captioned illustrations to describe medieval life. It includes information on the social hierarchy, the plants and animals, and the preparations for a feast.

Book Talk Material and Activities

Studying medieval times is frequently part of social studies programs. Many children are fascinated with the ceremonies and customs of the time. Lords and ladies, serfs and peasants, minstrels, and jugglers are part of this colorful period. Children enjoy creating their own coat of arms, dressing in costumes of the time, and organizing their own medieval feast. Aliki's book provides many details about the preparation for a feast, including how the food was served and how the guests behaved. In some of the illustrations, the borders surrounding the picture depict plants and animals that were common to this time. Some will be familiar to children but others will need to be researched. Children could try this style of illustration in other areas of study. For example, a science study of the pond could have a central picture of the pond and border illustrations showing pond life. It would be a good project for a group of children to work on cooperatively, with the finished product being a bulletin board display. Examining how an author/illustrator uses different formats and techniques to present information provides children with ideas for their own work.

Library services should be coordinated with classroom activities, and school and public librarians need to be familiar with the school curriculum. Bibliographies, programs, and class visits are more effective when they meet the immediate needs of the group being served. School and public librarians should establish regular communication with classroom teachers and, if possible, serve on committees that are making decisions about curriculum.

Audiovisual Adaptation

A Medieval Feast. Random House Media, cassette/book, 1983; filmstrip/cassette, 1984.

Related Titles

Anno's Medieval World written and illustrated by Mitsumasa Anno. Philomel, 1980. Detailed illustrations and a brief text present many aspects of life during the Middle Ages. An appended note provides information about the Ptolemic theory, in which the earth is the center of the universe. A chronology is also included.

Castle written and illustrated by David Macaulay. Houghton Mifflin, 1977. Macaulay describes the construction of a mythical castle, including many details about the building materials and procedures.

Chanticleer and the Fox by Geoffrey Chaucer. Illustrated by Barbara Cooney. Crowell, 1958. In this 1959 Caldecott-Award-winning book, Cooney includes details about plants, animals, and the way of life during the Middle Ages.

Dick Whittington and His Cat retold and illustrated by Marcia Brown. Scribner, 1950. During medieval times, Dick Whittington finds a way to rid the country of rats. He is rewarded with caskets of riches and eventually becomes the Lord Mayor of London.

Life in a Medieval Village by Gwyneth Morgan. Lerner, 1982. A small book packed with information about medieval life. Some topics include peasant life in the village, clothes, the church, the lord, and the courts.

Looking into the Middle Ages written and illustrated by Huck Scarry. Harper & Row, 1985. An intriguing pop-up book about the Middle Ages presents details about castles, battles, tournaments, and cathedrals. The paper engineering allows some pages to be manipulated, and others pop up into three-dimensional buildings.

The Luttrell Village: Country Life in the Middle Ages written and illustrated by Sheila Sancha. Crowell, 1983. Focusing on the village owned by Sir Geoffrey Luttrell in the fourteenth century, Sancha describes everyday life. Special terms highlighted in bold type in the text are included in a glossary. A very useful book for the research needs of students in the upper elementary grades.

Merry Ever After: The Story of Two Medieval Weddings written and illustrated by Joe Lasker. Viking, 1976. Two weddings are described, the marriage of a merchant's daughter and a nobleman's son, and a peasant wedding. Information is included about the customs and behavior of the nobles and the peasants.

About the Author and Illustrator

ALIKI (BRANDENBERG)

Illustrators of Children's Books: 1957–1966, Vol. III, comp. by Lee Kingman, Grace Allen Hogarth, and Harriet Quimby. Horn Book, 1968, pp. 72, 206; *1967– 1976, Vol. IV,* 1978, pp. 94–95, 177–178.

Something about the Author, ed. by Anne Commire. Gale, 1971, Vol. 2, pp. 36–38; 1984, Vol. 35, pp. 49–55.

Third Book of Junior Authors, ed. by Doris de Montreville and Donna Hill. Wilson, 1972, pp. 8–9.

Anderson, Joan.   *The First Thanksgiving Feast*
Photographs by George Ancona. Clarion, 1984
Suggested Use Level: Gr. 3–4   Reading Level: Gr. 7

Plot Summary

Plimoth Plantation is now a reconstructed museum where "interpreters" reenact the daily life of the Pilgrims and Native Americans. The black-and-white photographs in this book follow these interpreters as they re-create the preparations for the celebration of a successful harvest. The text includes dialogue, which, although fictional, is based on historical accounts from the era.

Governor Bradford and his assistants discuss the need for a harvest festival similar to those that the Pilgrims had celebrated in England. Although the first year in the New World has been a difficult one, the harvest has been successful and the leaders of the settlement see that the villagers need an opportunity to rejoice and give thanks. Several Pilgrims, including John Alden and Myles Standish, give brief statements about their experiences as settlers. The entire community prepares for the feast, which will also include Massasoit and other Native Americans who have befriended the Pilgrims. On the first day of the celebration, Governor Bradford begins with a blessing, and the Pilgrims and Native Americans share foods that they have prepared. Recreation after the meal includes "pillow pushing" (women sit on logs and try to push each other off by swinging pillows), dancing, and singing. The feasting and other activities continue for three days.

Thematic Material

Using black-and-white photographs of the reconstructed settlement at Plimoth Plantation, this book presents historical information about the preparations for the first Thanksgiving.

Book Talk Material and Activities

Celebrating holidays, especially those associated with America's history, is an integral part of school and public library programming. Thanksgiving Day, Presidents' Day, Columbus Day, and other American holidays provide opportunities for children to learn about the past. By doing research on the period and the people who lived then, children can broaden their understanding of the experiences of the colonists, patriots, and explorers. *The First Thanksgiving Feast* provides useful information about Thanksgiving for children in the middle and upper elementary grades. Joyce K. Kessel's *Squanto and the First Thanksgiving* (see this chapter) could be used in the primary grades.

In *The First Thanksgiving Feast,* the photographs of the restored village and of the interpreters help make the era more understandable to children. The dialogue reflects the language patterns of the time and provides details about the way of life. Children might want to use *The First Thanksgiving Feast* as a starting point for a presentation about the holiday. Some of the dialogue could be incorporated into a play or recitation for a school or library program. Librarians could also book talk other books, including *Meet the Real Pilgrims,* which contains more information about the Pilgrims and Thanksgiving.

Related Titles

Feast of Thanksgiving: The First American Holiday—A Play by June Behrens. Illustrated by Anne Siberell. Childrens, 1974. Teachers will find this play with 10 parts—including Father and Mother Goodwell and Squanto—useful when planning a class presentation about this holiday.

Meet the Real Pilgrims: Everyday Life on Plimoth Plantation in 1627. Photographs. Doubleday, 1979. The text is written as a tour of the reconstructed settlement at Plimoth Plantation. (The black-and-white photographs were taken at the site.) The tour guide introduces some of the different people at the settlement, including the soldiers at the fort, a family of settlers, and some indentured servants, and the guide describes their daily activities. The book concludes with an invitation to visit the real Plimoth Plantation and observe the people who work there (called interpreters), who demonstrate the way of life in the village during the seventeenth century.

Merrily Comes Our Harvest In: Poems for Thanksgiving edited by Lee Bennett Hopkins. Illustrated by Ben Shecter. Harcourt, 1978. The 20 poems in this collection express different moods for this holiday, including Dean Hughes's humorous poem about a turkey ("Turkey Time") and Myra Cohn Livingston's more serious poem about the origins of the holiday ("First Thanksgiving").

The Pilgrims of Plimoth written and illustrated by Marcia Sewell. Atheneum, 1986. Full-color paintings correlate with the descriptive text, which discusses the travels of the Pilgrims and their settlement at ·

Plimoth Plantation. Chapters that present information about the daily life and the struggle for survival include "Menfolk," "Womenfolk," and "Children and Youngfolk."

Turkeys, Pilgrims, and Indian Corn: The Story of the Thanksgiving Symbols by Edna Barth. Illustrated by Ursula Arndt. Clarion, 1975. Chapters such as "Indian Corn" and "Horn of Plenty" discuss the origins of some of the familiar items associated with Thanksgiving.

About the Author and Illustrator

ANCONA, GEORGE
Authors of Books for Young People: Supplement to the Second Edition, by Martha E. Ward and Dorothy Marquardt. Scarecrow, 1979, p. 5.
Something about the Author, ed. by Anne Commire. Gale, 1977. Vol. 12, pp. 10–12.

Baylor, Byrd. *The Best Town in the World*
Illus. by Ronald Himler. Scribner, 1983; pap., Macmillan, 1986
Suggested Use Level: Gr. 3–4   Reading Level: Gr. 4

Plot Summary

Father always described his childhood experiences as "the best." The town in Texas where he grew up was friendly and there was plenty to do. There was a creek nearby for swimming and fishing. There were caves to explore, trees to climb, and blackberries to pick and eat. The people in his town all knew each other. Even if you were a child, they would stop and talk to you, sometimes inviting you into their houses for a home-baked treat. The days in his town were full of activities, but the nights had something special about them. The night sky was lit with fireflies and stars, and music drifted across the fields. The store in his town was filled with wonderful things to buy, including "the best candy in the world." At town celebrations everyone shared in the food and festivities. People in his town shared at other times, too, such as when someone needed help with building a house or mending a fence. Father shared his memories of his town and what it was like to grow up there with his children and grandchildren, and they wonder if they will ever find a town like *The Best Town in the World.*

Thematic Material

The Best Town in the World describes a special memory of childhood experiences in Texas around the turn of the century.

Book Talk Material and Activities

Baylor describes the memories that a father (presumably her father) shared with his children about his childhood. This book could be shared with children in the third and fourth grades as part of a family history study. After hearing the story, each child could interview older relatives (for example, parents, aunts, uncles, and grandparents) to put together a story about his or her own family. Or, the children could just share some of their own favorite memories about childhood. At this age, children are able to "look back" at their early experiences and think about some of their special moments. *When I Was Young in the Mountains* and *My Album* are other books that could correlate with this activity.

Baylor has written many books for children that celebrate the heritage and natural beauty of the American Southwest. Librarians could book-talk some of Baylor's other books and encourage children to look at her description of the setting in each book. For example, children could compare her description of the canyon in Texas (in *The Best Town in the World*) with her description of the desert canyon (in *The Desert Is Theirs*). The children could also look for recurring themes in her books, such as reverence for the past (*When Clay Sings* and *Before You Came This Way*) and respect for nature (*Hawk, I'm Your Brother*). By comparing some of Baylor's many books children could see how different illustrators (including Ronald Himler, Peter Parnall, and Tom Bahti) have interpreted her words.

Related Titles

Before You Came This Way by Byrd Baylor. Illustrated by Tom Bahti. Dutton, 1969. Baylor writes about the ancient drawings that can still be seen on canyon walls. These messages from the past tell of another time and another people. Bahti's illustrations evoke the images of prehistoric cave paintings.

The Desert Is Theirs by Byrd Baylor. Illustrated by Peter Parnall. Scribner, 1975. People and animals of the desert canyon are described in this poetic text. Parnall's illustrations received a Caldecott Honor Medal in 1976.

Family Scrapbook written and illustrated by M. B. Goffstein. Farrar,

Straus, 1978. Seven essays illustrated with small line drawings describe some special family moments. One essay describes "The Night We Got a Pickup Truck."

Hawk, I'm Your Brother by Byrd Baylor. Illustrated by Peter Parnall. Scribner, 1976. Rudy Soto, a young Native American boy, dreams of flying. By helping an injured hawk and then setting it free, Rudy is able to feel the joy of flight as the hawk soars through the sky. Parnall's illustrations received a Caldecott Honor Medal in 1977.

I'm in Charge of Celebrations by Byrd Baylor. Illustrated by Peter Parnall. Scribner, 1986. The girl in this book creates her own special celebrations honoring the beauty of her desert world. Included are "Rainbow Celebrations Day" and "Coyote Day." Bright colors streak across the page and evoke a feeling of joy for each celebration.

My Album written and illustrated by Eleanor Schick. Greenwillow, 1984. A little girl looks at photographs of herself and her family and describes each scene. The "photographs" are actually drawings, and children could prepare a similar project using real photographs or their own drawings.

When Clay Sings by Byrd Baylor. Illustrated by Tom Bahti. Scribner, 1972. The images that remain on fragments of clay pots used by the desert people of long ago provide information about their lives. Bahti based his drawings on the images on the pottery of prehistoric Native Americans to interpret Baylor's poetic text.

When I Was Young in the Mountains by Cynthia Rylant. Illustrated by Diane Goode. Dutton, 1982. The repetition of the title phrase evokes a sense of nostalgia and yearning as the author describes childhood moments. The illustrations for this memoir received a Caldecott Honor Medal in 1983.

About the Author and Illustrator

BAYLOR, BYRD

Authors of Books for Young People: Supplement to the Second Edition, by Martha E. Ward and Dorothy Marquardt. Scarecrow, 1979, p. 19.

Fourth Book of Junior Authors and Illustrators, ed. by Doris de Montreville and Elizabeth D. Crawford. Wilson, 1978, pp. 31–32.

Something about the Author, ed. by Anne Commire. Gale, 1979, Vol. 16, pp. 33–35.

HIMLER, RONALD

Illustrators of Children's Books: 1967–1976, Vol. IV, comp. by Lee Kingman, Grace Allen Hogarth, and Harriet Quimby. Horn Book, 1978, pp. 126, 192.

Something about the Author, ed. by Anne Commire. Gale, 1974, Vol. 6, p. 114.

Carrick, Carol. *What Happened to Patrick's Dinosaurs?*
Illus. by Donald Carrick. Clarion, 1986; pap., 1988
Suggested Use Level: Gr. 1–3　　　Reading Level: Gr. 3

Plot Summary

Patrick and his brother, Hank, are in their yard raking leaves. While they work, they start to talk about Patrick's favorite subject—dinosaurs. Patrick wonders about what happened to the dinosaurs. Hank suggests some logical possibilities, but Patrick does not want to be logical. Instead, Patrick begins a fantastic explanation of how dinosaurs and people once shared the earth. In his story, the dinosaurs were very skilled and helpful. They performed important services for people and the people relied on them. Patrick suggests that, eventually, the dinosaurs became tired of being responsible for everything, so they built a spaceship and left. The people did not know how to care for all the cars, houses, stores, airplanes, and other inventions that the dinosaurs had given them and they had to move into caves. The cities deteriorated and the people forgot about the dinosaurs. As Patrick finishes his story, it is evening. Patrick and Hank think about dinosaurs. They look at the sky and they see dinosaur shapes in the stars. This book is a sequel to *Patrick's Dinosaurs*.

Thematic Material

In this story there is a blending of fantasy and reality. Patrick's explanation of what happened to the dinosaurs is creative and imaginative, but it also includes some accurate scientific information about different kinds of dinosaurs.

Book Talk Material and Activities

Using this book in a story or book talk program leads very naturally to the study of dinosaurs. Because Patrick's explanation about what happened to dinosaurs is so fantastic, children will want to read other, more plausible explanations. Dinosaurs are one of the most popular subjects with children and many fine nonfiction books are available. Some of the information about dinosaurs has been revised, so it is important to highlight resources that are up-to-date. Seymour Simon's *The Largest Dinosaurs* and Aliki's *Dinosaurs Are Different* are two recent books that provide current information. The changes in what is known about dinosaurs provide teachers and librarians with an opportunity to talk about the importance of accuracy in nonfiction books. It is often helpful to keep a copy of a canceled book to compare with the revision. This not only encourages the critical examination of books, but also demonstrates that revision is an important part of the writing process. Children can see that published authors often return to work that was "finished" to improve it. This provides them with a model for their own writing efforts.

In *What Happened to Patrick's Dinosaurs?*, Patrick sees dinosaur shapes in stars and clouds. Children will enjoy closing their eyes, marking dots or swirls on a blank piece of paper, and then trying to find a dinosaur. This will build on their knowledge of dinosaurs and also encourage their creativity.

Related Titles

Dinosaurs by Mary Lou Clark. Illustrated. Childrens, 1981. Part of the New True Book series, this text will be accessible to many beginning readers. Features such as a contents, a glossary, and an index make it a good example when talking about nonfiction books.

Dinosaurs and Their Young by Russell Freedman. Illustrated by Leslie Morrill. Holiday House, 1983. This clearly written nonfiction book discusses a recent discovery that has influenced scientists' beliefs about some dinosaurs.

Dinosaurs Are Different written and illustrated by Aliki. Crowell, 1985. A visit to the museum prompts a discussion of dinosaurs. Included is a clear explanation of "bird-hipped" and "lizard-hipped" dinosaurs. Aliki's *My Visit to the Dinosaurs* (Crowell, 1985) is also up-to-date using "apatosaurus," the new term for brontosaurus.

Dinosaurs Walked Here and Other Stories Fossils Tell by Patricia Lauber. Illustrated. Bradbury, 1987. Even though this book, with its background information about archaeology and paleontology, is a challenge for younger readers, many children will be attracted by the clear color illustrations and fascinated by the facts.

A First Look at Dinosaurs by Millicent E. Selsam and Joyce Hunt. Illustrated by Harriett Springer. Walker, 1982. The First Look series introduces children to many subjects, including fish, insects, flowers, plants, and, in this case, dinosaurs.

The Largest Dinosaurs by Seymour Simon. Illustrated by Pamela Carroll. Macmillan, 1986. Provides recent information about "apatosaurus" (formerly called brontosaurus). Ask students if they know that there is new information about the shape of the dinosaur's skull. Simon's *The Smallest Dinosaurs* (Crown, 1982) is a companion book.

Patrick's Dinosaurs by Carol Carrick. Illustrated by Donald Carrick. Clarion, 1983. In this first book about Patrick and his interest in dinosaurs, Patrick's imagination leads him to see dinosaurs all around him.

The Trouble with Tyrannosaurus Rex written and illustrated by Lorinda Bryan Cauley. Harcourt, 1988. Two dinosaurs are frightened by the violent Tyrannosaurus Rex. They devise a plan to frighten him away.

Tyrannosaurus Rex by Millicent Selsam. Illustrated. Harper & Row, 1978. Patrick wonders about the size and behavior of many dinosaurs. More can be learned about this very violent creature in Selsam's nonfiction book.

About the Author and Illustrator

CARRICK, CAROL
Fourth Book of Junior Authors and Illustrators, ed. by Doris de Montreville and Elizabeth D. Crawford. Wilson, 1978, pp. 69–71.
Something about the Author, ed. by Anne Commire. Gale, 1975, Vol. 7, pp. 39–40.
CARRICK, DONALD
Fourth Book of Junior Authors and Illustrators, ed. by Doris de Montreville and Elizabeth D. Crawford. Wilson, 1978, pp. 71–72.
Illustrators of Children's Books: 1967–1976, Vol. IV, comp. by Lee Kingman, Grace Allen Hogarth, and Harriet Quimby. Horn Book, 1978, pp. xiii, 106, 183.
Something about the Author, ed. by Anne Commire. Gale, 1975, Vol. 7, p. 40.

Coerr, Eleanor. *The Josefina Story Quilt*
Illus. by Bruce Degen. Harper & Row, 1986
Suggested Use Level: Gr. 1–3   Reading Level: Gr. 2

Plot Summary

In 1850, Faith, her parents, and her brother, Adam, are preparing to travel by covered wagon to California. Faith is dismayed to be told that she cannot take her beloved pet chicken, Josefina. As Faith's family packs the wagon, she tries to find a good home for Josefina, but no one is willing to keep a hen as a pet. The wagon is finally loaded and Faith tries to say good-bye to Josefina. Her parents see her sadness and agree to let Josefina come with them.

On the wagon train, Faith stays busy working on a rag quilt and trying to keep Josefina out of trouble. Despite Faith's efforts, Josefina nearly causes a stampede and then falls into the river and must be rescued. Just as Pa is prepared to leave Josefina behind, she cackles and lays an egg. Now, because she can contribute to the family's needs, Pa allows her to stay.

The journey continues, and food and water become scarce. Faith continues to work on her quilt, making patches to commemorate moments on the trip—a wagon wheel, a desert, an egg. One night, robbers enter the camp. Josefina's squawking rouses the pioneers, but the effort is too much for her. Faith is saddened by the death of her pet and sews a pine tree to remember where Josefina has been buried. At the end of the journey, Faith and her family piece together the patches, creating a quilt that chronicles their adventures.

Thematic Material

This book presents accurate historical information about the pioneering experience in America, both in the story and also in an Author's Note. It is an adventure story, as Faith and her family face the hardships of their journey, which has a feeling of family togetherness as well.

Book Talk Material and Activities

The Josefina Story Quilt offers many possibilities for discussion and activities. Children who hear this story read aloud could focus on the concepts of "then and now," listing items on a chalkboard under each category. For example, "Then: Faith and her family traveled by covered wagon. Now: We travel by car, bus, and plane." The Author's Note provides additional information about the pioneering experience.

Another question for discussion is "What would you take on this trip?" Faith and her family must make some difficult decisions about what items will be needed and what will fit into the covered wagon. Children enjoy planning what they would need and could relate this to a time when they prepared for family vacations.

In his illustrations, Degen has drawn some of the patches that Faith sewed to commemorate the trip. Children could draw their own story quilts by folding a piece of paper into fourths, opening it, and drawing a different picture in each square. Quilts could be drawn to show favorite books, memorable scenes from one book, family memories, school memories, or other ideas that the children might suggest. Other quilt books, such as *The Patchwork Quilt* by Valerie Flournoy (see Chapter 1), can be discussed.

Related Titles

Becky and the Bear by Dorothy Van Woerkom. Illustrated by Margot Tomes. Putnam, 1975. Based on a true adventure, this book tells of Becky's bravery and ingenuity when she confronts a bear. Details about life in colonial Maine are woven into the story. How is Becky like Faith (in *The Josefina Story Quilt*)?

Cobblestone: The History Magazine for Young People. Cobblestone, 1980– . Each issue of this magazine has a subject theme and includes articles, stories, maps, and activities.

Dakota Dugout by Ann Turner. Illustrated by Ronald Himler. Macmillan, 1985. A woman remembers her life in a sod house on the prairie.

The Drinking Gourd by F. N. Monjo. Illustrated by Fred Brenner. Harper & Row, 1970. Tommy and his family become involved in helping some runaway slaves escape to Canada. This I Can Read History book is accessible to younger readers.

Joshua's Westward Journal by Joan Anderson. Photographs by George Ancona. Morrow, 1987. Photographs re-create the pioneer experiences of a young boy and his family on their journey to Illinois; the text is written in the form of the boy's journal.

Sarah, Plain and Tall by Patricia MacLachlan. Harper & Row, 1985. This 1986 Newbery-Award-winning book tells of Anna and Caleb and their life on the American prairie. The arrival of their father's mail-order bride, Sarah, changes their lives.

She'll Be Comin' Round the Mountain retold and illustrated by Robert Quackenbush. Lippincott, 1973. A lively song illustrated with characters from a Wild West show arriving in town on the railroad. Singing American folk songs is a fun way to introduce a discussion about American history. *The Erie Canal* (Doubleday, 1970), illustrated by Peter Spier, and *Old MacDonald Had a Farm* (Dial Books, 1984), illustrated by Tracey Campbell Pearson, are some other songs to share.

Wagon Wheels by Barbara Brenner. Illustrated by Don Bolognese. Harper & Row, 1978. A good book to compare with *The Josefina Story Quilt*, it tells the story of a black family's westward journey. Many parallels can be found between the two family stories.

About the Author and Illustrator

COERR, ELEANOR
Authors of Books for Young People: Supplement to the Second Edition, by Martha E.
   Ward and Dorothy Marquardt. Scarecrow, 1979, p. 49.
Something about the Author, ed. by Anne Commire. Gale, 1971, Vol. 1, p. 64.
DEGEN, BRUCE
Something about the Author, ed. by Anne Commire. Gale, 1987, Vol. 47, p. 73.

Fisher, Leonard Everett. *The Great Wall of China*
   Illus. by the author. Macmillan, 1986
   Suggested Use Level: Gr. 3–4   Reading Level: Gr. 4

Plot Summary
   During the reign of Ch'in Shih Huang Ti, the Mongols attacked many
villages and overran the countryside. The emperor commanded that a
wall be built to stop the barbarians. More than one million people
worked on the Great Wall, many of them unwillingly. After 10 years, the
wall was completed and it helped control the Mongols for more than
1,000 years.

Thematic Material
   The Great Wall of China presents accurate information about a real
place. Details about the empire of Ch'in Shih Huang Ti are included,
showing how the emperor could force people to do his work.

Book Talk Material and Activities
   The Great Wall of China is a book about real people who lived in China
more than 2,000 years ago. In many schools, it would correlate with the
study of ancient civilizations in the social studies curriculum. Additional
books about ancient China can be included in a program to introduce
children to some of the resources that are available. Folktales often incorporate information about a country's history and culture. Compare these
two versions of the same story—*The Enchanted Tapestry* and *The Weaving
of a Dream*—and look for details about China and its history.
   Fisher has written and illustrated more than 200 books for children
(see Related Titles, which follows, for some of the books illustrated by
Fisher). As children examine the work of an author/illustrator, they can

see the range of topics and treatments that have been presented. An in-depth study of Fisher's work reveals his use of different illustrative techniques to meet the needs of different texts, and the various types of books that he has illustrated, including picture books, poetry, and historical nonfiction. Questions for discussion include: What are some of the techniques and media that Fisher uses? Does Fisher change his technique to illustrate different types of books and, if so, how? and What is your (the child's) reaction to Fisher's illustrations?

Related Titles

The Alamo written and illustrated by Leonard Everett Fisher. Holiday House, 1987. A well-researched account of the importance of the Alamo to the history of Texas and Mexico. The illustrations include reproductions of historical materials and scratchboard pictures by Fisher.

Alphabet Art: 13 ABCs from Around the World written and illustrated by Leonard Everett Fisher. Four Winds, 1978. Historical information about 13 alphabets, including Arabic, Cyrillic, Gothic, and Japanese. Additional titles in this format include Fisher's *Number Art* (Four Winds, 1982); *Symbol Art* (Four Winds, 1985); and *Calendar Art* (Four Winds, 1987).

Boxes! Boxes! written and illustrated by Leonard Everett Fisher. Viking, 1984. Bright, colorful pictures show a variety of boxes and their uses. The background is uncluttered and helps focus attention on the boxes.

The Enchanted Tapestry: A Chinese Folktale retold by Robert D. San Souci. Illustrated by Laszlo Gal. Dial, 1987. A woman weaves beautiful tapestries to support herself and her three sons. She weaves a special tapestry that is blown away by the wind and each son must search for it.

The Railroads written and illustrated by Leonard Everett Fisher. Holiday House, 1979. Part of a series about nineteenth-century America that focuses on aspects of daily life. Other titles in the series are Fisher's *The Hospitals* (Holiday House, 1980) and *The Newspapers* (Holiday House, 1981). Black-and-white scratchboard illustrations capture the feeling of the time period.

Sky Songs by Myra Cohn Livingston. Illustrations by Leonard Everett Fisher. Holiday House, 1984. One of a series of collaborations between Livingston and Fisher. The moods of the sky are explored in Livingston's poems, such as "Shooting Stars," "Storm," and "Sunset." Fisher's full-color paintings capture the movement of the stars, the jagged lightning, and the changing colors of the sky.

The Weaving of a Dream: A Chinese Folktale retold and illustrated by Marilee Heyer. Viking, 1986. A woman who weaves beautiful tapestries buys a picture of a lovely palace and takes it home to her three sons. The painting brings her joy and comfort and she begins to weave a tapestry of it. The tapestry is blown away and each son must search for it.

About the Author and Illustrator

FISHER, LEONARD EVERETT
Authors of Books for Young People: First Supplement, by Martha E. Ward and Dorothy Marquardt. Scarecrow, 1967, pp. 96–97.
Illustrators of Children's Books: 1946–1956, Vol. II, comp. by Lee Kingman, Grace Allen Hogarth, and Harriet Quimby. Horn Book, 1958, pp. 111, 223; *1957–1966, Vol. III,* 1968, pp. 5, 15, 108, 200, 218; *1967–1976, Vol. IV,* 1978, pp. 66, 118, 188.
Something about the Author, ed. by Anne Commire. Gale, 1973, Vol. 4, pp. 84–87; 1984, Vol. 34, pp. 87–97.
Third Book of Junior Authors, ed. by Doris de Montreville and Donna Hill. Wilson, 1972, pp. 84–85.

Hendershot, Judith. *In Coal Country*
Illus. by Thomas B. Allen. Knopf, 1987
Suggested Use Level: Gr. 3–4   Reading Level: Gr. 5

Plot Summary

In this memoir, a girl recalls her father and his work in the coal mines of Ohio. Even though Papa's work was dangerous and dirty, he took pride in it. He worked all night to provide for his family. Their house was in a row of houses built by the mining company. Living near the coal mines meant that the houses were always dirty and the water was often contaminated. Hills of dirt carried out from the mines dotted the landscape. The presence of the coal mines was felt and seen everywhere, but the girl also remembers the warmth of her father's smile, the care and attention of her mother, and the happiness of playing with friends. She remembers the rye bread Mama baked and the food that came from the garden. She remembers playing in the cool spring water to escape the summer heat, collecting nuts in autumn, and riding homemade sleds in the winter. Christmas is a special memory filled with Mama's cooking,

Papa staying home for the day, and the wonderful feeling of a loving family being together.

Thematic Material

This book is a family reminiscence that celebrates both the family and the past. The daughter's love and respect for her parents is very evident.

Book Talk Material and Activities

Cynthia Rylant's *When I Was Young in the Mountains* is very similar to *In Coal Country* and makes a good comparison story. Both books are by women who are reminiscing about their early years in the hills of Ohio (Hendershot) and West Virginia (Rylant). Although both describe some of the difficult moments, they focus on the strength and love of their families. Their experiences, although sometimes harsh, are treasured memories.

The illustrations provide a contrast. In Diane Goode's illustrations for *When I Was Young in the Mountains,* white space dominates the page. Indistinct borders make the illustrations seem to exist in a cloud, like a remembered moment that is clear at the center but hazy around the edges. Goode includes details about Appalachian life that are never mentioned in the text—kerosene lanterns, country stores, primitive furniture. Allen's illustrations for *In Coal Country* seem to capture very specific moments. Done in pastels and charcoal, the pictures are outlined with black lines and assembled in an album format. It is almost as if these moments had been photographed and the author is now looking at and talking about them.

Some children would enjoy asking for old family photographs. They could then try to draw a picture based on the photograph and write a story to go with it. A group of children could use the same photograph and compare the finished projects, which could be displayed on a bulletin board.

Like many good poems or picture books, *In Coal Country* and *When I Was Young in the Mountains* are deceptively simple. Their depth of feeling touches readers of all ages. Children can enjoy visiting the past and feeling the warmth and humor of these families. They can find satisfaction in the everyday details and compare them with their own lives.

Audiovisual Adaptation

In Coal Country. Random House Media, filmstrip/cassette, 1988; cassette/book, 1989.

Related Titles

Family Scrapbook written and illustrated by M. B. Goffstein. Farrar, Straus, 1978. Seven essays illustrated with small line drawings describe some special family moments. Memoirs like "The Night We Got a Pickup Truck" and "My Friend, Mr. Johnson" express the feelings of friendship, love, and togetherness.

Grandpa's Slide Show by Deborah Gould. Illustrated by Cheryl Harness. Lothrop, 1987. Visiting Grandpa always meant watching his slide show. Now that Grandpa has died, Douglas and Sam remember him as they watch the slides together.

In My Mother's House by Ann Nolan Clark. Illustrated by Velino Herrara. Viking, 1941. Details about growing up in a pueblo are lovingly recounted. As in *When I Was Young in the Mountains,* there is some repetition of the title phrase. Compare the everyday life described in this book with the experiences in *When I Was Young in the Mountains* and *In Coal Country.*

Papa's Lemonade written and illustrated by Eve Rice. Greenwillow, 1976. This old-fashioned family of dogs enjoys being together and sharing simple moments. They save pennies, plan a garden, take a walk, and drink lemonade. What kind of memoirs would these pups write about their father?

When I Was Young in the Mountains by Cynthia Rylant. Illustrated by Diane Goode. Dutton, 1982. The illustrations for this memoir received a 1983 Caldecott Honor Medal.

About the Author and Illustrator

ALLEN, THOMAS B.
Something about the Author, ed. by Anne Commire. Gale, 1986, Vol. 45, pp. 27–29.

Hopkins, Lee Bennett, ed. *Dinosaurs: Poems*
Illus. by Murray Tinkelman. Harcourt, 1987
Suggested Use Level: Gr. K–4   Reading Level: NA

Plot Summary
In this collection, there are 18 poems about dinosaurs, fossils, paleontology, and other related topics—poems with humor and whimsy, like Lillian M. Fisher's "I'm Glad I'm Living Now, Not Then!"; and poems expressing wonder and awe, like "To the Skeleton of a Dinosaur in the Museum" by Lilian Moore. The index lists authors, titles, and first lines, making it easy to find specific poems.

Thematic Material
The poems in this collection present different images about dinosaurs, those huge creatures from the past that fascinate children.

Book Talk Material and Activities
The poems about dinosaurs collected by Lee Bennett Hopkins would correlate well with a classroom or library program on dinosaurs and other prehistoric life. Picture books like Carol Carrick's *What Happened to Patrick's Dinosaurs?* (see this chapter) and Lorinda Bryan Cauley's *The Trouble with Tyrannosaurus Rex* could be read aloud, followed by some of the poems from the collection. Jack Prelutsky's collection of poems, *Tyrannosaurus Was a Beast,* is an additional poetry resource.

One activity that relates poetry to science is to have children do research on a specific dinosaur and then compare the facts that they find with the information in poems about that dinosaur. The apatosaurus is a good choice because recent scientific research has resulted in its name being changed from brontosaurus, and there are several poems about the brontosaurus. Children could discuss how the details in the poems relate to the facts that they have gathered.

Related Titles
Dinosaurs written and illustrated by Gail Gibbons. Holiday House, 1987. Colorful illustrations combine with a clearly written text to present information about dinosaurs. Fourteen dinosaurs are highlighted, including the Tyrannosaurus rex and the apatosaurus.

A First Look at Dinosaurs by Millicent E. Selsam and Joyce Hunt. Illustrated by Harriett Springer. Walker, 1982. The First Look series introduces children to many subjects, including fish, insects, flowers, plants, and, in this case, dinosaurs.

Pterosaurs, the Flying Reptiles by Helen Roney Sattler. Illustrations by Christopher Santoro. Lothrop, 1985. Full-color illustrations highlight the relationship between the fossil remains of pterosaurs and the reconstructed images that paleontologists have prepared. The text describes some things scientists have learned about pterosaurs.

The Trouble with Tyrannosaurus Rex written and illustrated by Lorinda Bryan Cauley. Harcourt, 1988. Two dinosaurs that are frightened by the violent Tyrannosaurus rex devise a plan to frighten him away.

Tyrannosaurus Was a Beast: Dinosaur Poems by Jack Prelutsky. Illustrated by Arnold Lobel. Greenwillow, 1988. Fourteen dinosaurs are featured in 14 poems, including the stegosaurus, triceratops, and allosaurus.

Tyrannosaurus Wrecks: A Book of Dinosaur Riddles by Noelle Sterne. Illustrated by Victoria Chess. Crowell, 1979. The title answers the question "What do you get when dinosaurs crash their cars?" The many riddles add enjoyment to the study of dinosaurs.

About the Author and Illustrator

HOPKINS, LEE BENNETT
Authors of Books for Young People: Supplement to the Second Edition, by Martha E. Ward and Dorothy Marquardt. Scarecrow, 1979, p. 134.
Fifth Book of Junior Authors and Illustrators, ed. by Sally Holmes Holtze. Wilson, 1983, pp. 155–157.
Something about the Author, ed. by Anne Commire. Gale, 1972, Vol. 3, pp. 85–87.

TINKELMAN, MURRAY
Illustrators of Children's Books: 1967–1976, Vol. IV, comp. by Lee Kingman, Grace Allen Hogarth, and Harriet Quimby. Horn Book, 1978, pp. 164, 211.
Something about the Author, ed. by Anne Commire. Gale, 1977, Vol. 12, pp. 224–225.

Kessel, Joyce K.   *Squanto and the First Thanksgiving*
Illus. by Lisa Donze. Carolrhoda, 1983
Suggested Use Level: Gr. K–2   Reading Level: Gr. 2

Plot Summary

Squanto was a member of the Patuxet Native American tribe. When the English colonists first came to Plymouth, they captured Squanto and some other braves, sent them to England, and sold them as slaves. There, Squanto learned to speak English. He was set free and returned to his homeland, but he was again captured and sold into slavery. This time he was sent to Spain. Again, he was set free and returned home, only to find that all the people in his tribe had died from smallpox. Squanto went to live with another tribe, and watched while another group of English settlers arrived in Plymouth—the Pilgrims. He observed their struggle to survive the hardships in the new land, in which many of them died, and decided to help them. Squanto taught the Pilgrims how to use the natural resources. After a successful harvest, the Pilgrims invited Squanto and the other Native Americans to join them in a celebration of thankfulness. Together, they ate, played games, and gave thanks for the harvest. This celebration was the origin of Thanksgiving Day.

Thematic Material

In her book, Joyce Kessel presents historical information about Squanto and the role he played in helping the Pilgrims.

Book Talk Material and Activities

Native Americans, Pilgrims, and Thanksgiving are included in the social studies curriculum of most elementary schools. The Thanksgiving holiday is celebrated in schools and libraries with food, arts and crafts, and special programs. Among other things, children learn about the importance of corn in America, they make pictures of turkeys, and they learn songs and poems about being thankful. Many fine books could be booktalked to support this curriculum study. Younger children would find the information in *Squanto and the First Thanksgiving* understandable, and older children could use Joan Anderson's *The First Thanksgiving Feast* (see this chapter). Both books present information about the hardships and cruelty that the Native Americans and the colonists faced, both from the environment and from mutual suspicion. The Thanksgiving celebration is all the more meaningful because of what had to be overcome. Gail Gibbons's *Thanksgiving Day* provides additional background information for young children.

Many schools hold Thanksgiving assemblies, where food is collected for social agencies and classes present skits or say poems about the holiday. The poems in *Merrily Comes Our Harvest In* and *It's Thanksgiving* are suitable for choral reading and group presentations.

Related Titles

Arthur's Thanksgiving written and illustrated by Marc Brown. Little, Brown, 1983. Arthur's class is putting on a Thanksgiving play and Arthur is the director. As children work on their own holiday programs, they will enjoy hearing about Arthur's problems.

It's Thanksgiving by Jack Prelutsky. Illustrated by Marylin Hafner. Greenwillow, 1982. Twelve poems express the different moods of Thanksgiving. Family togetherness, school activities, and eating turkey are some of the topics covered in Prelutsky's poems.

Merrily Comes Our Harvest In: Poems for Thanksgiving edited by Lee Bennett Hopkins. Illustrated by Ben Shecter. Harcourt, 1978. Myra Cohn Livingston's poem "First Thanksgiving" is especially appropriate to share with *Squanto and the First Thanksgiving*. The collection has 19 other poems.

Thanksgiving by Cass R. Sandak. Illustrated by Carla Bauer. Watts, 1980. This nonfiction book focuses on the Pilgrims and also provides historical information about Thanksgiving. It is a fine companion for *Squanto and the First Thanksgiving*.

Thanksgiving Day written and illustrated by Gail Gibbons. Holiday House, 1983. Through a simple text and colorful illustrations, Gibbons tells about the origins of Thanksgiving and the different ways in which it is celebrated now.

About the Author and Illustrator

KESSEL, JOYCE K.
Something about the Author, ed. by Anne Commire. Gale, 1985, Vol. 41, pp. 116–117.

Levinson, Riki. *Watch the Stars Come Out*
Illus. by Diane Goode. Dutton, 1985; pap., Macmillan, 1987
Suggested Use Level: Gr. 1–4   Reading Level: Gr. 2

Plot Summary

A girl listens as her grandma tells her a special story. When the grandma was a little girl, she and her brother left their home and traveled by boat to America. Her parents and sister were already there and were to meet them. Life on the boat was very difficult and some people died on the journey, but the girl and her brother stayed together and survived. As the boat approached the shore, the children were excited to see the Statue of Liberty. After passing through the health inspection area, the two children were reunited with their family. Together they went to their new home, filled with the hope and promise of the new land. As the story closes, the little girl is back in her room hoping that her grandma will share another special memory.

Thematic Material

The immigrant experience is an important part of U.S. history. Children need to see the relationship between their everyday lives and what happened in the past. In many families, there is a great appreciation for the courage and spirit of their ancestors. This book shows the importance that one family places on its history.

Book Talk Material and Activities

America is a land of immigrants, and their experiences are an important part of school and library programs. The journeys of the first explorers, the coming of the Pilgrims, the forced movement of African slaves, and the travels of European immigrants have all contributed to the "melting pot" that is America. Books about these experiences correlate with the social studies curriculum in many schools and are excellent for book talks. Several titles deal with the 1986 centennial celebration of the Statue of Liberty, and the ongoing restoration of Ellis Island, which marks its centennial in 1992, continues to focus attention on the immigrant experiences.

Molly's Pilgrim, which brings the immigrant experience into the present, is a good book to compare with *Watch the Stars Come Out*. A discussion could center around the possible reasons each family had for making its journey, how America is depicted in Levinson's book, and Molly's experiences. The styles of the illustrators could also be examined and discussed.

Audiovisual Adaptation

Watch the Stars Come Out. Random House Media, cassette/book, 1986; filmstrip/cassette, 1986. Also "Reading Rainbow," Great Plains National Instructional Television Library, videorecording, 1986.

Related Titles

Ellis Island: Gateway to the New World written and illustrated by Leonard Everett Fisher. Holiday House, 1986. A photoessay that provides excellent historical information about the experiences of those passing through this reception station (which was in use from 1892 until 1954).

How They Built the Statue of Liberty by Mary J. Shapiro. Illustrated by Huck Scarry. Random House, 1985. An oversized book with large illustrations (including diagrams and close-ups) that presents information about the construction of the Statue of Liberty.

The Long Way to a New Land written and illustrated by Joan Sandin. Harper & Row, 1981. A family journeys from Sweden to America to escape the famine and harsh conditions in its homeland. A comparison can be made between this journey and the one described in *Watch the Stars Come Out.*

Molly's Pilgrim by Barbara Cohen. Illustrated by Michael J. Deraney. Lothrop, 1983. Molly and her family have come to America from Russia, and Molly feels like an outsider. When her class studies Thanksgiving and the Pilgrims, Molly begins to see her place in her new homeland.

The Statue of Liberty written and illustrated by Leonard Everett Fisher. Holiday House, 1985. Facts and photographs highlight the history and restoration of "Miss Liberty."

About the Author and Illustrator

GOODE, DIANE
Fifth Book of Junior Authors and Illustrators, ed. by Sally Holmes Holtze. Wilson, 1983, pp. 134–135.
Illustrators of Children's Books: 1967–1976, Vol. IV. comp. by Lee Kingman, Grace Allen Hogarth, and Harriet Quimby. Horn Book, 1978, pp. 123, 190.
Something about the Author, ed. by Anne Commire. Gale, 1979, Vol. 15, pp. 125–127.

Longfellow, Henry Wadsworth. *Hiawatha*
Illus. by Susan Jeffers. Dial, 1983.
Suggested Use Level: Gr. 3–4   Reading Level: NA

Plot Summary
The verses in this book are excerpted from Longfellow's epic poem "The Song of Hiawatha." They are the ones that begin with the familiar line "By the shores of Gitche Gumee" and tell the story of the young Hiawatha and his early years with his grandmother, Nokomis. Nokomis taught Hiawatha the ways of their people, their myths, and their legends. She also told him of the ways of the animals of the forest. Together, they rejoiced in the natural world and revered their heritage. As Hiawatha grew older, he learned to imitate the sounds of many animals and developed a relationship with the woodland creatures built on respect and trust.

Thematic Material
Hiawatha conveys a sense of respect for nature and for the cultural heritage of Native Americans.

Book Talk Material and Activities
Hiawatha could be correlated with the study of Native Americans that is part of the social studies curriculum at many schools. Students who are learning about Native American tribes and how they lived will find details in both the poem and the illustrations. Many teachers encourage children to use a variety of materials when they are researching a topic, and poetry by and about Native Americans could be booktalked to extend children's understanding of the cultural heritage of these peoples. Books with poetry by Native Americans include *The Trees Stand Shining* and *Our Fathers Had Powerful Songs*.

Jeffers's illustrations for *Hiawatha* are very detailed, showing plants and animals referred to in the poem. In *Hiawatha's Childhood*, Errol Le Cain has illustrated the same verses with a very different style. Where Jeffers's illustrations are detailed and full of light, Le Cain used darker, more somber colors. Children could be asked to examine both interpretations and discuss their reactions. A teacher or librarian may want to read the poem aloud without showing any illustrations and ask children to talk about the images that they would expect to find in an illustrated version. Other poems that have been illustrated as picture books could be booktalked, including *Paul Revere's Ride* and *Casey at the Bat*. Another activity is to have the children compare *Hiawatha* with other poetry picture books illustrated by Susan Jeffers, such as *Stopping by Woods on a Snowy Evening* and *Wynken, Blynken, and Nod,* and discuss the different styles and techniques Jeffers used to interpret different poems.

Related Titles

Casey at the Bat: A Ballad of the Republic, Sung in the Year 1888 by Ernest Lawrence Thayer. Illustrated by Wallace Tripp. Coward, McCann, 1978. In the whimsical illustrations for this poem about the most famous strikeout in baseball, animals are playing the game, and Casey is a powerful bear. Casey's strikeout is all the more dramatic because of how he is depicted.

Hiawatha's Childhood by Henry Wadsworth Longfellow. Illustrated by Errol Le Cain. Farrar, Straus, 1984. Another illustrated version of selected verses from Longfellow's poem. Compare the illustrations with those done by Jeffers for *Hiawatha*.

Our Fathers Had Powerful Songs by Natalia Belting. Illustrated by Laszlo Kubinyi. Dutton, 1974. Belting has written lyrical verses based on the legends and writings of different Native American tribes.

The Owl and the Pussy Cat by Edward Lear. Illustrated by Paul Galdone. Clarion, 1987. In this well-known poem of the romance and marriage of an owl and a pussy cat, other characters are depicted as animals, including the pig who performs the ceremony and the turkey who is an admiral. Galdone's illustrations are lively.

Paul Revere's Ride by Henry Wadsworth Longfellow. Illustrated by Nancy Winslow Parker. Greenwillow, 1985. Colorful illustrations enhance this famous poem about the American Revolution. Two pages of "Geographical and Military Notes" help explain some of the references in the poem.

Stopping by Woods on a Snowy Evening by Robert Frost. Illustrated by Susan Jeffers. Dutton, 1978. Soft gray lines combine with the white of snow, birch trees, and a horse to interpret Robert Frost's well-known poem. Children could compare Jeffers's illustrations for this book with those she did for *Hiawatha*.

The Trees Stand Shining: Poetry of the North American Indians selected by Hettie Jones. Illustrated by Robert Andrew Parker. Dial, 1971. A recurring theme in these poems collected from many different tribes is respect for the natural world.

Wynken, Blynken, and Nod by Eugene Field. Illustrated by Susan Jeffers. Dutton, 1982. Field's classic bedtime poem is illustrated in shades of blue that create a restful mood. Ask children to compare Jeffers's illustrations for this book with those for *Hiawatha.*

About the Author and Illustrator

LONGFELLOW, HENRY WADSWORTH
Authors of Books for Young People, Second Edition, by Martha E. Ward and Dorothy Marquardt. Scarecrow, 1971, p. 324.
Something about the Author, ed. by Anne Commire. Gale, 1980, Vol. 19, pp. 181–204.

JEFFERS, SUSAN
Fourth Book of Junior Authors and Illustrators, ed. by Doris de Montreville and Elizabeth D. Crawford. Wilson, 1978, pp. 198–199.
Illustrators of Children's Books: 1967–1976, Vol. IV, ed. by Lee Kingman, Grace Allen Hogarth, and Harriet Quimby. Horn Book, 1978, pp. 10, 11, 131, 176, 195.
Something about the Author, ed. by Anne Commire. Gale, 1979, Vol. 17, pp. 86–88.

O'Kelley, Mattie Lou. *From the Hills of Georgia: An Autobiography in Paintings*
Illus. by the author. Little, Brown, 1983; pap., 1986
Suggested Use Level: Gr. 3–4   Reading Level: Gr. 7

Plot Summary

Through paintings with brief captions, Mattie Lou O'Kelley shares memories of her early life. Born in 1908, Mattie Lou was part of a large family living on a farm in rural Georgia. The whole family shared in the responsibilities on the farm—Mama worked in the fields; her sister, Gert, took care of the farmyard birds; Papa cleared the land for plowing; the boys cared for the tools; and everyone helped with the planting and harvesting of the crops. Daily life included summer picnics, playing games, having a "pound supper," where each guest brings a pound of food to share, visiting the country store, and going to school.

Thematic Material

Mattie Lou O'Kelley has written and painted a memoir of rural life at the turn of the century with a strong sense of family. Her folk paintings capture many details of her childhood, allowing readers to see rural life through her eyes.

Book Talk Material and Activities

Sharing this book with children can help them see the relationship between art and children's literature. O'Kelley has written autobiographical captions to accompany some of her paintings. While children study the work of an artist, they can also look for details about the artist's life.

The format of O'Kelley's book is similar to that of William Kurelek's prairie memoirs, *A Prairie Boy's Summer* and *A Prairie Boy's Winter*. Both artists reflect on their childhood experiences primarily through their paintings, and both write captions to tell the "story." As the time period for these books is similar (the early 1900s) but the setting is different (rural Georgia for O'Kelley and rural Canada for Kurelek), comparing them would be an interesting activity. Some possible topics to consider are the setting, the daily experiences, and the family's activities. For example, O'Kelley describes a "Late Snow in Georgia," capturing the sense of surprise and delight. Her painting shows a crowd of nearly 20 people, many farm animals, buildings, snow-covered hills, and trees. In Kurelek's "Snowball Weather," a crowd of children is rolling in the snow, but the surrounding area is a stark, flat plain. Every picture in O'Kelley's book is almost cluttered with details, but Kurelek's summer and winter scenes are dominated by the open space of the prairie. After looking at these different interpretations of childhood, children may want to look through some of their own art projects and try writing descriptive captions. A classroom teacher could keep a folder of work for each child during the year to have available for this project.

Related Titles

Emanuel Leutze: Washington Crossing the Delaware by Ernest Goldstein. Illustrated. Garrard, 1983. Part of the Let's Get Lost in a Painting series, this title uses close-up details from the famous painting of George Washington to show the relationship between history and art.

The Farm Book story and pictures by E. Boyd Smith. Houghton Mifflin, 1982. Although not autobiographical, Smith's paintings and text present detailed information about American farm life in the early 1900s.

Ox-Cart Man by Donald Hall. Illustrated by Barbara Cooney. Viking, 1979. This 1980 Caldecott-Award-winning book describes the everyday experiences of a farmer and his family in nineteenth-century New England. Look at the illustrations for details about New England and then compare them to O'Kelley's description of Georgia.

Pieter Brueghel's "The Fair" by Ruth Craft. Illustrated by Pieter Brueghel. Lippincott, 1975. Using Brueghel's "The Fair," Craft wrote a story of the gossip that is going on and the reasons for different activities. It is a book that encourages children to look carefully at a painting and imagine what is happening, a good springboard for a writing activity.

A Prairie Boy's Summer paintings and story by William Kurelek. Houghton Mifflin, 1975. Each illustration is accompanied by a description of the daily activities being depicted. On the Canadian prairie during the summer, children played baseball and went swimming, but they also watched the swallows chase the cat, raked and burned weeds off the fields, and harvested grain.

A Prairie Boy's Winter paintings and story by William Kurelek. Houghton Mifflin, 1973. Winter activities on the Canadian prairie included playing ice hockey and having snowball fights, as well as bringing in hay from the frozen fields, bringing in firewood, and cleaning the chicken coop.

A Winter Place by Ruth Yaffe Radin. Paintings by Mattie Lou O'Kelley. Little, Brown, 1982. Compare the many winter scenes in this book with those by Kurelek. Radin's poetic text captures the joy of winter.

About the Author and Illustrator

O'KELLEY, MATTIE LOU
Something about the Author, ed. by Anne Commire. Gale, 1984, Vol. 36, p. 151.

Provensen, Alice, and Provensen, Martin. *The Glorious Flight: Across the Channel with Louis Blériot, July 25, 1909*
Illus. by the authors. Viking, 1983; pap., Penguin, 1987
Suggested Use Level: Gr. 3–4   Reading Level: Gr. 4

Plot Summary

Louis Blériot lives with his family in France. While out for a ride in the family car, Blériot is distracted by a noise. His car swerves into a wagon full of pumpkins and there is chaos on the village street. As the muddle continues, a large airship passes overhead. It is the early 1900s and air travel is still very experimental. Everyone forgets the scattered pumpkins and stares at the wonderful sight. Louis Blériot is enchanted. He becomes determined to create his own flying machine. His many efforts are inventive and comic and, finally, on his seventh attempt, successful. As he continues to perfect his aircraft, Blériot decides to accept the challenge of Lord Northcliff and the *London Daily Mail*. On July 25, 1909, Blériot successfully pilots Blériot XI across the English Channel.

Thematic Material

The Glorious Flight is the story of a man with an adventurous spirit. Louis Blériot was one of the pioneers of flight. He had the courage to take risks and the spirit to succeed.

Book Talk Material and Activities

This nonfiction picture book could be the focus of a program on pioneers in technology. Many other fine nonfiction books focus on the contributions of scientists and inventors. Sally Ride's *To Space and Back* brings the story of pioneers of flight into today's world. Biographies of Henry Ford (*We'll Race You, Henry*); Buckminster Fuller (*More with Less*); and Charles Goodyear (*Oh, What an Awful Mess!*) provide insights into the development of technologies that are a part of everyday life. Many schools participate in science fairs and invention conventions, and this program could be coordinated with children's efforts to come up with their own inventions.

Another fun activity to try is a paper airplane flying contest. Seymour Simon's *The Paper Airplane Book* provides some ideas for designs. Read a book like *Bored—Nothing to Do*, a humorous look at some modern-day pioneers of flight.

The Glorious Flight received the Caldecott Award in 1984, one of the few nonfiction titles that has been honored in this way. Children could research the Caldecott Medal and examine some of the other nonfiction books that have received it, perhaps beginning with *Cathedral: The Story of Its Construction* (honor book, 1974); *Moja Means One: Swahili Counting Book* (honor book, 1972); *Ashanti to Zulu: African Traditions* (Caldecott Medal, 1977); and the many folktales that have been honored.

Audiovisual Adaptation

The Glorious Flight. Live Oak Media, cassette/book, 1987; filmstrip/cassette, 1984; videorecording, 1987.

Related Titles

Ashanti to Zulu: African Traditions by Margaret Musgrove. Illustrated by Leo Dillon and Diane Dillon. Dial, 1976. Each letter of the alphabet introduces another group of African people. Information about their customs and location is included in the brief description and in the illustration.

Bored—Nothing to Do written and illustrated by Peter Spier. Doubleday, 1978. Two boys, surrounded by toys, cannot find anything to do. When they find an old airplane propeller in the barn, their adventure begins.

Cathedral: The Story of Its Construction written and illustrated by David Macaulay. Houghton Mifflin, 1973. Large, detailed illustrations describe the construction of a cathedral during the thirteenth and fourteenth centuries.

Moja Means One: Swahili Counting Book by Muriel Feelings. Illustrated by Tom Feelings. Dial, 1971. The illustrations of the numbers 1 to 10 include details about life in Africa.

More with Less: The Future World of Buckminster Fuller by Nathan Aaseng. Lerner, 1986. Fuller's contributions in the areas of architecture, automotive engineering, and creative thinking are profiled in this biography.

Oh, What an Awful Mess! A Story of Charles Goodyear written and illustrated by Robert Quackenbush. Prentice-Hall, 1980. Charles Goodyear's discovery of vulcanization revolutionized the rubber industry. Quackenbush presents a humorous portrait of Goodyear and his achievements.

The Paper Airplane Book by Seymour Simon. Illustrated by Byron Barton. Viking, 1971. Clear instructions and illustrations for making paper airplanes.

To Space and Back by Sally Ride with Susan Okie. Lothrop, 1986. Sally Ride gives a personal account of her experiences in space in this beautifully illustrated photoessay.

We'll Race You, Henry: A Story about Henry Ford by Barbara Mitchell. Illustrated by Kathy Haubrich. Carolrhoda, 1986. Part of the Creative Minds series. Other titles focus on George Eastman, George Washington Carver, and Jan Matzeliger.

About the Author and Illustrator

PROVENSEN, ALICE, AND PROVENSEN, MARTIN
Illustrators of Children's Books: 1744–1945, Vol. I, comp. by Lee Kingman, Grace
    Allen Hogarth, and Harriet Quimby. Horn Book, 1947, pp. 21, 25, 38, 168;
    1957–1966, Vol. III, 1968, pp. 161, 236; *1967–1976, Vol. IV,* 1978, pp. 152, 205.
Something about the Author, ed. by Anne Commire. Gale, 1976, Vol. 9, pp. 154–155.
Third Book of Junior Authors, ed. by Doris de Montreville and Donna Hill. Wilson,
    1972, pp. 231–232.

Roop, Peter, and Roop, Connie.   *Buttons for General Washington*
   Illus. by Peter E. Hanson. Carolrhoda, 1986; pap., Lerner, 1987
   Suggested Use Level: Gr. 1–4   Reading Level: Gr. 3

Plot Summary

It is 1777. In Philadelphia, the Darragh family worries about Charles,
who is serving in General Washington's army. Charles's parents and his
brother, John, are Quakers who, despite their religious beliefs, are help-
ing the Revolutionary army by delivering secret messages to Charles.
The messages are in code and are sewn into the buttons on John's coat.
Using his pass to visit his aunt, John is able to leave the city and look for
Washington's camp. On this trip, however, John gets into a fight with a
Loyalist and is then stopped at a British guard post. After inspecting
John's pass, the British soldier allows him to continue. John is well on his
way when he discovers that he has lost one button, probably in the fight.
He returns to the city, finds the button, and hurries to find his brother,
taking a shortcut through the woods. There, he is stopped by a stranger
who thinks John is a spy. The man takes John to an army camp, which
turns out to be Washington's camp. John delivers his messages and is
commended by General Washington for his patriotism.

Thematic Material

Set during the American Revolution, this story includes a famous
historical figure, George Washington. The Darragh family are Quakers
who are going against the peaceful concepts of their religion to help the
revolutionaries.

Book Talk Material and Activities

During patriotic holidays, such as Washington's Birthday, younger children often find it difficult to relate to the concept of "long ago." Books can help them develop an understanding of the way of life during different periods in the past. In this Revolutionary War story, children are introduced to the concepts of patriots and tories and the involvement of many citizens in the war, some supportive and some not. The Author's Note at the beginning of the book gives some background on Quakers, as well as information about the war. *Buttons for General Washington* is based on a real Quaker family that acted as spies for Washington's army. Other books about the Revolutionary War, including *Sam the Minuteman* and *Six Silver Spoons*, should be on display for children to select.

In many historical fiction books, the illustrations add information about the way of life during the period. Peter E. Hanson's illustrations show what people wore and how they traveled. There is a picture of a cobblestone street in Philadelphia and one of General Washington talking to John Darragh in a tent lit by a candle. Brinton Turkle's books about Obadiah Starbuck and his family, such as *Obadiah the Bold,* also provide information about a Quaker family in colonial America. Although Turkle's books are not set during the Revolutionary War, they do provide a picture of family life in early America. As children hear and read more historical fiction, they are able to use both the text and the illustrations to gather information about the time period.

Related Titles

George the Drummer Boy by Nathaniel Benchley. Illustrated by Don Bolognese. Harper & Row, 1977. A British drummer boy participates in the battles of Lexington and Concord. His point of view of the Revolutionary War contrasts with John's in *Buttons for General Washington* and with Sam's in *Sam the Minuteman.*

Jack Jouett's Ride written and illustrated by Gail E. Haley. Viking, 1973. In Virginia, Jack Jouett observed British troops on their way to capture American patriots. He rode faster than the British troops and warned the revolutionaries, including Thomas Jefferson and Patrick Henry. Compare this patriotic ride to *Paul Revere's Ride.*

Obadiah the Bold written and illustrated by Brinton Turkle. Viking, 1965. Life in Nantucket during colonial times is fairly strict, but Obadiah Starbuck's imagination gets him into many adventures. Look at the illustrations for details about clothing, furniture, and houses during this time.

Paul Revere's Ride by Henry Wadsworth Longfellow. Illustrated by Nancy Winslow Parker. Greenwillow, 1985. This well-known poem is illustrated with colorful line and watercolor pictures. The appended Geographical and Military Notes extends the reader's understanding of the references in the poems. Look at *Jack Jouett's Ride* for the story of another patriot.

Sam the Minuteman by Nathaniel Benchley. Illustrated by Arnold Lobel. Harper & Row, 1969. Sam's friend John is injured during a battle in the Revolutionary War—another story that looks at the impact of the war on a young American patriot.

Six Silver Spoons by Janette Sebring Lowrey. Illustrated by Robert Quackenbush. Harper & Row, 1971. More information about colonial America comes from the I Can Read History series. The format is accessible to younger readers.

Steven Kellogg's Yankee Doodle written by Edward Bangs. Illustrated by Steven Kellogg. Parent's Magazine Press, 1976. There is much American history in this patriotic song.

About the Author and Illustrator

ROOP, PETER, AND ROOP, CONNIE
Something about the Author, ed. by Anne Commire. Gale, 1987, Vol. 49, p. 176.

Stevenson, James. *When I Was Nine*
Illus. by the author. Greenwillow, 1986
Suggested Use Level: Gr. 3–4   Reading Level: Gr. 4

Plot Summary

Walking alone, a man reminisces about his childhood. He remembers his dog, his family, his neighborhood, and some of the everyday activities of his childhood, including printing a neighborhood newspaper. On one special summer vacation, his family traveled out west to a ranch in New Mexico. Returning home, the man remembers how he felt. Even though the neighborhood looked the same, it seemed different. His new experience had helped him grow and change.

Thematic Material

When I Was Nine is a story of personal reminiscence and appreciation for the past, but it is also a story of growing up that includes details about the relationships within a family.

Book Talk Material and Activities

Several books that look back and reflect on childhood experiences could serve as models for similar memory books for children and their families. This would be especially appropriate for children in the middle elementary grades (grades 3 and 4) who are beginning to have a sense of their own past. They can remember when they were younger and recall some of their first experiences—their first bike, their first day at school, and their first best friend. Working on an illustrated memory book could be a project for children and their families. As part of a school or library activity, children could prepare their own books, using *When I Was Nine* as a model. They may want to focus on a much younger age, for example, "When I Was Five." Parents, grandparents, siblings, and other family members could be interviewed and these reminiscences illustrated by the children and bound together into generation books.

Stevenson has illustrated *When I Was Nine* with small impressionistic watercolor pictures. Some children may want to experiment with watercolors or use other media to illustrate their books.

Related Titles

Don't You Remember? by Lucille Clifton. Illustrated by Evaline Ness. Dutton, 1973. A five-year-old girl remembers things that are important to her, but the rest of her family seems to ignore them. The everyday experiences of this black family provide a contrast to *When I Was Nine*, as does the little girl's perspective on what is important to her now.

Higher on the Door written and illustrated by James Stevenson. Greenwillow, 1987. Stevenson continues to look back on his childhood, remembering a train ride to the city and watching an ocean liner leave port.

My Album written and illustrated by Eleanor Schick. Greenwillow, 1984. A little girl looks at photographs of herself and her family and describes each scene. The "photographs" are actually drawings, and children could prepare a similar project using real photographs or their own drawings.

On Mother's Lap by Ann Herbert Scott. Illustrated by Glo Coalson. McGraw-Hill, 1972. Although not a reminiscence, this story does capture a special feeling that many children will remember. The illustrations depict an Eskimo family, which highlights the universal nature of family experiences.

When I Was Little by Lyn Littlefield Hoopes. Illustrated by Marcia Sewell. Dutton, 1983. As a mother, daughter, and new baby take a walk, the daughter asks about when she was little. The mother talks about waiting for her to be born and the joy of finally seeing her. They talk of their hopes for the new baby and the love they will always feel for each other.

When I Was Young in the Mountains by Cynthia Rylant. Illustrated by Diane Goode. Dutton, 1982. The repetition of the title phrase evokes a sense of nostalgia and yearning as the author describes childhood moments.

When You Were a Baby written and illustrated by Ann Jonas. Greenwillow, 1982. Another model for children's writing and illustrations about themselves.

About the Author and Illustrator

STEVENSON, JAMES
Authors of Books for Young People: Supplement to the Second Edition, by Martha E. Ward and Dorothy Marquardt. Scarecrow, 1979, p. 262.
Fifth Book of Junior Authors and Illustrators, ed. by Sally Holmes Holtze. Wilson, 1983, pp. 303–304.
Illustrators of Children's Books: 1967–1976, Vol. IV, comp. by Lee Kingman, Grace Allen Hogarth, and Harriet Quimby. Horn Book, 1978, pp. 161–162, 210.
Something about the Author, ed. by Anne Commire. Gale, 1984, Vol. 34, p. 191; 1986, Vol. 42, pp. 180–184.

6

Learning about the World
Around You

CHILDREN wonder about other people and other places. They want to
learn about plants, animals, and seasons. Their curiosity covers topics
from outer space to the outdoors, and they ask questions about the moon
and the planets as well as about bugs and animals. The books in this
chapter help children discover more about the world around them.
Teachers and librarians can relate these books to science and social studies activities.

Andrews, Jan. *Very Last First Time*
Illus. by Ian Wallace. Atheneum, 1985
Suggested Use Level: Gr. 1–4   Reading Level: Gr. 4

Plot Summary

Eva Padlyat is an Inuit girl living in northern Canada. She is preparing
for a special adventure. In her village, gathering mussels in the winter is
a very unusual experience. After the surface of the sea has frozen, the
tide continues to rise and fall. When the tide is out, villagers climb down
through a hole in the ice and gather mussels from the seabed. Today will
be Eva's first time gathering mussels alone. The ice overhead makes the
seabed look eerie and frightening as Eva begins her task. Soon, in the
flickering light of her candles, Eva realizes how happy she is to be alone.
After her job is done, she goes exploring and is awed by the beauty of the
seabed. Eva wanders farther and farther from her starting point and is
momentarily lost when she drops her candle. She overcomes her fear,
lights a new candle, and goes triumphantly back to her mother. Eva

realizes that this first time for gathering mussels alone will be an experience that she will remember forever.

Thematic Material

This story gives children a look at the life of a child in another land. Details about the Inuit culture are included as is information about the way of life in northern Canada.

Book Talk Material and Activities

A book talk or story program on the Inuit and Eskimo cultures could be developed using *Very Last First Time* as the focus. Other titles could present information about their legends, folklore, history, food, art, and crafts. Understanding the land and climate of northern Canada is very important. Many children are unfamiliar with the location of the story and will need to use a map to see where they are in relationship with where the story is set.

Ian Wallace's illustrations provide many details that could enhance children's understanding of the story. Eva's home is covered with snow. A fur skin is stretched on a frame beside the house and snowshoes are on the walls. A big metal drum is attached to the house, perhaps holding fuel oil. Inside the house is a more familiar scene. The kitchen has many ordinary items—including a box of Kellogg's Corn Flakes on the table. Children could study the pictures to discover more facts about Eva's life and to compare what they observe with their own experiences.

Some important information is presented in the text but additional details come from the illustrations. By examining how the author and illustrator have collaborated, children become more aware of the contributions of each. They will be able to discuss their observations and develop more critical skills for analyzing books.

Related Titles

The Art of the Eskimo by Shirley Glubok. Photographs. Harper & Row, 1964. Masks, carvings, dolls, and prints are described along with the habitat and way of life of the Eskimos. Snow knives made of ivory and intricately carved scrapers for animal hides are two of the many fascinating artifacts presented.

The Eskimo: The Inuit and Yupik People by Alice Osinski. Photographs and drawing. Childrens, 1985. As part of the New True Book series, this book presents current information about the land, customs, and daily life of Eskimos—good background information for studying them. A map shows the general location of the Inuits and the Yupiks, and a glossary is included.

An Eskimo Family by Bryan Alexander and Cherry Alexander. Photographs. Lerner, 1985. Focusing on one Eskimo family, the authors describe some of their typical activities. Color photographs show many modern activities like going to school and to the dentist.

Eskimos edited by Henry Pluckrose. Illustrated by Maurice Wilson. Gloucester, 1980. Colorful illustrations add to the textual information about Eskimos. Many double-page spreads focus on specific aspects of Eskimo life, such as the animals in the Arctic, the types of transportation, and recreational activities.

On Mother's Lap by Ann Herbert Scott. Illustrated by Glo Coalson. McGraw-Hill, 1972. Mother's lap is a special place with room for everyone and everything. The illustrations show the love that is shared in this Eskimo home.

Up North in Winter written and illustrated by Deborah Hartley. Dutton, 1986. A boy's father tells of a time when it was so cold that his father (the boy's grandfather) walked across the frozen lake to get home. About halfway across the lake, he found a frozen fox, which he carried home, wrapped around his neck. The man's warmth revived the fox, who ran away, but Grandpa was glad to be warm and at home.

Whale in the Sky written and illustrated by Anne Siberell. Dutton, 1982. This Northwest Native American legend uses woodcuts to tell the story of how Thunderbird saved the salmon from the whale. The people had the story carved into a totem pole. The final page of the book shows carving tools and discusses how natural materials were used to produce colors.

About the Author and Illustrator

ANDREWS, JAN
Something about the Author, ed. by Anne Commire. Gale, 1987, Vol. 49, p. 35.

Anno, Mitsumasa. *Anno's U.S.A.*
Illus. by the author. Philomel, 1983
Suggested Use Level: Gr. 1–4   Reading Level: NA

Plot Summary

In this wordless book, a man in a boat rows toward shore passing an Eskimo with his dog sled (Alaska) and an island with native dancers (Hawaii). In a fishing village, he is directed to follow the trail leading over the hill. In the distance is the Golden Gate Bridge and the skyline of San Francisco. The man seems to be moving through different periods of American history. In some scenes, there is a curious mixture of the past and the present, as boys play basketball near Native Americans living in teepees. As the man continues his journey, however, he moves further back into America's past. He also travels further east, passing wagon trains in the Old West, a frontier settlement, a Mississippi River boat, the Liberty Bell, and modern-day New York City filled with people in old-fashioned clothes. He reaches New England just as Columbus is approaching the shore. The traveler continues his journey as he rows out into the Atlantic Ocean and a new adventure.

Thematic Material

This is a wordless book that includes many details about past and present life in America. It is part of the series of journey books that includes *Anno's Italy* (Collins, 1978); *Anno's Journey* (Collins-World, 1977); and *Anno's Britain* (Philomel, 1982).

Book Talk Material and Activities

Wordless books offer children many opportunities for close observation, imaginative interpretation, and creative writing. In *Anno's U.S.A.* there are many familiar American characters and landmarks for children to find. This and other journey books in the series are especially good to share with children in the upper elementary grades, because they build on a basic knowledge of history and geography. Even junior and senior high school students would enjoy the humor and history in these books.

Anno's journey books could be available in a library or classroom for students to examine and write about. Children enjoy writing about the same picture and then comparing their stories. In the process, they learn from and about each other. They talk about trips that they have taken and what they have seen. They often ask for other books about the place and time in the picture, so that they will be able to identify more details. Some children compete to find the most hidden details in a picture. Many teachers have correlated these books with the social studies curriculum. Other wordless books by Anno also encourage children to study the illustrations carefully. These books allow children to use their own imagination and create their own stories. A display of Anno's books would attract both children and adults.

Related Titles

Anno's Alphabet: An Adventure in Imagination written and illustrated by Mitsumasa Anno. Crowell, 1974. Each letter of the alphabet has been drawn to look like it has been carved out of wood and is paired with a drawing of an object that represents that letter. The borders around each letter and object have more objects hidden in the foliage.

Anno's Animals written and illustrated by Mitsumasa Anno. Collins, 1977. A wordless book where animals are hidden in the leaves and trees in the forest. The final page tells what an observant person should have been able to find.

Anno's Counting House written and illustrated by Mitsumasa Anno. Philomel, 1982. Instructions are included for how to use this book to play a counting game. Addition, subtraction, and counting are some of the skills that are developed as children play the game.

Anno's Flea Market written and illustrated by Mitsumasa Anno. Philomel, 1984. Many familiar figures appear in these intricate illustrations of a flea market. Look for Laurel and Hardy by the vegetables and for Alice (from Wonderland) wandering through the tools. The time period of the flea market changes with each page.

Anno's Magical ABC: An Anamorphic Alphabet written and illustrated by Mitsumasa Anno and Masaichiro Anno. Philomel, 1980. Two sheets of mirror paper, a reflecting silver sheet (included with the book), must be used to turn each misshapen illustration into one that is in more normal perspective. The capital letters of the alphabet are illustrated in one half of the book and then the book is reversed to illustrate the lowercase letters. Instructions are included on "How to Do an Anamorphic Drawing."

In Shadowland written and illustrated by Mitsumasa Anno. Orchard, 1988. Anno has created two worlds, a real one and a shadow world. Only one person, the watchman, can cross between the two. One day, he leaves Shadowland to help a little match girl, and when he returns, he brings her with him. The unusual illustrations of Shadowland are cut from a single piece of paper.

Topsy-Turvies: Pictures to Stretch the Imagination written and illustrated by Mitsumasa Anno. Walker/Weatherhill, 1970. In this book, shifting perspectives and visual tricks challenge the viewer to study each picture. Anno's *Upside-Downers: More Pictures to Stretch the Imagination* (Weatherhill, 1971) continues the visual challenge.

About the Author and Illustrator

ANNO, MITSUMASA
Fourth Book of Junior Authors and Illustrators, ed. by Doris de Montreville and Elizabeth D. Crawford. Wilson, 1978, pp. 11–12.
Illustrators of Children's Books: 1967–1976, Vol. IV, comp. by Lee Kingman, Grace Allen Hogarth, and Harriet Grimby. Horn Book, 1978, pp. 55–56.
Something about the Author, ed. by Anne Commire. Gale, 1973, Vol. 5, pp. 6–7; 1985, Vol. 38, pp. 24–32.

Bennett, Olivia. *A Family in Brazil*
Photographs by Liba Taylor. Lerner, 1986
Suggested Use Level: Gr. 3–4   Reading Level: Gr. 8

Plot Summary

Eliane Leonardelli lives with her family in Sao Marcos, Brazil, which is in southern Brazil. Her father's job as a truck driver means that he is often away from home. Eliane and her brother and sister work to make their father's time at home special. With their mother, they plan a Sunday barbecue (*churrascou*), which is cooked in a small room beside the house. Eliane's father cooks the meat, usually beef from the nearby cattle ranches, on skewers. After the meal, the family often watches soccer on television. Attending Mass at the Catholic church or going to the village festival are also common Sunday activities.

The Leonardelli family is very close to other relatives. Some of Eliane's relatives work at local businesses, such as the winery, the plastic factory, and the glass factory, and others work in their homes. Eliane often helps her grandmother on her farm, where there are chickens, rabbits, cows, and pigs. Sometimes Eliane packs grapes and figs that her grandmother has grown. Carnival, which is right before Lent, is a special time for Eliane, her family, and friends, as they celebrate with music, dancing, food, costumes, and parades.

Thematic Material

The information in this nonfiction book is current and up-to-date. By focusing on just one family, children learn specific details about everyday life in Brazil.

Book Talk Material and Activities

Books like *A Family in Brazil* and others in this Families the World Over series provide information about everyday life in other countries. They help children see the similarities and differences between people and places and are often the focus of social studies programs. A culminating activity for the study of other countries could be an all-school program, such as an "International Night." Each class or group picks a country to study and then learns about the daily life, food, songs, stories, climate, animals, industry, and activities in that country. As many library resources are used, especially nonfiction and reference books, this can be a timely opportunity for discussing encyclopedias, almanacs, and atlases. Often, guest speakers from the community are invited to discuss their visits to the country, or to demonstrate crafts, music, dance, or cooking. Student projects could be displayed at the program, and each group could perform songs and dances. After the program, the children and their guests could sample some foods from the different countries, perhaps as part of a fund-raising project for a parent organization.

School or public librarians should be especially aware of such special programs as an "International Night" that might be part of school, church, or club activities. Services such as a speaker's bureau or an up-to-date vertical file are very useful to these groups. Book selection and programming are much more effective if they are coordinated with the needs of community groups.

Related Titles

Brazil by Wilbur Cross and Susanna Cross. Photographs. Childrens, 1984. The Enchantment of the World series is most appropriate for students in the upper elementary and middle grades, also providing good background information for teachers and librarians as they work with younger children.

Children Are Children Are Children: An Activity Approach to Exploring Brazil, France, Iran, Japan, Nigeria and the U.S.S.R. by Ann Cole, Carolyn Haas, Elizabeth Heller, and Betty Weinberger. Illustrated by Lois Axeman. Little, Brown, 1978. Any study of Brazil would be enhanced by some of the projects in this book, such as making a terrarium to simulate an Amazon rain forest or making a *jangada* (fisherman's raft). Children will also enjoy making and testing some of the recipes, like *cocadas* (coconut candy).

The Legend of the Palm Tree written by Margarida Estrela Bandeira Duarte. Illustrated by Paulo Werneck. Grosset, 1968. A legend from Brazil tells of a drought that destroyed everyone in a tribe except a boy and his parents, who travel in search of a new land. On the trip the boy encounters a magic palm tree that helps him and his parents survive.

South America by D. V. Georges. Photographs and drawings. Childrens, 1986. "The Amazon Rain Forest" and "Highlights of Brazil" are two chapters in this book, which is part of the New True Book series and accessible to younger readers. The contents, maps, glossary, and index make it a good nonfiction book for beginners.

Take a Trip to Brazil by Keith Lye. Photographs. Watts, 1984. Another series of books for young readers that focuses on countries. Color photographs help make this a very attractive book. Other books in the series include information on China, Thailand, Greece, and Russia.

Branley, Franklyn M. *Comets*
Illus. by Giulio Maestro. Crowell, 1984; pap., Harper & Row, 1985
Suggested Use Level: Gr. 1–4   Reading Level: Gr. 3

Plot Summary

Comets are described relative to other objects in the solar system. The formation of comets, their movement, and the most famous comet, Halley's, are discussed. Some superstitions about comets are included. The importance of the gravity of the sun and the planets is also presented.

Thematic Material

This is a nonfiction science book about comets that includes some general information about outer space and the Earth's solar system. It is part of the Let's-Read-and-Find-Out series and is designed as an introductory nonfiction book for beginning readers.

Book Talk Material and Activities

Just as there are fiction books that are part of a series (see Harry Allard and James Marshall's *Miss Nelson Has a Field Day,* Chapter 4), there are also nonfiction series such as the Let's-Read-and-Find-Out series. *Comets* has a relatively brief text and clearly labeled illustrations depicting the information in the text. Ample space between words and lines makes the print easier for younger readers to focus on. Librarians who use this book in a story or book talk program could show other books in the series, such as *What Happens to a Hamburger; Gravity Is a Mystery; Wild and Woolly Mammoths;* and *Flash, Crash, Rumble, and Roll.* A number of these titles have been recently revised and updated, and librarians might want to show some of the improvements that have been made. It is an excellent opportunity to illustrate how science books are kept up-to-date and how revisions are issued as information changes.

Librarians and teachers could plan a program to talk about other nonfiction series. Working in small groups children can examine several books in a series and list the features of the series. (Sample books from different series can be found in the "Related Titles" section.) This will help children develop their knowledge about books and think about the ways in which different books can meet their reading and research needs. While working together, children can talk about books and make decisions about their strengths and weaknesses. When examining nonfiction books, children can look for such research aids as a contents, an index, a glossary, and appendixes. The books in the Let's-Read-and-Find-Out series do not have these aids, and children can discuss why, looking at the needs of beginning readers versus the needs of researchers.

Audiovisual Adaptation

Comets. Listening Library, cassette/book, 1987.

Related Titles

Egg to Chick by Millicent E. Selsam. Illustrated by Barbara Wolff. Harper & Row, 1970. A Science I Can Read book similar in format to the

I Can Read fiction books. The print is large with ample space between words and lines for beginning readers to focus on the print. Detailed scientific information about chickens and eggs is presented in the text and in the large illustrations.

Flash, Crash, Rumble, and Roll (revised edition) by Franklyn M. Branley. Illustrated by Barbara Emberley and Ed Emberley. Crowell, 1985. Basic information about weather and storms. The revised edition has updated illustrations, which are more colorful than those in the original edition.

Football, You Are the Coach by Nate Aaseng. Photographs and drawings. Lerner, 1983. One of the You Are the Coach books, a series that also includes books about baseball and hockey. In these books, students are given a sports scenario and then must decide the correct play. Information about actual games is provided, and the "solution" is listed in a section called "Here's What Happened." Once children find these books, they like to read them all. They enjoy the similarity to the Choose Your Own Adventure series and the Encyclopedia Brown fiction series.

The Foxes by Mark E. Ahlstrom. Photographs and drawings. Crestwood, 1983. Part of the Wildlife, Habits, and Habitat series, which also has focused on the grizzly bear, raccoon, and alligator, among other animals. Like books in the Wonders of . . . series (see *Wonders of Foxes*), *The Foxes* has reference aids (contents, glossary, maps) that make it a useful book for young researchers.

Gravity Is a Mystery (revised edition) by Franklyn M. Branley. Illustrated by Don Madden. Crowell, 1986. Gravity is a difficult concept for many children in the primary grades. The text and illustrations in this book provide clear information using examples that young children can understand.

Pioneers by Dennis B. Fradin. Photographs and drawings. Childrens, 1984. The books in the New True Book series cover a variety of topics, including airplanes, animals, countries, and nature. They are a good introduction to nonfiction books, because they have a contents, index, and glossary. In *Pioneers,* children can read about the reasons many people became pioneers and learn about some well-known ones.

What Happens to a Hamburger (revised edition) by Paul Showers. Illustrated by Anne Rockwell. Crowell, 1985. Children learn about the digestive process as they read this book and perform some of the suggested activities. The illustrations are colorful and clearly labeled to aid in explaining concepts in the text.

Wild and Woolly Mammoths written and illustrated by Aliki. Crowell,

1977. Prehistoric times are fascinating to children, so a book with facts that they can read and understand will be exciting to them. It also contains a great deal of information about how people lived and survived in the Stone Age.

Wonders of Foxes by Sigmund A. Lavine. Photographs and drawings. Dodd, Mead, 1986. The books in the Wonders of . . . series follow a similar pattern in the presentation of information. They each focus on an animal and give facts about the way of life, physical characteristics, and behavior of that animal. Some of the folklore or superstition surrounding the animal is also given. Other animals that have been presented include badgers, giraffes, pigs, sharks, and turkeys. The books have a contents and an index, and they are illustrated with black-and-white photographs and drawings. Children in the upper elementary grades find this series useful for research.

About the Author and Illustrator

BRANLEY, FRANKLYN M.
More Junior Authors, ed. by Muriel Fuller. Wilson, 1963, pp. 24–25.
Something about the Author, ed. by Anne Commire. Gale, 1973, Vol. 4, pp. 32–34.
MAESTRO, GIULIO
Authors of Books for Young People: Supplement to the Second Edition, by Martha E. Ward and Dorothy Marquardt. Scarecrow, 1979, p. 183.
Something about the Author, ed. by Anne Commire. Gale, 1976, Vol. 8, pp. 123–124.

Branley, Franklyn M. *What the Moon Is Like*
Illus. by True Kelley. Crowell, 1986; pap., Harper, 1986
Suggested Use Level: Gr. K–3   Reading Level: Gr. 3

Plot Summary

From the Earth, the moon seems to have shadows that many have said are shapes of animals and faces. Learning more about the moon's surface explains what causes the shadows seen from the Earth. Drawings and photographs depict the surface of the moon, showing the craters and seas. Information about the manned voyages to the moon is provided, including a map showing the locations of the six lunar landings. The astronauts who made these voyages and investigated the surface of the moon brought back rock samples and verified that there is no water or life on the moon. These astronauts needed to wear space suits for life support as well as protection from the wide variations in temperature on the moon. A comparison between the Earth and the moon provides information about gravity, weather, and atmosphere. Possibilities for future exploration and colonization of the moon are suggested.

Thematic Material

This nonfiction book presents information about the moon, contrasting it with the Earth, as well as about lunar explorations. It is part of the Let's-Read-and-Find-Out series.

Book Talk Material and Activities

The moon, the planets, the sun, and outer space are popular subjects with children. In order to ensure that books and other literature provide accurate information, librarians need to evaluate and update their collections in this area. *What the Moon Is Like* provides current information in a format that is accessible to children in the primary grades. An earlier version of the book was published in 1963, long before the lunar expeditions, but the publishers do not call the 1986 publication a revised edition because the earlier version was completely rewritten and reillustrated. When sharing *What the Moon Is Like* with children, teachers and librarians could read the jacket information, which discusses some of the changes that were made. Children could suggest other subject areas that need to be revised and updated, such as medicine and sports.

The illustrations in *What the Moon Is Like* include drawings and photographs. Seymour Simon's books about space, for example, *Earth* and *The Moon*, are illustrated primarily with photographs and could be booktalked to encourage children to read more about the planets and outer space.

Audiovisual Adaptation

What the Moon Is Like. Listening Library, cassette/book, 1987.

Related Titles

Earth by Seymour Simon. Photographs. Four Winds, 1984. The information about Earth in this book provides a good contrast to the details in *What the Moon Is Like*. Children could be asked to describe the similarities and differences between Earth and its moon.

The Long View into Space by Seymour Simon. Photographs. Crown,

1979. Black-and-white photographs combine with a clearly written text to describe the universe. Part of the book focuses on Earth and the moon.

The Moon by Seymour Simon. Photographs. Four Winds, 1984. The text in *The Moon* could add to children's knowledge of Earth's satellite. The black-and-white photographs could be contrasted with the illustrations and photographs in *What the Moon Is Like*.

The Moon Seems to Change, revised edition by Franklyn M. Branley. Illustrated by Barbara Emberley and Ed Emberley. Crowell, 1987. In contrast to *What the Moon Is Like*, which provides information about the moon and its surface, *The Moon Seems to Change* provides information about how the moon looks from Earth.

Moon, Sun, and Stars by John Lewellen. Photographs and drawings. Childrens, 1981. The focus here is on the relationship between Earth, the moon, and the sun. Chapters include "How the Moon Moves" and "Earth Is a Planet." The simple text makes the book accessible to beginning readers.

The Sun by Seymour Simon. Photographs and drawings. Morrow, 1986. Color photographs depict some of the dramatic occurrences on the sun's surface, including "prominences," which are eruptions of magnetic forces. Children could be asked to compare the sun's surface with that of the moon.

About the Author and Illustrator

BRANLEY, FRANKLYN M.
More Junior Authors, ed. by Muriel Fuller. Wilson, 1963, pp. 24–25.
Something about the Author, ed. by Anne Commire. Gale, 1973, Vol. 4, pp. 32–34.
KELLEY, TRUE
Something about the Author, ed. by Anne Commire. Gale, 1985, Vol. 35, p. 120; 1985, Vol. 41, pp. 114–116.

Bunting, Eve. *Clancy's Coat*
Illus. by Lorinda Bryan Cauley. Warne, 1984
Suggested Use Level: Gr. 1–3   Reading Level: Gr. 5

Plot Summary

One morning, Tippitt is surprised to see Clancy coming up the road to his house. Ever since Tippitt's cow got into Clancy's garden, the two former friends have been feuding. Tippitt is a tailor and Clancy has decided that, despite their differences, he will let Tippitt mend his coat. The two men snap at each other as they talk about the coat, but Tippitt agrees to do the work by the following Saturday. It is unusually cold during the week and Tippitt uses Clancy's coat to cover his cow, so it is not ready on Saturday. To distract Clancy's attention from the coat, Tippitt gives him a cup of tea and promises to be finished with the coat in another week. During the week, however, it is cold again, and Tippitt uses the coat to cover a broken window. Again, it is not ready on Saturday, or the next or the next. With each passing week, the two men renew their friendship as they share food and memories. At the end of the book, the coat is still not mended, but the friendship is.

Thematic Material

This story, set in Ireland, is about friendship. Even though Tippitt and Clancy have had an argument, they realize that their friendship is still important to them. There is humor in this story, as Tippitt must make up new excuses for why the coat is not ready.

Book Talk Material and Activities

Most familiar stories from Ireland are folktales involving leprechauns or telling about legendary figures like Fin M'Coul. *Clancy's Coat* is a more contemporary story of friendship. Tippitt and Clancy continue to be angry with each other long after the original problem has been solved. The book could be compared to other stories about friendship, such as *Best Friends* by Steven Kellogg (see Chapter 1).

Clancy's Coat is a good story to read aloud or tell as part of a program on Ireland. The expressive cadence of the conversations between Clancy and Tippitt captures the feeling of the language and provides a challenge to a storyteller or reader. The storyteller will need to practice to tell the story effectively. Even though the book does not include many details about Ireland, it is still a good springboard to a study of the country's history and geography. Irish names and references to the weather and food provide a starting point for additional study, and the humor of the story will capture children's interest.

Related Titles

Daniel O'Rourke: An Irish Tale told and illustrated by Gerald Mc-Dermott. Viking, 1986. Daniel O'Rourke goes to a party, stuffs himself with food, and dances until he can dance no more. On the way home, he has a series of unusual adventures, only to find that they are all part of a dream.

A Family in Ireland by Tom Moran. Photographs. Lerner, 1986. By looking at the experiences of one specific family living near a seaside resort town on Galway Bay, children learn about the schools in Ireland, how the drivers stay on the left side of the road, and the kind of work that is available. Details about the climate, countryside, and food are also presented. Color photographs make this a very attractive book, and charts of pronunciation and additional facts are also useful.

Fin M'Coul: The Giant of Knockmany Hill retold and illustrated by Tomie de Paola. Holiday House, 1981. In de Paola's lively version of the legend of this Irish giant, Fin and his wife, Oonagh, outwit the giant Cucullin.

The Leprechaun's Story by Richard Kennedy. Illustrated by Marcia Sewell. Dutton, 1979. A tradesman meets a leprechaun and, of course, is entitled to his pot of god. The man keeps his eyes on the leprechaun while the leprechaun tries to trick the man into looking away from him. They travel through many dangers, but the man never looks away, until the leprechaun tells him a sad story that makes him close his eyes and cry.

The Republic of Ireland by Dennis B. Fradin. Photographs. Childrens, 1984. Part of the Enchantment of the World series, this book is most appropriate for children in the upper elementary and middle grades, but it will provide good background information for teachers and librarians. Facts about the history, geography, and people are included.

About the Author and Illustrator

BUNTING, EVE (ANNE EVELYN BUNTING)
Authors of Books for Young People: Supplement to the Second Edition, by Martha E. Ward and Dorothy Marquardt. Scarecrow, 1979, p. 36.
Fifth Book of Junior Authors and Illustrators, ed. by Sally Holmes Holtze. Wilson, 1983, pp. 60–61.
Something about the Author, ed. by Anne Commire. Gale, 1980, Vol. 18, pp. 38–39.
CAULEY, LORINDA BRYAN
Something about the Author, ed. by Anne Commire. Gale, 1986, Vol. 43, p. 53; 1987, Vol. 46, pp. 49–50.

Carrick, Carol. *Dark and Full of Secrets*
Illus. by Donald Carrick. Clarion, 1984; pap., 1987
Suggested Use Level: Gr. 1–2   Reading Level: Gr. 4

Plot Summary

Christopher and his father go out on the pond in the canoe. When Christopher's father suggests that they go swimming later, Christopher expresses his fear of the shadows at the bottom of the pond. Christopher's father is somewhat amused by his fears and buys them both snorkeling equipment to show Christopher that there is nothing to be afraid of. When they go snorkeling together, Christopher begins to see some of the beauty of the pond. Now that he can see the bottom of the pond, he realizes that his fears were groundless. Later in the day, Christopher goes snorkeling on his own while his father watches from the porch. He follows a bass as it swims along at the bottom of the pond. When Christopher stops to clear the water from his mask, he finds that he has drifted out too far. As Christopher struggles in the water and begins to cough, his dog, Ben, swims up beside him. Christopher grabs his tail and is towed to where he can stand up. Christopher's father comes down from the porch to help him, and he reminds Christopher of how important it is to be careful in the water. Even though Christopher is subdued by his experience, he tells his father of some of the wonderful things that he has seen.

Thematic Material

In this story, which is part of a series of stories about Christopher and his family, Christopher must face his fear of the pond and overcome it.

Book Talk Material and Activities

All of the books about Christopher and his family focus on their experiences at their summer cottage. They are warm family stories that convey a feeling of respect for the beauty of nature. In *Dark and Full of Secrets*, Christopher is afraid of the pond because he cannot see the bottom. He is afraid of the unknown. Once he sees the bottom of the pond, he is fascinated by the plants and animals that he sees. He forgets his fears and wants to explore and learn more about this underwater world. After reading *Dark and Full of Secrets* to children, librarians and teachers could booktalk the other books about Christopher and his family. They could highlight some of the themes presented in these books, including the death of a pet (*The Accident*), accepting a new pet (*The Foundling*), and facing new situations (*Sleep Out*).

Related Titles

Here are some other books about Christopher and his family written by Carol Carrick and illustrated by Donald Carrick.

The Accident. Clarion, 1976. Christopher's dog, Bodger, is accidentally hit by a truck and dies. Although his parents try to comfort him, it takes some time for Christopher to adjust to his loss.

Ben and the Porcupine. Houghton Mifflin, 1981. Christopher's new dog, Ben, finds a porcupine in the woods and will not leave it alone. When Ben comes home with quills in his nose, Christopher is upset. He worries that Ben will not be safe on the island, but then he realizes that Ben will have to learn to adjust to the island and the creatures who live there.

The Foundling. Clarion, 1977. Ever since his dog, Bodger, was killed (*The Accident*), Christopher's parents have wondered if he might want another dog. His father takes him to the animal shelter, but Christopher cannot accept another dog. Back at their house, Christopher notices a puppy that has strayed over from the neighbor's house. When Christopher takes the dog to his neighbor, he finds that the puppy does not belong there. Christopher decides to keep the puppy, and names him Ben.

Lost in the Storm. Houghton Mifflin, 1974. Christopher and his dog, Bodger, take the ferry out to the island to visit Christopher's friend, Gray. Out on the island, the boys have fun playing on the beach. When a storm begins, they realize that Bodger is not with them. Christopher and Gray stay in the house and worry about Bodger, even though Gray's parents try to reassure them. In the morning, the boys search for Bodger and are happy when they find that he is safe.

Sleep Out. Seabury, 1973. Christopher has a new sleeping bag and he cannot wait to leave the city for a vacation at the cottage in the country. Once there, Christopher takes his sleeping bag, hikes into the woods, and picks a camping place. Although it is exciting to be outside at night, Christopher feels lonely after a while. Then, the night noises scare him. When it begins to rain, he hurries to an abandoned house and spends the night there, joined by his dog, Bodger. The next morning, he returns home, and his father agrees that they will pitch a tent and sleep out together.

The Washout. Clarion, 1978. Christopher and his mother are already at the family's vacation cottage in the country. Christopher's father is still at work in the city. During their first night there, a big storm knocks down trees and power lines and the road is washed out. Christopher promises to be careful and is given permission to try to get to town to get help and pick up some food. After several hours, he manages to reach the general store. One of the men takes him back to where the road is washed out and helps him across the creek. His mother has been waiting there, worrying about him. Although Christopher is sorry to have worried her, he is proud of his accomplishment.

About the Author and Illustrator

CARRICK, CAROL
Fourth Book of Junior Authors and Illustrators, ed. by Doris de Montreville and Elizabeth D. Crawford. Wilson, 1978, pp. 69–71.
Something about the Author, ed. by Anne Commire. Gale, 1975, Vol. 7, pp. 39–40.
CARRICK, DONALD
Fourth Book of Junior Authors and Illustrators, ed. by Doris de Montreville and Elizabeth D. Crawford. Wilson, 1978, pp. 71–72.
Illustrators of Children's Books: 1967–1976, Vol. IV, comp. by Lee Kingman, Grace Allen Hogarth, and Harriet Quimby. Horn Book, 1978, pp. xiii, 106, 183.
Something about the Author, ed. by Anne Commire. Gale, 1975, Vol. 7, p. 40.

Cazet, Denys. *A Fish in His Pocket*
Illus. by the author. Orchard, 1987
Suggested Use Level: Gr. K–3   Reading Level: Gr. 3

Plot Summary

A young bear named Russell leaves home and walks to school. Along the way, he stops at the pond to look at the fish. His math book falls out of his book bag and into the water, so Russell pulls it out and takes the soggy book to school. His teacher is understanding but reminds Russell to be more careful. While Russell is cleaning out his book, he finds a dead fish, and is even more upset by what has happened. Russell puts the dead fish in his pocket and tries to think of what to do. Throughout the day, Russell is pensive and withdrawn. During art time, Russell decides what to do. After school, he returns to the pond and, placing the fish on a paper boat that he has made, he launches the boat, which he has named "Take Care."

Thematic Material

Russell learns about death and the importance of being careful with living things. He sees the cycle of life and death in nature. Ecology and caring for the environment are related themes in this book.

Book Talk Material and Activities

Animals are a part of the science program and activities in many schools and libraries. Many classrooms have aquariums and cages for gerbils, hamsters, and other small pets. When teachers and librarians have to discuss the death of one of these creatures, a book like *A Fish in His Pocket* can help children talk about their feelings. Other books, like *The Accident, The Dead Bird,* and *The Tenth Good Thing about Barney,* also deal with the death of an animal.

In many communities, children visit nature centers and parks as part of school, library, or club programs. *A Fish in His Pocket* could promote a discussion about nature and ecology—children often want to pick plants or take home small animals that they have found. Russell's message "Take Care" would help the children think about the needs of the natural world and what they can do to keep their environment clean and to protect the animals that live around them. Books about ecology and conservation could be displayed in the library.

Related Titles

The Accident by Carol Carrick. Illustrated by Donald Carrick. Clarion, 1976. When Christopher's dog is hit by a truck, Christopher cannot accept his loss. It takes much understanding and patience from Christopher's family before he begins to deal with his grief.

The Dead Bird by Margaret Wise Brown. Illustrated by Remy Charlip. Young Scott, 1958. A group of children finds a dead bird and they decide to bury it. They hold a ceremony to commemorate the bird. Like Russell in *A Fish in His Pocket,* these children feel chastened by their encounter with death.

The Dead Tree by Alvin Tresselt. Illustrated by Charles Robinson. Parent's Magazine Press, 1972. Beautiful illustrations and a poetic text combine to describe the life cycle of an oak tree. Even as the tree decays, it provides food and a home for other creatures in the forest. Around the tree, acorns begin to sprout and grow.

The Desert Is Theirs by Byrd Baylor. Illustrated by Peter Parnall. Scribner, 1975. A book that celebrates the plants and animals of the desert, describing the respect that desert people feel for this environment and how they protect it.

Oak and Company by Richard Mabey. Illustrated by Clare Roberts. Greenwillow, 1983. The life story of an oak includes information about the creatures that depend on the tree for food and shelter.

Professor Noah's Spaceship written and illustrated by Brian Wildsmith. Oxford University Press, 1980. The animals are distressed by the increasing pollution of their environment. Professor Noah offers to take them with him in his spaceship to look for another place to live. As in *A Fish in His Pocket,* this story stresses the importance of caring for the natural world.

The Tenth Good Thing about Barney by Judith Viorst. Illustrated by Erik Blegvad. Atheneum, 1971. When a little boy's cat, Barney, dies, he tries to think of 10 good things that he remembers about him. His family helps him cope with his grief and to discover one last good thing about Barney.

About the Author and Illustrator

CAZET, DENYS
Something about the Author, ed. by Anne Commire. Gale, 1985, Vol. 41, p. 73; 1988, Vol. 52, pp. 26–28.

Daly, Niki. *Not So Fast Songololo*
Illus. by the author. Atheneum, 1985; pap., Penguin, 1987
Suggested Use Level: Gr. 1–4   Reading Level: Gr. 3

Plot Summary

Malusi lives with his family near a big city in South Africa. There are many people in his family and his home is full of noise and movement.

Being one of the younger children means that Malusi wears the old shoes—"tackies"—that his brother Mongi has outgrown. Today Malusi is going to the city with his grandmother, Gogo. Malusi and Gogo move slowly to the bus stop.

In the city, the noise and traffic are distracting, but so are the displays in the store windows. Malusi sees toys, games, and bright red shoes. After Gogo is finished with her shopping, she and Malusi walk past the display windows again. Seeing the new shoes, Gogo looks at Malusi's old "tackies" and buys him a new pair. Malusi is so proud of his new shoes that he quickly walks ahead of Gogo, until she uses her special nickname for him and calls, "Not so fast, Songololo." They ride home on the bus sharing the satisfaction of their day together.

Thematic Material

Not So Fast Songololo takes place in South Africa and details the every-day life of Malusi and his loving black family. Special emphasis is given to the relationship between Malusi and his grandmother.

Book Talk Material and Activities

This book includes some language and details from its South African setting, but it is basically a delightful story of a little boy and his grand-mother. Malusi is proud to help his grandmother. He likes to move slowly and so does she. They enjoy their time together. Most children will identify with how Malusi feels about his old, hand-me-down tennis shoes, but they won't be familiar with the word "tackies" and will enjoy adding the word to their vocabularies. Teachers and librarians often help children make lists and labels of familiar items, and "tackies" could be added to the footwear list (for example, boots, tennis shoes, high tops, loafers, and so on).

Discussions could focus on the relationship between Malusi and his grandmother. Ask children to tell how Malusi's grandmother makes him feel special and about a time when someone made them feel special. This kind of discussion helps children relate Malusi's story to their own lives. As with any story set in another country, the illustrations here could be compared with the children's familiar surroundings. Older children could coordinate their reading of this book with current events studies of South Africa, examining the illustrations for indications of apartheid (for example, all the people on the bus are black).

Related Titles

Abiyoyo: Based on a South African Lullaby and Folk Song by Pete Seeger. Illustrated by Michael Hays. Macmillan, 1986. A boy and his father are outcasts until they find the way to trick Abiyoyo, the giant.

Jafta by Hugh Lewin. Illustrated by Lisa Kopper. Carolrhoda, 1981. In this first book in a series about Jafta and his family, aspects of Jafta's lively personality are compared with animals that are a familiar part of his South African home. Compare Jafta's experiences to Malusi's in *Not So Fast Songololo.*

Jafta and the Wedding by Hugh Lewin. Illustrated by Lisa Kopper. Carolrhoda, 1981. Jafta and other village children do a "songololo" dance. ("Songololo" is defined at the end of the book as "taken from the Zulu word for centipede or millipede.") Many children will enjoy seeing Songololo's name in another story.

Jafta—The Journey by Hugh Lewin. Illustrated by Lisa Kopper. Carolrhoda, 1983. Jafta is going to visit his father. It is not an easy trip, but everyone works together and Jafta feels the joy of being held in his father's arms.

Jafta—The Town by Hugh Lewin. Illustrated by Lisa Kopper. Carolrhoda, 1983. Jafta and his mother have traveled to town for the funeral of an uncle. Jafta misses the animals and birds that he is used to, but he is happy to see his father, who must live in town in order to have a job.

Jafta's Father by Hugh Lewin. Illustrated by Lisa Kopper. Carolrhoda, 1981. Jafta's father lives in town, where there is work. He can only come home for a visit every few months. Jafta thinks of how much he misses his father and how much he loves him.

Jafta's Mother by Hugh Lewin. Illustrated by Lisa Kopper. Carolrhoda, 1981. Jafta describes his mother and the activities that are part of her life. Unusual terms that are used in the story, such as "hoopoe" (a bird) and "mealies" (corn-on-the-cob), are explained on the last page of the book.

About the Author and Illustrator

DALY, NIKI (NICHOLAS)
Something about the Author, ed. by Anne Commire. Gale, 1985, Vol. 37, pp. 52–54.

Friedman, Ina R. *How My Parents Learned to Eat*
Illus. by Allen Say. Houghton Mifflin, 1984; pap., 1987
Suggested Use Level: Gr. 1–3   Reading Level: Gr. 2

Plot Summary

A young girl whose mother is Japanese and whose father is American tells about her family. Her parents met in Japan when her father was serving in the navy. As her parents' relationship slowly developed, each was apprehensive about eating with the other. Each worried about offending the other by not knowing the correct customs and behaviors. When the sailor received his orders to leave, he decided to learn how to eat with chopsticks. Meanwhile, the schoolgirl decided to learn about Western ways. When they finally went to dinner together, they realized that they had been sharing the same worries. The daughter's reminiscence explains why her family still sometimes eats with chopsticks and sometimes with knives and forks.

Thematic Material

Children are introduced to another way of life here—another culture with different manners and customs. They see that, despite differences, people from different backgrounds can learn to get along. This book is also a reminiscence, as the young girl shares a family memory.

Book Talk Material and Activities

How My Parents Learned to Eat is an opportunity to explore Japanese culture and to talk about family history. Although the story is a reminiscence, it is not set in the distant past. Many details about the manners and customs in Japan are still relevant today.

Libraries often offer travel programs for adults and keep a file on available speakers who have traveled or lived in Japan. A speaker could be invited to meet with a group of children either at the public or school library. Preparing some Japanese food, using chopsticks, and learning some simple Japanese phrases could all be part of the program. Some children may want to do more research on Japan. Additional resources about Japan could then be displayed and booktalked. *Children Are Children Are Children* is a collection of activities, projects, and information about six countries. The presentation on Japan includes details on a

Japanese tea ceremony, some recipes, several games and crafts, and information about the country and language. The facts about the country need to be updated but the rest of the information would be very helpful for planning a program.

Say's illustrations in *How My Parents Learned to Eat* provide many additional details about Japan that children should be encouraged to observe and discuss. Some questions could include: Looking at the setting, what is different from our homes? What is similar? How does the clothing compare to what we wear? Looking at the first and last pages, can you describe what you observe?

Audiovisual Adaptation

How My Parents Learned to Eat. "Reading Rainbow." Great Plains National Instructional Television Library, videorecording, 1986.

Related Titles

The Bicycle Man written and illustrated by Allen Say. Houghton Mifflin, 1982. Two American soldiers visit the Japanese school on Sportsday and add to the fun of that special day in this memoir of the author's experience as a first-grader. Compare Allen Say's illustrations in this book with those in *How My Parents Learned to Eat.*

Children Are Children Are Children: An Activity Approach to Exploring Brazil, France, Iran, Japan, Nigeria and the U.S.S.R. by Ann Cole, Carolyn Haas, Elizabeth Heller, and Betty Weinberger. Illustrated by Lois Axeman. Little, Brown, 1978. Great suggestions for projects and activities that would extend children's understanding of these countries. Plan a Japanese festival to celebrate Shogatsu (New Year's Day) or Tanabata (Festival of the Stars).

Cooking the Japanese Way by Reiko Weston. Photographs by Robert L. Wolfe and Diane Wolfe. Lerner, 1983. After a brief introductory overview of Japan, Weston presents recipes for some typical Japanese foods. Sections describing "A Japanese Table" and "Eating with Chopsticks" could be compared with *How My Parents Learned to Eat.*

A Family in Japan by Peter Otto Jacobsen and Preben Sejer Kristensen. Bookwright, 1984. The everyday experiences of one family in Japan are the focus here. Information is given about their home, work, school, food, and recreation.

Journey to Japan by Joan Knight. Illustrated by Kinuko Craft. Viking, 1986. Children are fascinated by pop-up books, and this one gives some basic information about Japanese life and customs. Paper engineering demonstrates the movement on an assembly line, a drum being played at a festival, and workers exercising.

Take a Trip to Japan written and photographed by Gwynneth Ashby. Watts, 1980. Color photographs and a brief text provide an overview of Japan for younger children. Included is a section of facts about Japan.

About the Author and Illustrator

FRIEDMAN, INA R.
Authors of Books for Young People: Supplement to the Second Edition, by Martha E. Ward and Dorothy Marquardt. Scarecrow, 1979, p. 92.
Something about the Author, ed. by Anne Commire. Gale, 1985, Vol. 41, pp. 85–86; 1987, Vol. 49, p. 101.
SAY, ALLEN
Something about the Author, ed. by Anne Commire. Gale, 1982, Vol. 28, p. 179.

Gibbons, Gail. *Zoo*
Illus. by the author. Crowell, 1987
Suggested Use Level: Gr. K–3   Reading Level: Gr. 5

Plot Summary

Colorful illustrations and a clearly written text combine to present information about the jobs and responsibilities at the zoo. Some of the preparations for the visitors include opening the sales booth and cleaning the exhibit areas. Once the visitors enter the zoo, the keepers have other jobs to do, such as preparing the food for the different animals. They also monitor the behavior of the animals and assist them when they are sick or injured. The managers of the zoo work hard to provide each animal with an appropriate environment, and they plan special exhibits to meet the needs of different visitors, like having a farm display where young children can visit and feed some familiar animals. As the visitors leave the zoo, the workers check that everything is secure, and a guard patrols the zoo throughout the night.

Thematic Material

The basic information in this nonfiction book about a typical day at the zoo includes facts about the workers at the zoo and the jobs they do.

Book Talk Material and Activities

Going to the zoo is an exciting experience for young children. Often, a school or library will organize a trip to the zoo or invite a speaker to give a program on zoo animals. Gail Gibbons's *Zoo* could be read before one of these activities to provide children with background information about the zoo. After the children have visited the zoo, they could make a mural of the different areas at the zoo, showing the animals that they saw, and perhaps write down some of the sounds that the animals made. Children would enjoy illustrating the mural either with their own drawings or with pictures from magazines. They also would enjoy hearing the animal sounds in *Roar and More* and *Jungle Sounds*.

Audiovisual Adaptation

Zoo. Live Oak Media, filmstrip/cassette, 1988.

Related Titles

A Children's Zoo written and illustrated by Tana Hoban. Greenwillow, 1985. Each color photograph of a zoo animal is accompanied by three descriptive words about the animal's behavior and appearance. Some of the animals in the book are the zebra, the seal, the lion, and the elephant. The last page of the book has a chart with more information about the animals, including the kinds of food they eat.

Dear Zoo written and illustrated by Rod Campbell. Four Winds, 1983. The narrator writes the zoo for a pet and receives many zoo animals that aren't suitable as pets, for example, a giraffe. Finally, the zoo sends a puppy. Readers lift flaps to find out what animal has been sent from the zoo.

Jungle Sounds by Colin Hawkins and Jacqui Hawkins. Crown, 1986. Six animals, including a panther and a bear, are depicted in cartoon-style drawings. Each animal is shown making a sound (such as "snarl"), and the children are encouraged to imitate these and other jungle sounds they know.

Roar and More written and illustrated by Karla Kuskin. Harper & Row, 1956. The rhyming text presents 11 animals and their sounds, including the lion and the snake.

Sam Who Never Forgets written and illustrated by Eve Rice. Greenwillow, 1977. Sam is the zookeeper who is responsible for feeding the animals and he never forgets to bring them just what they like best.

Zoo Babies written and photographed by Donna K. Grosvenor. National Geographic Society, 1978. Color photographs show many young animals in the zoo, and the text describes some of their daily activities and how they are cared for.

About the Author and Illustrator

GIBBONS, GAIL
Something about the Author, ed. by Anne Commire. Gale, 1981, Vol. 23, pp. 77–78.

Hopkins, Lee Bennett, ed. *The Sky Is Full of Song*
Illus. by Dirk Zimmer. Harper & Row, 1983; pap., 1987
Suggested Use Level: Gr. 1–4   Reading Level: NA

Plot Summary

The 38 poems in this collection celebrate the seasons. Some of the poems deal with holidays like Thanksgiving and the Fourth of July, and others capture the moods and feelings that come with the changing seasons. Poems about the weather and activities that occur throughout the year are also presented. Included are poems from many well known poets, such as Aileen Fisher, Lilian Moore, David McCord, Gwendolyn Brooks, and Dorothy Aldis.

Thematic Material

The Sky Is Full of Song offers poems that describe the many different moods of the seasons.

Book Talk Material and Activities

Poetry should be an integral part of school and library programs. Many of the poems in this collection could be correlated with seasonal activities and displayed on bulletin boards or charts. Children enjoy illustrating these displays with their own interpretation of the seasons. Aileen Fisher's poem "How?" talks about animal migration and could be a part of science studies. Her poem "Fall Wind" could encourage children to look for signs of fall. Other poems in this collection could be read before group activities. "New Sounds" by Lilian Moore is perfect before a walk in the leaves, and Karla Kuskin's "Days That the Wind Takes Over" is great for a windy day.

Reading poems can enhance story programs and provide a different perspective on a subject. In Gwendolyn Brooks's poem "Tommy," the main character plants a seed and then waits for it to grow. Read the poem with *The Carrot Seed* or "The Garden" from *Frog and Toad Together* and discuss how these characters feel about what they have planted. Or read Ilo Orleans's "The Shadow Tree" along with *A Tree Is Nice* and describe some of the different feelings about trees that come from these authors. All of these poems could be discussed relative to a science study of the seasons, using books like *Sunshine Makes the Seasons* and *A Book of Seasons*.

Related Titles

A Book of Seasons written and illustrated by Alice Provensen and Martin Provensen. Random House, 1976. A picture book that describes the weather and some of the activities that occur in each season.

The Carrot Seed by Ruth Krauss. Illustrated by Crockett Johnson. Harper & Row, 1945. A little boy plants a seed and waits for it to grow. No one in his family is very encouraging. They are all surprised when he grows a very large carrot.

Celebrations by Myra Cohn Livingston. Illustrated by Leonard Everett Fisher. Holiday House, 1985. With 16 holiday poems and paintings, Livingston and Fisher provide for a year of holidays.

A Circle of Seasons by Myra Cohn Livingston. Illustrated by Leonard Everett Fisher. Holiday House, 1982. Poems and paintings capture the mood of the changing seasons. How do the images compare with those in *The Sky Is Full of Song?*

Frog and Toad Together written and illustrated by Arnold Lobel. Harper & Row, 1971. Like Tommy, the title character in Gwendolyn Brooks's poem, Toad is watching his garden, but he is not very patient.

Sunshine Makes the Seasons by Franklyn M. Branley. Illustrated by Giulio Maestro. Crowell, 1985. Some scientific information about the seasons and why they change is presented in a format that is attractive and accessible to children in the primary grades.

A Tree Is Nice by Janice May Udry. Illustrated by Marc Simont. Harper & Row, 1956. This 1957 Caldecott-Award-winning book tells a simple story about trees, including how they change through the seasons.

About the Author and Illustrator

HOPKINS, LEE BENNETT

Authors of Books for Young People: Supplement to the Second Edition, by Martha E. Ward and Dorothy Marquardt. Scarecrow, 1979, p. 134.

Fifth Book of Junior Authors and Illustrators, ed. by Sally Holmes Holtze. Wilson, 1983, pp. 155–157.

Something about the Author, ed. by Anne Commire. Gale, 1972, Vol. 3, pp. 85–87.

McPhail, David. *Farm Morning*
Illus. by the author. Harcourt, 1985
Suggested Use Level: Gr. PreK–1   Reading Level: Gr. 2

Plot Summary

A little girl and her father wake very early to begin their chores on the farm. After they get dressed, they start out to take care of the animals. They are greeted by a chorus of familiar noises: cows moo, horses whinny, and geese honk. As each group of animals is being fed, the father talks to the animals and to his daughter. Finally, the morning chores are done, and the girl and her father sit down to their breakfast together.

Thematic Material

Farm Morning gives information about farms and farm animals within the framework of a story about a girl and her father. The relationship between the girl and her father is indicated through their conversations and the expressive illustrations.

Book Talk Material and Activities

Using this book along with those books mentioned in the Related Titles (see below) that invite children to join in on the noise is a fun way for children to learn about familiar animals and their sounds. Children could then make a farm mural that includes the animals from all the books discussed. Which book presents the most animals? *"Quack!" Said the Billy Goat,* which pokes fun at the more traditional books, is a good book to share at the end of this activity. *Farm Morning* and those books mentioned as Related Titles are also wonderful to read and discuss before a visit to a farm. Children could compare the illustrations in the books with the photographs in a nonfiction book. Which book has the most realistic illustrations? A class or library group could make their own books of other animals (such as zoo animals or birds) and the sounds they make.

Many children will want to talk or write about their own early morning routines. The girl and her father follow a pattern as they feed the animals—rabbits first and the pig last. Children could make a list of some of the things that they do every morning. "The List" in *Frog and Toad Together* correlates with this activity.

Related Titles

Cock-a-Doodle-Doo by Franz Brandenberg. Illustrated by Aliki. Greenwillow, 1986. Farm animals make their usual noises in this colorful picture book. Ask the children what the farmer and his wife say.

Early Morning in the Barn written and illustrated by Nancy Tafuri. Greenwillow, 1983. The only text is the sound that each animal makes.

Farm Animals by Karen Jacobsen. Photographs. Childrens, 1981. A simple nonfiction book that provides background information about chickens, cows, pigs, sheep, goats, and horses.

Farmyard Sounds written and illustrated by Colin Hawkins and Jacqui Hawkins. Crown, 1986. The sounds of familiar farmyard animals are presented in a format that encourages participation.

Frog and Toad Together written and illustrated by Arnold Lobel. Harper & Row, 1971. Toad decides that he will be more efficient if he follows a list of activities in the morning. When the list blows away, he does not know what to do.

Our Animal Friends at Maple Hill Farm written and illustrated by Alice Provensen and Martin Provensen. Random House, 1974. Here is a close-up look at the animals on the farm—a good book to share before a visit to a farm.

"Quack!" Said the Billy Goat by Charles Causley. Illustrated by Barbara Firth. Lippincott, 1986. In this rhyming text, animals make mixed-up sounds. Ask the children if they know the real noises.

Spot Goes to the Farm written and illustrated by Eric Hill. Putnam, 1987. Spot and his father look for baby animals on the farm. This lift-the-flap format is ideal for Dad's questions and Spot's answers. The children can become involved in guessing what Spot will reply.

About the Author and Illustrator

McPHAIL, DAVID

Fifth Book of Junior Authors and Illustrators, ed. by Sally Holmes Holtze. Wilson, 1983, pp. 213–214.

Illustrators of Children's Books: 1967–1976, Vol. IV, comp. by Lee Kingman, Grace Allen Hogarth, and Harriet Quimby. Horn Book, 1978, pp. 4, 5, 143, 200.

Something about the Author, ed. by Anne Commire. Gale, 1983, Vol. 32, p. 137; 1987, Vol. 47, pp. 150–165.

Parker, Nancy Winslow, and Wright, Joan Richards. *Bugs*

Illus. by Nancy Winslow Parker. Greenwillow, 1987; pap., Morrow, 1988

Suggested Use Level: Gr. 1–4   Reading Level: Gr. 6

Plot Summary

Sixteen bugs are each introduced using a riddle: the horsefly, cicada, ant, tick, flea, slug, spider, moth, mosquito, centipede, roach, cricket, termite, louse, firefly, and dragonfly. The authors then tell where the bug is found, how it behaves, and what it eats. Also included are the scientific name and a clearly labeled illustration of each bug. The picture glossary describes metamorphosis, the difference between bugs and insects, and the stages in the growth of bugs. A taxonomy chart and bibliography also are included.

Thematic Material

Bugs presents factual details in both the text and illustrations about bugs that are familiar to most children.

Book Talk Material and Activities

A book like *Bugs* could be read aloud or featured in a book talk to show children that books contain information. Such an activity should be part of all library programs, and could be coordinated with a class visit for a science curriculum assignment. In addition to reading parts (or all) of the book aloud, children should be introduced to some of its special features, including a picture glossary, a taxonomy chart, and a bibliography. Each should be described to acquaint children with its purpose. The book's attractive format makes it accessible to many age groups. Each bug is presented on a two-page spread, with a humorous rhyming riddle about the bug on the left page, and a large, clearly labeled illustration of the bug with a paragraph of text on the right. Younger children will appreciate the large illustration, and older children will find sufficient information in the brief text to satisfy their initial curiosity.

Mary Ann Hoberman's *Bugs: Poems* includes poems about many of the bugs in Parker and Wright's book. Read aloud Hoberman's poem "Cricket" and compare its scientific information with the paragraph in *Bugs.* Or look at her description in "Spiders," in which she lists the reasons why spiders are not insects, and compare her list with the one in Parker and Wright's book (p. 37). The accurate information in *Bugs: Poems* makes it a valuable resource for science and writing projects. Other poems about bugs reflect different moods. David McCord (*One at a Time*), Aileen Fisher (*Out in the Dark and Daylight*), and Norma Farber (*Never Say Ugh to a Bug*) have written playful, quiet, descriptive, and humorous poems, demonstrating that when different poets look closely at ordinary things, they can present different images.

Audiovisual Adaptation

Bugs. "Reading Rainbow." Great Plains National Instructional Television Library, videorecording, 1988.

Related Titles

Bugs: Poems by Mary Ann Hoberman. Illustrated by Victoria Chess. Viking, 1976. The poems in this collection are both humorous and scientifically accurate.

Busy Bugs written by Ada Graham and Frank Graham. Illustrated by D. D. Tyler. Dodd, Mead, 1983. Fifteen bugs are described. More information is provided here than in *Bugs.* Some of the bugs discussed are the field cricket, dragonfly, house fly, honeybee, and monarch butterfly.

Insects: A Close-Up Look by Peter Seymour. Illustrated by Jean Cassels Helmer. Macmillan, 1984. A pop-up book that gives a three-dimensional look at the grasshopper, mosquito, ant, and dragonfly. Lifting flaps and pulling tabs reveal more information.

Never Say Ugh to a Bug by Norma Farber. Illustrated by Jose Aruego. Greenwillow, 1979. Twenty poems describe the behavior of different bugs.

One at a Time by David McCord. Illustrated by Henry B. Kane. Little,

Brown, 1977. A collection of poems from five previously published titles that includes poems about crickets, grasshoppers, and other insects.

Out in the Dark and Daylight by Aileen Fisher. Illustrated by Gail Owens. Harper & Row, 1980. A collection of poems that expresses feelings of delight and wonder for the natural world.

The Very Hungry Caterpillar written and illustrated by Eric Carle. Collins-World, 1969. The main character here is a bug. Ask the children some of these questions: Does the caterpillar in the story act like a bug? What does a real caterpillar eat? Can you think of other stories with bugs as important characters?

About the Author and Illustrator

PARKER, NANCY WINSLOW

Fifth Book of Junior Authors and Illustrators, ed. by Sally Holmes Holtze. Wilson, 1983, pp. 233–235.

Illustrators of Children's Books: 1967–1976, Vol. IV, comp. by Lee Kingman, Grace Allen Hogarth, and Harriet Quimby. Horn Book, 1978, pp. 149, 203–204.

Something about the Author, ed. by Anne Commire. Gale, 1976, Vol. 10, pp. 113–114.

Patterson, Francine. *Koko's Kitten*
Photographs by Ronald H. Cohn. Scholastic, 1985; pap., 1987
Suggested Use Level: Gr. 3–4   Reading Level: Gr. 4

Plot Summary

Because of an illness, Koko the gorilla was separated from the other gorillas in the San Francisco Zoo. Francine Patterson made arrangements to work with Koko as part of a research project that lasted 14 years. In that time, Koko learned to use sign language and hundreds of words. This book describes how Koko asked for a kitten as a present. Koko had heard several stories about cats and kittens and wanted one. At first, she was given a toy cat, but she was not satisfied. Finally, the people who cared for Koko decided to give her a real kitten, which she named "All Ball." When the kitten visited, Koko often treated him like a baby gorilla. In time, Ball, who had been separated from his mother at birth, grew to be an aggressive and playful cat. Koko and Ball played games together, and Koko would use sign language to communicate with her keepers about Ball. As Ball grew older, he roamed about freely in and out of Koko's compound. Unfortunately, Ball was hit by a car and killed. After that, Koko became extremely unhappy. As she mourned her lost kitten, she communicated her sadness through sign language and her physical behavior. Her caretakers decided to get her a new kitten, which she now cares for and protects.

Thematic Material

In *Koko's Kitten*, children learn about animal communication and intelligence. Koko learns to communicate with humans using American Sign Language. She shows her sensitivity by caring for her pet kitten and by grieving for him when he is killed.

Book Talk Material and Activities

Koko's Kitten, a nonfiction photoessay that introduces children to a very special animal, could be included in a book talk program on animal communication with humans. *Cindy, a Hearing Ear Dog; A Dolphin Goes to School; Working Dogs;* and *The Story of Nim* are other titles that could be included.

Many children try to learn sign language from books. Some books are excellent for introducing children to the alphabet and the signs for words. *Handtalk Birthday* uses signs to tell a simple story, which children could learn and retell. *Handmade ABC* is a more straightforward look at the sign language alphabet. Children interested in learning more about Koko will want to read *Koko's Story*, which describes Koko's early years and how she learned to sign. It also tells some of Koko's activities since the publication of *Koko's Kitten*.

Related Titles

Cindy, a Hearing Ear Dog by Patricia Curtis. Photographs by David Cupp. Dutton, 1981. Cindy is trained to be the "ears" of a deaf person. When she hears noises like the telephone or the doorbell, she alerts her owner. In the course of this story, readers learn about the program for training such dogs.

A Dolphin Goes to School: The Story of Squirt, a Trained Dolphin by Elizabeth Simpson Smith. Illustrated by Ted Lewin. Morrow, 1986. Squirt is learning tricks to be a performer for a water arena show. The book shows the process of acquiring dolphins, training them, preparing them for performances, and providing for their needs.

Handmade ABC: A Manual Alphabet written and illustrated by Linda

Bourke. Addison-Wesley, 1981. Finger-spelling positions for the letters of the alphabet are drawn clearly enough for children to follow.

Handtalk Birthday: A Number and Story Book in Sign Language by Remy Charlip, Mary Beth, and George Ancona. Photographs. Four Winds, 1987. Both sign language and finger spelling are included in this birthday story. The colorful photographs capture the enthusiasm of the characters as they celebrate Mary Beth's birthday.

Koko's Story by Francine Patterson. Photographs by Ronald H. Cohn. Scholastic, 1987. Koko learns sign language and has a friendship with another gorilla. One chapter tells of Koko and her pets (including All Ball from *Koko's Kitten*), and the last chapter describes Koko's daily activities.

The Story of Nim: The Chimp Who Learned Language by Anna Michel. Photographs by Susan Kiklin and Herbert S. Terrace. Knopf, 1980. Like Koko, Nim was able to learn American Sign Language to communicate with people. The emphasis here is on the language learning process, in contrast with *Koko's Kitten*, which is about the friendship between the gorilla and her kitten.

Working Dogs by George S. Fichter. Photographs. Watts, 1979. Sled dogs, seeing eye dogs, and police dogs are some of the dogs included in this well-organized presentation on the many ways that dogs help people.

Plotkin, Gregory, and Plotkin, Rita. *Cooking the Russian Way*
Photographs by Robert Wolfe and Diane Wolfe. Lerner, 1986
Suggested Use Level: Gr. 3–4   Reading Level: Gr. 10

Plot Summary

The Plotkins' cookbook includes traditional Russian recipes for breakfast, dinner, and supper. The introduction briefly describes the Soviet Union and its people, focusing on the Slavic republics of Russia, and includes some information about the history and food resources of these regions. A menu shows some typical meals (with a pronunciation guide), and a glossary describes cooking utensils, cooking terms, and special ingredients. Some of the recipes are: blini (pancakes), boiled potatoes, chicken Kiev, beef Stroganoff, and honey spice cake. Accompanying many recipes are brief comments about Russian life and customs. The full-color photographs show some of the prepared foods as well as familiar Russian objects, such as a "Matryoshka" doll.

Thematic Material

Although this nonfiction book does give some information about daily life in Russia, it centers on only one aspect of the country's life—its food—and should be introduced to children as a cookbook.

Book Talk Material and Activities

Several activities could be coordinated with this book. It could be the focus of a book talk program on cookbooks or cooking around the world, or part of a display of books on daily life in the Soviet Union. It also could be correlated with a classroom unit on geography.

Cooking the Russian Way could help familiarize children with the cookbook genre of nonfiction. For example, the recipes in the book list all the ingredients first, then a numbered list of steps to follow. After reading one recipe aloud, it would be fun to make the dish following the directions and then taste the finished dish. The recipe for "Vegetable Salad Vesna," which uses some readily available ingredients (such as radishes, cucumbers, and scallions) and does not require cooking, is relatively easy to demonstrate. As the recipe is being prepared, ask the children to think about the directions. Could they be followed by a beginner or does one need some basic knowledge about the kitchen? Are the ingredients familiar? When the dish is completed, let the children who want to, take a taste and talk about their reactions. How does this vegetable salad compare with other salads they have eaten? What did they like or dislike about it? Compare the recipes in *Cooking the Russian Way* with those in another cookbook. "Cucumber Nut Salad" in *Kids Cooking Without a Stove* would be a good comparison. Some possible questions to ask are: Do the recipes seem easy or difficult? How are the books illustrated? What kinds of foods are included? Children might enjoy writing down some of their own favorite recipes and making a cookbook.

A program correlating *Cooking the Russian Way* with a study of Russia would help children learn about the climate and the types of food available there. It would also be a good opportunity to share some folktales, especially ones with food in them. *The Gossipy Wife* and *The Night It Rained Pancakes* are two versions of the same story that could be compared and contrasted. A recipe for pancakes (blini) is given in the Plotkins' cookbook. *Cooking the Russian Way* is part of the Easy Menu Ethnic Cookbooks series. Some other books in the series describe food from France, Greece, India, Japan, Poland, and Vietnam.

Related Titles

Children Are Children Are Children: An Activity Approach to Exploring Brazil, France, Iran, Japan, Nigeria and the U.S.S.R. by Ann Cole, Carolyn Haas, Elizabeth Heller, and Betty Weinberger. Illustrated by Lois Axeman. Little, Brown, 1978. The activities include cooking, planning a circus, playing games, and making simple crafts. A separate section has a list of some Russian words and how to pronounce them.

A Family in the U.S.S.R. by Peter Otto Jacobsen and Preben Sejer Kristensen. Photographs. Bookwright, 1985. The simple text and color photographs make this an attractive book to share with younger children, and the chapter "Mealtime" adds to the information given in *Cooking the Russian Way*.

The Gossipy Wife adapted and illustrated by Amanda Hall. Bedrick/ Blackie, 1981. When Ivan finds a chest of gold coins, he is worried. If the landlord hears of his find, Ivan will lose the gold. How can Ivan keep his wife from gossiping about his discovery? Using his wits and his wife's pancakes, Ivan tricks both his wife and the landlord.

Kids Cooking Without a Stove: A Cookbook for Young Children by Aileen Paul. Illustrated by Carol Inouye. Doubleday, 1975. None of the recipes needs cooking over a stove. Children would enjoy making "Blackberry Patch Salad" or "Arabian Dates."

The Night It Rained Pancakes adapted by Mirra Ginsburg. Illustrated by Douglas Florian. Greenwillow, 1980. In this version of *The Gossipy Wife*, Ivan's brother Stepan is the one who cannot keep a secret.

We Live in the European U.S.S.R. by E. Ryabko. Illustrated. Bookwright, 1984. The 26 people profiled include a student, a winemaker, and a schoolteacher. Each brief biographical sketch has details about everyday life in the Soviet Union.

Provensen, Alice, and Provensen, Martin.　*Town and Country*
Illus. by the authors. Crown, 1984
Suggested Use Level: Gr. 1–4　　Reading Level: Gr. 6

Plot Summary

Readers are given a guided tour of a city and a home near a rural town. Large buildings and hundreds of people are shown in the city, as well as many different modes of transportation—train, boat, car, and bus. Children see that something is always happening in the city: people are hurrying to work and then home; buildings are being built and demolished; and children are going to school, the park, the zoo, the library, the museum, the aquarium, and the planetarium. A variety of restaurants and stores serve many different kinds of food, and festivals celebrate special occasions. The city is shown to be crowded, bright, and noisy but it is some people's home, and where they want to be.

Although a farm has lots of open space, it also has lots of activity. Farm animals are cared for, fields are plowed, and crops are planted and harvested. Children play on the hills and in the fields; help with the chores; and go to school, on field trips, and to the store. The work is hard, but it is their home.

Thematic Material

Reading about the contrasts between life in the city and the country helps children learn about the world around them.

Book Talk Material and Activities

Town and Country is a good model for writing and illustrating similar contrast books. After hearing the book in a story session, children could suggest other contrasting situations, such as land and ocean, earth and space, and inside and outside. Using their own drawings or magazine pictures, children could illustrate these situations and then write captions to describe the contrasts. Peter Spier's *People* could be read to help children find out about other people and places.

Several other stories extend the city/country theme. Read several versions of *The Town Mouse and the Country Mouse* and ask children to discuss how each mouse feels about its home and why. *A Country Tale* shows the adventures of a simple village cat that visits the city home of an elegant cat. As children learn more about different places, they might enjoy making a simple concept book about a place, for example, a city counting book, or a city/country transportation book. Rachel Isadora's *City Seen from A to Z* and Jane Miller's *Farm Counting Book* provide some ideas.

Related Titles

City Seen from A to Z written and illustrated by Rachel Isadora. Greenwillow, 1983. Apartment buildings and crowded streets are the settings for some of the black-and-white drawings that illustrate the letters of the alphabet. "E" is for the "entrance" to the subway and "U" is for the "umbrella" over a vendor's cart, for example. Compare the drawings with the photographs in *Hey, Look at Me!*

A Country Tale written and illustrated by Diane Stanley. Macmillan, 1985. Cleo, a country cat, is happy with her simple life until she meets a grand cat from the city. Mrs. Snickers seems so elegant, and Cleo thinks her own life is dull in comparison. Cleo's trip to the city is a disaster, and she comes to realize the importance of being herself. Children can discuss how the author describes life in the city, and how she writes about the country.

Farm Counting Book written and illustrated by Jane Miller. Prentice-Hall, 1983. Color photographs of farm animals and objects illustrate the numbers 1 to 10, and many other photographs encourage children to count on their own in this companion to Jane Miller's *Farm Alphabet Book* (Prentice-Hall, 1984).

Hey, Look at Me! A City ABC by Sandy Grant. Photographs by Larry Mulvehill. Bradbury, 1973. Black-and-white photographs capture city images to illustrate the letters of the alphabet with action words. "E" shows people "eating," "S" shows a child "splashing," and "W" shows a bus load of people "waving."

People written and illustrated by Peter Spier. Doubleday, 1980. Spier provides information about the similarities and differences among people. For example, all people have noses but they come in different shapes, colors, and sizes.

The Town Mouse and the Country Mouse retold and illustrated by Lorinda Bryan Cauley. Putnam, 1984. In this version of Aesop's fable, the text and illustrations are very detailed. Children can compare it with the version illustrated by Galdone.

The Town Mouse and the Country Mouse retold and illustrated by Paul Galdone. McGraw-Hill, 1971. In this version of Aesop's fable, the town mouse dresses as a court dandy, and the country mouse dresses as a monk. Children can make a list of what each mouse likes about its home.

About the Author and Illustrator

PROVENSEN, ALICE, AND PROVENSEN, MARTIN
Illustrators of Children's Books: 1744–1945, Vol. I, comp. by Lee Kingman, Grace Allen Hogarth, and Harriet Quimby. Horn Book, 1947, pp. 21, 25, 38, 168; *1957–1966, Vol. III*, 1968, pp. 161, 236; *1967–1976, Vol. IV*, 1978, pp. 152, 205.
Something about the Author, ed. by Anne Commire. Gale, 1976, Vol. 9, pp. 154–155.
Third Book of Junior Authors, ed. by Donna de Montreville and Donna Hill. Wilson, 1972, pp. 231–232.

Rylant, Cynthia. *Night in the Country*
Illus. by Mary Szilagyi. Bradbury, 1986
Suggested Use Level: Gr. PreK–1   Reading Level: Gr. 4

Plot Summary
In the country, the night is filled with animals and sounds—swooping owls and singing frogs—as people and animals move slowly through the night. Other animals are shown settling down with their young. It is so quiet that you can hear an apple fall from the tree. Then slowly, as the light begins to change and new noises are heard, night animals grow quiet and a new day begins.

Thematic Material
Night in the Country celebrates the simple beauty of nature and captures the sounds and feelings of the dark country night.

Book Talk Material and Activities
Many public libraries offer evening story hours, and *Night in the Country* is a unique book to read aloud to children and their parents. After the story, the group could even meet outside and listen to the evening noises around them. Each parent–child pair could make a list of the sounds they hear as they walk around. Then the group could get back together and share the sounds that they heard and compare them with the ones in the book. Each child could illustrate one of the sounds he or she heard, and the pictures could be assembled into a book or library display on "A Night at the Library."

Night in the Country could also be coordinated with a science curriculum study of night animals. After reading the book aloud, have children list some animals that are active at night. Read other stories, such as *The Goodnight Circle,* and add to the list. As the list grows, collect some nonfiction books about night animals and have children work together in pairs or small groups to gather more information about specific animals. Each group could list two or three facts about its animal and report back to the group either orally or through a written and illustrated sheet for display. This kind of activity helps children learn about the variety of materials and information available in the library. It is an especially good opportunity to look at fiction and nonfiction and to help children learn about working on reports.

Related Titles

All in the Woodland Early: An ABC Book by Jane Yolen. Illustrated by Jane Breskin Zalben. Collins, 1979. Each letter of the alphabet is represented by an animal commonly found in the woods. Children could make a day animal/night animal alphabet book with the day animals illustrated on yellow paper and the night animals on blue or black paper.

City Night by Eve Rice. Illustrated by Peter Sis. Greenwillow, 1987. The text describes the noises and activities of the city. The illustrations show a dark blue sky with yellow light coming from windows and street lamps. How do the pictures and descriptions compare with those in *Night in the Country*?

Creatures of the Night by Judith E. Rinard. Photographs. National Geographic Society, 1977. Full-color photographs correlate with the text to describe the behavior of several night animals.

The Goodnight Circle by Carolyn Lesser. Illustrated by Lorinda Bryan Cauley. Harcourt, 1984. Deer, foxes, turtles, and frogs all prepare to go to sleep, but owls, beavers, opossums, and raccoons are busy throughout the night.

The Moon's the North Wind's Cooky: Night Poems edited and illustrated by Susan Russo. Lothrop, 1979. Poems by Nikki Giovanni, Myra Cohn Livingston, Karla Kuskin, and others express the many different moods of the night.

Only the Cat Saw written and illustrated by Ashley Wolff. Dodd, Mead, 1985. As the sun is setting, the cat begins to prowl around the countryside. Parallel information shows what is happening inside the house and what the cat observes outside.

Raccoons and Ripe Corn written and illustrated by Jim Arnosky, Lothrop, 1987. During the night, a family of raccoons comes into the cornfield and eats the corn. As morning comes, they hurry back to the woods.

Wait Till the Moon Is Full by Margaret Wise Brown. Illustrated by Garth Williams. Harper & Row, 1948. A young raccoon wants to go out into the night, but his mother tells him to wait. While he waits, he hears night noises—an owl, the wind, and the branches. His mother describes the wonders of the night until, finally, the moon is full and the young raccoon goes outside.

About the Author and Illustrator

RYLANT, CYNTHIA
Something about the Author, ed. by Anne Commire. Gale, 1986, Vol. 44, pp. 167–168; 1988, Vol. 50, pp. 182–188.

Simon, Seymour. *Saturn*
 Photographs and drawings. Morrow, 1985; pap., 1988
 Suggested Use Level: Gr. 1–4   Reading Level: Gr. 4

Plot Summary
 Saturn is one of the titles in Seymour Simon's group of books about the large planets. In it, Simon describes the relative position of Saturn in the earth's solar system and discusses explorations that have added to existing knowledge of this planet. Facts about the size, length of day, and gravity of Saturn are explained in terms of experiences on Earth. The temperature, climate, and atmosphere of Saturn are also compared with current information about Earth. Detailed information about Saturn's rings is accompanied by photographs and drawings. Saturn's many moons are discussed, with a few described in detail, including Titan, the only moon that has an atmosphere.

Thematic Material
 This nonfiction photoessay about one of the larger planets in the Earth's solar system includes facts about space exploration and travel as well as historical information about the discovery of Saturn.

Book Talk Material and Activities
 The space books by Seymour Simon are excellent to read aloud in a program about space and the solar system. They are also wonderful as an introduction to the nonfiction photoessay genre. Simon's child-centered books relate information about the planets to children's familiar experiences on Earth. They answer many questions about life on other planets, such as: Could people live there? How far away is it? and How long would it take to reach it from Earth? The clear and colorful photographs are large enough to be visible when shown to a group of children.
 Librarians or classroom teachers may want to set up a science center

using Seymour Simon's books. Along with the books, they should have some prepared cards to encourage children to read for details. Working individually or in pairs, children could read some of Simon's books and then use the cards to organize the facts that they have learned. A sample card is given here. The card provides a framework for children that teaches them to note the author and title of the book along with their facts. The structure is especially useful for students who are just beginning to do research, who will then be able to apply the approach to other research efforts. Finished cards could be included in a display on doing research or on Simon's books.

In Seymour Simon's _____

                                    TITLE

I learned that _____

_____

_____

                          _____

                                    NAME

Seymour Simon has written a wide variety of books for young people. Sharing his books with children provides an opportunity to talk about nonfiction science books, including the photoessay and such science-fiction books as his _Einstein Anderson, Science Sleuth_. Simon has also written books about dinosaurs, optical illusions, paper airplanes, animals, and other science related topics.

Related Topics

Earth: Our Planet in Space by Seymour Simon. Photographs and drawings. Four Winds, 1984. Simon describes the planet Earth, its position in space, its atmosphere, and its structure. This is a good book to share at the beginning of a study of other space books, most of which make some reference to Earth. Drawings and black-and-white photographs help children visualize some of the concepts.

Einstein Anderson, Science Sleuth by Seymour Simon. Illustrated by Fred Winkowski. Viking, 1980. In each of 10 stories in this first book in the series about Adam "Einstein" Anderson, Einstein is able to solve a problem by using his knowledge of scientific principles.

Galaxies by Seymour Simon. Photographs. Morrow, 1988. Focusing on the Milky Way galaxy, Simon describes the size, shape, and formation of galaxies, and also includes information about supernovas and magnetic clouds. The dramatic full-color photographs will attract many children to the book.

Jupiter by Seymour Simon. Photographs and drawings. Morrow, 1985. How many planet Earths could fit into the planet Jupiter? (Answer: More than 1,300.) What is it like on the surface of Jupiter? (Answer: It is an ocean of liquid hydrogen.) These are among the facts presented in this book—just the ones children want to know. Simon's description of the red spot on Jupiter is aided by the color photographs.

Mars by Seymour Simon. Photographs and drawings. Morrow, 1987. How many planets the size of Mars could fit into the planet Earth? (Answer: Seven.) What is it like on the surface of Mars? (Answer: It is dusty and there are violent storms.) Color photographs from the *Mariner* and *Viking* spacecrafts enhance Simon's description of Earth's neighbor.

The Moon by Seymour Simon. Photographs. Morrow, 1984. Black-and-white photographs from lunar explorations, including ones of astronauts on the moon, add to the drama of this book, which describes Earth's only natural satellite in detail. As every other planet book includes some mention of the planet's moons, the children can discuss how the moons of other planets are like or unlike the Earth's moon.

Stars by Seymour Simon. Photographs and drawings, 1986. Children can read this book along with Simon's *The Sun* to find out the similarities and differences between these huge, hot balls.

The Sun by Seymour Simon. Photographs and drawings. Morrow, 1986. How many planet Earths could fit inside the sun? (Answer: 1.3 million.) What is it like on the surface of the sun? (Answer: It is a continuous series of nuclear explosions.) This book will encourage children's fascination with the sun.

Uranus by Seymour Simon. Photographs and drawings. Morrow, 1987. How many planet Earths could fit inside Uranus? (Answer: 50.) What is it like on the surface of Uranus? (Answer: Scientists think Uranus has a hot, watery atmosphere.) In addition to the information common to the other books in the series, Simon describes Uranus's rings and how scientists found out about them.

About the Author and Illustrator

SIMON, SEYMOUR
Authors of Books for Young People: Supplement to the Second Edition, by Martha E. Ward and Dorothy Marquardt. Scarecrow, 1988, p. 252.

Fifth Book of Junior Authors and Illustrators, ed. by Sally Holmes Holtze. Wilson, 1983, pp. 292–294.
Something about the Author, ed. by Anne Commire. Gale, Vol. 4, pp. 191–192.

Tejima. *Fox's Dream*
Illus. by the author. Philomel, 1985
Suggested Use Level: Gr. 1–3   Reading Level: Gr. 5

Plot Summary

One winter night, a fox is walking through the snow-filled forest searching for food, but the frozen land has little to offer. After chasing a rabbit, which he does not catch, the fox discovers that he has run to a part of the forest that he has never seen. The trees overhead are frozen, and animal shapes seem to be suspended in the icy branches. In one tree he sees antelopes; in another he sees birds; and in yet another foxes. Seeing the foxes makes him remember his own family and the warmer time when they were together. As he approaches a field, the fox sees a shape in the distance, which turns out to be a vixen. The fox goes to her, and the two foxes stand together in the frozen field.

Thematic Material

The fox's fantasy is combined with the reality of the harsh winter and the promise of spring and a new generation. As the lonely and isolated fox begins his journey, he dreams of other foxes. At the end of his dream, he meets one. The combination of fantasy and reality could be discussed with children.

Book Talk Material and Activities

Teachers often have their students write reports about animals, because it is an easy topic for children to research. One library activity that supports this process is to discuss the difference between a story and a nonfiction book about that same animal. *Fox's Dream* could be correlated with *Foxes* by Kay McDearmon as part of a discussion of realistic fiction and nonfiction. *Foxes* includes information about several foxes as well as such details as the animal's habitat, food, and behavior. Make a chart that lists some facts about foxes. Then, as children read fiction books with a fox character, compare the fox's behavior with the factual information.

Does the fox act like a real fox? For example, in many stories the fox character talks. *The Foxes* and *Wonders of Foxes* are two other nonfiction books that could be used for more information, and *Fox in Love* and *One Fine Day* are fiction books with fox characters.

The school librarian could have children look for story books about animals to share during the discussion time. Depending on the children, they could work on this project individually or in small groups. Animal fiction and nonfiction books also make an informative display. Children could identify the common features of the books in each category and post them with the books. These activities encourage children to develop and apply criteria for examining and using books, and are also an opportunity for them to work together and learn from each other.

Audiovisual Adaptation

Fox's Dream. Random House Media, filmstrip/cassette, 1988.

Related Titles

Fox in Love by Edward Marshall. Illustrated by James Marshall. Dial, 1982. Fox is a cool character with sunglasses and many neat hats. Although he does not want to, he must take his sister, Louise, to the park, where he meets Raisin, a beautiful vixen. Ask the children whether this fox acts like a real fox.

The Foxes by Mark E. Ahlstrom. Photographs. Crestwood, 1983. The basic facts here include details about where foxes are found, their life cycle, how they hunt for food, and who their enemies are. The contents, glossary, and maps make this a useful book for beginning researchers.

Foxes by Kay McDearmon. Photographs. Dodd, Mead, 1981. Clear black-and-white photographs and a well-spaced text make this an easy book to read. Although the main emphasis is on the red fox, some information about the gray, kit, and Arctic foxes is included.

One Fine Day written and illustrated by Nonny Hogrogian. Macmillan, 1971. When a thirsty fox comes out of the forest and drinks the old woman's milk, she cuts off his tail and will not sew it back on unless he replaces her milk. Each character that the fox asks for help demands something in return. Ask the children whether this fox behaves like a real fox.

Wonders of Foxes by Sigmund A. Lavine. Photographs and drawings.

Dodd, Mead, 1986. Lavine provides facts about the fox's physical characteristics and behavior as well as some superstitions about them.

Yabuuchi, Masayuki. *Whose Baby?*
Illus. by the author. Philomel, 1985
Suggested Use Level: Gr. PreK–1   Reading Level: Gr. 1

Plot Summary
The text and illustrations in this book follow a pattern. The picture of a young animal (for example, a fawn) comes first with a question about "whose baby" it is. The next page shows the young animal with its parents and the correct terminology for the male and female animal. Six animals are presented: the deer, the peacock, the fox, the lion, the seal, and the bison.

Thematic Material
Whose Baby? provides information about animals and their young.

Book Talk Material and Activities
After reading *Whose Baby?* young children could have fun making a bulletin board display of their own baby pictures. They could try to guess who is who and add their names to the display later. Other books about animals and their young could be booktalked and shown near the bulletin board display for children to sign out. The book talks could highlight such fiction books as Marc Brown's *Arthur's Baby* (see Chapter 1) and nonfiction books such as *Zoo Babies.* Young children might also enjoy *Whose Footprints?*, the companion book to *Whose Baby?* After the book is shared with children, they could make handprints and footprints with fingerpaint. Both *Whose Baby?* and *Whose Footprints?* introduce children to simple facts about animals.

Related Titles
Baby Animals by Illa Podendorf. Photographs. Childrens, 1981. Besides discussing the special needs and behavior of young animals, this book

also provides information about how young animals are cared for, grow, and change.

How to Hide a Butterfly and Other Insects written and illustrated by Ruth Heller. Grosset, 1985. The rhyming text describes different camouflaged animals, including a butterfly, a moth, and a grasshopper. Ruth Heller has written and illustrated several other similar books, including *How to Hide a Whip-poor-will and Other Birds* (Grosset, 1986).

Whose Footprints? written and illustrated by Masayuki Yabuuchi. Philomel, 1985. Animal footprints are depicted with a question about whom they belong to. Children turn the page to find out the animal whose footprints are shown. Some of the animals include a duck, a cat, and a bear.

Zoo Babies written and photographed by Donna K. Grosvenor. National Geographic Society, 1978. Color photographs show many young animals in the zoo, and the text describes some of their daily activities and how they are cared for.

Zoo Babies: The Nursery Babies by Georgeanne Irvine. Photographs by Ron Garrison. Childrens, 1983. Clear color photographs enhance the text, which describes the special care that young animals receive at the zoo.

Yolen, Jane. *Owl Moon*
Illus. by John Schoenherr. Philomel, 1987
Suggested Use Level: Gr. 1–4   Reading Level: Gr. 2

Plot Summary

The first time that the little girl goes owling with her father, they walk through the moonlit winter night. At the beginning, it seems quiet, but as their walk continues, the little girl begins to hear sounds—a train whistle, dogs barking, and feet crunching in the snow. Her father stops near the pine trees and calls to the owls, but there is no answer, so they continue to walk into the woods. Again he stops, and again there is no sign of any owls. The little girl is cold and tired, but she knows that she must be patient. When they reach a moonlit clearing in the woods and her father calls for the owls again, this time there is an answering call. As the owl flies closer, the owl and her father exchange calls, and the little girl stands waiting and hoping. Finally the owl lands on a branch above the little girl, and her father shines a light on the owl. Time seems suspended while the owl is looking down at them. Then the owl flies away, and the little girl and her father walk home together.

Thematic Material

Owl Moon shows a deep sense of respect and appreciation for the natural world. The little girl and her father enjoy their time together as they look at the beauty around them. John Schoenherr received the 1988 Caldecott Medal for his illustrations.

Book Talk Material and Activities

When showing *Owl Moon* to the students for the first time, try having them look at the illustrations before reading the story. Ask the children to think about what they feel as they look at the pictures. They can try to predict what the book will be about. Children who are already familiar with other Caldecott Award-winning books will have a better understanding of the relationship between the beautiful illustrations and the poetic text. A boy in one group of third graders suggested that on many pages the words looked like footprints in the snow. Another child saw the faces of the people looking at the owl before she saw the face of the owl. The group talked about the different expressions on the characters' faces— the little girl and her father had looks of surprise and wonder, and the owl looked proud but somewhat curious. After hearing the story, the children believed that the author and illustrator had actually been owling. They were pleased to read the author and illustrator information on the dust jacket, which confirmed their expectations. Several children commented on the use of open space in the book. With details only provided on some parts of each page, they felt that the open space really seemed like the snow and the moonlit winter sky. This group of children went on to study owls, and a naturalist visited their classroom to discuss the behavior of owls. *Owl Moon* has remained one of their favorite books.

Tejima's *Owl Lake* is an excellent book to contrast with *Owl Moon*. In *Owl Lake,* Father Owl flies across the lake in search of food for his family. He stops on a log and listens to the sounds around him, but eventually he resumes his flight, swooping down on the lake and catching a fish, which he takes back to his family. The illustrations are woodcuts with a black background that provide a very different feeling from the brightly lit images in *Owl Moon*. Both books have dramatic pictures of owls and communicate a sense of wonder about the natural world.

John Schoenherr has illustrated other books that have a nature theme. *The Barn*, which he also wrote, has detailed black-and-white illustrations that children can compare with the paintings in *Owl Moon*. How is the owl presented in each book?

Audiovisual Adaptation

Owl Moon. Weston Woods, cassette/book, 1988; filmstrip/cassette, 1988.

Related Titles

About Owls by May Garelick. Illustrated by Tony Chen. Four Winds, 1975. By describing three owls—the elf owl, the barn owl, and the great horned owl—the author provides information about the habits and behavior of owls.

The Barn written and illustrated by John Schoenherr. Little, Brown, 1968. As a skunk searches for food, he becomes the target of a hungry owl in this realistic story of a predator and his prey.

The Man Who Could Call Down Owls by Eve Bunting. Illustrated by Charles Mikolaycak. Macmillan, 1984. The mysterious man who can call down owls is viewed with awe and fear, but his unusual skill places him in great danger from a sinister stranger who wants his power. This is an unusual and disquieting story of greed and cruelty.

Owl in the Garden by Bernice Freschet. Illustrated by Carol Newsom. Lothrop, 1985. Blue Jay's peanut is missing and Owl and the other animals try to find out who has taken it. Only the squirrel, who is gathering food, including peanuts, for the winter, is too busy to help.

Owl Lake written and illustrated by Tejima. Philomel, 1987. At night Father Owl flies over the trees and the lake searching for food for the hungry owl family and brings back a fish. Then, as morning comes, the owls go to sleep.

Your Owl Friend by Crescent Dragonwagon. Illustrated by Ruth Bornstein. Harper & Row, 1977. A boy who goes outside one night is joined by an owl. Their night is filled with love as the owl protects and shelters the boy. The owl is like a great spirit who watches over the boy, and their relationship has a dreamlike quality.

About the Author and Illustrator

YOLEN, JANE

Fourth Book of Junior Authors and Illustrators, ed. by Doris de Montreville and Elizabeth D. Crawford. Wilson, 1978, pp. 356–358.

Something about the Author, ed. by Anne Commire. Gale, 1973, Vol. 4, pp. 237–239; 1985, Vol. 40, pp. 217–231.

SCHOENHERR, JOHN (CARL)

Fourth Book of Junior Authors and Illustrators, ed. by Doris de Montreville and Elizabeth D. Crawford. Wilson, 1978, pp. 306–308.

Illustrators of Children's Books: 1957–1966, Vol. III, comp. by Lee Kingman, Grace Allen Hogarth, and Harriet Quimby. Horn Book, 1968, pp. 170, 239; *1967–1976, Vol. IV,* 1978, pp. 61, 157, 208.

Something about the Author, ed. by Anne Commire. Gale, 1985, Vol. 37, pp. 166–170.

7

Analyzing Illustrations

In picture books, text and illustration are combined to present a unified whole. Authors and illustrators challenge children with their words and pictures. Illustrations add details to the presentation that are not in the text. Children become involved in examining illustrations and develop an appreciation for the creative contribution of the artists.

The books in this chapter have imaginative illustrations. Artists have experimented with light, shadow, color, and perspective, and have used different techniques, such as batik, collage, and linoleum block printing. Some have an unusual format, including Janet Ahlberg and Allan Ahlberg's *The Jolly Postman: Or Other People's Letters,* which actually has the letters that a postman is delivering. These books show that picture books can be works of art.

Ahlberg, Janet, and Ahlberg, Allan.　*The Jolly Postman: Or Other People's Letters*
　Illus. by the authors. Little, Brown, 1986
　Suggested Use Level: Gr. K–4　　Reading Level: NA

Plot Summary
　The rhyming text tells how the postman delivers the mail. A letter he brings to the home of the Three Bears is an apology from Goldilocks and an invitation to her birthday party. Next, he delivers an advertising circular for witch supplies to the gingerbread house of the witch. A postcard from Jack to the Giant is his next delivery, followed by a book to Cinderella. The wolf receives a letter from Red Riding Hood's lawyer, and Goldilocks receives a birthday card from Mrs. Bunting and baby. At each stop, the postman enjoys some tea while the characters read their

mail. When the postman completes his deliveries, he goes home for more tea.

The format of the book is very creative. Some pages are designed as envelopes (complete with addresses, postmarks, and stamps) that open at the top to allow the reader to take out the items that are being sent. Each piece of mail that is delivered is actually inside one of the envelopes, so readers enjoy holding and reading the witch's advertising flier and Goldilocks's birthday card.

Thematic Material

This book's unusual and imaginative format correlates well with the story of a postman delivering the mail.

Book Talk Material and Activities

After hearing *The Jolly Postman,* children could suggest replies to some of the letters. For example, how might the wolf respond to the letter from Red Riding Hood's lawyer? What supplies might the witch order? Children could also think of characters from other books and write letters from or to them. Such nursery rhyme characters as Jack and Jill or the Old Woman in the Shoe could be a starting point. *Tomie de Paola's Mother Goose* is a good source for nursery rhymes. Children might want to look at other stories where characters write to each other. For example, in *Frog and Toad Are Friends,* Frog sends Toad a letter, and in *A Letter to Amy,* Peter invites Amy to his party. *Stringbean's Trip to the Shining Sea* is a collection of postcards from Stringbean and his brother, Fred, describing their vacation, which children could also use as a writing model.

One first-grade class read *The Jolly Postman* and decided to learn more about how the mail is delivered. They invited the school's mail carrier to a "Jolly Postman" party. The mail carrier talked about his job and read them one of his favorite children's books. For more information about mail delivery the class read Gail Gibbons's *The Post Office Book.*

Related Titles

Frog and Toad Are Friends written and illustrated by Arnold Lobel. Harper & Row, 1970. Here are five stories about two good friends, Frog and Toad. In one, Toad feels sad because he does not get any mail, so his friend, Frog, writes him a letter.

A Letter to Amy written and illustrated by Ezra Jack Keats. Harper &

Row, 1968. Peter invites Amy to his birthday party. Children might want to talk about what information needs to be included in an invitation.

The Post Office Book written and illustrated by Gail Gibbons. Crowell, 1982. The activities performed by postal employees that are described include sorting mail, loading it onto trucks and planes, and delivering it.

Stringbean's Trip to the Shining Sea by Vera B. Williams. Illustrated by Vera B. Williams and Jennifer Williams. Greenwillow, 1988. Most pages in this book are designed to look like postcards, which Stringbean and his brother, Fred, send home to their family in Kansas.

Tomie de Paola's Mother Goose illustrated by Tomie de Paola. Putnam, 1985. Among many familiar Mother Goose rhymes included here, are "Old Mother Hubbard" and "Humpty Dumpty." Children could think of letters that these characters would send or receive.

About the Author and Illustrator

AHLBERG, JANET
Fifth Book of Junior Authors and Illustrators, ed. by Sally Holmes Holtze. Wilson, 1983, pp. 4–5.
Something about the Author, ed. by Anne Commire. Gale, 1983, Vol. 32, p. 25.
AHLBERG, ALLAN
Fifth Book of Junior Authors and Illustrators, ed. by Sally Holmes Holtze. Wilson, 1983, pp. 4–5.
Something about the Author, ed. by Anne Commire. Gale, 1984, Vol. 35, p. 23.

Baker, Jeannie. *Home in the Sky*
Illus. by the author. Greenwillow, 1984
Suggested Use Level: Gr. 1–3   Reading Level: Gr. 3

Plot Summary

Mike cares for a flock of pigeons in the city. He even built them a coop on the roof of an old building. One day, one of the pigeons, Light, flies away from the flock. As he flies high over the city, he observes the activity below. When he tries to share some food with the street pigeons and they push him away, he wanders through the city confused and hungry. Accidentally, he boards a train, where a boy finds and comforts him. When the boy takes Light home and releases him, Light flies back to Mike and his own coop.

Thematic Material

The focus of this story is on the journey of a pigeon who seems to want an adventure. When the pigeon leaves his home, he discovers that the world can be dangerous as well as exciting.

Book Talk Material and Activities

Jeannie Baker's illustrations are unusual collage constructions. Using fabric, clay, hair, twigs, grass, feathers, and other objects, she has created realistic pictures of the city that have a feeling of depth and texture. After seeing and discussing these interesting illustrations, children might want to experiment with different materials. Books such as *Foxtails, Ferns, and Fish Scales* and *Pebbles and Pods* provide information about how to gather and use natural material for art projects.

Many books have characters who take a journey. Often, such characters want to find some excitement only to realize that the adventure is not what they expected. They are usually happy to return home. Ping in *The Story about Ping* could be compared to Light. Children will find many similarities between them. For example, they are both birds, they both leave their safe homes, and they both find that the outside world is confusing and not what they expected. Ask children to suggest other books whose characters look for adventure but come to regret leaving home. Some possibilities are *The Little House, The Whingdingdilly,* and *Hey, Al!* Classic stories like *Alice's Adventures in Wonderland* and *The Wizard of Oz* might also be mentioned.

Related Titles

Alice's Adventures in Wonderland by Lewis Carroll. Illustrated by S. Michael Wiggins. Knopf, 1983. The illustrations for this classic story are in full color. Children can be asked the following questions: How does Alice's adventure begin? How does it end? Is her story similar to Light's?

Foxtails, Ferns, and Fish Scales: A Handbook of Art and Nature Projects by Ada Graham. Illustrated by Dorothea Stoke. Four Winds, 1976. The author describes many projects using materials from the seashore, the forest, and the neighborhood. Prints, mosaics, pressings, plaques, and sculptures are some suggested ideas.

Hey, Al! by Arthur Yorinks. Illustrated by Richard Egielski. Farrar, Straus, 1986. Al is not happy with his life, but when he is taken to an island in the sky, he realizes that his life was not so bad. This book received the 1987 Caldecott Medal.

The Little House written and illustrated by Virginia Lee Burton. Houghton Mifflin, 1942. A little house in the country dreams of the bright lights and fast life of the city. Eventually, the city surrounds the little house and she wishes she were back in the country. This book received the 1943 Caldecott Medal.

Pebbles and Pods: A Book of Nature Crafts by Goldie Taub Chernoff. Illustrated by Margaret Hartelius. Walker, 1973. One suggested activity is a shadow box using outdoor objects. Children might enjoy working on several shadow boxes and then making up a story about them.

The Story about Ping written and illustrated by Marjorie Flack and Kurt Wiese. Viking, 1933. When Ping is separated from his family, he has an unpleasant adventure, but he is willing to receive his punishment in order to get back home.

The Whingdingdilly written and illustrated by Bill Peet. Houghton Mifflin, 1970. Scamp is jealous of Palomar, a prize-winning horse. He wishes he were something special, but when he is transformed into a "Whingdingdilly" his life becomes unbearable. Scamp learns that it is important to be yourself.

The Wizard of Oz by L. Frank Baum. Illustrated by Michael Hague. Holt, Rinehart, 1982. The beautiful color illustrations will attract many children to this classic story. Children can answer the following questions: How does Dorothy's adventure begin? How does Dorothy feel when it is over? Is Dorothy's story like Light's?

About the Author and Illustrator

BAKER, JEANNIE
Something about the Author, ed. by Anne Commire. Gale, 1981, Vol. 23, pp. 3–5.

Bang, Molly. *The Paper Crane*
Illus. by the author. Greenwillow, 1985; pap., Morrow, 1987
Suggested Use Level: Gr. 3–4   Reading Level: Gr. 4

Plot Summary

The once busy restaurant is now empty. The new highway that bypasses the restaurant has changed the fortune of the man who owns it.

Yet even though the restaurant is failing, the kindness of the owner is not diminished. When a poor stranger comes to the empty restaurant, the owner feeds him in grand style. The stranger pays for his meal with a folded paper crane that comes to life and dances. Many people come to the restaurant to see the magical dancing crane, and once again the owner becomes prosperous. After many months, the stranger returns and plays his flute. The crane dances and then flies away with the stranger on his back. However, people still come to the restaurant and talk of the stranger and the magical crane.

Thematic Material

The Paper Crane is an imaginative blend of reality and fantasy, in which the kindness of the restaurant owner is magically rewarded by the stranger. The three-dimensional paper cutouts that illustrate the book create a feeling of shadowy depth and enhance the unusual story.

Book Talk Material and Activities

This subtle story provides an opportunity for children to read about and discuss unusual characters. Even with very little description, the character of the man who owns the restaurant is evident, as is the character of the stranger. Ask children to describe each character. How does the author describe the character in the text? How do the illustrations contribute to what is known about the character? Why does the child think the stranger came to the restaurant? As children examine the characters, they learn to look for details in the text and illustrations to support their ideas. Arnold Lobel's *Fables* provides additional opportunities to look at the nuances in character development. With very little text and one illustration, Lobel has created characters that are independent and have spirit.

Molly Bang's paper cutout illustrations for *The Paper Crane* are special. The layers of paper and the shadows that they cast provide a feeling of depth. These illustrations could be compared with the ones in Jeannie Baker's *Home in the Sky* (see this chapter). Another book that could be compared with *The Paper Crane* is *Perfect Crane*. In both stories, a folded paper crane that is magically brought to life brings prosperity to the main characters, and although the crane leaves, the happiness of the characters continues. A folded paper crane is an obvious prop to use when sharing these books. Librarians could also booktalk origami books like *Easy Origami* or *Paper Pandas and Jumping Frogs*.

The crane, a symbol of good fortune and longevity, is seen in many traditional tales from the Orient. *The Crane Maiden, The Crane Wife,* and *Dawn* are all versions of the traditional Japanese legend of the Crane Wife, in which a crane takes the shape of a woman and brings success to the man who has helped her, but the greed and curiosity of the characters force her to return to her own people. *Sadako and the Thousand Paper Cranes* is a more modern story of a Japanese schoolgirl who dies of leukemia following the dropping of the atom bomb. Before her death, she tried to fold 1,000 paper cranes, because in Japan the crane is a symbol of long life. After her death, her classmates finish the cranes.

Audiovisual Adaptation

The Paper Crane. Random House Media, cassette/book, 1987; filmstrip/cassette, 1987. Also "Reading Rainbow," Great Plains National Instructional Television Library, videorecording, 1987.

Related Titles

The Crane Maiden by Miyoko Matsutani. Illustrated by Chihiro Iwasaki. Parent's Magazine Press, 1968. In this version of the Japanese Crane Wife legend, a poor old man rescues a crane. Later, he and his wife meet a lovely maiden who weaves them a beautiful cloth, which they sell for a fine price. But the wife's curiosity forces the maiden to become a crane again and leave them.

The Crane Wife retold by Sumiko Yagawa. Illustrated by Suekichi Akaba. Morrow, 1979. In this version of the Japanese Crane Wife legend, a poor young man rescues a crane who returns to him as a maiden and eventually becomes his wife. The beautiful cloth she weaves brings them much wealth, but the woman insists that no one may watch her weaving. When the husband's curiosity causes him to open the doorway and see his wife as a crane weaving cloth from her feathers, the wife becomes a crane again and flies away.

Dawn written and illustrated by Molly Bang. Morrow, 1983. Although this story is similar to *The Crane Maiden* and *The Crane Wife,* Molly Bang has chosen New England for its setting. A shipbuilder saves a Canada goose. Later, a woman appears and becomes the man's wife. She weaves him a special cloth, which he uses for the sails of his ship.

Easy Origami by Dokuohtei Nakano. Illustrated. Viking, 1985. The many simple paperfolding activities in this book include butterflies, birds, and flying saucers.

Fables written and illustrated by Arnold Lobel. Harper & Row, 1980. Twenty fables teach lessons about pleasing oneself, how to act in public, and finding happiness. The characters show many different personality traits, from thoughtfulness to greed to simple dignity.

Paper Pandas and Jumping Frogs by Florence Temko. Illustrated by Paul Jackson and Florence Temko. China Books, 1986. The ideas in this well-designed resource on paperfolding would enhance the telling of many stories. For example, make a "jumping frog" to use with *Jump, Frog, Jump!* by Robert Kalan (Greenwillow, 1981), or a paper crane to use with *The Paper Crane.*

Perfect Crane by Anne Laurin. Illustrated by Charles Mikolaycak. Harper & Row, 1981. A magician folds a paper crane and then uses his magic to bring it to life. Eventually, the crane must leave him to fly with other birds.

Sadako and the Thousand Paper Cranes by Eleanor Coerr. Illustrated by Ronald Himler. Putnam, 1977. A book based on the true story of Sadako Sasaki, a young girl who died of leukemia caused by the radiation from the bombing of Hiroshima.

About the Author and Illustrator

BANG, MOLLY
Fifth Book of Junior Authors and Illustrators, ed. by Sally Holmes Holtze. Wilson, 1983, pp. 20–21.
Something about the Author, ed. by Anne Commire. Gale, 1981, Vol. 24, pp. 37–39.

Browne, Anthony. *Piggybook*
Illus. by the author. Knopf, 1986
Suggested Use Level: Gr. 3–4   Reading Level: Gr. 3

Plot Summary

The Piggott family lives together in a lovely home. Mr. Piggott and his sons, Simon and Patrick, are loud and demanding. Mrs. Piggott is over-worked and frustrated. She does all the cooking, cleaning, and shopping without any consideration from her husband and sons. Finally, Mrs. Piggott has had enough. "You are pigs," she writes, and she leaves the men to fend for themselves. Mr. Piggott and the boys are at first pigs in their behavior, but eventually in appearance as well. Their noses become snouts and their eyes become beady; they snuffle and grunt, and images of pigs appear all around the house. When Mrs. Piggott comes home, Mr. Piggott and the boys beg her to stay. She does, but after that everyone helps around the house, so that Mrs. Piggott has time for herself and her interests, including fixing the family car.

Thematic Material

Piggybook takes a humorous look at stereotypes, as the men in the Piggott family expect Mrs. Piggott to do all of the traditional "woman's work." The illustrations are especially imaginative—familiar items are transformed into pig shapes and shadows.

Book Talk Material and Activities

Piggybook is a humorous and perceptive book that pokes fun at human selfishness and insensitivity. It is a great discussion book for children in the upper elementary grades, when children are able to understand the issues of stereotypes and prejudices. They may have personally experienced some discrimination based on their age, gender, religion, or race. After hearing this story, many children will want to discuss their own feelings about discrimination. It could also serve as a springboard for a study of human rights, perhaps focusing on the women's movement or black civil rights efforts. *Sleeping Ugly* is another humorous story that deals with stereotyped expectations.

Anthony Browne's illustrations for the book are special. Every group that has heard the story has enjoyed the humor of the text, but once children notice the transformations that are occurring in the illustrations, they begin to move closer to the book, and even shout out the changes that they see. Pigs appear in the wallpaper, the light switch, the fireplace tiles, and the andirons. Mr. Piggott's hands become pig's feet, and he and his sons begin to move about the house on their hands and knees. Children clamor to be first to sign out the book after the story session, and they look for other books by Anthony Browne. One teacher who does a unit on pig books with her fourth-grade class has the children read *The Book of Pigericks* and try to write their own pig limericks. They also look for other picture and fiction books with pigs as important characters. Special favorites include *Piggins* and *Interstellar Pig*.

Audiovisual Adaptation

Piggybook. Random House Media, cassette/book, 1988.

Related Titles

The Amazing Bone written and illustrated by William Steig. Farrar, Straus, 1976. Pearl the pig, dressed in a lovely pink frock, finds a bone with magical powers.

The Book of Pigericks: Pig Limericks written and illustrated by Arnold Lobel. Harper & Row, 1983. Elaborately dressed pigs illustrate the limericks. After hearing these read aloud, children can vote for their favorites.

Interstellar Pig by William Sleator. Dutton, 1984. Barney is on vacation with his parents when strange things start to happen. The people they meet seem sinister, and the game they are playing is becoming dangerous. What are the powers of "The Piggy?" This is not a picture book, but it is an intriguing book to read aloud or booktalk with older children.

Piggins by Jane Yolen. Illustrated by Jane Dyer. Harcourt, 1987. Piggins is Mr. and Mrs. Reynard's very proper butler. He keeps their household organized and running in tip-top shape from upstairs to downstairs. When Mrs. Reynard's diamonds are stolen, Piggins exposes the thieves—Lord and Lady Ratsby.

Pigs from A to Z written and illustrated by Arthur Geisert. Houghton Mifflin, 1986. Students can try to find the seven hidden pigs on each page of this alphabet book. Also, they can look for the five different forms of each letter.

Sleeping Ugly by Jane Yolen. Illustrated by Diane Stanley. Coward, McCann, 1981. To poke fun at the story of Sleeping Beauty and the stereotyped expectations based on appearance, Jane Yolen's Plain Jane is kind but ugly, and Princess Miserella is mean but beautiful. Children can decide which one *really* deserves the prince.

Yummers, Too! written and illustrated by James Marshall. Houghton Mifflin, 1986. Emily Pig, whose unsuccessful weight-loss program was described in *Yummers!* (Houghton Mifflin, 1973), is back. In this adventure, her appetite creates problems again. Emily is a pig who really acts like one.

About the Author and Illustrator

Browne, Anthony

Something about the Author, ed. Anne Commire. Gale, 1986, Vol. 44, p. 56; 1986, Vol. 45, pp. 48–53.

Carle, Eric. *The Very Busy Spider*
Illus. by the author. Philomel, 1984
Suggested Use Level: Gr. PreK–1   Reading Level: Gr. 1

Plot Summary

As a spider is spinning her web in the farmyard, farm animals come to talk to her—first a horse, then a cow, a sheep, a goat, a pig, a dog, a cat, a duck, and a rooster. Each animal asks the spider to leave her work, but she will not. The spider finishes her web and catches a fly. When it is night, an owl speaks to the spider, but she has fallen asleep after her busy day.

Thematic Material

The spider is able to finish her web because she keeps working despite all the interruptions. As a result of her work, the spider not only catches the fly but also has a place to sleep; thus she is rewarded for her perseverance. Eric Carle used his familiar collage technique for the illustrations, but the spider, her web, and the fly were printed on the pages with raised lines so that they could be felt.

Book Talk Material and Activities

Eric Carle has written and/or illustrated some of the most popular books for children. Young children have learned about the days of the week, colors, and counting while listening to *The Very Hungry Caterpillar;* they have used his illustrations for *Brown Bear, Brown Bear What Do You See?* to follow a sequence of colors and animals; and they have learned about counting and the zoo from *1, 2, 3 to the Zoo.* His books often have an unusual format, like the fold-out pages in *Papa, Please Get the Moon for Me.* Children certainly would enjoy learning more about this author/illustrator.

Studying some of Eric Carle's books is a great opportunity for the library and an artist or the school art department to work together. Children could experiment with the raised-line design of *The Very Busy Spider* using paper, string, and glue. After reading many books by Eric Carle and talking about his illustrations with her class, one teacher had her class make different kinds of textured paper. They made sponge paintings, experimented with printing techniques, and also made designs with tissue paper. The pictures were then cut into random shapes to be used for collages, and children were encouraged to experiment with the different shapes and textures. The children in the class became familiar with the sequencing in many of Carle's books by charting the days of the weeks and the foods in *The Very Hungry Caterpillar* and the farm animals and sounds in *The Very Busy Spider*. The patterns in Carle's books (such as the days of the week or the sequence of colors) became a part of the art and stories that they were creating.

Related Titles

Brown Bear, Brown Bear What Do You See? by Bill Martin, Jr. Illustrated by Eric Carle. Holt, Rinehart, 1967. A brown bear sees a red bird, who sees a yellow duck, who sees a blue horse, and so on. Each animal is depicted with bright colors on a two-page spread, making this a fine book to share with a group of children.

Do Bears Have Mothers, Too? written by Aileen Fisher. Illustrated by Eric Carle. Crowell, 1973. Poems about baby animals are illustrated with large, colorful pictures of the young animals and their mothers. Like *Brown Bear, Brown Bear What Do You See?*, it is great to share with a group of children. Compare the pictures of the bears on the covers of the two books.

Feathered Ones and Furry by Aileen Fisher. Illustrated by Eric Carle. Crowell, 1971. Poems about animals are illustrated with linoleum cuts, some filling a page and others adding a small detail. The bear on page 36 can be compared with others in Carle's pictures.

1, 2, 3 to the Zoo written and illustrated by Eric Carle. Philomel, 1968. In this wordless book, a train chugs by carrying animals headed for the zoo. Each car carries one more animal than the car before it, beginning with 1 elephant and ending with 10 birds. The last page folds out to show all the animals in the zoo. As with other books by Eric Carle, this one has an extra feature—a miniature picture of the train appears at the bottom of the page, showing all the cars that have been presented so far.

Papa, Please Get the Moon for Me written and illustrated by Eric Carle. Picture Book Studio, 1986. When a little girl asks her papa for the moon, he climbs a ladder and brings it to her. The pictures fold out, becoming larger and larger, until the full moon is pictured, then decreasing in size as the moon wanes.

The Very Hungry Caterpillar written and illustrated by Eric Carle. Collins-World, 1969. The little caterpillar eats and eats until he is full.

Then he builds a cocoon and rests before becoming a butterfly. The die-cut holes in the book are perfect for showing the caterpillar's progress through the food he eats.

About the Author and Illustrator

CARLE, ERIC

Fourth Book of Junior Authors and Illustrators, ed. by Doris de Montreville and Elizabeth D. Crawford. Wilson, 1978, pp. 68–69.

Illustrators of Children's Books: 1967–1976, Vol. IV, comp. by Lee Kingman, Grace Allen Hogarth, and Harriet Quimby. Horn Book, 1978, pp. 11, 105–106, 183.

Something about the Author, ed. by Anne Commire. Gale, 1973, Vol. 4, pp. 41–43.

Crews, Donald. *Parade*

Illus. by the author. Greenwillow, 1983; pap., Morrow, 1987
Suggested Use Level: Gr. PreK–1   Reading Level: NA

Plot Summary

With colorful pictures and a simple text, Crews shows the preparations for and experiences at a parade. The crowd gathers and waits for the parade to begin. The color guard, carrying flags of many nations, leads the parade. The drum major and marching band are next, followed by a float, a baton-twirling team, cyclists, old cars, and another float. The parade ends with the appearance of a new fire engine. As the people leave the parade route, the street-cleaning machine picks up streamers and confetti.

Thematic Material

Parade shows the excitement and activity that accompany one.

Book Talk Material and Activities

Being in a parade is an exciting experience for children. In one kindergarten program, the teachers organized a circus. The children acted as clowns and other circus performers. Some children even dressed up as circus animals and performed tricks, for example, a seal playing a horn. *Parade* was shared with classes to help them prepare to march into the big top (usually the gymnasium). Some children played kazoos, and others used tin pans for cymbals as they marched through the halls and around the gym. Parents and other classes in the school were the audience.

Before the circus, the teachers read poems and stories about the circus, including *The Circus* and *Harriet Goes to the Circus*. The classes made a mural to decorate the long wall in the gym, using Crew's *Parade* for ideas about colors and design.

Related Titles

The Balancing Act: A Counting Song written and illustrated by Merle Peek. Clarion, 1987. In this counting songbook, animals at the amusement park ride the ferris wheel and the roller coaster, and watch elephants balancing on a high wire. Children like to act out the words to the song as part of their circus.

The Circus by Mabel Harmer. Photographs. Childrens, 1981. The simple text and clear photographs provide children with facts about the circus. Some of the chapters describe "Circus Animals," "Show Time," and "Between Shows."

Circus by Jack Prelutsky. Illustrated by Arnold Lobel. Macmillan, 1974. In this poetry book, the circus opens with a poem about a band of monkeys and ends with one about a parade of the performers.

Circus! Circus! Poems edited by Lee Bennett Hopkins. Illustrated by John O'Brien. Knopf, 1982. Seventeen poems highlight different activities at the circus.

Harriet Goes to the Circus written and illustrated by Betsy Maestro and Giulio Maestro. Crown, 1977. Harriet the elephant and her animal friends stand in line for the circus. Harriet hopes to be first, but she is disappointed when the door opens on the other side of the tent.

Parade! by Tom Shachtman. Photographs by Chuck Saaf. Macmillan, 1985. Children will be fascinated by this behind-the-scenes look at the preparations for Macy's Thanksgiving Day Parade. Color photographs show the large balloons of many familiar characters that are part of the parade.

About the Author and Illustrator

CREWS, DONALD
Fifth Book of Junior Authors and Illustrators, ed. by Sally Holmes Holtze. Wilson, 1983, pp. 88–90.

Illustrators of Children's Books: 1967–1976, Vol. IV, comp. by Lee Kingman, Grace
   Allen Hogarth, and Harriet Quimby. Horn Book, 1978, pp. 110, 185.
Something about the Author, ed. by Anne Commire. Gale, 1983, Vol. 30, p. 88;
   1983, Vol. 32, pp. 58–60.

Grifalconi, Ann.   *Darkness and the Butterfly*
Illus. by the author. Little, Brown, 1987
Suggested Use Level: Gr. 1–3   Reading Level: Gr. 5

Plot Summary

Osa, a young girl, lives in Africa. During the day, she is happy and
carefree, but at night, she is filled with fear. Everything about the dark
frightens Osa, and no one in her family can convince her that there is
nothing to fear. One afternoon, Osa leaves her village to wander
through the valley. After a while, she realizes that she is lost. She looks
around her and sees brightly colored bottles hanging from some trees.
The sunlight sparkles on the bottles, and Osa follows the shining colors
to the home of the Wise Woman. The Wise Woman greets Osa and they
begin to talk. Osa tells the Wise Woman of her fear of the dark and the
Spirits that lurk there. The Wise Woman holds Osa and shows her a
butterfly that, even though it is a small creature, flies on through day and
night. As Osa falls asleep, she dreams of the night. In her dream, she
flies like a butterfly through a sky lit by the stars and the moon. When
she awakens, the memory of her dream comforts her. She can now face
the night without fear. Osa hurries home through the dusk. When she
arrives at home, she tells her family what has happened and there is a
joyous celebration.

Thematic Material

Osa learns to overcome her fear of the dark. The story is set in Africa
and shows a warm, supportive black family.

Book Talk Material and Activities

In *Darkness and the Butterfly,* shades of yellow and orange depict the
daytime, and shades of blue are used for the night. Osa's facial expressions reflect her moods, from fearful to joyous. Sharing this book with
children could encourage them to look at how illustrators use colors to

enhance the mood of a story. Librarians could booktalk other books in which the colors used in the illustrations are related to the feelings in the story. For example, in both *Dawn* and *Grandfather Twilight,* colors are used to distinguish between day and night. In *The Village of Round and Square Houses,* a somber story of the aftermath of a volcano, shadowy gray tones are used to depict the ash-covered people. Children could talk about their feelings about certain colors and try to find other books where, as in *Darkness and the Butterfly,* colors extend the mood of the story.

Related Titles

Dawn written and illustrated by Uri Shulevitz. Farrar, Straus, 1974. A boy and his grandfather spend the night outside, waking just before dawn and watching the sun rise. The illustrations begin as a small blue and black oval and grow in size to fill the pages with bright green, blue, and yellow.

Grandfather Twilight written and illustrated by Barbara Berger. Philomel, 1984. A man carries a special pearl to the sea. As he walks, he leaves the soft light of twilight behind him.

I Wish I Were a Butterfly by James Howe. Illustrated by Ed Young. Harcourt, 1987. A young cricket is dissatisfied with his life and longs to be a butterfly. Other animals try to convince him to be himself, but he ignores them. Finally, the spider helps the cricket feel good about being a cricket. Young's illustrations are filled with colors, light, and shadows.

Storm in the Night by Mary Stolz. Illustrated by Pat Cummings. Harper & Row, 1988. During a storm that has cut off the electricity, a grandfather and his grandson sit together in the dark and enjoy the sounds, smells, and feelings of the rain. The grandfather describes a stormy night from his childhood and how he had to overcome his fear of the dark. Like *Darkness and the Butterfly,* this book describes a loving relationship in a black family. The illustrations are in shades of blue.

The Village of Round and Square Houses written and illustrated by Ann Grifalconi. Little, Brown, 1986. This story, based on an African folktale, describes the volcanic explosion that led to men living in square houses and women in round ones. Grifalconi's illustrations capture the drama of the volcano and the ash-covered grayness of its aftermath. The book received the Caldecott Honor Medal in 1987.

When the Sun Rose written and illustrated by Barbara Helen Berger. Philomel, 1986. In this fanciful story, the sun is a golden rose that is pulled in a cart by a shining lion. The illustrations glow with a golden light.

About the Author and Illustrator

GRIFALCONI, ANN

Illustrators of Children's Books: 1957–1966, Vol. III, comp. by Lee Kingman, Grace Allen Hogarth, and Harriet Quimby. Horn Book, 1968, pp. 3, 17, 222; *1967–1976, Vol. IV,* 1978, pp. 68, 124, 191.

Something about the Author, ed. by Anne Commire. Gale, 1971, Vol. 2, pp. 125–126.

Third Book of Junior Authors, ed. by Doris de Montreville and Donna Hill. Wilson, 1972, pp. 111–113.

Jonas, Ann. *Reflections*
Illus. by the author. Greenwillow, 1987
Suggested Use Level: Gr. 1–3   Reading Level: Gr. 2

Plot Summary

A young child describes her day, beginning with watching the sun rise over the sea. She sees the ferry arrive and watches a summer storm before going to the boatyard, the beach, and on through the birch grove. In the forest, the girl turns around (and the book is turned upside down). On her way back she visits the carnival and the campgrounds. Before she eats dinner, she feeds the ducks and flies kites with her family. As the sun sets, she listens to a concert and goes to bed.

Thematic Material

The little girl in this book celebrates simple, everyday moments. The creative illustrations show reflections of different moments as the book is read and then turned upside down.

Book Talk Material and Activities

Round Trip is a "turn around" book that Ann Jonas wrote and illustrated in black and white. For *Reflections,* she created "turn around" illustrations in color. Both books challenge children to look closely at each picture. After sharing *Reflections* with a group of children, teachers and librarians should encourage them to talk about what they have seen and how they feel about it. Children often ask to look at specific pages again, and it helps to have two copies of the book available so that both sides of a picture can be viewed at once. As children look at the pictures and study the different images, they can discuss how they perceive them and try to "see" what Jonas has suggested in the text, such as sailboats in a storm, a family flying kites, or the boatyard/campground. Children sometimes look away from the pictures and then quickly look back, trying to "surprise their eyes" into seeing something new.

Many other books provide children with information about art and perception. The books of Mitsumasa Anno are visually challenging and often suggest activities for children. *Anno's Magical ABC: An Anamorphic Alphabet* describes the process of creating anamorphic drawings and encourages children to try to make their own. Books such as *The Optical Illusion Book,* which give suggestions for creating optical illusions, fascinate children. *Ed Emberley's Picture Pie* encourages children to create pictures using full and divided circles, demonstrating the relationships between shapes. A booktalk or display of these titles after reading *Reflections* and *Round Trip* will provide children with the opportunity to choose a book that challenges their creativity.

Related Titles

Anno's Magical ABC: An Anamorphic Alphabet written and illustrated by Mitsumasa Anno and Masaichiro Anno. Philomel, 1980. Two sheets of mirror paper must be used to turn the misshapen illustration into one that is in more normal perspective.

Ed Emberley's Picture Pie: A Circle Drawing Book written and illustrated by Ed Emberley. Little, Brown, 1984. Using circles and parts of circles, Emberley shows how to create hundreds of designs. The same two shapes, for example, can make a clown wearing a hat or a fish with a tail. Children enjoy rearranging the shapes into many different objects.

If at First You Do Not See written and illustrated by Ruth Brown. Holt, Rinehart, 1982. Turn this book around and see the unusual creatures that the caterpillar meets in the vegetables, the ice cream, even the hamburgers—another story of a very strange trip.

The Optical Illusion Book by Seymour Simon. Illustrated by Constance Ftera. Four Winds, 1976. Beginning with the chapter "How You See," Simon describes several optical illusions and explains why the eye is tricked by them. Children can experience the visual trickery through the book's many illustrations.

Round Trip written and illustrated by Ann Jonas. Greenwillow, 1983. Black-and-white illustrations create a "turn around" story that challenges the imagination.

The Turn About, Think About, Look About Book written and illustrated by Beau Gardner. Lothrop, 1980. The book's bold graphic designs can be interpreted in a number of different ways as the book is turned around. Gardner suggests four possibilities for each picture.

The Upside Down Riddle Book compiled and edited by Louis Phillips. Illustrated by Beau Gardner. Lothrop, 1982. The answers to these rhyming riddles are found when the pictures are turned upside down.

About the Author and Illustrator

JONAS, ANN
Something about the Author, ed. by Anne Commire. Gale, 1986, Vol. 42, p. 122; 1988, Vol. 50, pp. 106–109.

Jonas, Ann. *The Trek*
  Illus. by the author. Greenwillow, 1985
  Suggested Use Level: Gr. K–3   Reading Level: Gr. 3

Plot Summary

  Walking to school, a little girl imagines that she sees animals all around her. Bushes look like sheep and gorillas, the stone walk is an alligator, and giraffes hide by the chimney. The girl meets her friend, and they continue to walk through the imagined dangers, until they reach their school, where two posters of animals on the wall provide some background on the girls' imaginative adventure.

Thematic Material

  Ann Jonas's creative illustrations capture the imaginative spirit of the young girls, as they "see" animals in the bushes, trees, fences, and buildings on their walk. The story is also about friendship, as seen in the girls' playful behavior and willingness to pretend together.

Book Talk Material and Activities

Jonas has given children a great deal to look at in her book, and they should be encouraged to spend time examining each page. *The Trek* would be especially good as part of a book talk program featuring books with inventive illustrations. Such a program might also include *There Was a Hill; Is This a Baby Dinosaur?; Elephant Buttons; Alphabatics; Pigs from A to Z; Who's Hiding Here?;* and *Take Another Look.* After all the books have been presented through brief book talks, have the children get together in groups of two or three, and let each group pick a book. Ask the children to read and look at the book together, and to pick one illustration to share with the other children. What attracted them to that picture? What is happening in the picture that makes it special? How does the picture relate to the story? Children need opportunities to talk about books, to develop their ability to evaluate books, and to share their ideas with their peers. Librarians and teachers can promote the development of critical thinking skills by providing children with many such opportunities.

Related Titles

Alphabatics written and illustrated by Suse MacDonald. Bradbury, 1986. The letters of the alphabet twist and bend like acrobats to form objects that represent each letter. For example, the lowercase "h" becomes a house, and the uppercase "Y" becomes the horns of a yak. The book received the 1987 Caldecott Honor Medal.

Elephant Buttons written and illustrated by Noriko Ueno. Harper & Row, 1973. A wordless visual treat that is sure to spark creative responses. An elephant is unbuttoned to reveal a horse. When the horse is unbuttoned, a lion appears. The final character is a mouse, who is unbuttoned to reveal . . . an elephant!

Is This a Baby Dinosaur? and Other Science Picture Puzzles by Millicent Selsam. Photographs. Harper & Row, 1971. Black-and-white photographs show a close-up view of an object, and a question is posed. Photographs on following pages answer the question.

Pigs from A to Z written and illustrated by Arthur Geisert. Houghton Mifflin, 1986. Hidden in each illustration are seven pigs and five designs of the letter being presented. The forms are revealed at the end of the book.

Take Another Look photographs by Tana Hoban. Greenwillow, 1981. Each black-and-white photograph in this wordless book is preceded by a plain white page with a die-cut hole in the center. Children are challenged to guess what object is on the next page. Like *The Trek*, this book encourages children to look closely at their world.

There Was a Hill written and illustrated by Lark Carrier. Picture Book Studio, 1985. Shapes are transformed into animals as half-pages are turned. The soft pencil illustrations could be contrasted with the bolder color illustrations in *The Trek*.

Who's Hiding Here? written and illustrated by Yoshi. Picture Book Studio, 1987. The title is repeated as die-cut pages reveal a part of the animal on the next page. On two pages at the end of the book, Yoshi talks about animal camouflage.

About the Author and Illustrator

JONAS, ANN
Something about the Author, ed. by Anne Commire. Gale, 1986, Vol. 42, p. 122; 1988, Vol. 50, pp. 106–109.

Leaf, Margaret. *Eyes of the Dragon*
Illus. by Ed Young. Lothrop, 1987
Suggested Use Level: Gr. 2–4   Reading Level: Gr. 6

Plot Summary

In a small village in China, the people decide to build a wall around their village to protect them from harm. When the wall is completed, everyone is filled with pride, until someone observes that the wall is very plain. Ch'en Jung, an artist from the city, is selected to come to the village to paint a dragon on the wall. The artist agrees to do the work, but has several conditions, one of which is that the villagers will not ask him to change his finished work. The villagers agree and Ch'en Jung begins to paint. As the days pass, the villagers watch Ch'en Jung work. When at last he is finished, the people are awed by the magnificence of his work, but they notice that the dragon has no eyes. Although Ch'en Jung reminds them that they should not ask him to change his painting, they insist that he paint eyes on the dragon. He does so and then hurries away to his home in the city, leaving the villagers to admire their beautifully painted wall. As the villagers watch, the dragon comes to life and begins to move, destroying the wall and disappearing into a huge, menacing cloud that hovers over the village.

Thematic Material

A promise is broken in this dramatic story. When the people of the town go back on their word to the painter, they are punished with the destruction of their wall as the dragon comes to life.

Book Talk Material and Activities

There are several possibilities for extending children's involvement with this book. For example, they could investigate other stories about dragons. Booktalking such books as *Saint George and the Dragon* and *Everyone Knows What a Dragon Looks Like* encourages children to see how other authors and illustrators portray dragons. In *Saint George and the Dragon,* the dragon must be destroyed, but in *Everyone Knows What a Dragon Looks Like,* the dragon saves the city of Wu. In *Eyes of the Dragon,* the dragon is a powerful image that, when brought to life, is very destructive.

The illustrations in *Eyes of the Dragon* are filled with bright colors and shadows. Children might want to look at other books illustrated by Ed Young, including Rafe Martin's *Foolish Rabbit's Big Mistake* (see Chapter 8) and Jane Yolen's *The Girl Who Loved the Wind.* They could discuss his illustrations, considering how they change with each book, as well as looking for common images. Examining an illustrator's contribution to a book helps children develop an appreciation for the creativity that artists bring to picture books.

Related Titles

The Emperor and the Kite by Jane Yolen. Illustrated by Ed Young. World, 1967. The emperor's youngest daughter, Djeow Seow, is so tiny that she is often ignored. When her father is imprisoned, Djeow Seow makes a special kite to save him. The use of white space in the illustrations draws attention to the details of the kite.

Everyone Knows What a Dragon Looks Like by Jay Williams. Illustrated by Mercer Mayer. Four Winds, 1976. The dragon appears from an unusual source and saves the town from the enemy's attack.

The Girl Who Loved the Wind by Jane Yolen. Illustrated by Ed Young. Crowell, 1972. A wealthy merchant wants to protect his only daughter from all the pain and cruelty in the world. He keeps her secluded from the world, but the wind tells her that life is both good and bad. Spurred by her curiosity about the world, she rides away on a current of wind. The illustrations are lush, detailed, and filled with intricate patterns and designs.

I Wish I Were a Butterfly by James Howe. Illustrated by Ed Young. Harcourt, 1987. A young cricket is dissatisfied with his life and longs to be a butterfly. Other animals try to convince him to be himself, but he ignores them. Finally, the spider helps the cricket feel good about being a cricket. Young's illustrations are filled with colors, light, and shadows.

Saint George and the Dragon retold by Margaret Hodges. Illustrated by Trina Schart Hyman. Little, Brown, 1984. George needs all his strength to slay the huge and fierce dragon. Hyman's illustrations won the Caldecott Medal in 1985.

Yeh-Shen: A Cinderella Story from China retold by Ai-Ling Louie. Illustrated by Ed Young. Philomel, 1982. Yeh-Shen is befriended by a magic fish, which is later destroyed by her stepmother. Young's illustrations incorporate the shape of a fish into each page.

About the Author and Illustrator

YOUNG, ED

Illustrators of Children's Books: 1967–1976, Vol. IV, comp. by Lee Kingman, Grace Allen Hogarth and Harriet Quimby. Horn Book, 1978, pp. 170, 214.

Something about the Author, ed. by Anne Commire. Gale, 1976, Vol. 10, pp. 205–206.

Third Book of Junior Authors, ed. by Doris de Montreville and Donna Hill. Wilson, 1972, pp. 309–310.

Lionni, Leo. *It's Mine! A Fable*
Illus. by the author. Knopf, 1986
Suggested Use Level: Gr. 1–3   Reading Level: Gr. 3

Plot Summary

Three frogs—Milton, Rupert, and Lydia—live on an island in the middle of a beautiful pond. Surrounded by beauty, the frogs only quarrel and fight. A toad lectures them about their behavior, but the frogs continue their disagreeable ways. When it begins to storm, the frogs find that they are comforted by being together. After the storm clears, they remember the good feelings that they had when they showed how they cared for each other. They continue to behave kindly and find peace and contentment.

Thematic Material

Leo Lionni has written a fable that children will be able to understand and relate to. The importance of caring for others is stressed as the greedy frogs find that they need each other.

Book Talk Material and Activities

It's Mine could be booktalked as part of a program on fables, including some from Aesop (*Borrowed Feathers*) as well as original fables like those by Arnold Lobel (*Fables*). Lionni has also written other fables, including *Cornelius* and *Six Crows*. Another activity that correlates well with this book is to look at the collage illustrations in Lionni's books. One first-grade class that heard and read many books by Leo Lionni looked at the different textures of materials that he uses in his collages, including tissue paper and paper with patterns and designs. The children discussed how sometimes the paper was cut for the picture, but other times it was torn, and noticed that most of his books are illustrated on a clean, white background. After examining and discussing many books, children can experiment with collage, collecting different kinds of paper, fabric, and other materials and trying to make their own designs. They might especially like to try to make mice similar to those in Lionni's *Alexander and the Wind-Up Mouse* and *Frederick*. Their designs could be put on a mural and used as backdrop for a display of Lionni's books.

Audiovisual Adaptation

It's Mine! Random House Media, cassette/book, 1986; filmstrip/cassette, 1988. Also Distribution Sixteen, 16mm film, 1986; videorecording, 1986.

Related Titles

Alexander and the Wind-Up Mouse written and illustrated by Leo Lionni. Pantheon, 1969. Alexander, a real mouse, is envious of Willie, a toy mouse, until he discovers that Willie is about to be thrown away. Alexander finds a way to turn Willie into a real mouse. Children notice that the paper used for Willie when he is a wind-up mouse is cut cleanly, but when he is a real mouse it is torn so that the edges are rough.

Borrowed Feathers and Other Fables edited by Bryna Stevens. Illustrated by Freire Wright and Michael Foreman. Random House, 1977. Here are seven fables from Aesop. The story of the greedy milkmaid could be compared with *It's Mine!*

Cornelius written and illustrated by Leo Lionni. Pantheon, 1983. Cornelius feels left out because the other crocodiles don't appreciate his special skills. Children could write their own moral to this story.

Fables written and illustrated by Arnold Lobel. Harper & Row, 1980. Animals are depicted in human situations and present important lessons about behavior in the 20 original fables in this collection.

Frederick written and illustrated by Leo Lionni. Pantheon, 1967. While the other mice are getting ready for winter, Frederick appears to be doing nothing. Yet, on the coldest, darkest winter days, Frederick's supplies prove very valuable.

Nicholas, Where Have You Been? written and illustrated by Leo Lionni. Knopf, 1987. When Nicholas, a mouse, is grabbed by a bird, he fears for his life. After he escapes, he is befriended by some birds and realizes that not all birds are bad. Nicholas learns a lesson about prejudice and shares his understanding with his mouse friends.

Pezzettino written and illustrated by Leo Lionni. Pantheon, 1975. Pezzettino is a small orange square that is looking for where it belongs. Children enjoy making collages that imitate Lionni's mosaiclike illustrations.

Six Crows written and illustrated by Leo Lionni. Knopf, 1988. A farmer and some crows battle over a field of wheat. They succeed in scaring each other and nearly ruin the wheat. An owl helps them realize that they would do better as friends than as enemies.

About the Author and Illustrator

LIONNI, LEO

Authors of Books for Young People, Second Edition, by Martha E. Ward and Dorothy Marquardt. Scarecrow, 1971, p. 319.

Illustrators of Children's Books: 1957–1966, Vol. III, comp. by Lee Kingman, Grace Allen Hogarth, and Harriet Quimby. Horn Book, 1968, pp. 3, 16, 140, 229; *1967–1976, Vol. IV,* 1978, pp. 7, 11, 139–40, 198.

Something about the Author, ed. by Anne Commire. Gale, 1976, Vol. 8, pp. 114–115.

Third Book of Junior Authors, ed. by Muriel Fuller. Wilson, 1963, pp. 179–180.

Lobel, Arnold. *Whiskers and Rhymes*
Illus. by the author. Greenwillow, 1985; pap., Morrow, 1988
Suggested Use Level: Gr. 1–3   Reading Level: NA

Plot Summary

Lobel has written 35 original nursery rhymes and illustrated them with humorous pictures showing exquisitely clothed cats. They are short verses, most of them funny, like the one that tells of a character who brushes his teeth with a paste that turns them green. A few have a more serious tone, as the one in which a bewhiskered cat is sitting in front of a pile of books reading and thinking of all the things the books have to offer.

Thematic Material

Lobel's poems are original verses written in the style of nursery rhymes.

Book Talk Material and Activities

The imaginative verses in *Whiskers and Rhymes* could be included in activities with nursery rhymes. Teachers and librarians might want to point out that they are original rhymes written in the style of nursery rhymes. Children often appreciate seeing how authors get ideas from other books, using them as models. Some children may even want to try writing their own nursery rhymes. Lobel used cats to depict the characters in the illustrations for *Whiskers and Rhymes*. In *The Book of Pigericks*, he wrote about and drew pigs. In *The Ice-Cream Cone Coot and Other Rare Birds*, he invented creatures using familiar items. For example, the "Steampresser Sparrow" has flatirons for feet. Children might enjoy looking at Lobel's illustrations in other poetry books to see how his pictures capture the images in the poems.

Audiovisual Adaptation

Whiskers and Rhymes. Random House Media, cassette/book, 1986; filmstrip/cassette, 1986; videorecording, 1988.

Related Titles

The Book of Pigericks: Pig Limericks written and illustrated by Arnold Lobel. Harper & Row, 1983. Children like limericks, and Lobel's fancy pigs and inventive humor are delightful. Children can compare the pigs' outfits with what the cats wear in *Whiskers and Rhymes.*

Circus by Jack Prelutsky. Illustrated by Arnold Lobel. Macmillan, 1974. In this poetry book, the circus begins with a poem about a band of monkeys and ends with one about a parade of all the performers. Many of Lobel's illustrations are in panels that show a sequence of action. For example, five pictures show the human cannonball doing his act.

Gregory Griggs and Other Nursery Rhyme People edited and illustrated by Arnold Lobel. Greenwillow, 1978. These nursery rhymes are all about people. The illustrations capture the personality of each individual, from "Gregory Griggs" to "Flying-man."

The Ice-Cream Cone Coot and Other Rare Birds written and illustrated by Arnold Lobel. Parent's Magazine Press, 1971. Poems about some very unusual birds include "The Drippet" and "The Sharpsaw Macaw." Lobel has created creatures out of ordinary objects, such as a dripping faucet and a saw.

Tyrannosaurus Was a Beast: Dinosaur Poems by Jack Prelutsky. Illustrated by Arnold Lobel. Greenwillow, 1988. Fourteen dinosaurs are featured in the poems, including the stegosaurus and triceratops. Lobel's illustrations capture the whimsical tone of Prelutsky's poems.

About the Author and Illustrator

LOBEL, ARNOLD
Authors of Books for Young People: Supplement to the Second Edition, by Martha E. Ward and Dorothy Marquardt. Scarecrow, 1979, p. 321.
Illustrators of Children's Books: 1957–1966, Vol. III, comp. by Lee Kingman, Grace Allen Hogarth, and Harriet Quimby. Horn Book, 1968, pp. xvi, 141, 229; *1967–1976, Vol. IV*, 1978, pp. 17–18, 140, 173, 199.
Something about the Author, ed. by Anne Commire. Gale, 1974, Vol. 6, pp. 147–148.
Third Book of Junior Authors, ed. by Muriel Fuller. Wilson, 1963, pp. 181–182.

Mahy, Margaret. *17 Kings and 42 Elephants*
Illus. by Patricia MacCarthy. Dial, 1987
Suggested Use Level: Gr. K–2   Reading Level: NA

Plot Summary

Kings and elephants are traveling through the jungle. Rhyming text with humorous word plays describes their adventures with crocodiles, tigers, pelicans, flamingos, and other jungle creatures. The illustrations are batik paintings that colorfully portray the rollicking fun.

Thematic Material

Mahy's text is a nonsense rhyme with imaginative word plays. Full-color batik paintings depict the jungle animals and lush foliage that the kings and elephants see.

Book Talk Material and Activities

When *17 Kings and 42 Elephants* was shared in a story program, the children enjoyed hearing the rhyme of "elephants" and "umbrella-phants" and "crocodiles" and "rockodiles." Many children tried the rhyming word play on their own. Some poems from Laura E. Richards (*Piping Down the Valleys Wild*) that also use made-up words for a humorous effect extended the fun of the story session. Children liked hearing one of Richards's poems, "Eletelephony," about an elephant who wants to use the telephone, after the rhymes in *17 Kings and 42 Elephants*.

The illustrations in *17 Kings and 42 Elephants* are batik paintings. As children may be unfamiliar with batik, an art teacher or local artist could be asked to demonstrate the technique. If learning to do batik is part of the children's art curriculum, *17 Kings and 42 Elephants* could be shared with the art teacher as an example of the technique. *Rennie the Fish* is another story with batik illustrations, and *Tie Dying and Batik* is a nonfiction book about the process.

Related Titles

May I Bring a Friend? by Beatrice Schenk de Regniers. Illustrated by Beni Montresor. Atheneum, 1964. Each day of the week, the king and queen invite a young boy to tea, and each day he brings a guest with him. Lions, monkeys, and other animals enjoy tea with the king and queen until, finally, the king, the queen, and the little boy join the animals for tea at the zoo. The rhyming text adds to the enjoyment of the book, which received the Caldecott Medal in 1965.

Oh What a Noise! written and illustrated by Uri Shulevitz. Macmillan, 1971. The rhyming text describes the noisy animals that a little boy sees while getting ready for bed.

Piping Down the Valleys Wild: Poetry for the Young of All Ages edited with a new introduction by Nancy Larrick. Illustrated by Ellen Raskin. Delacorte, 1985. This classic poetry collection originally published in 1968 includes many humorous poems by Laura E. Richards. The word play of "Eletelephony" and "The Giraffe and the Woman" would extend the humor of *17 Kings and 42 Elephants*.

Rennie the Fish written and illustrated by Emmy Howe. Van Nostrand Reinhold, 1972. The story of Rennie the fish who leaves his fishbowl, travels through the water pipes of the city, and comes out the faucet back in his own home was written and illustrated by Emmy Howe when she was 15. After the story comes a description of how the batik illustrations were prepared.

Tie Dying and Batik by Astrith Deyrup. Illustrated by Nancy Lou Gahan. Doubleday, 1974. The first half of the book discusses tie-dyeing. The second half gives step-by-step instructions for different batik projects and designs. Chapters include "Brush Strokes," "Crayon Batik," and "Experimenting with Batik."

Tikki Tikki Tembo retold by Arlene Mosel. Illustrated by Blair Lent. Holt, Rinehart, 1968. Tikki Tikki Tembo's complete name is so long that he nearly drowns because his younger brother cannot say it fast enough to get him rescued. Children enjoy hearing his long name and then saying it themselves.

About the Author and Illustrator

MAHY, MARGARET

Authors of Books for Young People: Supplement to the Second Edition, by Martha E. Ward and Dorothy Marquardt. Scarecrow, 1979, p. 184.

Fourth Book of Junior Authors and Illustrators, ed. by Doris de Montreville and Elizabeth D. Crawford. Wilson, 1978, pp. 248–250.

Something about the Author, ed. by Anne Commire. Gale, 1978, Vol. 14, pp. 129–131.

Ormerod, Jan. *The Story of Chicken Licken*
Illus. by the author. Lothrop, 1985
Suggested Use Level: Gr. 1–3   Reading Level: NA

Plot Summary

With the audience assembled and the curtain closed, a narrator appears to announce the beginning of the play "The Story of Chicken Licken." As the familiar story is told, the illustrations depict children in costumes taking the various parts. The illustrations also show the members of the audience, including the antics of an unattended baby. When the play is finished, the actors take their bows and the audience applauds. Meanwhile, the baby has crawled up to the stage and joins the children.

Thematic Material

The Story of Chicken Licken is based on a folktale that has many variations. The book's unusual premise places the story in the context of a school play, with the dramatic activities on the stage telling the story, while more humorous activities can be observed in the audience.

Book Talk Material and Activities

Ormerod's book tells two stories. The familiar story of the chicken who thinks that "the sky is falling" takes place on stage, while the illustrations tell the story of what is happening in the audience. *The Story of Chicken Licken* could be compared and contrasted with other folktale versions, including Rafe Martin's *Foolish Rabbit's Big Mistake* (see Chapter 8).

Presenting the story in the form of a play adds an inventive twist that children enjoy. As the activities in the audience are never discussed in the text, children can tell their own stories about what is happening. In most of the illustrations, the audience, except for the baby, is depicted as silhouettes, and children must look carefully at each illustration to see what is changing. Children can compare *The Story of Chicken Licken* with other stories that are presented as plays, such as *The Comic Adventures of Old Mother Hubbard and Her Dog* and *Who's in Rabbit's House?*, answering such questions as: Does the play format add to the retelling? and Why do you think the author and illustrator chose to present the story as a play?

After reading Jan Ormerod's book, children might enjoy putting on a simple play of their own. Librarians could booktalk and display collections of plays and work with classroom teachers on a presentation. *Little Plays for Little People* and *Fried Onions and Marshmallows* have some simple plays, and *Presenting Readers' Theater* gives suggestions for organizing a performance.

Related Titles

The Comic Adventures of Old Mother Hubbard and Her Dog illustrated by Tomie de Paola. Harcourt, 1981. Familiar nursery rhyme characters fill the audience to watch Old Mother Hubbard and her dog act out their rhyme. In the oval pictures on either side of the stage are scenes from other nursery rhymes that children enjoy finding and saying.

Fried Onions and Marshmallows and Other Little Plays for Little People by Sally Melcher Jarvis. Illustrated by Franklin Luke. Parent's Magazine Press, 1968. These 13 simple plays originally appeared in *Humpty Dumpty* magazine and are easy enough for primary-grade children. Some, like "Trip-Trap! Trip-Trap!" are based on familiar stories.

Little Plays for Little People from the Editors of Humpty Dumpty's Magazine for Little Children. Illustrated by Ilse-Margaret Vogel. Parent's Magazine Press, 1965. The illustrations for these simple and appropriate plays for young children give suggestions for some easy props and costumes.

Presenting Readers' Theater: Plays and Poems to Read Aloud by Caroline Feller Bauer. Illustrated by Lynn Gates Bredeson. Wilson, 1987. Bauer provides practical suggestions for involving children in dramatic reading activities. Included are more than 50 poems and stories in play format.

Who's in Rabbit's House? A Masai Tale retold by Verna Aardema. Illustrated by Leo Dillon and Diane Dillon. Dial, 1977. Readers see the villagers gather for the performance of the story and observe the actors finishing their preparations. As the curtain opens, the perspective shifts, and the readers become the audience. What impact does the play format have on the presentation of this folktale?

About the Author and Illustrator

ORMEROD, JAN (JANETTE LOUISE ORMEROD)
Something about the Author, ed. by Anne Commire. Gale, 1986, Vol. 44, p. 140.

Small, David. *Paper John*
Illus. by the author. Farrar, Straus, 1987
Suggested Use Level: Gr. 3–4   Reading Level: Gr. 6

Plot Summary

John is an unusual man with a special skill. He can fold paper into wonderful objects—flowers, hats, boats, even a house. He settles in a new town and folds a paper house for himself. As a stranger in town, John's talent and gentle personality win him the affection of the townsfolk, who call him Paper John. One day, Paper John finds a strange little man tangled in his fishing line. The man is a devil who disrupts John's life and causes trouble in the town. When John realizes the evil work the devil is doing, he uses his paper-folding skill to capture him. The angry devil is taken to jail, where he conjures the winds to destroy the town. Once again, John uses his talent to help others as he folds a boat and rescues the townsfolk. The devil is blown away, the townspeople rebuild their town, and John folds a new paper house for himself.

Thematic Material

Paper John is the story of a kind man with an independent spirit, who is happy to be himself and live according to his own simple needs and values. It is also the story of a talented character who uses his talent to help others. The illustrations depict the many objects that John creates, showing the texture and line of the paper.

Book Talk Material and Activities

For Children's Book Week or National Library Week, many school and public libraries invite guest readers to share stories with children. Community members, parents, and grandparents become involved in library activities while celebrating books and reading. Guests often ask for suggestions of what to read to help make their visit special. With some very simple preparations, *Paper John* is a great book to suggest. Imagine a guest reader who comes in wearing a paper hat and carrying some paper flowers, sits down, and begins to read *Paper John*. After the reading, the guest could give away the paper flowers. The librarian could extend the reading by booktalking and displaying books about paper folding, perhaps demonstrating a few simple examples. This is also an opportunity for the librarian to show children where the arts and crafts books are located. Booktalking a few books about origami and paper crafts would introduce children to this nonfiction area.

Children enjoy comparing *Paper John* with *Louis the Fish* by Arthur Yorinks, another book about an independent man, and talking about Louis and John. They can be asked various questions, such as: In what ways are Louis and John alike? What makes them different from other people? Are they happy being different? Can you find examples from the books to show why or why not? Do you feel that you can do what you want? Can you give some reasons to support your answer? Children develop a better understanding of what they read when they can relate it to their own lives. Discussing *Paper John* and *Louis the Fish* helps them think about their choices and opportunities.

Related Titles

Cut and Tell: Scissor Stories for Fall; Cut and Tell: Scissor Stories for Spring; Cut and Tell: Scissor Stories for Winter written and illustrated by Jean Warren. Totline Press, 1984. Three manuals give instructions for creating paper props to accompany stories, poems, and finger plays. Librarians and teachers will find this a useful source of ideas to "jazz up" story sessions.

Easy Origami by Dokuohtei Nakano. Illustrated. Viking, 1985. These origami projects are more difficult than those in *Paperfolding to Begin With*, and there are many more of them, with two sections of "Origami to Play With," and one section each of "Origami to Use" and "Origami for Display."

Exciting Things to Make with Paper by Ruth Thomson. Illustrated by Carol Lawson. Lippincott, 1977. Colorful illustrations help with each step to make simple pop-up cards, jewelry, and flowers.

Louis the Fish by Arthur Yorinks. Illustrated by Richard Egielski. Farrar, Straus, 1980. Louis has spent his life pleasing other people. At last, he is able to live his life his own way—as a fish.

Paper Cutting by Florence Temko. Illustrated by Steve Madison. Doubleday, 1973. Do you need to know how to make some tissue flowers to use as props for *Paper John*? This book has clear instructions and illustrations for paper flowers as well as paper lanterns, fish, and stars.

Paperfolding to Begin With by Florence Temko and Elaine Simon. Illustrated by Joan Stoliar. Bobbs-Merrill, 1968. Although this is a fairly old title, the projects really are just right for beginners. A simple sailboat, a kite, a hat, and a tulip correlate well with *Paper John.*

About the Author and Illustrator

SMALL, DAVID
Something about the Author, ed. by Anne Commire. Gale, 1987, Vol. 46, p. 202; 1988, Vol. 50, pp. 203–206.

Van Allsburg, Chris. *The Polar Express*
Illus. by the author. Houghton Mifflin, 1985
Suggested Use Level: Gr. 1–4   Reading Level: Gr. 4

Plot Summary

It is Christmas Eve, and a young boy who is too excited to sleep waits in his room for sounds of Santa. Instead, he hears the noise of a large locomotive that has mysteriously appeared outside his house. The boy goes outside and boards the train, which is filled with other children and bound for the North Pole. Along the way, the train passes through woods, travels up mountains, and crosses vast icy plains, until it reaches the North Pole. There the children hurry to meet Santa, and the boy is chosen to receive the first gift of Christmas. He selects one of the silver bells from Santa's sleigh. On the way home, however, the boy discovers that he has lost the bell. Although saddened by the loss, he is still eager to celebrate Christmas. The next morning as he opens his presents he finds a small box. Inside it is the bell, which Santa had found. As the boy shakes the bell, his parents cannot hear the jingling. The boy and his sister can hear it, for they still believe in the spirit of Christmas.

Thematic Material

The Polar Express is a Christmas story, but it is also a story of imagination. The illustrations create a mood of wonder that is very different from the feeling in Van Allsburg's other books.

Book Talk Material and Activities

This perfect holiday book, filled with the joy and wonder that are the best part of Christmas, celebrates the spirit of the season. Like the other books by Chris Van Allsburg, it is a joy to read aloud because it challenges the imagination. The North Pole is not just a little workshop for Santa and his elves. Van Allsburg shows a more believable North Pole—a city filled with factories and hundreds of elves. And how else would one get there but on a train that appears out of nowhere, travels thousands of miles, and returns home before morning. From the very first page, children know that the story is a magical one.

The variety and creativity in Van Allsburg's books make them very effective for library programs. Children could compare the color paintings in *The Polar Express* to the black-and-white pencil drawings in *Jumanji*. Both books have unusual plot twists that capture the interest of children, and both received the Caldecott award (*Jumanji* in 1982 and *The Polar Express* in 1986). *Jumanji* was Van Allsburg's second book for children and many children are surprised to learn that Van Allsburg won the award so early in his career, but they are even more surprised to find out that he won the Caldecott Honor Medal in 1980 for his first book, *The Garden of Abdul Gasazi*. Looking at these books could lead to a discussion of the Caldecott Medal and a discussion of some of the other illustrators who have received it. Sharing Van Allsburg's books can also help children develop an appreciation for the different media and techniques an artist uses to interpret different stories.

Audiovisual Adaptation

The Polar Express. Random House Media, cassette/book, 1986; filmstrip/cassette, 1986; videorecording, 1988.

Related Titles

Ben's Dream written and illustrated by Chris Van Allsburg. Houghton Mifflin, 1982. While Ben is studying for his geography test, it begins to rain. Listening to the pouring rain, Ben falls asleep. Suddenly, he seems to wake up and discover that the world is flooded. As he is floating away in his house, he looks out the window and sees many famous landmarks, including Mount Rushmore, where George Washington tells him to wake up. The shift in perspective of the black-and-white ink drawings adds to the unusual mood during the dream.

The Garden of Abdul Gasazi written and illustrated by Chris Van Allsburg. Houghton Mifflin, 1979. While watching a neighbor's dog, Alan Mitz accidentally enters the forbidden garden of a retired magician, who turns the dog into a duck. Back home, when Alan tries to explain what happened to his neighbor, the dog reappears, making Alan think it was just a trick. Or was it? This is Chris Van Allsburg's first book, which received a Caldecott Honor Medal in 1980. The shadows in the black-and-white drawings create just the right mood of mystery.

Jumanji written and illustrated by Chris Van Allsburg. Houghton Mifflin, 1981. Two children find a board game and take it home. When they play it, the game seems like any other, until the jungle adventures actually begin to happen. A lion attacks them, monkeys get into the kitchen, and the living room is flooded. At last they escape from the jungle and end the game. When everything is back to normal, the children wonder if their adventures were just a dream. Black-and-white pencil drawings capture the details of the jungle animals and make the experience seem real. *Jumanji* was awarded the Caldecott Medal in 1982.

The Mysteries of Harris Burdick written and illustrated by Chris Van Allsburg. Houghton Mifflin, 1984. Van Allsburg's inventive premise is that an artist left his portfolio containing some black-and-white drawings and suggested chapter titles and captions with a publisher and then never returned. The rest of the story is left to the reader's imagination. Each drawing has a slight twist, sometimes sinister, sometimes magical. The book is often used to start creative-writing projects.

The Stranger written and illustrated by Chris Van Allsburg. Houghton Mifflin, 1986. A man is accidentally hit by a car and cannot remember who he is. The farmer who hit him takes him home and hopes he will someday remember. Weeks pass, but the stranger's memory does not return. Summer seems to be lasting longer than ever before, however, and unusual things seem to happen when the stranger is nearby. Finally, one day, the stranger remembers who he is and leaves the farmer and his family. Now the stranger can continue his work. The realism of the full-color illustrations in orange and yellow, which set the mood of Indian summer, contrasts with the fantasy in the story.

The Wreck of the Zephyr written and illustrated by Chris Van Allsburg. Houghton Mifflin, 1983. An old man tells a fantastic story filled with magic sails and flying boats, about how a small sailboat came to be wrecked high on the cliffs above the sea. A boy who had learned the secret of the flying boats but refused to listen to the advice of the sailor who taught him flew his boat alone and crashed it into the cliffs. The full-color illustrations make the flying boats seem real.

The Z Was Zapped: A Play in Twenty-Six Acts Performed by the Caslon Players written and illustrated by Chris Van Allsburg. Houghton Mifflin,

1987. This alphabet book is filled with the creativity and mystery that is evident in Van Allsburg's books. Black-and-white drawings show each letter on a stage with something unusual happening to it.

About the Author and Illustrator

VAN ALLSBURG, CHRIS
Fifth Book of Junior Authors and Illustrators, ed. by Sally Holmes Holtze. Wilson, 1983, pp. 316–317.
Something about the Author, ed. by Anne Commire. Gale, 1985, Vol. 37, pp. 204–207.

Wildsmith, Brian. *Daisy*
Illus. by the author. Pantheon, 1984
Suggested Use Level: Gr. K–2   Reading Level: Gr. 3

Plot Summary

Farmer Brown and his cow, Daisy, both enjoy watching television. One day, Farmer Brown forgets to close the farm gate, and Daisy leaves the farm, searching for the adventurous life she has seen on television. When Daisy accidentally walks from the hillside onto the roof of a church, her rescue from the roof is filmed by a camera crew, and she becomes famous. A film producer sees Daisy's rescue and arranges with Farmer Brown to take her to Hollywood, where her life is filled with films, fans, advertisements, and banquets. Daisy's life is exciting, but she realizes that she misses her old life. The producer decides to make a movie about Daisy's return home. Daisy stays on the farm with Farmer Brown, content that she has fulfilled her dreams, but happy to be back home.

Thematic Material

Daisy wants to lead a more exciting life, but after she is famous, she misses her simple life. Daisy learns to be satisfied with her own life. Children will enjoy the half-page illustrations.

Book Talk Material and Activities

The half-page illustrations draw extra attention to this story. Wildsmith has arranged his text so that events occur sequentially and correlate with the half-page illustrations. For example, in one sequence, Daisy is on the church roof, and when children flip the half page, she is being rescued. After reading other Wildsmith books (for example, *Pelican* and *Give a Dog a Bone*), children often want to experiment with this technique. They can take a piece of paper, fold one-third of it over, and make a drawing in which the fold lifts up to reveal another picture. Teachers and librarians may want to have a variety of materials on hand, including markers, chalk, and paints, for the children to use. Booktalking other books in which illustrators used this technique, including *Is Anyone Home?* and *Where Can It Be?*, gives children more ideas for their own drawings.

Related Titles

Give a Dog a Bone written and illustrated by Brian Wildsmith. Pantheon, 1985. Every bone that the dog Stray finds is lost before she can enjoy it. Finally, Stray finds a bone to keep and a new home. The half-page style is perfect for showing how Stray finds her bones and what happens to them.

Goat's Trail written and illustrated by Brian Wildsmith. Knopf, 1986. A goat who lives in the mountains is curious about the noises from the town below. On his way to town, he is joined by some sheep, a cow, a pig, and a donkey. The noises from the animals added to the noises from the town make this a very noisy book. Sections are cut out of pages to allow children to peek through to the next page.

In My Garden written and illustrated by Ron Maris. Greenwillow, 1987. A young girl takes the reader on a visit to her garden. The half-page style shows the movement of the animals and the people in the story.

Is Anyone Home? written and illustrated by Ron Maris. Greenwillow, 1985. A young child opens doors to see who is at the farm. The doors are really half pages that reveal different farm animals, including chickens, cats, and horses.

Pelican written and illustrated by Brian Wildsmith. Pantheon, 1982. A boy named Paul finds a box with an egg inside that has fallen off a truck. The egg hatches into a pelican that causes problems until Paul and his family help her learn to be on her own. The detailed half-page illustrations blend so well with the underlying page that children are often surprised to find that they can be turned.

Where Can It Be? written and illustrated by Ann Jonas. Greenwillow, 1986. As a little girl searches for her blanket, children lift pages that seem to open doors, pull down blankets, and lift up tablecloths.

About the Author and Illustrator

WILDSMITH, BRIAN
Illustrators of Children's Books: 1957–1966, Vol. III, comp. by Lee Kingman, Grace
    Allen Hogarth, and Harriet Quimby. Horn Book, 1968, pp. 36–37, 50, 53,
    192, 203, 247; 1978, pp. 26, 38, 70–71, 169, 214.
Something about the Author, ed. by Anne Commire. Gale, 1979, Vol. 16, pp. 277–
    283.
Third Book of Junior Authors, ed. by Doris de Montreville and Donna Hill. Wilson,
    1972, pp. 300–301.

Williams, Vera B.   *Cherries and Cherry Pits*
   Illus. by the author. Greenwillow, 1986
   Suggested Use Level: Gr. K–3   Reading Level: Gr. 3

Plot Summary

   Bidemmi loves to draw. As she draws with markers, she tells stories
about her pictures. One story is about a strong man with dark brown skin
who brings bright red cherries home to his children. Another story is
about a white woman who brings home sour cherries to share with her
parrot. The third story is about a black boy who gives a dark red cherry
to his little sister. In the next story, Bidemmi buys her own cherries,
saving the pits and planting trees. The last story tells about how cherry
trees grow, and Bidemmi imagines how everyone in the neighborhood
will enjoy "eating cherries and spitting out the pits."

Thematic Material

   The artwork in this story is especially effective. Vera B. Williams used
watercolors to show Bidemmi working on her drawings with markers,
but the pictures that correlate with Bidemmi's stories were done with
markers to appear to have been done by Bidemmi.

Book Talk Material and Activities

   There are many possibilities for using this story with children, especially in cooperation with the school art department. The story-within-a-
story pattern is supported by Williams's use of different media to illustrate the story about Bidemmi and those by her.
   The following activity is from the experiences of Jeanette Throne,

Mercer Elementary School, Shaker Heights, Ohio, with *Cherries and Cherry Pits*. It was one of eight winning entries in the "Children's Books Open Doors" competition, sponsored by the National Council of Teachers of English and the Children's Book Council. When Ms. Throne's kindergarten class heard *Cherries and Cherry Pits,* the children began drawing borders around some of their pictures, imitating the colorful borders in many of the book's illustrations, and they enjoyed chanting the refrain "eating cherries and spitting out the pits." They drew and wrote their own cherry stories using markers, and put them into a class book, which they dedicated "To our class for working on this book." One child wrote about a rock star who had a bag of cherries. Another drew a picture of a cherry orchard with all his friends eating cherries and saving the pits to plant cherry trees. Still another wrote: "I was walking in the woods and a big cherry fell on me. I put my hands up to get it, and I put it down so I could eat it. Then when I got home, I was full from eating that big cherry." After hearing this story, the class decided to make it the last story in the book, which the class named *The Littlest Cherries First and the Biggest Cherry at the End of This Book.*

Bidemmi's story and pictures about saving and planting cherry pits led to a variety of science activities in Ms. Throne's class. After tasting different kinds of cherries, the children voted for their favorites, and of course, they planted the cherry pits. They used library books to learn more about how cherries grow and compared that information with what they knew about other plants. They also read stories about other children who planted things, such as *Titch* and *The Carrot Seed*. The kindergarten teacher helped the children extend their knowledge of books and the world by encouraging them to reflect on and integrate their own experiences with those in books.

Related Titles

The Carrot Seed by Ruth Krauss. Illustrated by Crockett Johnson. Harper & Row, 1945. When a little boy plants a carrot seed and waits for it to grow, his family is interested but not encouraging. Still, the boy cares for his plant and, finally, is rewarded with a carrot so large that he must move it in a wheelbarrow. Children enjoy a story in which the littlest person grows the biggest thing. A comparison can be made with *Titch*.

Eat the Fruit, Plant the Seed by Millicent E. Selsam and Jerome Wexler. Photographs. Morrow, 1980. Clear directions are given for growing plants from the seeds in avocado, papaya, citrus fruits, mango, pomegranate, and kiwi. Photographs help children see the process of finding and saving the seeds and then cultivating the plants.

Frog and Toad Together written and illustrated by Arnold Lobel. Harper & Row, 1971. There are five stories in this book. In "The Garden," Frog has a beautiful garden, and Toad wants one too. After planting his seeds, Toad becomes impatient and yells at his garden. But Frog urges him to take care of his garden and to be kind to the plants, and, at last, Toad's garden grows.

Seeds and More Seeds by Millicent E. Selsam. Illustrated by Tomi Ungerer. Harper & Row, 1959. Once Benny, who experiments by planting a pebble, a stone, a marble, and a seed, sees that only the seed will grow, he continues his experiment by planting many different kinds of seeds. This book in the I Can Read Science series makes information about seeds and growing things accessible to many young readers.

Titch written and illustrated by Pat Hutchins. Macmillan, 1971. Titch is the youngest in his family. His older brother and sister seem so much bigger and more important. When Titch plants his tiny seed, he surprises everyone with the huge plant that he grows.

About the Author and Illustrator

WILLIAMS, VERA B.
Fifth Book of Junior Authors and Illustrators, ed. by Sally Holmes Holtze. Wilson, 1983, pp. 327–328.
Something about the Author, ed. by Anne Commire. Gale, 1983, Vol. 33, p. 230.

Wolff, Ashley.   *A Year of Birds*
Illus. by the author. Dodd, Mead, 1984
Suggested Use Level: Gr. PreK–1   Reading Level: NA

Plot Summary

A young girl watches the birds that visit her house throughout the year. The months of the year provide the framework for block prints of many birds, including cardinals, hummingbirds, and wrens.

Thematic Material

Using linoleum block illustrations, Ashley Wolff presents information about birds and the months of the year.

Book Talk Material and Activities

After sharing *A Year of Birds* with children, teachers and librarians could show Wolff's *A Year of Beasts* and *The Bells of London,* which also have linoleum block illustrations. Once the prints are made, the pictures are hand-tinted with vivid colors that are all the more striking because of the dark black outlines from the block prints. In many schools, children learn simple printing techniques as part of the art program. An art teacher could be asked to demonstrate linoleum block printing to a group at a school or public library. A related activity is to have children make some simple prints, perhaps just using potatoes. *Potato Printing* offers some good suggestions for different techniques.

A Year of Birds could also be related to the study of birds and the seasons. Stories, poetry, and nonfiction books about birds could be booktalked, including *A Child's Book of Birds* and *Flocks of Birds.*

Related Titles

The Bells of London written and illustrated by Ashley Wolff. Dodd, Mead, 1985. Colorful linoleum block prints illustrate Wolff's version of the traditional rhyme about the activities in London during the Elizabethan Age.

A Child's Book of Birds by Kathleen N. Daly. Illustrated by Fred Brenner. Doubleday, 1977. Familiar birds, including the cardinal and the quail, briefly described and illustrated (many in color).

Feathered Ones and Furry by Aileen Fisher. Illustrated by Eric Carle. Crowell, 1971. These poems are about animals, including the pelican, squirrel, robin, duck, and raccoon. They could be shared with *A Year of Birds.*

Five Nests by Caroline Arnold. Illustrated by Ruth Sanderson. Dutton, 1980. The simple text describes how five birds—robins, redwinged blackbirds, rheas, Mexican jays, and cowbirds—care for their young.

Flocks of Birds by Charlotte Zolotow. Illustrated by Ruth Lercher Bornstein. Crowell, 1965. A little girl is not ready to fall asleep, so her mother tells her to think of birds. As her mother talks about birds soaring in the sky, the little girl falls asleep.

Going Barefoot by Aileen Fisher. Illustrated by Adrienne Adams. Crowell, 1960. These poems about animals and their tracks, including rabbits, deer, kangaroos, and birds, also describe the changing weather through the seasons.

It's Time Now! by Alvin Tresselt. Illustrated by Roger Duvoisin.

Lothrop, 1969. Here is a picture-book story about the changing seasons. Children could compare Duvoisin's pictures of the seasons with Wolff's in *A Year of Birds*.

Potato Printing written and illustrated by Helen R. Haddad. Crowell, 1981. Clear instructions and illustrations describe different techniques for potato printing. Chapters include "Papers for Printing," "Reversal," "Fabric Printing," and "Creating Backgrounds."

When Birds Change Their Feathers by Roma Gans. Illustrated by Felicia Bond. Crowell, 1980. Most of this book, which is part of the Let's-Read-and-Find-Out Science series, describes how and why birds lose their feathers.

A Year of Beasts written and illustrated by Ashley Wolff. Dutton, 1986. Like in *A Year of Birds*, months of the year are used as a framework for presenting information, in this case, about animals. The linoleum block prints produce clear black lines that draw attention to details in the illustrations.

Wood, Audrey.   *Heckedy Peg*
Illus. by Don Wood. Harcourt, 1987
Suggested Use Level: Gr. 2–4   Reading Level: Gr. 4

Plot Summary

A mother lives in a cottage with her seven children, who are named for the days of the week. Although they are poor, they help each other. One day, before going to the market, the mother lets each child request something special. She promises to bring them what they have requested and reminds them that they must not speak to strangers or touch the fire while she is gone. After the mother leaves for the market, a witch, Heckedy Peg, comes to their cottage and asks for a flame to light her pipe. At first, the children refuse, but when the witch offers them gold, they let her into the house. The witch lights her pipe and uses it to cast a spell on the children, changing each of them into something to eat or drink and carrying them off in her basket. When the mother returns home, she discovers her children are missing. A blackbird leads her to Heckedy Peg's hut, where the mother must identify her bewitched children so that they can be returned to their original form. The mother succeeds, and she and her children chase Heckedy Peg away.

Thematic Material

Many elements in this original story are associated with a folktale, including a witch and magical transformations.

Book Talk Material and Activities

Although not about Halloween, *Heckedy Peg* could be shared in October with other books about witches. Children could look for stories with witches in them and discuss how the witches are portrayed in the text and illustrations. For example, the story has very little description of Heckedy Peg, but the illustrations depict her as having a wrinkled face and wearing worn, ragged clothes. Her home is depicted as cavernous and dark. Librarians and teachers may want to provide a starting point for students by booktalking some books with witches. They could include the traditional folktale witches in such stories as *Hansel and Gretel* and *Rapunzel;* some stories where witches are not evil, such as *Strega Nona;* and such stories of contemporary witches as *The Witch Who Lives Down the Hall* (see Chapter 2). A writing activity that could correlate with this project is to have the children write descriptions of the witches based on the illustrations.

Audiovisual Adaptation

Heckedy Peg. Random House Media, filmstrip/cassette, 1988.

Related Titles

Jorinda and Joringel by the Brothers Grimm. Illustrated by Adrienne Adams. Scribner, 1963. A young man and a young woman, Joringel and Jorinda, who plan to be married, go for a walk in the forest and become lost. Jorinda is turned into a bird by the witch who lives in the forest, but Joringel eventually breaks the enchantment and rescues her and all the other maidens that the witch had captured. Children could compare the witch in this story with *Heckedy Peg.*

Hansel and Gretel by the Brothers Grimm. Illustrated by Lisbeth Zwerger. Morrow, 1970. In this classic folktale, Hansel and Gretel are abandoned by their father and stepmother and captured by a witch. Children could compare the description of the witch in the text with the one in the illustrations.

Hansel and Gretel retold by Rika Lesser. Illustrated by Paul O. Zelinsky. Dodd, Mead, 1984. The text has very little description of the witch, but Zelinsky depicts her as an old woman, wrinkled and bent, with grasping clawlike hands. The illustrations received the Caldecott Honor Medal in 1985.

Rapunzel from the Brothers Grimm. Retold by Barbara Rogasky. Illustrations by Trina Schart Hyman. Holiday House, 1982. To save his wife, the husband steals food from the witch's garden. When he is caught, he promises to give his daughter to the witch, who locks her in a tower. In this version, the witch loves Rapunzel but will not allow her to be free.

Strega Nona retold and illustrated by Tomie de Paola. Prentice-Hall, 1975. Poor Big Anthony does not know how to make Strega Nona's magic pasta pot stop cooking. Strega Nona is a witch who helps others with her magic. She even saves the town from Big Anthony's foolishness.

About the Author and Illustrator

WOOD, AUDREY
Something about the Author, ed. by Anne Commire. Gale, 1986, Vol. 44, p. 214; 1988, Vol. 50, pp. 218–224.

WOOD, DON
Something about the Author, ed. by Anne Commire. Gale, 1986, Vol. 44, p. 214; 1988, Vol. 50, pp. 224–231.

8

Focusing on Folktales

FOLKTALES represent the cultural heritage of many different people. With origins in the oral tradition, folktales can be especially effective when told or read aloud. The cadence of their language, with its many chants, spells, and repeated phrases, helps make them memorable. Characters in folktales can accomplish great tasks or be transformed into creatures of wonder or fear. Folktales can include such larger-than-life figures as giants, witches, and magicians. In this chapter, there are stories from many lands, including China, Vietnam, Africa, and the West Indies; legends from Native-American tribes; and stories of bravery, trickery, and foolishness. Reading these books will introduce children to some of the traditional literature that is shared around the world.

Aardema, Verna.   *Oh, Kojo! How Could You! An Ashanti Tale*
Illus. by Marc Brown. Dial, 1984, pap., 1988
Suggested Use Level: Gr. 2–4   Reading Level: Gr. 3

Plot Summary

In Ashantiland, a lonely woman, Tutuola, asks the River Spirit for a son. In granting her wish, the River Spirit tells her that her son will bring her joy but problems, too. Tutuola is happy to have a son, whom she names Kojo, but as the River Spirit warned, Kojo causes problems—by spending Tutuola's money and not working. One day, Kojo is preparing to leave Tutuola to go to the sea. However, before Kojo leaves, Tutuola warns him to beware of their fellow villager Ananse and his tricks. Nevertheless, when Kojo meets Ananse, Ananse tricks him into giving him all of his gold in exchange for a dog, which Ananse says will gather firewood, but, of course, will not. Back home, Kojo's mother is dismayed that Kojo listened to Ananse. On market day, Kojo again leaves the house and, again, Ananse tricks him and takes his gold, selling him a cat. The next market day, Kojo is tricked into buying a dove from Ananse, but this time the dove turns out to be a queen. When Kojo returns the dove to her flock, the queen rewards him with a magic ring, which Kojo uses to make himself a rich chief with a village of his own. Ananse hears of Kojo's good fortune and devises a plan to steal the ring. He sends his beautiful niece to take the ring from Kojo, which she does. When Kojo sends his cat and dog to get the ring back, Ananse tricks the dog, but the cat succeeds in recovering the ring. To this day, cats are treated with respect and dogs are disdained.

Thematic Material

The character Ananse appears in various African folktales. Other elements of *Oh, Kojo! How Could You!* are also common to many folktales, such as magic, trickery, and things happening in threes.

Book Talk Material and Activities

Oh, Kojo! How Could You! could be the featured story in a program on stories about Ananse, which would also include *A Story, A Story* and *Anansi the Spider.* In some books, like *Oh, Kojo! How Could You!*, Ananse is a devious trickster; in others, including *A Story, A Story,* he is clever but not evil. Children enjoy seeing Ananse depicted as a spider and reading other West African spider stories, such as *The Adventures of Spider.*

Some Ananse stories answer a question, often about the natural world. *Oh, Kojo! How Could You!* describes why dogs are often kept outside and cats are treated more kindly. In *Anansi the Spider,* Anansi and his sons find a globe of light, which they give to the Sky God to keep, thus explaining how the moon got into the sky. Other common folktale elements in the Ananse stories are magic, trickery, and the number three. Teachers and librarians might want to organize a series of activities using folktales to encourage children to look for other common elements.

Audiovisual Adaptation

Oh, Kojo! How Could You! An Ashanti Tale. Random House Media, cassette/book, 1986; filmstrip/cassette, 1986.

Related Titles

The Adventures of Spider: West African Folk Tales retold by Joyce Cooper Arkhurst. Illustrated by Jerry Pinkney. Scholastic, 1964. Six stories about Spider including "Why Spiders Live in Dark Corners."

Ananse the Spider: Tales from an Ashanti Village by Peggy Appiah. Illustrated by Peggy Wilson. Pantheon, 1966. A collection of 13 stories about Ananse. "Why Kwaku Ananse Stays on the Ceiling" could be compared with the story in *More Adventures of Spider*, which also describes why spiders stay on the ceiling.

Anansi the Spider: A Tale from the Ashanti adapted and illustrated by Gerald McDermott. Holt, Rinehart, 1974. After Anansi's sons rescue him from the fish and the falcon, Anansi finds a beautiful globe of white light in the jungle. He wants to give this light to one of his sons, but he cannot decide which one is the most deserving. Anansi gives the globe to the God who lives in the sky and the God keeps it there. Anansi is not a trickster in this story, which describes how the moon came to be in the sky.

More Adventures of Spider: West African Folk Tales retold by Joyce Cooper Arkhurst. Illustrated by Jerry Pinkney. Scholastic, 1972. These six stories about Spider include "Why Spiders Live on the Ceiling," which could be compared with the story in *Ananse the Spider*, which also describes why spiders stay on the ceiling.

A Story, A Story retold and illustrated by Gail E. Haley. Atheneum, 1970. Ananse must perform three tasks before the Sky God will sell his stories. Although Ananse uses trickery to accomplish his tasks, he is not portrayed as an evil character here.

About the Author and the Illustrator

AARDEMA, VERNA

Authors of Books for Young People: Supplement to the Second Edition, ed. by Martha E. Ward and Dorothy Marquardt. Scarecrow, 1979, p. 1.

Fifth Book of Junior Authors and Illustrators, ed. by Sally Holmes Holtze. Wilson, 1983, pp. 1–2.

Something about the Author, ed. by Anne Commire. Gale, 1973, Vol. 4, pp. 1–3.

BROWN, MARC

Fifth Book of Junior Authors and Illustrators, ed. by Sally Holmes Holtze. Wilson, 1983, pp. 54–55.

Something about the Author, ed. by Anne Commire. Gale, 1976, Vol. 10, pp. 17–18.

Brett, Jan, reteller.   *Goldilocks and the Three Bears*
Illus. by the reteller. Dodd, Mead, 1987
Suggested Use Level: Gr. PreK–3   Reading Level: Gr. 4

Plot Summary

In Jan Brett's version of a familiar story, three bears—a little bear, a middle-sized bear, and a huge bear—live in a very comfortable house in the forest. They each have their own bowls, chairs, and beds. One day, they leave the house while their porridge is cooling in their bowls. While they are gone, a little girl named Goldilocks comes into the house, tastes their porridge, and eats all the porridge from the little bear's bowl. She sits in each of their chairs and breaks the little bear's chair. Then she rests on each of their beds and falls asleep in the little bear's bed. When the bears return home, they are upset to see that their belongings have been disturbed. They find Goldilocks in the little bear's bed and are annoyed with her. Goldilocks wakes up when she hears their voices and runs off into the woods.

Thematic Material

Brett's illustrations for her retelling of a familiar folktale are colorful and detailed.

Book Talk Material and Activities

Many children already know the story of *Goldilocks and the Three Bears.* Librarians and teachers might want to read this and other books about the three bears to allow children to predict what they expect to happen. Before reading *Goldilocks and the Three Bears,* ask children to retell the story, and write their version of the story on the chalkboard or on a large piece of paper. One group of children said that the story should always include three bears and that the bears should be big, medium, and small. After some discussion, the group decided that the bears should be called Papa Bear, Mama Bear, and Baby Bear, and that everything the bears have should be in three sizes—big, medium, and small—including their voices, their bowls, their chairs, and their beds. Goldilocks should always have long blond hair, and when the bears leave the house and Goldilocks comes, she should spoil their food, mess up their chairs and beds, and break everything that belongs to Baby Bear. The group expected a pattern to what the bears say when they return home, for example, "Somebody's been sitting in my chair." After the children discussed their expectations, they heard several Three Bears stories and compared them with their predictions, focusing on two aspects of the story: what the bears were called, and what they said when they found their bowls, chairs, and beds. The children were interested in seeing how each story had been adapted by the author, and they were pleased that, for the most part, their predictions were confirmed.

When comparing illustrated versions of the same story, children can discuss what details the illustrator chose to include and decide which illustrated versions they find the most appealing. For example, in Brett's illustrations for *Goldilocks and the Three Bears,* the bears wear patterned tunics; in Stevens's version they wear clothes, and in Galdone's version they do not. Children can decide which presentation they prefer and why.

Related Titles

Deep in the Forest written and illustrated by Brinton Turkle. Dutton, 1976. Turkle's wordless book depicts the familiar Three Bears story but with a twist. A baby bear goes into a log cabin and wreaks havoc on the food, chairs, and beds of a papa, a mama, and a baby. When the three settlers return to their cabin, they find the bear cub in the little girl's bed and chase him out into the woods.

Goldilocks and the Three Bears retold and illustrated by Lorinda Bryan Cauley. Putnam, 1981. Details in the illustrations add humor to the familiar story of the Three Bears. The bears lead a comfortable life in a lovely home. Father smokes his pipe and reads while mother works on her embroidery and drinks tea. The baby bear sits in a wicker chair, reading a book and drinking a glass of milk.

Goldilocks and the Three Bears retold and illustrated by Janet Stevens. Holiday House, 1986. The Three Bears live in a cozy house and have comfortable clothing and furniture. Stevens has used many different patterns and colors on the fabrics in the bears' house.

The Three Bears retold and illustrated by Paul Galdone. Seabury Press, 1972. Galdone's bears are very bearlike—large and furry. Goldilocks is missing a front tooth and looks mischievous. When the bears speak, the size of the print reflects the size of the bear, for example, large letters for the Great Big Bear.

The Three Bears illustrated by Robin Spowart. Knopf, 1987. The soft colors in the illustrations give a feeling of warmth. The bears' home is a little cottage decorated with simple country furnishings.

About the Author and Illustrator

BRETT, JAN
Something about the Author, ed. by Anne Commire. Gale, 1986, Vol. 42, pp. 38–39.

Bryan, Ashley.   *The Cat's Purr*
Illus. by the author. Atheneum, 1985
Suggested Use Level: Gr. 1–3   Reading Level: Gr. 2

Plot Summary

Cat and Rat live happily as friends and neighbors. They even work together on their farm and are planning a feast to celebrate their harvest. One day, Cat's uncle visits him and gives him a Cat family drum, which has a secret to playing it. When it is gently stroked, it produces a soft purring sound. After Cat's uncle leaves, Rat comes to visit and hears the wonderful drum. He wants to play it but Cat refuses to let him, so he becomes very upset and decides to find a way to play the drum. Rat pretends to be sick, and as soon as Cat leaves him alone to rest and goes off to the fields, Rat plays the drum. Cat hears him and returns, but quick and clever Rat jumps back into Cat's bed and continues his pretense of illness. Again Cat goes to the field and again he hears the drum and returns, only to find Rat still in bed. The third time, however, Cat outwits Rat and catches him playing the drum. With his mouth wide open showing his sharp teeth, Cat chases Rat. Rat panics, pushes the drum into Cat's mouth and Cat swallows it. Cat and Rat have been enemies ever since. Now, when you softly stroke a cat, you can hear the Cat drum.

Thematic Material

In *The Cat's Purr,* Ashley Bryan has a version of a West Indian folktale as it appeared in a book from the American Folklore Society of New York City in 1936. Like many folktales, this one answers a question—Why do cats purr?—and its language has a special cadence that makes it excellent for storytelling.

Book Talk Material and Activities

The Cat's Purr is good to use when discussing the features that are common to many folktales. For example, events often happen in threes. In *The Cat's Purr*, Rat tries to trick Cat three times, but is found out the third time. In other stories, characters get three wishes (as in *The Three Wishes*), they blow three kisses (as in *Strega Nona*), or they must perform three tasks (as in *A Story, A Story*). Other folktales answer questions, for example, *Why Mosquitoes Buzz in People's Ears* and *Why the Sun and the Moon Live in the Sky*. In *The Cat's Purr*, readers are given one possible reason why cats purr. Children could compare *The Cat's Purr* with other folktales, while they look for additional common folktale elements, such as the number seven, the use of magic and chants, and folktale creatures (such as trolls and dragons). This activity would be especially effective for children to do independently or in small groups and then report back to the large group. By discussing many folktales, children become more familiar with this type of literature.

Ashley Bryan's retelling includes repetition and sounds that add to the flavor of the story and make it memorable for storytelling. As the drum is stroked in the story, the teller could stroke a small drum while children participate by making the purring sound of a cat's drum. Because of the small size of the book and the difficulty for a very large group of seeing the illustrations, a dramatic reading or retelling is even more appropriate. The brown-and-white illustrations emphasize the personalities of Cat and Rat and enhance the story for individuals or small groups.

Audiovisual Adaptation

The Cat's Purr. Random House Media, cassette/book, 1987.

Related Titles

A Story, A Story retold and illustrated by Gail E. Haley. Atheneum, 1970. Ananse wants to buy the Sky God's stories. To do so, he must perform three tasks. A good question to ask children is: Will Ananse meet the Sky God's demands?

Strega Nona retold and illustrated by Tomie de Paola. Prentice-Hall, 1975. Big Anthony has a problem. Strega Nona's pasta pot will not stop cooking until he sings the magic song *and* blows three kisses.

The Three Wishes: An Old Story retold and illustrated by Margot Zemach. Farrar, Straus, 1986. If the peasant does not use his third wish wisely, he will have a sausage on his nose forever! Sometimes, three wishes are not enough.

Why Mosquitoes Buzz in People's Ears retold by Verna Aardema. Illustrated by Leo Dillon and Diane Dillon. Dial, 1975. In this sequential story, a mosquito's silly behavior creates fear in the jungle. Now we know why mosquitoes are such annoying pests.

Why the Sun and the Moon Live in the Sky: An African Folktale retold by Elphinstone Dayrell. Illustrated by Blair Lent. Houghton Mifflin, 1968. When the Sun and the Moon invite everyone to their home, they find that they must jump up into the sky to make room for their guests. Have children write their own stories explaining other natural phenomena.

About the Author and Illustrator

BRYAN, ASHLEY
Fifth Book of Junior Authors and Illustrators, ed. by Sally Holmes Holtze. Wilson, 1983, pp. 57–59.
Illustrators of Children's Books: 1967–1976, Vol. IV, comp. by Lee Kingman, Grace Allen Hogarth, and Harriet Quimby. Horn Book, 1978, pp. 105, 182.
Something about the Author, ed. by Anne Commire. Gale, 1983, Vol. 31, pp. 44–45.

Cole, Joanna. *Bony-Legs*
Illus. by Dirk Zimmer. Four Winds, 1983; pap., Scholastic, 1986
Suggested Use Level: Gr. 1–3   Reading Level: Gr. 2

Plot Summary

A cruel witch named Bony-Legs who lives deep in the forest captures and eats any children who wander near her house (which stands on chickens' feet). One day, a little girl named Sasha is walking through the woods and sees the witch's house. To reach the house, Sasha must open a gate. The hinges on the gate creak so badly that she kindly stops to grease it. She gives her bread to a hungry dog and then shares her meat with a hungry cat. When Sasha reaches the door of the house, the witch opens it and invites Sasha inside, planning to eat her. The witch tells Sasha to bathe, so that she will be clean enough to eat, and locks Sasha in the bathroom while she goes to gather wood for the fire. The witch's cat, whom Sasha had befriended, gives Sasha a magic mirror and then helps her escape. The witch's dog gives her a magic comb and lets her run past, and the witch's gate does not squeak when she runs through it. When the witch discovers that Sasha is gone and that her cat, dog, and gate have helped her escape, she is enraged. She chases after Sasha but is stopped when Sasha throws the magic mirror, which becomes a wide lake. The witch runs around the lake but is then stopped when Sasha throws the magic comb, which becomes a high thick wall. Bony-Legs returns to her house and Sasha hurries home to safety.

Thematic Material

Bony-Legs is a folktale based on the Baba Yaga stories from Russia. As in many folktales, an innocent child shows kindness to others and triumphs over a cruel witch.

Book Talk Material and Activities

Several aspects of this story are common to many folktales: The story includes both a cruel witch and magical objects, and the good character triumphs over the evil one. Learning about these folktale conventions extends children's understanding of other folktales. As they read and discuss other folktales with similar features, they can compare them with *Bony-Legs*. One group might want to list the characteristics of witches in folktales, perhaps naming all the books they know that have witches and then describing how the witches behave. Another activity is to look at the unusual houses in folktales. Bony-Legs's house stands on chickens' feet; in some stories, the house can run through the forest. Read another Baba Yaga story (like "Baba Yaga's Geese" or *Baba Yaga*) and gather more information about the witch and her house. Or describe the different houses, including one from a *Hansel and Gretel* story. Other stories with unusual houses are *The Maid and the Mouse and the Odd-Shaped House* and *The Three Little Pigs*. Children could build a collection of stories with different kinds of houses. Each of these activities encourages children to read many books and work together to find common features, applying the information about folktales that they have learned in story sessions. Through discussion, children learn from each other and make decisions about what they are reading.

Librarians could display other folktales that, like *Bony-Legs*, are in the format of a beginning reader. The print size in these books is larger than in a typical picture book, with usually only one or two sentences per page and more space between the words and the lines of text, so that beginning readers can focus more easily on the print. *The Pancake; King*

Rooster, Queen Hen; The House of Five Bears; Pecos Bill; and *Sally Ann Thunder Ann Whirlwind Crockett* are other folktales that are accessible to beginning readers.

Audiovisual Adaptation

Bony-Legs. Random House Media, cassette/book, 1985.

Related Titles

Baba Yaga by Ernest Small. Illustrated by Blair Lent. Houghton Mifflin, 1966. While looking for turnips, Marusia enters Baba Yaga's forest and encounters the evil witch. The description of the witch and her house includes many details.

"Baba Yaga's Geese" in *Baba Yaga's Geese and Other Russian Stories* translated and adapted by Bonnie Carey. Illustrated by Guy Fleming. Indiana University Press, 1973. Baba Yaga sends her geese to capture Marya's little brother and joins them in their chase by flying in an enormous bowl.

Hansel and Gretel by the Brothers Grimm. Illustrated by Adrienne Adams. Scribner, 1975. Look at the description of the witch and her house. How do they compare with the description and illustrations in Susan Jeffers's version?

Hansel and Gretel written by the Brothers Grimm. Illustrated by Susan Jeffers. Dial, 1980. Here are another witch and an unusual house to add to the list.

The House of Five Bears by Cynthia Jameson. Illustrated by Lorinda Bryan Cauley. Putnam, 1978. Jameson's version of a Russian folktale has an easy-to-read format. The large print and careful spacing make it accessible to younger children.

King Rooster, Queen Hen written and illustrated by Anita Lobel. Greenwillow, 1975. This beginning-reader folktale has some similarities with the Henny Penny stories, such as Jan Ormerod's *The Story of Chicken Licken* (see Chapter 7). The rooster and hen think they want to be king and queen. Children can discuss what changes their minds.

The Maid and the Mouse and the Odd-Shaped House adapted and illustrated by Paul O. Zelinsky. Dodd, Mead, 1981. The unusual house is not as safe as it seems. The maid and the mouse find that their house is really a cat!

The Pancake written and illustrated by Anita Lobel. Greenwillow, 1978.

The Gingerbread Boy story is told in a format for beginning readers. A pancake runs away from a woman and her children. As they chase it, they are joined by other animals, until the pig catches the pancake and eats it.

Pecos Bill written and illustrated by Ariane Dewey. Greenwillow, 1983. The story of the famous American cowboy is retold in the format of a beginning reader.

Sally Ann Thunder Ann Whirlwind Crockett retold by Caron Lee Cohen. Illustrated by Ariane Dewey. Greenwillow, 1985. In this beginning reader, children can find out how Sally Ann, the wife of Davy Crockett, beats Mike Fink.

The Three Little Pigs illustrated by Erik Blegvad. Atheneum, 1980. The unusual houses of these pigs do not protect all of them from the wolf.

About the Author and Illustrator

COLE, JOANNA

Fifth Book of Junior Authors and Illustrators, ed. by Sally Holmes Holtze. Wilson, 1983, pp. 77–78.

Something about the Author, ed. by Anne Commire. Gale, 1985, Vol. 37, p. 50; 1987, Vol. 49, pp. 68–74.

The Gingerbread Boy
Illus. by Scott Cook. Knopf, 1987
Suggested Use Level: Gr. PreK–1   Reading Level: Gr. 4

Plot Summary

In this version of a familiar story, a little old woman bakes a Gingerbread Boy because she and her husband are lonely. When the boy is done, he jumps out of the oven and runs away. The little old couple chase the boy, but they cannot catch him. He continues to run, passing a cow, a horse, some threshers, and some mowers, who all join in the chase. As the boy passes each group, he says a chant about how he has succeeded in staying ahead of all who are chasing him. Then the Gingerbread Boy comes to a fox, who cleverly says that he does not want to catch the boy and helps him cross the river. When they reach the other side, however, the fox shows that he has tricked the Gingerbread Boy by eating him.

Thematic Material

Events in *The Gingerbread Boy* occur in a sequence. The story is also about food that runs away from its owner.

Book Talk Material and Activities

There are many other versions of the Gingerbread Boy story, as well as books about foods that run away, such as *The Funny Little Woman* and *The Rolling Rice Ball*. Reading one book aloud and then booktalking the others gives children a choice of titles to sign out. In one kindergarten class, the teacher read several Gingerbread Boy books and the children voted for their favorite. At the beginning of the year, the teacher organized an activity that correlates with the stories, in which gingerbread cookies are available for a snack. After the stories have been read, the children go out for recess and the cookies are taken to the library. When the children return and find their cookies gone, the teacher takes them on a tour of the school building. They visit the office and meet the principal and the secretary. They visit the art room, meet the art teacher, and so on. In each place, they find a note from the Gingerbread Boy that repeats the "you can't catch me" chant. The last place they visit is the library, where the librarian reads another Gingerbread Boy book and shares the cookies with the children. The children discuss why the cookies "ran" to the library—because that is where the Gingerbread stories are. This activity allows kindergarten children to tour the school and meet different people, thus becoming more familiar with the school building and the people who work there. It is also a positive introduction to the library program and the activities that children will be participating in throughout the year.

Related Titles

The Bun: A Tale from Russia written and illustrated by Marcia Brown. Harcourt, 1972. A woman makes a bun for her husband that, like the Gingerbread Boy, runs away. Children could list the animals that the bun runs away from and compare their list to the sequence in *The Gingerbread Boy*.

The Funny Little Woman retold by Arlene Mosel. Illustrated by Blair Lent. Dutton, 1972. A woman makes a rice dumpling that rolls away from her. When she chases it, she ends up a prisoner of the oni, wicked creatures that live underground. For his illustrations, Lent received the 1973 Caldecott Medal.

The Gingerbread Boy retold and illustrated by Paul Galdone. Seabury Press, 1975. Children could compare the chant in this version of the story with the one in other versions.

Journey Cake, Ho! by Ruth Sawyer. Illustrated by Robert McCloskey. Viking, 1953. A journey cake, similar to a pancake, rolls away from a boy, who chases it. Various farm animals see the journey cake and join in the chase. They all end up back at the home of a poor farmer and his wife, who are happy to have all the animals come to stay on their farm. The farmer, his wife, and the boy eat the journey cake.

The Pancake written and illustrated by Anita Lobel. Greenwillow, 1978. A pancake runs away from a woman, her seven children, a farmer, a goose, a cat, a sheep, and a goat, but is then eaten by a pig.

The Rolling Rice Ball by Junichi Yoda. Illustrated by Saburo Watanabe. Parent's Magazine Press, 1969. The old man's rice ball rolls down a hole where it is eaten by some mice. The man shares the rest of his rice balls with the mice and is rewarded for his kindness. Later, a greedy man tries to get a reward from the mice, but he is punished.

You Can't Catch Me! by Joanne Oppenheim. Illustrations by Andrew Shachat. Houghton Mifflin, 1986. A fly runs away from many different animals chanting that they cannot catch him. Unfortunately, he chooses to rest on a turtle's shell and is caught.

Goble, Paul. *Buffalo Woman*
    Illus. by the author. Bradbury, 1984; pap., Macmillan, 1986
    Suggested Use Level: Gr. 2–4   Reading Level: Gr. 4

Plot Summary

A young man, who is a great hunter, knows the ways of the buffalo. One day, while waiting near a stream, he sees a buffalo turn into a beautiful woman, who has come from the Buffalo Nation to be his wife. They marry and have a son, Calf Boy. But the young man's people distrust his wife and berate her, so she takes Calf Boy and runs away. When the young man follows and finds her, she tells him that she must return to her people, but that he cannot join her. During the night, she takes Calf Boy and continues her journey. Once again, the young man finds them and, again, his wife warns him to stay away. The next morning, she and Calf Boy are gone. Still, the young man follows them, until he reaches the Buffalo Nation. Calf Boy, who is now a calf, warns his father that he is in danger, but the young man knows he must stay. The old bull who is chief of the Buffalo Nation challenges the young man. He must find his wife and son from among all the buffaloes. When he succeeds, he is accepted into the Buffalo Nation and transformed into a buffalo.

Thematic Material

Buffalo Woman is a story of courage and sacrifice—the young man risks his life to be with his wife and child. Based on legends from several Native-American tribes of the Great Plains, the story also conveys a sense of respect for the natural world.

Book Talk Material and Activities

In many Native-American legends the relationship between the people in the tribes and the animals around them is a positive one. Even when the animals are hunted for food, as in *Buffalo Woman,* the feeling is one of respect and appreciation. The young man in *Buffalo Woman* is a great hunter, but he knows that his tribe needs the buffalo to survive. Goble has written and illustrated other books based on Native-American legends that convey a respect for the natural world and often describe a relationship between the people of a tribe and the animals around them, for example, *The Friendly Wolf* and *The Girl Who Loved Wild Horses.* As children study Native Americans, they should be encouraged to look at their legends and poems. Book talks and displays of materials about Native Americans correlate with the social studies program and extend children's understanding of Native Americans.

Related Titles

The Friendly Wolf written by Paul Goble and Dorothy Goble. Illustrated by Paul Goble. Bradbury, 1974. Little Cloud and his sister, Bright Eyes, wander away from the camp, become lost on the mountain, and are befriended by a wolf, who helps them find their way home.

The Gift of the Sacred Dog written and illustrated by Paul Goble. Bradbury, 1980. A boy goes to the Great Spirit to get help for his hungry people. Because of his bravery, his people are given horses, "Sacred Dogs," to help them capture animals for food.

The Girl Who Loved Wild Horses written and illustrated by Paul Goble. Bradbury, 1978. A girl who has lived with the wild horses is eventually transformed into a beautiful mare, and her tribe rejoices in their kinship with the Horse People. This book received the Caldecott Medal in 1979.

Star Boy retold and illustrated by Paul Goble. Bradbury, 1983. A girl leaves her tribe to live in the Sky World with her husband, Morning Star. When she disobeys the Moon, she is sent back to Earth with her son, Star Boy, who is poor and ugly. After his mother's death, Star Boy must find a way to reach the Sun. He listens to the Sun and shows his people how to honor it.

The Trees Stand Shining: Poetry of the North American Indians selected by Hettie Jones. Illustrated by Robert Andrew Parker. Dial, 1971. A recurring theme in these poems from many different tribes is respect for the natural world.

About the Author and Illustrator

GOBLE, PAUL

Authors of Books for Young People: Supplement to the Second Edition, by Martha E. Ward and Dorothy Marquardt. Scarecrow, 1979, p. 101.

Fourth Book of Junior Authors and Illustrators, ed. by Doris de Montreville and Elizabeth D. Crawford. Wilson, 1978, pp. 150–151.

Illustrators of Children's Books: 1967–1976, Vol. IV, comp. by Lee Kingman, Grace Allen Hogarth, and Harriet Quimby. Horn Book, 1978, pp. 122, 190.

Something about the Author, ed. by Anne Commire. Gale, 1981, Vol. 25, pp. 120–122.

Haley, Gail E., reteller. *Jack and the Bean Tree*
Illus. by the reteller. Crown, 1986
Suggested Use Level: Gr. 3–4   Reading Level: Gr. 3

Plot Summary

One evening, Poppyseed gathers everyone around her and begins to tell a story about a boy named Jack who lived with his Maw in a cabin on the mountain. Jack and his Maw did not have much, but they survived by living off their land and drinking the milk of their cow, Old Milky Way.

One time, though, everything was going wrong. Even Old Milky Way stopped giving milk. So Maw sent Jack to the market to sell the cow. While walking to town, Jack met a stranger who gave him three magic beans for the cow. Jack's Maw was angry with him for taking beans instead of money, and she grabbed them and threw them out. They grew into a huge, twisting bean tree, which Jack could not resist climbing. At the top of the tree, Jack met Matilda, the giant's wife, who told him about her husband's habit of eating humans. Before Jack could leave, the giant, Ephidophilus, appeared, chanting a rhyme as he walked, which began: "Feee, fiii, fooo, fuuum! I smell the blood of an Englishman," but Matilda distracted him by bringing him his magic cloth. The giant said a chant, and the cloth magically filled with food. After the giant finished eating, he said another chant, and the food disappeared. Seeing all this from his hiding place, when the giant was asleep, Jack took the cloth and ran home. Jack returned to the giant's home twice more, and each time he brought home a new treasure. On the third trip, Ephidophilus woke up and chased Jack, who chopped down the bean tree and killed the giant.

Thematic Material

Haley's retelling is an Appalachian version of the well-known English folktale "Jack and the Beanstalk"; it is written in the style of a story being told and would correlate well with programs on storytelling.

Book Talk Material and Activities

Before reading *Jack and the Bean Tree,* be sure to talk about the tradition of storytelling. Children are used to television and radio, and many will not be familiar with families and friends spending an evening together listening to stories. In Gail Haley's book, an old lady named Poppyseed is telling the story. Like the grandfather in *Grandfather Tales,* she has the age and experience to know many stories. Some children will be surprised that *Jack and the Bean Tree* is based on versions of an English folktale that were told in the Appalachian Mountains. But when they are reminded of America's English heritage and the many settlements that were in the Appalachian Mountains, they will begin to see how the same story could enter different cultures. This is an effective story to learn to tell. The rhythm of the language with its chants and repetitions makes it memorable and adds to its flavor. Consider using the illustrations to enhance the storytelling.

Children who are familiar with other "Jack and the Beanstalk" stories will want to talk about the differences in Haley's version. Children could examine other books about Jack and decide on some areas to compare. For example, how does Jack get the beans? Is the giant's chant the same in each book? and Does Jack bring back the same treasures? The information could be assembled on a chart or just discussed in a group sharing session. Encourage children to think of other traditional stories or poems where the name Jack appears, such as "Jack Be Nimble" and "Jack and Jill," which could be found in a nursery rhyme book like *Tomie de Paola's Mother Goose* (Putnam, 1985). Introduce them to *The Jack Tales* by Richard Chase, which includes another version of "Jack and the Bean Tree."

Audiovisual Adaptation

Jack and the Bean Tree. Weston Woods, filmstrip/cassette, 1987.

Related Titles

Grandfather Tales compiled and retold by Richard Chase. Illustrated by Berkeley Williams, Jr. Houghton Mifflin, 1948. Some of these stories are excellent for memorizing and telling. "Soap, Soap, Soap" has the repetition seen in many folktales.

The History of Mother Twaddle and the Marvelous Achievements of her Son, Jack retold and illustrated by Paul Galdone. Seabury Press, 1974. In this rhyming version of "Jack and the Beanstalk," Jack makes only one trip up the beanstalk and kills the giant by cutting off his head.

Jack and the Beanstalk retold and illustrated by Lorinda Bryan Cauley. Putnam, 1983. An especially good choice for a beginning comparison activity—there are enough differences to discuss without being confusing.

The Jack Tales edited by Richard Chase. Illustrated by Berkeley Williams, Jr. Houghton Mifflin, 1943. The preface gives some fascinating background information on the origin of these stories.

Jim and the Beanstalk written and illustrated by Raymond Briggs. Coward, McCann, 1970. A helpful boy named Jim climbs a strange plant and meets an even stranger giant, but instead of stealing from the giant, Jim gives the giant three presents.

About the Author and Illustrator

HALEY, GAIL E.

Illustrators of Children's Books: 1967–1976, Vol. IV, comp. by Lee Kingman, Grace Allen Hogarth, and Harriet Quimby. Horn Book, 1978, pp. 125, 191.

Something about the Author, ed. by Anne Commire. Gale, 1982, Vol. 28, p. 123; 1986, Vol. 43, pp. 101–106.
Third Book of Junior Authors, ed. by Muriel Fuller. Wilson, 1963, pp. 117–118.

Lee, Jeanne M., reteller.   *Toad Is the Uncle of Heaven: A Vietnamese Folk Tale*
Illus. by the reteller. Holt, Rinehart, 1985
Suggested Use Level: Gr. 1–3   Reading Level: Gr. 4

Plot Summary

Toad has a comfortable life on Earth, but one year, there is a drought, and Toad watches everything around him wither and die. Worried that even his own pond will soon be gone, he decides to go to the King of Heaven and ask for rain. As Toad begins his journey, he meets some Bees, who are also worried about the drought and decide to accompany Toad on his trip to Heaven. The Rooster and the Tiger also join Toad. When the King of Heaven sees the lowly Toad in his palace, however, he orders him removed. The Bees, the Rooster, and the Tiger help Toad escape by attacking the King's guards, Thunder God, and hound. Finally, the King begs Toad to stop his friends, and he grants Toad's croaking request for rain by sending rain to earth. To this day, when toads croak, the King of Heaven will soon send rain.

Thematic Material

Toad Is the Uncle of Heaven is a Vietnamese folktale that has some similarities with other folktales. Toad takes a journey to make a request from a more powerful character and, even though he is weak, he accomplishes his task. The theme of the small creature succeeding against a larger creature is evident here.

Book Talk Material and Activities

Toad Is the Uncle of Heaven is a wonderful book to include in a story program of folktales from around the world. Many children are familiar with stories from Europe and Africa, but few know stories from Asia. Children will enjoy seeing the similarities between this story and other, more familiar stories. Toad begins his journey alone and is joined by other characters. All of them want rain from the King of Heaven. *Rum, Pum, Pum: A Tale from India; King Rooster, Queen Hen;* and *The Fool of the World and the Flying Ship: A Russian Tale* have similar structures. So do the stories about Henny Penny, such as *The Story of Chicken Licken* by Jan Ormerod (see Chapter 7) and *Foolish Rabbit's Big Mistake* by Rafe Martin (see this chapter). All of these books could be compared with *Toad Is the Uncle of Heaven.* A chart showing the points of comparison might list the reason for the journey, the characters that join the journey and why, and the resolution of the problem.

Many social studies classes study foreign countries, and *Toad Is the Uncle of Heaven* is one of the few stories from Vietnam available in picture-book format. Other Vietnamese stories that could be correlated with the social studies program are *In the Land of Small Dragon* and *The Brocaded Slipper: And Other Vietnamese Tales.* Like *Toad Is the Uncle of Heaven,* these books share similarities with some of the more familiar European folktales, and children could be encouraged to look for different versions of the same story.

Related Titles

The Brocaded Slipper: And Other Vietnamese Tales by Lynette Dyer Vuong. Illustrated by Vo-Dinh Mai. Addison-Wesley, 1982. Five stories from Vietnam demonstrate how different versions of a story can appear in many cultures. ("The Brocaded Slipper" is a Cinderella story.) An appendix provides some insight into the Vietnamese influences in these stories.

The Fool of the World and the Flying Ship: A Russian Tale retold by Arthur Ransome. Illustrated by Uri Shulevitz. Farrar, Straus, 1968. The youngest son, who is called the Fool of the World, sets out to win the czar's daughter. On his journey, he befriends several men who help him win his prize. This book won the 1969 Caldecott Medal.

In the Land of Small Dragon as told by Dan Manh Kha to Ann Nolan Clark. Illustrated by Tony Chen. Viking, 1979. Cám, the younger daughter, is jealous of her beautiful older stepsister, Tâm, who is her father's Number One Daughter. Cám tricks her sister out of her birthright. However, Tâm's kindness continues and, when the prince is searching for a bride, he chooses her.

King Rooster, Queen Hen written and illustrated by Anita Lobel. Greenwillow, 1975. The rooster has decided that he wants to be the king, and that the hen will be his queen. Other animals join their entourage, until they meet the fox, who has other plans for them.

Rum Pum Pum: A Folk Tale from India retold by Maggie Duff. Illustrated by Jose Aruego and Ariane Dewey. Macmillan, 1978. When the king takes Blackbird's wife, Blackbird makes war on him. On his journey, Blackbird is joined by Cat, the ants, Stick, and River, and when the king tries to destroy Blackbird, his companions come to his rescue.

Marshak, Samuel, reteller. *The Month-Brothers: A Slavic Tale*
Illus. by Diane Stanley. Morrow, 1983
Suggested Use Level: Gr. 3–4   Reading Level: Gr. 4

Plot Summary

A young girl lives with her stepmother and stepsister, both of whom are cruel to her. The little girl has a difficult life. One night, during a snowstorm, the stepmother orders the little girl to go outside and find some flowers. The girl wraps a worn shawl around her and goes out into the storm. In the forest, she can barely move because the wind is so strong and she is so cold, but in the distance, she is surprised to see a glowing light. She heads toward the light and finds that it is a campfire surrounded by a group of men. The men cannot believe that she is looking for flowers during a snowstorm in January, but they agree that they must help her. Each man is named for a month of the year. Brother January holds his icy crook and says a chant that allows it to become February. Brother February allows it to become March, and Brother March lets the snowdrop flowers bloom. The little girl fills her basket with the flowers and hurries home with them. Her stepmother and stepsister cannot believe that she has found the flowers, and they are even more surprised by her story of the Month-Brothers. They decide that they want more from these brothers, so the stepsister goes out into the woods. When she finds the Month-Brothers, she demands gifts from them. In response, Brother January calls forth a storm, and the stepsister is lost in the snow. Her mother goes to look for her and she, too, is lost. Released from their cruelty, the little girl grows up to lead a happy life.

Thematic Material

The Month-Brothers is a Slavic folktale from Czechoslovakia. As in many folktales, there is a relationship between a human and a natural phenomenon, in this case, the months of the year.

Book Talk Material and Activities

Folktales often include information about the natural world. Some tell about how the moon came to be in the sky (*Anansi the Spider* and *Why the Sun and the Moon Live in the Sky*). Another tells about how the rains came to Earth (*Bringing the Rain to Kapiti Plain*). In some cultures, people used stories to explain natural phenomena, or they included details about their climate and environment in their stories. *The Month-Brothers* is from an area in Eastern Europe where there are distinct changes in the seasons and where the winters are long and difficult. The environment of the region is reflected not only in the text but also in the illustrations, which include many features of the climate and the culture. The bitter cold is seen not just in the wind and snow but also in the expression of the little girl. The patterns of the cloth and the style of the characters' clothing have an Eastern European feeling. Two other versions of this tale, *Little Sister and the Month Brothers* and *The Twelve Months,* have some similarities with this retelling that children will enjoy finding and discussing.

Folktales from other lands often incorporate information about the climate. Look at a story from the Far North such as *Louhi, Witch of North Farm.* Read the text and study the illustrations to find specific details about the climate and the culture. Select stories from other regions and see how the author and illustrator include details to reflect the origins of the stories.

Related Titles

Anansi the Spider: A Tale from the Ashanti adapted and illustrated by Gerald McDermott. Holt, Rinehart, 1972. After Anansi's sons rescue him from the fish and the falcon, he finds a beautiful globe of white light in the jungle. He wants to give the light to one of his sons, but he cannot decide which one. Finally, Anansi gives the globe to the God who lives in the sky, and the God decides to keep it.

Bringing the Rain to Kapiti Plain: A Nandi Tale retold by Verna Aardema. Illustrated by Beatriz Vidal. Dial, 1981. In this cumulative rhyme, Ki-pat sees the drought around him. Using an eagle's feather for an arrow, he aims at the cloudy sky piercing the cloud and causing the rain to fall.

Little Sister and the Month Brothers retold by Beatrice Schenk de Regniers. Illustrated by Margot Tomes. Seabury Press, 1976. Little Sister is treated like a drudge by her stepmother and her stepsister. As in *The Month-Brothers*, Little Sister is sent out into the snow to look for flowers. Although other details are also similar to *The Month-Brothers*, there are enough differences to make this a good book for a comparison activity.

Louhi, Witch of North Farm retold by Toni Gerez. Illustrated by Barbara Cooney. Viking, 1986. In this Finnish tale, Louhi is a witch who has stolen the sun and the moon. Vainamoinen must find a way to get them back. Children can discuss whether these illustrations reflect the climate and culture of Finland.

The Twelve Months: A Greek Folktale retold and illustrated by Aliki. Greenwillow, 1978. A widow leaves her home to find food for her children. She meets 12 men who find a way to help her and to destroy her selfish neighbor.

Why the Sun and the Moon Live in the Sky: An African Folktale by Elphinstone Dayrell. Illustrated by Blair Lent. Houghton Mifflin, 1968. When the Sun and the Moon invite many guests to their home, it becomes so crowded that they must go up on the roof and then jump into the sky. This is a different story about why the moon is in the sky from the one in *Anansi the Spider*.

About the Author and Illustrator

STANLEY, DIANE
Illustrators of Children's Books: 1957–1966, Vol. III, comp. by Lee Kingman, Grace Allen Hogarth, and Harriet Quimby. Horn Book, 1968, pp. 183–184, 245.
Something about the Author, ed. by Anne Commire. Gale, 1983, Vol. 30, p. 190.

Marshall, James, reteller. *Red Riding Hood*
Illus. by the reteller. Dial, 1987
Suggested Use Level: Gr. 1–3   Reading Level: Gr. 3

Plot Summary

In this version of a familiar folktale, Red Riding Hood is a pleasant child who lives a happy life. When Red Riding Hood's mother sends her to visit her Granny and to take Granny some food, she is happy to go. As she leaves her house, her mother reminds her to be careful on her journey. Red Riding Hood enters the woods and meets a wolf, whose lovely manners convince her that he can be trusted. They begin to walk to Granny's together, but the wolf tricks Red Riding Hood into letting him get to Granny's first. He swallows Granny without chewing, then jumps into Granny's bed, and waits for Red Riding Hood. When she arrives, she comments on Granny's changed appearance ("big eyes," "long arms," and "big teeth"). The wolf eats Red Riding Hood and goes to sleep, but a hunter who hears the wolf's snoring comes to the house, kills the wolf, and frees Red Riding Hood and her Granny from the wolf's stomach.

Thematic Material

Marshall's retelling is similar to the German folktale, but it has humorous expressions and the illustrations are filled with many amusing details.

Book Talk Material and Activities

This very humorous retelling of a familiar story provides the perfect opportunity to look at the books of James Marshall and to talk about what makes a book funny. Marshall has written and illustrated the delightful George and Martha books, as well as *Three by the Sea, Fox on Wheels,* and *Space Case* (which he wrote under the name Edward Marshall). He has also illustrated other books that are popular with children, including *The Stupids Step Out,* and *Miss Nelson Is Missing.* After examining many of Marshall's books, children will be able to recognize some common elements in his illustrations, and they will enjoy looking for them in *Red Riding Hood.* As in many other Marshall illustrations, those in *Red Riding Hood* include numerous cats. His characters have beady little eyes, stringy hair, thin mouths that stretch across their faces, and flat noses. Their behavior is often zany, their clothing is unusual, and they often make expressive exclamations. For example, Fox says "Rats" (*Fox on Wheels*), Granny says "You horrid thing" (*Red Riding Hood*), and Emily Pig (*Yummers!*) says "Yummers." When children look closely at an author's style, they frequently begin to incorporate similar features into their own writings. Studying James Marshall's books could lead children to experiment with humorous expressions and foolish situations.

Sharing Marshall's humorous version of *Red Riding Hood* could also lead to a discussion of other, more traditional versions of the story. Trina Schart Hyman's version, which she retold and illustrated, received the 1984 Caldecott Honor Medal. In Hyman's retelling, Red Riding Hood is named Elisabeth and, as in Marshall's version, her polite behavior is almost her downfall. *Little Red Cap* is another version that might be unfamiliar to children and would make an interesting comparison.

Related Titles

Fox on Wheels by Edward Marshall. Illustrated by James Marshall. Dial, 1983. In three stories about Fox, he babysits his sister, acts out Aesop's fable of the fox and the grapes, and fools around with a cart at the market. Children can look for humorous details in the illustrations, for example, Fox's sticklike legs and strange clothing.

George and Martha written and illustrated by James Marshall. Houghton Mifflin, 1972. In this first book in the series about these two hippo friends, which has five stories, the illustrations add to the humor. For example, in "The Tub," Martha stops George from peeking in when she is in the bathtub. The text does not say how, but the illustration shows George with a bathtub on his head. Children can find other examples where the illustrations expand on the text.

Miss Nelson Is Missing written and illustrated by Harry Allard and James Marshall. Houghton Mifflin, 1977. When the kids in Room 207 act up, Miss Nelson takes action. She calls in that dreaded substitute Miss Viola Swamp.

Space Case by Edward Marshall. Illustrated by James Marshall. Dial, 1980. It is Halloween and a spaceship has landed on Earth. As everyone is in costume, no one pays any attention to it. Children can look at the picture at the breakfast table for some funny details.

The Stupids Step Out by Harry Allard. Illustrated by James Marshall. Houghton Mifflin, 1974. Every picture in this book pokes fun at this very stupid family. Children can look at the pictures on the Stupids' wall and how they have been captioned.

Three by the Sea by Edward Marshall. Illustrated by James Marshall. Dial, 1981. Lolly, Spider, and Sam tell stories using the simplified vocabulary from their reading book. Ask the children how the cat in this story compares with the ones in *Red Riding Hood.*

Yummers! written and illustrated by James Marshall. Houghton Mifflin, 1973. Emily Pig is trying to lose weight, so she is taking a walk. Of course, because she is exercising, she should be allowed to eat—sandwiches, corn on the cob, scones, eskimo pies, Girl Scout cookies, and more.

Other versions of Little Red Riding Hood include:

Little Red Cap written by the Brothers Grimm. Illustrated by Lisbeth Zwerger. Morrow, 1983.

Little Red Riding Hood adapted from the retelling by the Brothers Grimm. Illustrated by Paul Galdone. McGraw-Hill, 1974.

Little Red Riding Hood written by the Brothers Grimm. Retold and illustrated by Trina Schart Hyman. Holiday House, 1983.

About the Author and Illustrator

MARSHALL, JAMES

Authors of Books for Young People: Supplement to the Second Edition, by Martha E. Ward and Dorothy Marquardt. Scarecrow, 1979, p. 187.

Fourth Book of Junior Authors and Illustrators, ed. by Doris de Montreville and Elizabeth D. Crawford. Wilson, 1978, pp. 253–254.

Illustrators of Children's Books: 1967–1976, Vol. IV, comp. by Lee Kingman, Grace Allen Hogarth, and Harriet Quimby. Horn Book, 1978, pp. 5, 144, 201.

Something about the Author, ed. by Anne Commire. Gale, 1974, Vol. 6, pp. 160–161; 1988, Vol. 51, pp. 109–121.

Martin, Rafe. *Foolish Rabbit's Big Mistake*
Illus. by Ed Young. Putnam, 1985
Suggested Use Level: Gr. 1–3   Reading Level: Gr. 3

Plot Summary

A rabbit, dozing under an apple tree, wonders "What if the Earth broke up?" A sudden crash makes him think that this is actually happening and he runs away in terror. As he runs, he meets other animals—rabbits, bears, an elephant, and some snakes. All join the rabbit's mad rush, until the lion intervenes and discovers the truth. The foolish rabbit was frightened by the sound of a falling apple. The other animals are very angry with the rabbit, but the lion reminds them that they also ran away without knowing why. All the animals return to their activities in peace.

Thematic Material

Foolish Rabbit's Big Mistake is from a collection of Asian stories called jatakas. It is like the traditional tales about Henny Penny and Chicken Little, showing how similar stories appear in different versions around the world.

Book Talk Material and Activities

Children who have read or heard many folktales will immediately notice the parallels between *Foolish Rabbit's Big Mistake* and the "Henny Penny" stories. *Foolish Rabbit's Big Mistake* could be used in a folktale program in which children compare it with other books, formulating questions using *Foolish Rabbit* as the focus book. Some possible questions are: Who or what starts the running? Is there a chant or repeated phrase? Who joins in the running? and How is the problem solved? With these questions as a framework, children can then examine other books, such as *Henny Penny* by Paul Galdone and *Chicken Little* by Steven Kellogg, looking for the similarities and differences between the stories. Working in small groups, they can read and discuss one book and then report back to the large group. Responses could be written on a chart similar to Chart F.

Having discussion groups, making charts, and illustrating the sequence of stories encourage children to examine and analyze books. When making a mural of the characters in *Foolish Rabbit's Big Mistake* and other similar stories, children must learn about the characters and their correct order in the sequence. As children have the opportunity to see and discuss the relationships between stories, they begin to develop their own criteria for examining books.

Audiovisual Adaptation

Foolish Rabbit's Big Mistake. Random House Media, filmstrip/cassette, 1987.

Related Titles

Chicken Little retold and illustrated by Steven Kellogg. Morrow, 1985. The illustrations show animals wearing clothes and driving an ambulance and a helicopter. In Kellogg's retelling, Foxy Loxy is tried and sent to prison.

Chart F

COMPARING SIMILAR STORIES

Title	Who or what starts the running?	Chant or repetition	Who joins in?	How is the problem solved?
Foolish Rabbit's Big Mistake (Martin)	The rabbit	"The earth is breaking up"	Rabbits Bears Elephant Snakes	The lion finds out what happened
Henny Penny (Galdone)	Henny Penny	"The sky is falling"	Cocky Locky Ducky Lucky Goosey Loosey Turkey Lurkey	Foxy Loxy tricks them into his cave and eats them
Chicken Little (Kellogg)	Chicken Little	"The sky is falling"	Henny Penny Ducky Lucky Goosey Loosey Gosling Gilbert Turkey Lurkey	Foxy Loxy tricks them into his truck, but Hippo Hefty rescues them

Henny Penny retold and illustrated by Paul Galdone. Seabury Press, 1968. The foolishness of Henny Penny and her friends results in a big meal for Foxy Loxy.

The Story of Chicken Licken written and illustrated by Jan Ormerod. Lothrop, 1985. Some of the different characters in this version are Drake Lake, Gander Lander, and Foxy Woxy. (See Chapter 7.)

The Three Bears and 15 Other Stories selected and illustrated by Anne Rockwell. Crowell, 1975. In several stories, including another version of "Henny Penny," events happen in sequence.

Why Mosquitoes Buzz in People's Ears retold by Verna Aardema. Illustrated by Leo Dillon and Diane Dillon. Dial, 1975. The events in the story happen in a sequence. Compare how the mosquito upsets the animals in the jungle with what happens to the rabbit in *Foolish Rabbit's Big Mistake*.

About the Author and Illustrator

YOUNG, ED
Illustrators of Children's Books: 1967–1976, Vol. IV, comp. by Lee Kingman, Grace Allen Hogarth, and Harriet Quimby. Horn Book, 1978, pp. 170, 214.
Something about the Author, ed. Anne Commire. Gale, 1976, Vol. 10, pp. 205–206.
Third Book of Junior Authors, ed. by Doris de Montreville and Donna Hill. Wilson, 1972, pp. 309–310.

Mikolaycak, Charles, reteller. *Babushka: An Old Russian Folktale*
Illus. by the reteller. Holiday House, 1984; pap., 1988
Suggested Use Level: Gr. 1–4   Reading Level: Gr. 4

Plot Summary

In this retelling of the classic Russian Christmas story, a young woman named Babushka, who is known throughout the village for having the best kept home, is cleaning her cottage. As darkness falls and Babushka opens the door to sweep her steps, she smells a fragrant scent. A magnificent procession is marching past her house and stops, and three men come toward her. They tell Babushka of their mission to follow the star and find the King, and they ask her to join them. Babushka refuses, choosing to stay and keep her cottage neat. The next morning, however, regretting her decision, Babushka runs into the snow to search for the three men and the King, whom she has heard is a child. For years, she watches children, hoping to see the King. Even as an old woman, she carries treats with her and gives them to children, who come to know of Babushka and her search.

Thematic Material

Babushka tells of a familiar Christmas figure from another country. In Russia, Babushka, like Santa Claus, is responsible for bringing gifts to children.

Book Talk Material and Activities

Many schools and libraries celebrate Christmas by looking at how the holiday is celebrated in other countries. Librarians and teachers could discuss some of the characters associated with Christmas, for example, Santa Claus, Babushka, and Befana, and booktalk some books about them, including *The Night before Christmas, Baboushka and the Three Kings,* and *The Legend of Old Befana. The Truth about Santa Claus* provides information about other Christmas characters, including St. Nicholas. Children who read these books might want to compare *Babushka* and *The Legend of Old Befana,* which have many similar features, even though they come from different countries. Comparing them helps children see that different versions of the same story can be incorporated into the folklore of different countries.

Related Titles

Baboushka and the Three Kings by Ruth Robbins. Illustrated by Nicolas Sidjakov. Parnassus, 1960. In this version, Baboushka is an old woman who cannot join the search for the Child because she must finish her work, but the kings will not wait for her. When her work is done, Baboushka hurries after the kings, but she does not catch them. Her story is retold every year, and children receive gifts that are said to have come from Baboushka. Sidjakov's illustrations received the Caldecott Medal in 1961.

The Legend of Old Befana: An Italian Christmas Story retold and illustrated by Tomie de Paola. Harcourt, 1980. Old Befana is a bad-tempered woman who spends her time cleaning and cooking. One night, a bright star appears, and the next day, a procession comes following the star, which will lead it to a Child King. Old Befana cannot leave her sweeping to accompany the procession. Later, she bakes treats for the Child and tries to find the procession. She hurries so fast that she flies through the sky. Every year, she flies to homes with gifts for children, one of whom might be the Child King.

The Night before Christmas by Clement Moore. Illustrated by Tomie de Paola. Holiday House, 1980. De Paola's illustrations for the well-known Christmas poem are colorful. His Santa Claus is short, fat, and rosy cheeked.

The Night before Christmas by Clement C. Moore. Illustrated by Scott Gustafson. Knopf, 1985. In this illustrated version of the popular poem, the outside scenes are cold and blue, but in the houses the illustrator used warm reds and yellows.

The Story of the Three Wise Kings retold and illustrated by Tomie de Paola. Putnam, 1983. The story of how the three kings came to be searching for the Child, could be shared with *Babushka.*

The Truth about Santa Claus by James Cross Giblin. Photographs and prints. Crowell, 1985. Giblin provides background information about different Santa Claus figures, including St. Nicholas and Father Christmas. Other "gift-bringers" are also discussed, including Babushka.

About the Author and Illustrator

MIKOLAYCAK, CHARLES
Fifth Book of Junior Authors and Illustrators, ed. by Sally Holmes Holtze. Wilson, 1983, pp. 216–217.
Illustrators of Children's Books: 1967–1976, Vol. IV, comp. by Lee Kingman, Grace Allen Hogarth, and Harriet Quimby. Horn Book, 1978, pp. 16–17, 145, 202.
Something about the Author, ed. by Anne Commire. Gale, 1976, Vol. 9, pp. 143–144.

Steptoe, John. *Mufaro's Beautiful Daughters: An African Tale*
Illus. by the author. Lothrop, 1987
Suggested Use Level: Gr. 3–4   Reading Level: Gr. 6

Plot Summary

Mufaro has two beautiful daughters, Manyara and Nyasha. Nyasha is kind and considerate. Manyara is vain, proud, and bad-tempered, but she is always careful to be well-behaved in front of Mufaro, so he is unaware of her true personality. Because Nyasha is liked by the villagers and by the creatures that she has befriended, Manyara is jealous of her. Nyasha is saddened by her sister's attitude toward her, but does not complain. Instead, she works in her garden, caring for her plants and showing consideration for the animals, including Nyoka the snake. When the king announces that he is searching for a wife, Mufaro believes that both of his daughters should be considered. Manyara wants to be the king's choice, so she leaves the village during the night, planning to reach the king first and win his affections. As Manyara hurries to the city, she passes a boy, an old woman, a grove of laughing trees, and a man. She is disdainful toward each and continues toward the city. In the morning, Nyasha journeys toward the city. When she comes to the boy, the old woman, and the trees, she is gentle and kind. Arriving in the city, Nyasha is greeted by her sister. Manyara has been frightened by the king, whom she saw as a five-headed snake. When Nyasha enters the king's chambers, she meets her friend Nyoka the snake, who transforms himself into the king. He then tells Nyasha that each creature that she was kind to on her journey was really him, and asks her to be his wife. Nyasha agrees, Manyara stays to be her servant, and Mufaro is proud of both of his beautiful daughters.

Thematic Material

The kind, considerate character Nyasha triumphs over the greedy character Manyara in this African folktale, with elements of a Cinderella story. The illustrations, which were awarded the Caldecott Honor Medal in 1988, show details from the Zimbabwe region of Africa.

Book Talk Material and Activities

Many folktales have two sisters (or stepsisters) with different personalities where the kind sister is rewarded and the greedy sister is punished—the basic theme of many Cinderella stories. Children are fascinated to find that stories from different countries use similar themes. A librarian could plan a booktalk program of several versions of Cinderella, having the children examine and discuss each book in small groups. Through this activity children can build on their knowledge of a familiar story, by seeing how a story can be changed to reflect different cultures and experiences. Some areas that children could be asked to consider are the descriptions of the characters, the setting of the story, and the use of magic in the story. *Yeh-Shen* could be included in this activity. Both *Mufaro's Beautiful Daughters* and *Yeh-Shen* have animal characters that befriend the kind daughter and both are unfamiliar stories for many children. *Tattercoats* could also be examined as could some of the more familiar stories, such as *Cinderella* and *Cinderella; or The Little Glass Slipper*. There are also many fables in which kindness is rewarded or greedy, conceited behavior is punished, and as children continue to read folk literature, they could look for stories that continue this theme, such as *The Woman with the Eggs* and *Once a Mouse*.

The illustrations in *Mufaro's Beautiful Daughters* include animals and plants from the Zimbabwe region of Africa. Children could look for other folktales in which the illustrations reflect the origins of the tale. For example, illustrations in other Cinderella stories provide details about France (*Cinderella* and *Cinderella; or The Little Glass Slipper*), China (*Yeh-Shen*), and England (*Tattercoats*).

Audiovisual Adaptation

Mufaro's Beautiful Daughters. Weston Woods, cassette/book, 1988; filmstrip/cassette, 1988; 16mm film, 1988. Also "Reading Rainbow," Great Plains National Instructional Television Library, videocassette, 1988.

Related Titles

Cinderella by Charles Perrault. Translated and illustrated by Marcia Brown. Scribner, 1954. For its detailed illustrations this book received the Caldecott Medal in 1955. Like Manyara in *Mufaro's Beautiful Daughters,* Cinderella's stepsisters are jealous of her kindness.

Cinderella; or The Little Glass Slipper by Charles Perrault. Illustrated by Errol Le Cain. Bradbury, 1972. Children can compare the illustrations in this version with those in *Mufaro's Beautiful Daughters,* and other Cinderella stories and decide whether the illustrations in each case reflect the origins of the story.

Once a Mouse: A Fable Cut in Wood written and illustrated by Marcia Brown. Scribner, 1961. In this 1962 Caldecott award-winning book, a hermit transforms a mouse into ever larger animals, until the mouse (who is now a tiger) is overcome by his own pride.

Tattercoats: An Old English Tale told by Flora Annie Steel. Illustrated by Diane Goode. Bradbury, 1976. Instead of sisters or stepsisters, it is Tattercoats's grandfather who ignores her and forces her to live in rags. A gooseherd befriends Tattercoats and helps her to meet the prince.

The Woman with the Eggs by Hans Christian Andersen. Adapted by Jan Wahl. Illustrated by Ray Cruz. Crown, 1974. A proud, haughty woman envisions the fine life that she will have with the money that she makes from selling her eggs. Unfortunately, she forgets that the eggs are on her head when she raises her head to look down at everyone.

Yeh-Shen: A Cinderella Story from China retold by Ai-Ling Louie. Illustrated by Ed Young. Philomel, 1982. The cruelty of Yeh-Shen's stepmother and stepsister is punished with death after Yeh-Shen is chosen to marry the king.

About the Author and Illustrator

STEPTOE, JOHN (LEWIS)
Fourth Book of Junior Authors and Illustrators, ed. by Doris de Montreville and Elizabeth D. Crawford. Wilson, 1978, pp. 321–322.

Illustrators of Children's Books: 1967–1976, Vol. IV, comp. by Lee Kingman, Grace Allen Hogarth, and Harriet Quimby. Horn Book, 1978, pp. 161, 210.
Something about the Author, ed. by Anne Commire. Gale, 1976, Vol. 8, p. 198.

Steptoe, John, reteller.   *The Story of Jumping Mouse*
Illus. by the reteller. Lothrop, 1984
Suggested Use Level: Gr. 3–4   Reading Level: Gr. 3

Plot Summary

A young mouse listens to stories of the beauty and danger in the world. He decides to leave his safe home and journey through the world seeking his own adventures. At the river, the mouse meets Magic Frog, who shares his magic and gives him a name, Jumping Mouse. After crossing the river, Jumping Mouse comes to the desert where he watches the shadows over his head. Although he is frightened, he continues his journey and reaches a stream. He stays there a while, replenishing his strength and talking with a fat mouse, but realizes that he is not finished with his journey and moves on. On the plain, Jumping Mouse meets a bison who has been blinded and is dying. Jumping Mouse uses his magic to give his sight to the bison, and the bison then escorts him across the plain. In the mountains, Jumping Mouse meets a wolf who has lost his sense of smell. Again, Jumping Mouse uses his magic to give the wolf his ability to smell, and the wolf then helps Jumping Mouse cross the mountains. Now, Jumping Mouse is at the end of his journey, but he is blind and cannot smell. As he wonders how he will survive, he hears the voice of Magic Frog telling him to jump high and remember all that he has hoped for in his life. As Jumping Mouse jumps, he is given a new name—Eagle—and soars across the land looking, listening, smelling, hearing, and feeling the power of the world around him.

Thematic Material

In this Native-American legend, Jumping Mouse cares more for the needs of others than for his own needs. He is unselfish even when that means risking his own life. Although he is a small creature, he overcomes the trials that he faces. His perseverance is rewarded and he is given a new life. John Steptoe received the 1985 Caldecott Honor Medal for this book.

Book Talk Material and Activities

The Story of Jumping Mouse could be coordinated with social studies units on Native Americans. As children study the tribes and their ways of life, they often need to find out about the beliefs and legends of the different people. *The Story of Jumping Mouse* is a legend from the Plains Indians, which includes the Crow, Cheyenne, Comanche, and Sioux tribes. When sharing this book with children, librarians and teachers can help them see how the story incorporates information about the way of life on the plains. For example, the mouse, frog, snake, bison and wolf are all animals that could live on the plains. Stories from other areas would include different details. Compare *The Story of Jumping Mouse* with *Arrow to the Sun: A Pueblo Indian Tale* and discuss the similarities and differences. Both stories deal with transformations and the main character in both is tested and is ultimately triumphant because of his unselfish behavior and perseverance. The illustrations include details about the setting of each story. In other Native-American legends characters must also make sacrifices to prove their worth or help others. *The Legend of the Bluebonnets* and *The Gift of the Sacred Dog* could also be compared.

John Steptoe's black-and-white illustrations are very detailed with many shifts in perspective that add to the drama of the story. Comparing them with the bold, colorful graphics in *Arrow to the Sun* (which won the Caldecott Medal in 1975) helps children understand how illustrators use different styles to interpret different stories, often adapting their illustrations to reflect the story's origin.

Related Titles

Arrow to the Sun: A Pueblo Indian Tale adapted and illustrated by Gerald McDermott. Viking, 1974. A boy must survive four tests to prove his identity and find his father.

The Gift of the Sacred Dog written and illustrated by Paul Goble. Bradbury, 1980. A boy goes to the Great Spirit to get help for his hungry people. Because of the boy's bravery, the people are given horses, "Sacred Dogs," to help them capture animals for food.

Indians, revised edition, written and illustrated by Edwin Tunis. Crowell, 1979. Tunis provides information about many tribes, including the "Buffalo Hunters" of the plains.

The Legend of the Bluebonnets retold and illustrated by Tomie de Paola. Putnam, 1983. During a drought and famine, a young Native-American girl sacrifices her most cherished possession to the Great Spirits. Her generosity is rewarded as the rain returns and the hills are covered with beautiful blue flowers.

Plains Indians edited by Henry Pluckrose. Illustrated by Maurice Wilson. Gloucester, 1980. Some background information is provided about life on the plains and the Native-American tribes that lived there.

About the Author and Illustrator

STEPTOE, JOHN (LEWIS)

Fourth Book of Junior Authors and Illustrators, ed. by Doris de Montreville and Elizabeth D. Crawford. Wilson, 1978, pp. 321–322.

Illustrators of Children's Books: 1967–1976, Vol. IV, comp. by Lee Kingman, Grace Allen Hogarth, and Harriet Quimby. Horn Book, 1978, pp. 161, 210.

Something about the Author, ed. by Anne Commire. Gale, 1976, Vol. 8, p. 198.

Stevens, Janet, adapter. *The Tortoise and the Hare: An Aesop Fable*

Illus. by the adapter. Holiday House, 1984

Suggested Use Level: Gr. 1–4   Reading Level: Gr. 2

Plot Summary

Janet Stevens has adapted Aesop's well-known fable of the race between the slow-moving tortoise and the speedy hare. In her version, Hare teases the Tortoise about his plodding pace, but Tortoise ignores him and continues to sit at his kitchen table and eat his cereal. No matter what the activity, from picking flowers to shopping, Hare mocks Tortoise. Tortoise knows he is slow, yet when his animal friends insist that he stand up to Hare, he agrees to a race. Tortoise's friends help him train and then gather with many other animals to watch the confrontation. As the race begins, Hare hurries ahead, until he is so far in front of Tortoise that he stops to visit a friend. When Tortoise catches up to him, Hare leaves his friend's house and speeds past Tortoise. Once again, though, Hare stops at a friend's house, and once again Tortoise is able to catch up. This time, Hare is so overconfident that he decides to take a nap. When he wakes up and realizes that Tortoise is now far ahead of him, he frantically races to the finish line, arriving just in time to see Tortoise cross the line and win. Like many fables, this one ends with a moral: "Hard work and perseverance bring reward."

Thematic Material

Hare is punished for his mean treatment of Tortoise and his self-centered pride when he loses the race. The book is a fable in which the moral lesson is stated.

Book Talk Material and Activities

The Tortoise and the Hare could be included in a story or booktalk program on fables with other fables from Aesop, such as *Borrowed Feathers;* fables from La Fontaine, like *The Rich Man and the Shoe-Maker;* and perhaps Arnold Lobel's *Fables.* After looking at different fables, children could discuss their common features. For example, many fables have a stated moral lesson and animal characters that act like humans. Before sharing what the author has written, teachers and librarians could have the children try to state the moral.

Children could compare the similarities and differences between Caroline Castle's retelling of *The Hare and the Tortoise* and *The Tortoise and the Hare.* They could look at the illustrations in each book to decide whether the illustrator's interpretation influences the mood of the story.

Audiovisual Adaptation

The Tortoise and the Hare. Listening Library, cassette, 1985; filmstrip/cassette, 1985. Also "Reading Rainbow." Great Plains National Instructional Television Library, videorecording, 1987.

Related Titles

Borrowed Feathers and Other Fables edited by Bryna Stevens. Illustrated by Freire Wright and Michael Foreman. Random House, 1977. A picture book with seven fables from Aesop. The moral of "The Fox and the Goat" is similar to the moral of *The Tortoise and the Hare,* and children could compare the two stories.

Fables written and illustrated by Arnold Lobel. Harper & Row, 1980. Animals are depicted in human situations and learn important lessons about behavior in this collection of 20 original fables.

The Hare and the Tortoise retold by Caroline Castle. Illustrated by Peter Weevers. Dial, 1985. In this version of Aesop's fable, the athletic Hare is irritated by the scholarly Tortoise, but it is the Tortoise who first mentions a race. Children could look for other similarities and differences between this version and *The Tortoise and the Hare*.

The Rich Man and the Shoe-Maker: A Fable by Jean de La Fontaine. Illustrated by Brian Wildsmith. Watts, 1965. A very poor shoemaker is also very happy. When his rich neighbor gives him a bag of gold, he finds the wealth such a burden that he returns the gold and finds happiness again in his simple life. As this story has no stated moral, children might enjoy suggesting some.

Three Aesop Fox Fables written and illustrated by Paul Galdone. Seabury Press, 1981. In these three fables, the Fox learns lessons about greed and trickery, and then teaches a lesson about flattery.

Wolkstein, Diane.   *The Magic Wings: A Tale from China*
Illus. by Robert Andrew Parker. Dutton, 1983; pap., 1986
Suggested Use Level: Gr. 2–4   Reading Level: Gr. 4

Plot Summary

In China, a poor goose girl wishes she could fly over the hills and see the beauty of the world. Her desire to grow wings leads her to flap her arms, attracting the attention of a grocer's daughter. The goose girl is so convinced that she will grow wings that the grocer's daughter becomes envious of her. Back home, the grocer's daughter begins to flap her arms and attracts the attention of the judge's daughter. The judge's daughter believes that she should have wings, too, so she flaps her arms. Then the princess sees her and hears her story. If these common girls will grow wings and be able to fly, the princess believes that she will, too. Soon all the women in town, including the queen, are flapping their arms and hoping to grow wings. The "Spirit in Heaven Who Grows Wings" sees them and decides to choose one of them to receive wings. He chooses the goose girl, who soars with the wind and sees the beautiful spring flowers below her.

Thematic Material

In *The Magic Wings*, as in many folktales, the least significant character is chosen to receive a special gift. When the goose girl is given wings, she is also magically transformed.

Book Talk Material and Activities

The Magic Wings is one of many stories in which people are transformed into birds that could be included in a booktalk or story program. *The Painter and the Wild Swans* is another. They could also be correlated with Molly Bang's *The Paper Crane* (see Chapter 7) and related books like *The Crane Wife*. After reading several of these books, children could discuss why they think the characters are fascinated by birds. What qualities have the birds been given that make them seem special? A writing activity could be suggested in which children write a story from the point of view of a bird (or another animal, if they wish). A book that provides an interesting contrast to *The Magic Wings* is *Hey, Al*, in which a man and his dog are unhappy with their lives, but are even more upset when they find that they are becoming birds. *The Wild Swans* and *The Seven Ravens* are two other stories in which characters are turned into birds against their will.

Related Titles

The Crane Maiden by Miyoko Matsutani. Illustrated by Chihiro Iwasaki. Parent's Magazine Press, 1968. In this version of the Japanese legend of the Crane Wife, a poor old man rescues a crane. Later, he and his wife meet a lovely maiden, who is really the crane. She weaves them a beautiful cloth. The man and his wife sell the cloth and are no longer poor, but the wife's curiosity forces the maiden to become a crane again and leave them.

The Crane Wife retold by Sumiko Yagawa. Illustrated by Suekichi Akaba. Morrow, 1979. In this version of the Japanese legend of the Crane Wife, a poor young man rescues a crane, who returns to him as a maiden and eventually becomes his wife. The beautiful cloth she weaves brings them much wealth. The woman insists that no one may watch her weaving, but the husband's curiosity causes him to open the door and see his wife as a crane weaving cloth from her feathers. The wife becomes a crane again and flies away.

Hey, Al by Arthur Yorinks. Illustrated by Richard Egielski. Farrar, Straus, 1986. Al and his dog, Eddie, are dissatisfied with everything about their lives. When a big bird takes them to an island in the sky, they are delighted, until they realize that staying on the island means they will change into birds. Children could discuss why Al and Eddie don't want to be birds, and compare them to the goose girl in *The Magic Wings*.

The Painter and the Wild Swans by Claude Clément. Illustrated by Frédéric Clément. Dial, 1986. Teiji's talent as a painter is greatly admired. In his village in Japan, he is honored and respected. One day, Teiji watches a flock of swans fly over him. He is transfixed by their beauty and begins to search for them. His search takes him to a frozen island, where, cold and covered with snow, he is transformed into a swan.

The Seven Ravens: A Grimm's Fairy Tale retold and illustrated by Donna Diamond. Viking, 1979. Seven brothers are turned into ravens, and their sister must find the way to release them from the spell.

The Wild Swans by Hans Christian Andersen. Retold by Amy Ehrlich. Illustrated by Susan Jeffers. Dial, 1981. A wicked queen turns 11 princes into swans and sends them and their sister, Elise, away from the castle. Elise and her brothers are faced with many dangers until Elise finds the way to break the evil spell. This story is filled with cruelty and violence, which Elise must endure in silence in order to free her brothers.

About the Author and Illustrator

WOLKSTEIN, DIANE

Fifth Book of Junior Authors and Illustrators, ed. by Sally Holmes Holtze. Wilson, 1983, pp. 336–338.

Something about the Author, ed. by Anne Commire. Gale, 1975, Vol. 7, pp. 204–205.

PARKER, ROBERT ANDREW (WALDO T. BOYD)

Authors of Books for Young People: Supplement to the Second Edition, by Martha E. Ward and Dorothy Marquardt. Scarecrow, 1979, pp. 31 (see Waldo T. Boyd), 212.

Fourth Book of Junior Authors and Illustrators, ed. by Doris de Montreville and Elizabeth D. Crawford. Wilson, 1978, pp. 283–284.

Illustrators of Children's Books: 1967–1976, Vol. IV, comp. by Lee Kingman, Grace Allen Hogarth, and Harriet Quimby. Horn Book, 1978, pp. 3, 149, 204.

Something about the Author, ed. by Anne Commire. Gale, 1980, Vol. 18, pp. 35–36 (see Waldo T. Boyd).

Zelinsky, Paul O., reteller. *Rumpelstiltskin*
Illus. by the reteller. Dutton, 1986
Suggested Use Level: Gr. 1–4   Reading Level: Gr. 4

Plot Summary

In this retelling of the classic Brothers Grimm folktale, the miller brags about his daughter to the king saying she can spin straw into gold. The greedy king has the girl brought to his castle, puts her in a room full of straw, and threatens to kill her if the straw is not spun into gold. The girl is frightened and dismayed when, suddenly, a little man comes into the room and offers to help her. In return, she gives him her necklace. When the king sees the gold, he insists that the girl spin more straw and, again, the girl is aided by the little man. This time, she pays him with her ring. When the king sees this gold, he takes the girl to an even larger room and leaves her there to spin the straw into gold. Since she has nothing left to give the little man, he makes her promise to give him her first child. When the king sees this last room full of gold, he marries the miller's daughter and, one year later, they have a son. The queen is horrified when the little man returns to collect his payment. She begs him to release her from their bargain and he agrees that she may have three days to try and guess his name. If she succeeds, she can keep her child. The queen thinks of every possible name, but none is correct. Her servant sees the little man in the woods and overhears him say that his name is Rumpelstiltskin. The queen guesses his name and the little man flies out the window on a cooking spoon.

Thematic Material

This German folktale is available in many versions and, in an appended note, Zelinsky provides some background information on this version of the story. The illustrations were awarded the 1987 Caldecott Honor Medal.

Book Talk Material and Activities

Zelinsky's retelling of *Rumpelstiltskin* offers another opportunity for children to look at different versions of folktales and see how similar stories have become a part of the literature of different countries. The many other picture-book versions of the story include *Tom Tit Tot*, as well as those illustrated by Jacqueline Ayer, Donna Diamond, Paul Galdone, Edward Gorey, and William Stobbs. In a school or public library program on folktales, one of these books could be read aloud and then children could work in small groups to examine the others. As part of the story reading experience, the librarian could pose some specific questions for the children to consider and make a display of their answers. Some possible questions are: What does the girl use to pay the little man? How does the girl guess the little man's name? What happens to the little man at the end of the story? Do the illustrations provide different details about the story? Providing an initial framework for children to use helps them focus on specific aspects of a book and introduces them to different ways of examining literature. Doing comparison activities encourages children to return to the books that they are reading to look for details. They can start to learn about story conventions and patterns and to develop a familiarity with the recurring elements in folktales.

Audiovisual Adaptation

Rumpelstiltskin. Random House Media, cassette/book, 1988; filmstrip/cassette, 1988. Also "Reading Rainbow," Great Plains National Instructional Television Library, videorecording, 1988.

Related Titles

The following titles are versions of *Rumpelstiltskin* that can be used for comparison with Zelinsky's work.

Rumpelstiltskin by the Brothers Grimm. Illustrated by Jacqueline Ayer. Harcourt, 1967.

Rumpelstiltskin by the Brothers Grimm. Illustrated by William Stobbs. Walck, 1970.

Rumpelstiltskin by the Brothers Grimm. Retold and illustrated by Donna Diamond. Holiday House, 1983.

Rumpelstiltskin by the Brothers Grimm. Retold and illustrated by Paul Galdone. Clarion, 1985.

Rumpelstiltskin by the Brothers Grimm. Retold by Edith Tarcov. Illustrated by Edward Gorey. Four Winds, 1973.

Tom Tit Tot: An English Folk Tale illustrated by Evaline Ness. Scribner, 1965.

About the Author and Illustrator

ZELINSKY, PAUL O.
Something about the Author, ed. by Anne Commire. Gale, 1983, Vol. 33, p. 239; 1987, Vol. 49, pp. 218–224.

AUTHOR INDEX

An asterisk (*) precedes the primary titles for which full summaries and discussions appear. Authors of the primary titles as well as those authors listed under "Related Titles" are included in this index.

ILLUSTRATOR INDEX

An asterisk (*) precedes the primary titles for which full summaries and discussions appear. Illustrators of the primary titles as well as those illustrators listed under "Related Titles" are included in this index.

TITLE INDEX

An asterisk (*) precedes the primary titles for which full summaries and discussions appear. The primary titles as well as those titles listed under "Related Titles" are included in this index.

SUBJECT INDEX

This index includes only the primary titles fully discussed and summarized in *Primaryplots*. Additional titles relating to these subjects can be found under the "Related Titles" section that accompanies the discussion of the books listed here. The subject headings refer to the fictional treatment of the subject unless otherwise noted with the label nonfiction.

DATE D